Family Law in Context

FAMILY LAW IN CONTEXT

Edited by

Dr MAEBH HARDING

and

Dr DEIRDRE MCGOWAN

CLARUS
PRESS

Published by
Clarus Press Ltd,
Griffith Campus,
South Circular Road,
Dublin 8.
www.claruspress.ie

Typeset by
Gough Typesetting Services,
Dublin

Printed by
SprintPrint
Dublin

ISBN
978-1-911611-87-5

A catalogue record for this book is available from the British Library

Preface

This book is the result of a collaborative process involving ten academic family lawyers, all with experience of teaching family law at third level. It aims to presents legal rules in an accessible manner. At the same time, it offers contextual information to encourage students to think critically about how the law impacts individual lives. Whilst adopting a similar format, each chapter takes a slightly different approach to explaining the law and how it operates, reflecting the research interests and pedagogical approach of the individual authors. This diversity in approach evidences the richness of family law scholarship in Ireland and we hope will encourage similar projects in other areas of law.

We are very grateful to our collaborators for their invaluable contributions and for taking the time to commit to this project during their own busy lives. Every chapter provoked enjoyable and enriching discussions about family law, and we hope that the project will spark future co-operative projects.

The idea for the book came from a coffee chat at the Irish Association of Law Teachers annual conference in Cork. Dr Ruth Lamont very generously gave us invaluable advice on how to develop our ill formed idea into a collaborative textbook. Our respective institutions, Technological University Dublin and University College Dublin have provided important practical support and David McCartney at Clarus press has been an absolute joy to work with.

We hope lecturers and students will find the book both useful and interesting and that it will encourage readers to engage fully in any future proposals for family law reform.

Family Law in Context is presented as an accurate reflection of Irish law as it was in August 2023.

Maebh Harding and Deirdre McGowan
September 2023.

About the Contributors

Dr Lydia Bracken is a Senior Lecturer at the School of Law, University of Limerick. She researches the areas of child and family law and European human rights, with a particular focus on the legal recognition of 'non-traditional' and 'new' family forms. Lydia is the author of two books, *Same-Sex Parenting and the Best Interests Principle* (Cambridge University Press, 2020) and *Child Law in Ireland* (Clarus Press, 2018; second edition forthcoming), and has published her research in a range of high-ranking national and international journals.

Dr Fiona Broughton Coveney lectures law at Technological University Dublin. Her research areas include child law and children's rights, particularly within the health care setting. She has published in national and international legal journals including the International Journal on Children's Rights and the Medico-Legal Journal of Ireland, on a variety of child law issues. She has presented her research at national and international conferences.

Dr Maebh Harding is a lecturer in child and family law at UCD Sutherland School of Law. She worked in English academia for many years, most recently as Associate Professor at the University of Warwick. She is an established family law academic, co-editing of the seminal English Family Law text, *Cretney's Principles of Family Law* from 2015-2018 and publishing widely in internationally peer-refereed journals. She is a founding member of the Doing Feminist Legal Work (DFLW) network, which brings together legal scholars across Ireland, Northern Ireland and Britain and is funded by an Irish Research Council, Shared Island, New Foundations award.

Dr Connie Healy lectures at University of Galway. Her research interests include family law, children's rights and conflict resolution. Much of her focus has been on assessing appropriate methods of dispute resolution within the family court system, including the adversarial process and alternative methods, namely mediation and collaborative practice. As such, she has led discussions on human-centred design and was appointed to the Department of Justice, Family Justice Oversight Committee. She has published widely on mediation and collaborative practice including *Collaborative Practice: A Research Perspective* (Routledge, 2017).

Dr Susan Leahy is a Senior Lecturer in the School of Law at the University of Limerick. She lectures in family law, media law and criminology. Susan's primary research interests lie in the areas of criminal justice (with particular emphasis on sexual violence and the rights of victims of crime) and family law (specifically domestic abuse and marriage). Her research on domestic abuse and marriage have been published in national and international journals including the Irish Journal of Family Law, the Child and Family Law Quarterly and the International Journal of Law, Policy and the Family.

Dr Deirdre McGowan is a Senior Lecturer and Head of Law at Technological University Dublin. Her research focuses on the regulation of adult relationships and the impact of identity rights on familial relationships. Her work has been published in national and international journals as well as a number of edited collections. She has extensive experience of teaching family law at third level with a particular focus on law for social care professionals.

Dr Máire Ní Shúilleabháin is an Associate Professor of Law at University College Dublin, specialising in private international law/conflict of laws. She is the author/co-author of a number of books and journal articles in the area. She has a particular interest in family disputes with a cross-border dimension.

Dr Kathryn O' Sullivan is a Senior Lecturer at the School of Law at the University of Limerick. Kathryn's primary research interests lie in family law and property law. She has published widely in highly respected national and international journals and is the Corresponding Member for Ireland with the Cambridge Family Law Centre at the University of Cambridge.

Dr Fergus Ryan is the Head of the School of Law and Criminology at Maynooth University. A graduate of TCD and former Head of Law at TU Dublin, he has extensive teaching and research experience in family law. He is a former President of the Irish Association of Law Teachers and a former Chairperson of One Family.

Dr Brian Tobin Dr Brian Tobin is a Lecturer in Law at the University of Galway, where he has taught family and child law since 2014. His research focuses on the legal recognition of contemporary family forms and the position of children born via donor-assisted human reproduction and surrogacy. He is a frequent media contributor on these topical issues, and he has also contributed to policy development in these areas in the U.K. and Ireland, and at a European level. Dr Tobin's book, *The Legal Recognition of Same-Sex Relationships: Emerging Families in Ireland and Beyond*, was released by Hart Publishing in 2023.

Table of Contents

Table of Cases

Table of Legislation

BUNREACHT NA hÉIREANN
CONSTITUTION OF IRELAND

PRE-STATE

IRELAND – STATUTES

IRELAND – STATUTORY INSTRUMENTS

ENGLAND AND WALES – STATUTES

ENGLAND AND WALES – STATUTORY INSTRUMENTS

SCOTLAND – STATUTES

NEW ZEALAND – STATUTES

CANADA – STATUTES

AUSTRALIA – STATUTES

EUROPEAN DIRECTIVES

EUROPEAN REGULATIONS

INTERNATIONAL CONVENTIONS AND AGREEMENTS

Introduction

Maebh Harding and Deirdre McGowan

1. The pedagogic approach of this textbook

In the last 50 years, Irish family law and Irish social attitudes towards the family have changed beyond recognition. Although the constitutional idea of the family is still based on marriage, Irish family law now embraces and provides for a diversity of family forms. With the introduction of divorce and proper provision we have gone from a legal system which attached shame to the breakdown of marriage to one that provides for the reality of family life. The law now centers the rights of children and promotes a child-focused approach to dispute resolution. Family law is also the subject of significant evidence-based research. This textbook takes a new approach to teaching family law to students by grounding the law in its socially inclusive context. Each chapter is research-led, written by an Irish family law academic who is an active researcher in that particular field. A 'law in context' approach is taken throughout the text, examining the real-world context of each area of family law in Irish society.

This textbook provides a comprehensive but accessible account of current family law in Ireland. Each chapter provides a clear overview of the particular topic, outlining the most relevant legislation and case law. Each chapter starts with **learning objectives,** clearly outlining for the student what they will have learned after reading the chapter. At the end of each chapter, students will be encouraged to reflect on what they have learned and their own critical opinions about the topic through a **summary.** Students' learning is scaffolded throughout the text by the use of text boxes and emboldening in order to highlight important legal mechanisms such as **key legislation** and **key cases.** An important aspect of Irish family law is the exercise of judicial discretion with reference to **statutory 'checklists'** in order to determine what a subjective concept such as **proper provision** or the **best interests of the child** means in the particular circumstances of the case. Students are prompted to consider how these statutory checklists are applied and the tendencies of the courts in using their discretion. **Example cases** are used to help students understand how judicial discretion works and how legal principles are applied.

This textbook supports students and instructors in going beyond the descriptive to thinking critically about family law in Ireland and to develop analytical skills. Each chapter builds on the exposition of the current law by critically engaging with questions about the nature of family law, the inclusivity of family law and law's impact on the forms of family life it seeks to regulate. Research-led **critical thinking points** outline relevant issues in simple terms before familiarising students with the current family law context and leading academic commentary. The critical thinking points include debates, reflections, tensions, emerging ideas and contested points of law. A **further reading list** is included at the end of each chapter which showcases the breadth of Irish family law research and links to broader international research. This orientates students with a range of research-informed critical perspectives on the relationship between law and family life. We have considered whether the sources referenced can be easily accessed by Irish students through university resources and favoured open access resources wherever possible.

In the introduction we explain the law in context approach, the importance of historical context and how we have approached language and inclusion. In addition, we provide an overview of the operation of the family justice system, the *in camera* rule and sources of Irish family law. At the end of the introduction, we have provided a glossary of some key terms used in the book

2. What is Irish family law in context?

The 'law in context' approach considers how family law actually works in Irish society. This textbook discusses factors beyond legal rules that impact how the legal system is experienced by those who must use it. These include historical experiences and understandings that have shaped legal rules, social practices that challenge the limitations of existing laws, and systemic issues that impact access to justice and information.

The textbook engages with different perspectives on lived experiences of family law highlighting research that examines the experiences of individual family members within the legal process. Some of this research is carried out by non-governmental organisations and survivor groups and their perspectives are incorporated where relevant. Unfortunately, little is known about how family law impacts on minoritised groups such as Mincéirí and immigrant communities whose experiences have been historically marginalised.

Empirical evidence such as court statistics, census data and official statistics are introduced to help students understand the relevance and scale of each area of family law. Absences of evidence about how the law actually operates are also highlighted as well as the challenges presented by the *in camera* rule and an overburdened court system. This encourages students to consider how and by whom family law remedies are used and the inadequacies of the family justice system.

Although we prefer to discuss contemporary implications of family law, where necessary, the textbook explains the historical context in which laws arose. This is intended to help students understand the structure and shape of the current law and appreciate the historic wrongs inflicted on families who did not fit within the narrow marital paradigm preferred by the law.

3. The Modern Relevance of History

The goal of this book is to teach a modern version of family law within a current socially inclusive context. By starting with the law as it exists today, we hope that students' thinking about the law will not be shaped by obsolete and pejorative legal ideas and categories such as the idea that the 'unmarried family' should be treated differently or that a woman's place is in the home. However, historical context is crucial to understanding the shape of the current law, and structural divisions that affect different types of families. Short accounts of historical context are therefore provided where relevant to ensure that students gain important historical consciousness of contemporary legal rules.

In Chapter 1 we explain how historical and religious understandings shaped the constitutional definition of family. Ireland was one of the last countries in Europe to permit the dissolution of marriage through divorce and as discussed in Chapter 2, legislating for divorce required a constitutional amendment. Many people opposed the introduction of divorce both on ideological grounds and because of a fear that women and children would be impoverished by divorce. As a result, the proposal to amend the Constitution was accompanied by draft legislation that aimed to make divorce difficult and to reassure dependent spouses that they would be financially protected. Although this legislation remains largely as enacted, its content reflects the political and social concerns of the 1990s when many women did not work outside the home and divorce was much less acceptable than it is today. The understandable desire to protect dependent women and children has resulted in a cumbersome and expensive divorce process ill-suited to the needs of today's families.

Historical consciousness is also vital in understanding the modern law of child protection and adoption discussed in Chapters 10 and 11. In the early twentieth century the State provided support for children in need though a system of unsuitable and often abusive industrial and reformatory schools. The Child Care Act 1991, which remains in force, responded to these abuses by providing a more modern child-centred approach to child protection. The legislative framework governing care continues to improve, ameliorated more recently by constitutional change and the integration of international human rights standards. The legacy of institutionalisation is also very present in Irish adoption law. Some of the impacts of forced and illegal adoptions facilitated by the incarceration of pregnant unmarried women and their babies have just recently been addressed by the Birth Information and Tracing Act 2022. Ireland had no adoption law at all before 1952 and although we now have a modern and largely rights compliant framework for adoption, historical failures continue to impact the lives of many adopted people.

4. Language and inclusion

The language of family law has historically emphasised the 'naturalness' of the heterosexual marital family and stigmatised other family forms. In this book we have chosen to avoid using stigmatising terms wherever possible, even though some of these terms have, in the past, been used as legal terms of art (illegitimacy, unmarried mothers and fathers). Some of the legal sources drawn on in this text date from a time when Irish law was not inclusive or progressive and make use of such terms. This is particularly an issue with case law. We have chosen not to repeat these older terms within the text even though this may be a departure from how cases are habitually described. We think it is important for students to approach family law using modern progressive language.

Whether or not a person is married remains very important in certain aspects of family law. There is a fundamental structural division in family law between the legal rules and rights that attach to marital families and the rules apply to everyone else. The rules of legal parentage and guardianship also differ depending on the marital status of a parent. Throughout the text we contrast the marital family to the non-marital family. However, we acknowledge that in many areas of law, being unmarried has historically brought stigma and shame, particularly to mothers and children. We try to avoid defining individuals by their marital status. Where possible we refer to people as members of types of families rather than by reference to their or their parents' marital status. Where it is absolutely necessary for clarity, we attach the labels of marital and non-marital to parents rather than children. We hope that the reader will excuse some of the long-windedness this causes as we navigate clear inclusive terminology that accurately encompasses the structural divide between marital and non-marital families in Irish law.

We acknowledge that in many areas of family law appropriate terminology is contested. We use the terms 'people parenting alone', 'one parent families', 'non-resident parent' and 'resident parent' in accordance with the practice of One Family.[1] We are sensitive to concerns about the language used to explain the law of adoption.[2] In this context we use the terms, 'mother', 'father' or parent to refer to biological parents and 'adoptive parents' to describe the parents who raise the child after adoption. This reflects the practices of the Clann project[3] and the approach of the Hague Intercountry Adoption Convention.

5. The Irish family justice 'system'

Ireland does not have a specialised family justice system. Most decisions about family law take place in the District Court or Circuit Court with some first instance decisions made at High Court level.

The way that family law cases are treated by the District or Circuit Court is very different across Ireland. The Dublin Metropolitan District Court comes closest to a specialised family law court as it deals with high volumes of family law cases and there is continuity of personnel and practice directions about the management of family law cases. In other parts of Ireland, District and Circuit Courts may only deal with family law cases a few times a month on a 'family law day' or sometimes as part of a general list of cases. The court lists can be very long. In a recent report, the Child Law Project noted one District Court sitting day with a list of 139 cases. These cases were a mix of crime, general civil law, family law and child care law.[4] The volume of cases as well as the absence of case management systems in regional courts means that waiting times for court dates can be very long and adjournments are common. Unsuitable facilities exacerbate the difficulties for families using the courts. The lack

1 One Family, *Human Rights, Equality and One Parent Families: A Guide to Delivering Public Services* (2022) available at https://onefamily.ie/wp-content/uploads/2022/09/15783_OneFamily_HumanRights_Booklet_PublicSector.pdf [last accessed 3 August 2023].

2 Conor O'Mahony, *Proposals for a State Response to Illegal Birth Registrations in Ireland* (2022), 6 available at https://assets.gov.ie/218808/2ee2204e-6a16-4669-94cf-01902f8e63d9.pdf [last accessed 3 August 2023].

3 Claire McGettrick, Maeve O'Rourke and Loughlin O' Nolan, *Birth Information and Tracing Bill 2022 Briefing Note and Amendments* (2022) available at http://clannproject.org/wp-content/uploads/Clann_A8A-Briefing-Note_Information-Tracing-Bill_28-02-22.pdf [last accessed 3 August 2023].

4 Child Law Project, *Regional Report 2019,* 1 available at https://www.childlawproject.ie/wp-content/uploads/2019/03/CCLRP-regional-report-2019_FINAL.pdf [last accessed 3 August 2023]].

of specialisation and training among the judiciary, as well as significant pressure of work means that even when cases come to hearing they may not receive adequate care and attention. The National Women's Council recently highlighted additional issues arising within the justice system for people reporting domestic abuse. They may need to deal with three sets of court proceedings in the criminal courts, private family courts and if children are involved, the child protection system.[5] The shortcomings of the existing family justice system are well known and there is unanimity among practitioners, academics and the broader legal establishment that reform is urgently needed.[6]

In 2020 the Department of Justice established the Family Justice Oversight Group to develop a Family justice strategy as a first step toward wide ranging reform. Their recently published, *Family Justice Strategy 2022-2025*[7] acknowledges the long waiting times for family law hearings across the country, the unsuitability of the current court system and the need for increased use of interpreters and other support services to deal with the diverse reality of family life in Ireland. The aim of the strategy is to work with participants in the family justice system to identify the reforms necessary to produce a modern family justice system that is easy to navigate and appropriately meets the needs of users. A number of modernisation processes have already begun, including:

- **The Family Court Bill 2022** which, if enacted, will establish specialist family law jurisdictions within the District Court, Circuit Court and the High Court. (This is discussed below)
- **The Courts Service Modernisation Programme** – which will provide more family focussed services and information for those using the family courts.
- **A Modern Purpose-Built Family Court Complex** to be built at Hammond Lane. This will be the first court complex in Ireland specifically designed for the requirements of family law cases.
- **Review of Civil Legal Aid**[8] – commenced in 2022 this is

5 National Women's Council, *A Report on the Intersection of the Criminal Justice, Private Family Law and Public Law Child Care Processes in relation to Domestic and Sexual Violence* (2023) available at https://www.nwci.ie/learn/article/call_to_action_for_survivors_in_the_three_justice_systems [last accessed 3 August 2023].

6 See for example Law Reform Commission, *Report on Family Courts* (LRC 52-1996), Joint Oireachtas Committee on Justice and Equality *Report on Reform of Family Law System* (2019) available at https://data.oireachtas.ie/ie/oireachtas/committee/dail/32/joint_committee_on_justice_and_equality/reports/2019/2019-10-24_report-on-reform-of-the-family-law-system_en.pdf [last accessed 3 August 2023].

7 The Department of Justice, *Family Justice Strategy 2022-2025* (November 2022) available at https://www.gov.ie/en/collection/4790f-family-justice-strategy/ [last accessed 3 August 2023].

8 https://www.gov.ie/en/consultation/79e1d-public-consultation-on-the-review-of-

the first review of the civil legal aid scheme since it was established. Most civil legal aid is provided to people seeking assistance with family law issues.

5.1 The Family Courts Bill 2022

The Family Courts Bill 2022 provides for the establishment of a Family Court by creating specialist divisions;[9] the Family High Court, The Family Circuit Court and the Family District Court. Under the new Bill, judges may be assigned full time to the Family Court Divisions and will be required to participate in education and training.[10] The proposed reforms will allow more family law cases to be dealt with in the District Court. Significantly, the District Court will be able to rule on settlements made in family law cases, irrespective of the amount of money involved.[11]

One important new initiative is the requirement for the court and legal practitioners to have regard to **general guiding principles for the conduct of family law proceedings.** Part 6 of the Bill allows for the creation of a Family Law Rules Committee to create and apply specialist procedural rules to the family law courts embodying these principles. This is an important acknowledgment of the special nature of family law and family law proceedings and the need for specialised rules of procedure. This will be the first time that child centred principles have been enshrined in Irish procedural law. Proposed principles will ensure that the best interests of the child is a primary consideration in proceedings involving children and that children's views are ascertained and given due weight. The proposed principles also acknowledge the importance of encouraging and facilitating consensus and resolution of disputes. Active case management practices are encouraged, and proceedings must be conducted in a way that is user-friendly, minimises conflict and is likely to minimise the costs of proceedings.

At the time of writing the Family Courts Bill 2022 was before Seanad Éireann.

6. The in camera rule

Article 34.1 of the Constitution provides that justice 'save in such special and limited cases as may be prescribed by law, shall be administered in public'. Family law is one such special case. It deals with sensitive issues, often involving children and impacting the most private elements of

---

the-civil-legal-aid-scheme/ [last accessed 3 August 2023].

9 Part 3.

10 s 59.

11 s 69.

people's lives. In order to protect children and family privacy, all family law cases are held in private. Legislation refers to cases being held 'otherwise than in public' or ***in camera.***[12] Both phrases mean that all elements of the case including documents, correspondence and court hearings are private. Only the parties to the case and their legal representatives may attend the court and documents and orders relating to the case cannot be shared with non-parties without the consent of the court. Whilst this strict privacy approach protects family law litigants it can create significant difficulties for researching and studying family law.

Since 2004, there has been some relaxation of the strict privacy rule to allow accredited journalists and researchers to attend and report on family law cases.[13] Anonymised reports of cases do therefore occasionally appear in newspapers and there have been some research projects focused on gathering information from family court hearings. The Child Law Project, for example, attends and reports on child care proceedings.[14] The reach of reporting projects is limited meaning that that main source of information about family law cases for practitioners, researchers, students and the general public is written judgments of the courts. However, most family law cases are decided in the District and Circuit Court where written judgments are uncommon. This further reduces the available information to decisions of the superior courts – the High Court, the Court of Appeal and the Supreme Court. These cases are generally not representative of the bulk of family law cases and often deal with areas of law not litigated in the District and Circuit Court. The dearth of relevant case law is apparent throughout the book, and whilst we have attempted to provide sample cases illustrating the operation of the law throughout the text, this is not always possible.

Where case reports are available, they are anonymised. This means that all information that might identify the parties is removed. There is no published Court Service guidance on how specifically this should be done, meaning that different judges take different approaches. It had been the practice for many years to use initials instead of names in the title of the case, but recently some judges exclusively use 'X' and 'Y' or 'A' and 'B' for the party names. This can be confusing because it results in many cases having the same names with the citation being the only distinguishing

---

[12] For an overview of the relevant rules see Clare Craven-Barry, 'Transparency in Family and Child Law Proceedings: Disentangling the Statutory Techniques and Terminology' (2019) (3) Irish Judicial Studies Journal 88.

[13] Civil Liability and Courts Act 2004, s 40; Courts and Civil Law (Miscellaneous Provisions) Act 2013.

[14] Reports are available here: https://www.childlawproject.ie/latest-volume/ [last accessed 3 August 2023].

element. Anonymisation can also impact the text of the judgment with, for example, property valuations redacted.[15]

7. Irish family law sources

The sources of Irish family Law have improved substantially in recent years but can still be tricky for students to navigate.

7.1 Legislation

Some of the main family law statutes have been subject to multiple amendments over a number of decades (eg the Guardianship of Infants Act 1964, The Family Law (Maintenance of Spouses and Children) Act 1976, The Judicial Separation and Family Law Reform Act 1989, the Child Care Act 1991). Other Acts are subject to rapid changes. Students are advised to consult the **Revised Acts** which bring together all legal amendments and changes in a single text and are freely available on the Law Reform Commission website.[16] Where Acts are quoted in the book, we have used the most up to date versions and removed the annotations.

At the time of writing, some important provisions of family law had been enacted but not commenced. Students can check the up-to-date status of legislative provision through www.irishstatutebook.ie by searching for the relevant Act and checking the 'commencement, amendments, SIs made under the Act' tab.

7.2 Irish case law

Most family law judgments from the higher courts are now published and freely accessible on www.courts.ie or on www.irlii.org. Where possible, we have avoided using older unreported judgments which are not accessible to all students.

Most family law cases take place in the District or Circuit Court and are not routinely reported. Some District Court and Circuit Court cases are now reported on www.courts.ie. Court reports for a selection of public child law cases are published through the Irish Child Care Law Reporting Project https://www.childlawproject.ie/#

7.3 Irish family law journals

The main academic journal dedicated to articles on family law in Ireland is the *Irish Journal of Family Law* which is available through Westlaw.ie at

---

15 See for example *M v S* [2020] IEHC 562.

16 https://revisedacts.lawreform.ie/revacts/intro.

many Irish Universities. Family law issues are also discussed in the *Irish Judicial Studies Journal* which is freely available online and in general Irish law journals like *The Irish Jurist, Dublin University Law Journal* and the *Hibernian Law Journal.*

7.4 Contextual sources

This is a list of some of the useful sources of contextual data about Irish law used in this book:

- CSO statistics (www.cso.ie) Note that 2022 census results on households will be available from 31 August 2023.
- Court Service Reports (www.courts.ie/annual-report)
- TUSLA statistics (www.tusla.ie)
- Law Reform Commission (www.lawreform.ie)
- Law Society of Ireland Reports on legal issues (www.lawsociety.ie)
- Annual Reports of the Special Rapporteur on Child Protection (www.gov.ie)
- Reports by the Ombudsman for Children (www.oco.ie)
- Oireachtas Debates including Dáil Debates and Committee debates (www.oireachtas.ie)
- NGO reports available on the websites of non-governmental organisations -e.g. Women's Aid, (www.womesaid.ie), National Women's Council of Ireland (www.nwci.ie), Irish Human Rights and Equality Commission (www.ihrec.ie)
- Annual report of An tArd-Chláraitheoir on the operation of the Civil Registration Acts available through the 'Documents Laid' section of Oireachtas website (https://opac.oireachtas.ie)

8. Glossary of terms

- **Access:** The right of a child to maintain contact with their parents, siblings and other persons involved in their care and upbringing.
- **Ancillary Relief**: A collective term for court orders making financial arrangements for spouses on divorce or judicial separation.
- **Approbation**: This term is used in the context of nullity law to indicate acceptance by a spouse that their marriage is valid.
- **Applicant**: The person who makes the application in a family law case (equivalent to the plaintiff in an ordinary civil case).
- **Best interests of the child**: This principle requires the court

to ensure that best interests of the individual child before the court are paramount in the decision making process before the court. The best interests of the child are also protected by the UNCRC.

- **Bigamy**: Bigamy is a criminal offence that involves going through a ceremony of marriage whilst already married.
- **Burden of proof**: The burden of proof in family law proceedings is the normal civil standard of the balance of probabilities. The court must be satisfied that it is more likely that not that a particular event has occurred.
- **Civil partnership**: A legally recognised relationship similar to marriage, open to same sex couples between 2011 and 2016.
- **Cohabitant**: One of two adults living together in an intimate and committed relationship. The term is sometimes specifically defined or qualified for particular purposes in legislation.
- **Custody**: An adult right to exercise physical day to day care and control over a child who lives with them.
- **Deed of separation**: A deed of separation is a legally binding document which records the terms upon which spouses have agreed to separate. It is usually drafted by solicitors and signed by both parties.
- **Divorce**: A court order that dissolves marriage.
- **Domicile**: A person's domicile is the country in which they have a permanent home. This can be important in determining where proceedings should be brought and also with respect to the validity of foreign divorces.
- **Duress**: Physical, psychological or social force applied to a person with the effect of coercing them to choose a particular course of action or make a legal commitment.
- **Ecclesiastical Courts**: These were religious courts of the Church of Ireland which historically had exclusive legal jurisdiction over issues related to marriage. This jurisdiction was transferred to the Irish High Court by the Matrimonial Causes and Marriage Law (Amendment) Act (Ireland) 1870.
- **Guardianship**: This gives an adult rights, responsibilities and decision-making powers in respect of children.
- **Habitual residence**: This is the place where a person is currently living, where they have their centre of interest and everyday life.
- **Impediment**: An impediment is the legal term for specific facts that can prevent a marriage from going ahead. The existence of an impediment will allow a member of the public to object to a marriage before it is celebrated.

- ***In camera* rule**: This is an exception to the general principle that court hearings are open to the public. All family law cases are held in private or *in camera* and only certain people designated by law can attend.
- **Judicial separation**: This is an order of the court that suspends the obligation of married people to live together.
- **Lump sum orders**: These are orders made by the court that one person should pay a particular sum of money to another. They can arise in maintenance applications and in judicial separation and divorce cases.
- **Maintenance**: Maintenance is a sum of money paid by one person to another either for their own use or for the care of a child. Maintenance can be agreed or ordered by the court.
- **Marriage of convenience**: A marriage of convenience is one entered into for the sole purpose of gaining an immigration advantage for one or both spouses.
- **Nullity**: An order of the court declaring that a marriage does not exist and that the parties to marriage ceremony are not the spouses of each other.
- ***Obiter:*** An obiter statement is a comment made by a judge about the law that is not directly relevant to the facts of the case being decided.
- **Open adoption**: A type of adoption in which contact continues between parents, adoptive parents and children after an adoption order has been made.
- **Periodic payments**: These are payments of maintenance made weekly or monthly on an ongoing basis.
- **Polygamy**: The marriage of a man to more than one woman. Polyandry is the marriage of a woman to more than one man.
- **Pre-nuptial agreement**: An agreement made between a couple before they get married in which they agree how property and income will be dealt with during the marriage and in the event of a divorce. Parties may also agree non-financial issues such as the religion in which the children of the marriage will be raised.
- **Proper provision**: This term refers to the legislative or constitutional requirement that spouses and children are financially provided for on divorce or judicial separation. It is achieved through the making of court orders for the division of property or payment of maintenance.
- **Respondent**: The person who must respond to court proceedings served on them. The equivalent of the defendant in other types of legal proceeding.
- **Separation agreement**: An agreement between spouses in which they agree to live apart. It usually contains the terms

upon which they will live apart including the division of property, payment of maintenance and arrangements for children.

- **Threshold for state intervention:** The legal test that must be met before the State is legally and constitutionally permitted to intervene in family life to protect children.
- **Tusla/Child and Family Agency**: Established by the Child and Family Agency Act 2013, this is the state agency responsible for improving wellbeing and outcomes for children. The Child and Family Agency is the legal name and is used in court proceedings, but the agency is otherwise referred to as Tusla.

Chapter 1

What is the 'Family' in Irish Law?

Deirdre McGowan and Fergus Ryan

LEARNING OBJECTIVES

By the end of the chapter, students will be equipped to:

- Outline different understandings of the family.
- Explain and assess how 'Family' is defined in the Constitution.
- Critically discuss how the constitutional position of marriage has affected the legal regulation of family life in Ireland.
- Assess how the European Court of Human Rights interprets 'family life' under the European Convention on Human Rights.
- Consider contrasting approaches to the legal regulation of family.

CRITICAL THINKING POINT

- Should the law extend special protection to the family based on marriage?

1. Introduction

While most of us instinctively accept that we have families, that we are members of families and that we have familial relationships, our experiences of family will not be the same. The shape and structure of the emotional and biological connections that we each call 'family' differ, and our individual experience of family changes as we move through life. The law, however, has a particular family 'in mind';[1] in the Irish context this legal family is defined by the Constitution and in its judicial interpretation as the family based on marriage.

This chapter focuses on the debate around whether marriage *should* be the essential foundation for family life or whether households not based on marriage – such as those led by one parent or by unmarried cohabiting couples – should also be treated as a family for the purpose of the law. It explores how the priority given to the family based on marriage conflicts with the reality of family life for many, and how law reform has created

1 Alison Diduck, *Law's Families* (Lexis Nexis UK 2003) 1.

limited new opportunities for the recognition of diverse forms of family. It contrasts the restrictive approach the Irish courts have typically taken to the concept of family with the more expansive approach of the European Court of Human Rights. It refers also to recent cases and constitutional reform proposals that suggest a strong momentum for change in the understanding of 'Family' under the Constitution.

2. What is a family?

In everyday conversation we think of family in terms of people connected to us by intimacy, marriage, or biology, but also in terms of the quality of those relationships. We expect family to encompass committed relationships between adults and/or parent-child relationships and to involve a certain amount of affection and care.[2] Heterosexual marriage was once seen as central to the creation of family life, but this is no longer the case as one parent families, families led by same sex couples, and cohabitation become increasingly common. Although most children across Europe are raised in a 'nuclear family' with both of their parents, these families can consist of parents of the same or different sexes who are married, civilly partnered or cohabiting. Children in all families may be their parent's biological children, step-children, born through assisted human reproduction, adopted, or fostered. As people become increasingly mobile, live longer and further from blood relatives, they may form strong bonds with friends whom they consider family. Siblings commonly share households, caring for each other through illness and old age. This diversity in family practice led sociologists Bivens et al to describe the sociological family as 'two or more persons who share resources, share responsibility for decisions, share values and goals, and have commitment to one another over a period of time.'[3] They describe family as 'that climate that one comes home to' and it is 'that network of sharing and commitment that most accurately describes the family regardless of blood, legal ties, adoption or marriage.'[4]

This modern understanding of families based on care can be contrasted with the 'functionalist' family that dominated sociological and political thinking for most of the twentieth century. A family consisting of the heterosexual married couple and their biological children was seen as

2 Jane Gray, Ruth Geraghty, David Ralph, *Family Rhythms: The Changing Textures of Family Life in Ireland* (Manchester University Press 2016), see Introduction pp 1-12.

3 Gordon Bivens, Margaret Fitch, Gwendolyn Newkirk, Beatrica Paolucci, Em Riggs, Satenig St Marie and Gladys Vaughn, 'Home Economics: New Directions II' (1975) 67 Journal of Home Economics 26.

4 Gorden Bivens et al, 'Home Economics: New Directions II' (1975) 67 Journal of Home Economics 26.

the 'natural' unit group of society and basis of social organisation.[5] This family, with its income-earning father and home-making mother had a powerful influence on law and social policy across Europe. Supported by the teachings of the major Christian religions, the gendered marriage-based nuclear family was protected and given preferential treatment in most European legal systems, including in Ireland.

3. Modern families in Ireland

Current social practices have moved on from the centrality of the marriage-based family, although marriage remains a popular choice for many. Census figures offer a useful insight into how patterns of family life have gradually changed in Ireland. Marriage rates, expressed as the number of marriages in each year per 1,000 of the population, have declined gradually from high rates in the 1960s and 1970s, to lower rates throughout the 1980s and 1990s. This is illustrated in the graph below:

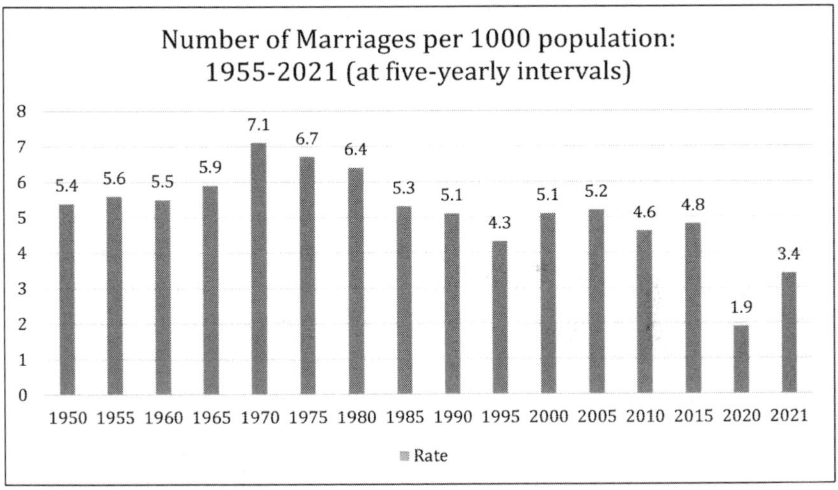

Fig. 1 Marriage rate expressed as the number of marriages each year per 1,000 of the population, 1960-2020 (at five-yearly intervals). Source: CSO Vital Statistics Yearly Summaries.[6]

Correspondingly, as illustrated by the graph below, the proportion of births that take place outside of marriage has increased from 2.7% of births in 1980 to 38.4% in 2020.

5 Deborah Chambers, *A sociology of Family Life: Change and Diversity in Intimate Relations* (Polity 2012) 22.

6 The sharp rate falls in 2020 and 2021 was most likely the result of restrictions imposed during the Covid 19 pandemic.

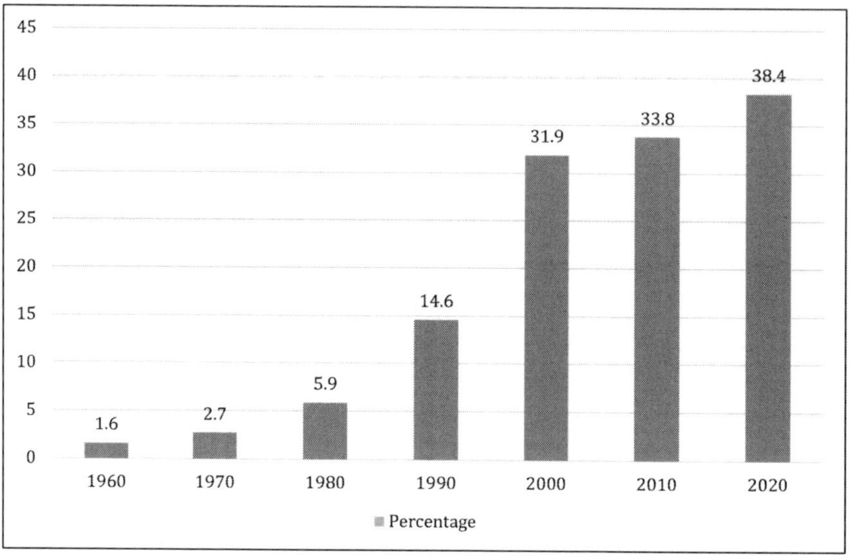

Fig. 2. Proportion of births that take place outside marriage, expressed as a percentage of all births (in 10-yearly intervals). Source: CSO Vital Statistics Yearly Summaries

None of this is to say that marriage is out of fashion. Even today, marriage remains popular and an important life goal for many, though it is evident that it is no longer seen as a vital element in the formation of new families. On average, people marry at an older age than in the past and many choose to live together either before getting married, or as an alternative to marriage. For instance, the number of unmarried cohabiting couples increased from around 31,300 in 1996 to 152,300 in 2016.

4. Who is, and is not, 'Family' for the purpose of Article 41?

Modern social understandings of family are significantly different to those of the 1930s when the Irish Constitution was adopted. Nonetheless, Article 41 of the Constitution and its judicial interpretation continues to reflect the ideas of functionalist sociology. The 'Family' is described as the fundamental unit group of society and women are allocated a defined role as mothers and homemakers. Article 41 does not expressly define 'Family,' but points to the family for constitutional purposes being – exclusively – based on marriage. Article 41.3.1° pledges the State 'to guard with special care the institution of Marriage, on which the Family is founded, and to protect it against attack.' The phrase 'on which the Family is founded' implies that the family springs from marriage. The Irish text of the Constitution makes this even more obvious: 'Ós ar an bPósadh atá an Teaghlach bunaithe' – because it is on marriage that the family is founded. Other parts of Article 41 confirm the central importance of marriage within the Constitution, with Article 41.3.2° setting out the conditions for divorce,[7] while Article 41.4 clarifies that marriage may be contracted in accordance with law 'by two persons without distinction as to their sex.'[8]

Key Constitutional provision – Article 41 'The Family'

ARTICLE 41

1 1° The State recognises the Family as the natural primary and fundamental unit group of Society, and as a moral institution possessing inalienable and imprescriptible rights, antecedent and superior to all positive law.

2° The State, therefore, guarantees to protect the Family in its constitution and authority, as the necessary basis of social order and as indispensable to the welfare of the Nation and the State.

2 1° In particular, the State recognises that by her life within the home, woman gives to the State a support without which the common good cannot be achieved.

2° The State shall, therefore, endeavour to ensure that mothers shall not be obliged by economic necessity to engage in labour to the neglect of their duties in the home.

3 1° The State pledges itself to guard with special care the institution of Marriage, on which the Family is founded, and to protect it against attack.

2° A Court designated by law may grant a dissolution of marriage where, but only where, it is satisfied that –

i there is no reasonable prospect of a reconciliation between the spouses,

ii such provision as the Court considers proper having regard to the circumstances exists or will be made for the spouses, any children of either or both of them and any other person prescribed by law, and

iii any further conditions prescribed by law are complied with.

3° Provision may be made by law for the recognition under the law of the State of a dissolution of marriage granted under the civil law of another state.

4 Marriage may be contracted in accordance with law by two persons without distinction as to their sex.

The Supreme Court has generally emphasised that the 'Family' to which Article 41 refers is the family based on marriage. As far back as 1966 and as recently as 2021 the Supreme Court reaffirmed its position that

7 As amended by the Fifteenth Amendment of the Constitution Act 1995 and the Thirty-eighth Amendment of the Constitution Act 2019. See also the Family Law (Divorce) Act 1996, as amended by the Family Law Act 2019.

8 Inserted by the Thirty-fourth Amendment of the Constitution Act 2015.

'Family' in Article 41 means only the family that emerges from a legally recognised marriage. A married couple without children are treated as a constitutionally recognised family.[9] Similarly, a separated married mother and her son,[10] a widow or widower and their children, and two orphans born to now-deceased married parents[11] have all been recognised as families for this purpose.

Key Supreme Court cases – defining family

In 1966, in *State (Nicolaou) v An Bord Uchtála*, Walsh J pronounced that the family in Article 41 'is the family which is founded on the institution of marriage and, in the context of the Article, marriage means valid marriage under the laws for the time being in force in the State.'[12]

In 1980, in *G v An Bord Uchtála*, O'Higgins CJ observed that the unmarried mother in that case 'is not the mother of a family, in the sense in which the term is used in the Constitution. Article 41 of the Constitution... refers exclusively to the family founded and based on the institution of marriage.'[13]

Sixteen years later, in *WO'R v EH*, Hamilton CJ agreed, noting how 'a de facto family, or any rights arising therefrom, is not recognised by the Constitution'.[14] In 2009, in *JMcD v PL and BM*, the Supreme Court ruled out recognizing an unmarried lesbian couple with a child as a 'Family' for the purposes of Irish law. Denham J reaffirmed that '[t]hroughout our case law the family is defined as the family based on marriage. ... Therefore, arising from the terms of the Constitution, "family" means a family based on marriage...'.[15]

In 2013, in *CO'S v Judge Doyle*, MacMenamin J remarked how '....it is very well established that the protection which is afforded to the family not only under Article 41 but also under Article 42 of the Constitution is based on the family as established by marriage.'[16] The unmarried mother in that case therefore could not claim that 'she and her son constituted a "family" recognised by the Constitution' as 'the law provides that the recognition given to the constitutional family is only one that is based on marriage.'[17]

---

9 *Murray v Ireland* [1985] IR 532 (High Court) and [1991] ILRM 465 (Supreme Court).
10 *Sinnott v Minister for Education* [2001] 2 IR 545.
11 See Walsh J (obiter) in *G v An Bord Uchtála* [1980] IR 32, 70.
12 [1966] IR 567, 643.
13 [1980] IR 32, 54.
14 [1996] IR 248, 265.
15 [2009] IESC 81, Denham J at [61]-[62] and again at [63]. She specifies 'the marriage of a man and a woman' but this approach has been superseded by the enactment of Art 41.4 and the Marriage Act 2015.
16 [2014] 1 IR 556, 568.
17 ibid.

In 2018, in *M v Minister for Justice and Equality*[18] Clarke CJ noted how the unmarried respondents in that case 'do not form a family unit within the meaning of that term as contained in Article 41 of the Constitution'.[19] Similarly, in *MIH v Minister for Justice and Equality*, in 2021, Charleton J observed that 'Article 41 protects the rights of the family based on marriage'.[20]

4.1 Impact of constitutional definition of 'Family'

The constitutional protection extended to marital families necessarily implies that such protection does not extend to other families. This means that a child with parents not married to each other do not together constitute a family for constitutional purposes. While single mothers and children born outside marriage enjoy constitutional rights in respect of their relationship (under Article 40.3 and 42A respectively), they fall outside the protection of Article 41. The Supreme Court has confirmed that the father of a child born to parents not married to each other has no constitutional entitlements in respect of his child either under Article 41 or Article 40.3. In *JK v VW* the Supreme Court acknowledged that the unmarried father may well have 'rights of interest or concern' but, unlike the mother of the child, he has no constitutionally protected rights in respect of his child.[21] Long term (unmarried) cohabiting couples are not 'Family' for the purposes of the Constitution even if they have children together. The Supreme Court has also exhibited reluctance to recognise extended family relationships outside the nuclear family.[22]

The constitutional preference for marriage has led to several further constitutional principles that prevent the Oireachtas from favouring the non-marital family over families based on marriage. Laws that penalise married couples for being married, by providing better conditions for unmarried couples over similarly positioned married couples, are likely to be unconstitutional.[23] For example, in *Hyland v Minister for Social Welfare*,[24] legislation imposing certain conditions in relation to the social

---

18 [2018] 1 IR 417.

19 ibid at 498.

20 [2021] IESC 32 [23]. See also Whelan J in the Court of Appeal in *In the Matter of Miss B, a minor* [2022] IECA 196 [86].

21 [1990] 2 IR 437, 447.

22 See *O(O) v Minister for Justice and Equality* [2015] IESC 26 [26], though for a different approach, see the High Court decision in *RX v Minister for Justice* [2010] IEHC 446. See also *Jordan v O'Brien* [1960] IR 363.

23 In *Murphy v Attorney General* [1982] IR 241, a law that resulted in double-income married couples paying more income tax than similarly-paid and similarly-positioned cohabiting unmarried couples was deemed to be in breach of Article 41, specifically of the 'pledge by the State to guard with special care the institution of marriage and to guard it against attack'.

24 [1989] IR 624.

welfare entitlements of married couples that did not apply to similarly-placed unmarried cohabitants were found to be in breach of Article 41's charge to guard with special care the institution of marriage. Some commentators and case law suggest that, in addition to laws that penalise marriage falling foul of the Constitution, laws that discourage marriage, that make it less attractive or that incentivise or 'induce' cohabitation may be unconstitutional.

As you will see throughout this book, the constitutional definition of 'Family' as that based on marriage has had a significant impact on how family life is regulated. The basic framework of the law is based around this family and the need to protect it. Restrictive divorce law enacted in the 1990s aimed to protect individual marriages by making divorce difficult.[25] In the 2010s a political desire to protect marriage meant that recognition of other forms of family life could only be done in a way that did not impinge upon marriage. Legislation providing for same sex civil partnership avoided creating a status equivalent to marriage. Limited protections extended to cohabitants were designed to ensure that the rights of spouses were protected[26] and a constitutional referendum was considered necessary to reflect changed social understandings of what marriage is and who may marry.[27]

The law governing the relationship between parents and their children is also constructed around an image of family based on marriage. This means that the legal relationships between parents and children are regulated differently depending on whether parents are married to each other or not. Men married to the mother of a child are assumed to be the father of the child and are automatic guardians of their children from birth. In contrast, fathers not married to the mother of their child do not enjoy automatic guardianship rights in respect of their children, though they may acquire them in accordance with a variety of processes including application to the court as set out in the Guardianship of Infants Act 1964.[28] Even with the possibility of a court order, the courts have emphasised that a father not married to the mother of a child merely has a right to apply to be a guardian and no automatic right to be appointed one. Questions around whether the threshold for state intervention to protect children was higher for children of married parents than for other children shaped the wording of Article 42A of the Constitution inserted by the Children's Rights Referendum in 2015.[29]

---

[25] Family Law (Divorce) Act 1996, facilitated by the Fifteenth Amendment of the Constitution Act 1995, discussed further in Chapter 3.

[26] Civil Partnership and Certain Rights and Obligations of Cohabitants Act 2010.

[27] Thirty-fourth Amendment to the Constitution (Marriage Equality) Act 2015.

[28] See Chapter 9.

[29] See Chapter 8.

4.2 Legislative recognition of families outside marriage

Legislation recognises different types of family situations and accords a variety of rights and protections to a range of family forms. An early example of this can be seen in the Family Law Act 1981, which regulates the legal ownership of wedding gifts as between engaged couples when a marriage does not go ahead. Although the measures apply to persons who at some point contemplated marriage, the Act recognises people who are, by definition, not yet married. Domestic violence legislation extends protection from abuse to people living together as cohabitants, parents living with adult children and others living together in a relationship that is 'not primarily contractual'.[30] The Civil Liability Act 1996 and Residential Tenancies Acts 2004- 2021 also recognise cohabiting partners in certain circumstances.

Substantive recognition and protection for some durable couple relationships outside marriage is provided by the Civil Partnership and Certain Rights and Obligations of Cohabitants Act 2010 ('the 2010 Act'). This legislation introduced two significant changes in the law for the benefit of cohabitants and same sex couples. First, it extended limited remedies to long-term financially dependent 'qualified cohabitants'. These remedies are similar, but significantly less extensive than those applicable to married couples (see Chapter 6). Secondly, it created the civil status of civil partnership as an alternative to marriage for same sex couples, but not for different-sex couples. This legislation was passed as a compromise solution in response to growing demand for marriage for same sex couples during the 2000s. With civil partnership, the State partially cloned marriage, though the clone was imperfect, and not universally welcomed. Indeed, because civil partnership compromised on the aim of marriage equality, it caused significant division within the LGBTI+ community between those who pragmatically viewed it as a significant step in providing legal protection for and recognition of same sex couples and those who, on principle, objected to what they saw as a second-class union denoting the inferiority of same sex partners in the eyes of the State.

The process for forming a civil partnership was entirely secular, with no role for religious groups, but otherwise bore many similarities to the process for entering a marriage. Couples seeking a civil partnership had to be of the same sex, aged 18 or over, not closely related by blood, and not already married or in another civil partnership. The process to register a civil partnership required the couple to make declarations before a registrar and was subject to the same notice and venue rules that applied to civil marriages. Civil partners enjoy many of the same rights, privileges

---

[30] Domestic Violence Act 2018, s 6(1)(a)(v). See Chapter 7.

and obligations as married couples. For instance, dealings with the 'shared home' of civil partners are subject to the same rules that apply to the family home of married couples.[31] The financial support provisions of the Act largely mirror the equivalent provisions that relate to spouses. In relation to succession, with some subtle differences, surviving civil partners have the same inheritance rights as surviving spouses. Civil partners are also treated the same as spouses for the purpose of domestic violence, tax, social welfare legislation and in respect of the acquisition of citizenship. Additionally, civil partners must be treated the same as spouses in relation to pensions.

There are differences between civil partnership and marriage, some of which underline the inferior legal status of civil partnership. A key difference is that civil partnership does not enjoy the constitutional protection that is afforded to the family based on marriage. Further the 2010 Act avoids using the term 'family' to describe civil partners, referring to their 'shared home' rather than the 'family home' of married couples. The process for dissolving a civil partnership was, until divorce reforms in 2019, easier than a dissolution of marriage and remains different in other respects, implying that the State is not as exercised about civil partners splitting up. Civil partners are also treated differently to spouses in other ways. For instance, judicial separation is not available to civil partners.

The Marriage Act 2015 ('the 2015 Act') introduced marriage for same sex couples and prevented further civil partnerships from being formed after May 2016. Between 2011 and 2016, 2,078 couples entered into civil partnership in Ireland. The 2015 Act repealed the provisions in the 2010 Act that had allowed new civil partnerships to be formed. This meant that only those who had given notice before the commencement of the 2015 Act in November 2015 could form new civil partnerships after commencement, and only for six months up to May 2016. This decision was likely motivated by a concern that continuing to offer civil partnerships to those who could now marry each other could dissuade couples from marrying. Civil partnership, it was argued, might act as competition to marriage, in possible breach of the guarantee in Article 41.3.1° that promises to safeguard marriage and protect it from attack. This contrasts with the approach in the UK. Following a successful legal challenge[32] and sustained campaigning from heterosexual couples who objected to marriage, in all jurisdictions in the UK both different sex and same sex couples can choose either marriage or civil partnership.[33]

31 Family Home Protection Act 1976, s 2.

32 *Steinfeld and Keidan v Secretary of State* [2018] UKSC 32.

33 See, for instance, the Civil Partnership Act 2004 as amended by the Civil Partnership (Opposite-sex Couples) Regulations 2019.

In Ireland, while the Marriage Act 2015 closed off the possibility of forming new civil partnerships, existing civil partnerships that were formed before 2016 and not dissolved or converted to marriages (of which there are about 1,200) remain intact for so long as civil partners choose to remain as such. Nonetheless, the 2015 Act incentivises civil partners to enter into marriage, by waiving the usual three months' notice requirement and offering a lower than normal notification fee. Approximately 650 couples converted their civil partnership to marriage between 2016 and 2020.

4.3 A broader constitutional perspective?

Recently, some judges have, in *obiter* comments (comments that are not relevant to the reasoning of the decision before the court), cast doubt on the primacy of the marriage-based family, suggesting that, in light of social change, a broader constitutional interpretation is possible. For instance, Article 41.2 of the Constitution speaks of the special position of women and mothers working within the home and caring for their families. Some judges have expressed the view that the 'woman' and 'mother' to whom Article 41.2 refers is not necessarily confined to the woman and mother in a family based on marriage.[34] In *Gorry v Minister for Justice*, O'Donnell CJ notes that unmarried parents are 'just as free to provide education in their homes or in private schools as married couples are and cannot be obliged by the State, in violation of their conscience, to send their children to schools established by the State or to any particular school designated by the State'.[35] Thus, it seems, while Article 42 may technically apply only to the constitutionally-recognised Family, it is unlikely that the courts would deny similar privileges to unmarried parents in respect of their children.[36]

In *IRM v Minister for Justice and Equality*,[37] Humphreys J, in the High Court, doubted the continuing force of older case law denying constitutional recognition to the non-marital family. Society, he said, had changed radically since some of these decisions, as reflected in the introduction of divorce, marriage for same sex couples and the new Article 42A, guaranteeing children's rights. Such reforms, he continued, justified 'a

---

[34] See, for instance, Justice Brian Walsh, 'The Constitution and Constitutional Rights' in Frank Litton (ed) *The Constitution of Ireland 1937-1987* (IPA 1988), 98. See also McCarthy and O'Flaherty JJ in *L v L* [1992] 2 IR 77, Abbott J in *AF v SF* [2007] 4 IR 326, and O'Donnell CJ in *Gorry v Minister for Justice* [2020] IESC 55 [66].

[35] [2020] IESC 55 [66].

[36] See also Gerard Hogan, Gerry Whyte, David Kenny and Rachael Walsh, *Kelly: The Irish Constitution*, (5th edn, Bloomsbury Publishing 2018) at 2265 who remark that 'it is clear that the Constitution affords protection to the autonomy of a stable non-marital family.'

[37] *IRM v Minister for Justice and Equality* [2016] IEHC 478.

recognition that members of a non-marital relationship, and non-marital parents of both sexes in particular, enjoy acknowledgement of inherent constitutional rights in relation to their children and each other on a wider basis than has been recognised thus far'.[38] The extension of marriage to same sex couples was, he added, 'a quantum leap in the extent to which the Constitution is oriented towards respect and protection for a diversity of private family relationships'.[39]

On appeal, however, the Supreme Court[40] concluded that the High Court judge's remarks were *obiter*. Clarke CJ added that 'they could not have the force of precedent on this point in light of the consistent case law of this Court to the contrary stretching back decades and reaffirmed on several recent occasions'.[41] Nonetheless, Clarke CJ left open the possibility of future reflection on the point in a more appropriate case: 'at some point in the future the question may arise as to whether the legal and constitutional position of unmarried parents, as between themselves and their children, should be afforded greater recognition than presently exists'.[42]

In *Gorry v Minister for Justice*,[43] O'Donnell CJ suggested that the distinction between the marital and non-marital family is less clear cut than some imagined it to be.[44] The comments are *obiter*; the parties before the court in *Gorry* had been married. O'Donnell CJ noted that while Article 41.3 references marriage, Articles 41 and 42, 'do not differentiate between the marital status of the couple involved or the families that are thereby created'.[45] He pointed out that even before Article 42A was enacted, the courts had recognised that non-marital children had the same constitutional rights as marital children.[46]

O'Donnell CJ challenged the narrow thinking around Article 41, suggesting that 'an intimate relationship of some permanence where the two people treat themselves, and are recognised by others, as a unit in addition to their standing as individuals is something of constitutional value'.[47] He pointed out the functional similarities between married couples and long term cohabitants suggesting that both units are 'capable of providing the basis of social order indispensable to the welfare of the nation and

---

38 ibid [99].
39 *IRM v Minister for Justice and Equality* [2016] IEHC 478 [99].
40 Now called *M v Minister for Justice and Equality* [2018] IESC 14.
41 ibid [239].
42 ibid [240].
43 *Gorry v Minister for Justice* [2020] IESC 55.
44 ibid [66].
45 ibid.
46 *Re M (an Infant)* [1946] IR 334.
47 [2020] IESC 55 [67].

the State'. As for the need to protect marriage, he argued that it was not necessary to treat cohabiting relationships as being of no value because they are not founded on marriage.[48] He concluded that long-term adult relationships 'must be valued and respected by a state which guarantees to protect individuals as human persons. It is not necessary for the exaltation of marriage that other pair-bonding nurturing relationships be humbled, still less ignored.'[49]

It is unclear whether O'Donnell CJ was proposing a reinterpretation of Article 41 to include all long-term adult relationships or whether he was suggesting that the rights of non-marital relationships reside elsewhere in the Constitution, perhaps, in the personal rights provisions of Article 40.3 (as is the case with the rights of the unmarried mother).

Judicial momentum in favour of change seems to be mounting. In *Re JJ,* McKechnie J (in the Supreme Court) also suggests that an alternative interpretation of Article 41 is possible; one that sweeps away the traditional distinction between marital and non-marital families. Nonetheless, he felt 'confined to approaching the issues [in that case] from the perspective that Article 41 rights apply to the marital family only.'[50] The other judges did 'not consider it necessary to express any view upon the wider issues.'[51]

These progressive judicial comments exist alongside the large body of clear legal precedent that the constitutional family is limited to the family based on marriage.

5. International dimensions – the European Convention on Human Rights

The legal understanding of family in article 41 of the Constitution conflicts with the stance of some international conventions in relation to family life. Most notably, Article 8 of the European Convention on Human Rights (ECHR) provides a more open interpretation of the concept of family that has evolved to reflect social change and includes diverse types of family not based on marriage. For the purpose of the ECHR, 'family life' is not confined to formal relationships such as those based on marriage but embraces a wide variety of family forms. In establishing whether family life exists, the European Court of Human Rights (ECtHR) looks to the substance and quality of family relationships rather than the form they take. Whether family life exists depends on the quality of the relationship

48 ibid.
49 ibid.
50 [2021] IESC 1 [168].
51 [2021] IESC 1 [100], O'Donnell CJ, Dunne J, O'Malley J and Baker J.

and bond, and closeness of personal ties. The ECtHR has recognised families bound by social rather than legal or genetic ties; the absence of any blood or legal tie is not a barrier to recognition of family relationships. The ECtHR case law therefore takes a more evolutionary and dynamic approach to family life than the Irish courts have broadly envisaged.

Key cases – Family life in the European Convention on Human Rights

In *Johnston v Ireland* the ECtHR affirmed that art 8 applies to the family life of unmarried couples and their children. The court determined that the 'absence of an appropriate legal regime reflecting the [child's] natural family ties amounts to a failure to respect her family life.'[52]

In *Marckx v Belgium*, the ECtHR recognised that 'family life' arose between an unmarried mother and her child and that it also encompassed the ties between near relatives such as grandchildren and grandparents who may play a considerable part in family life.[53]

In *Keegan v Ireland* the ECtHR confirmed that family life is recognised not only in a marital context and 'may encompass other de facto family ties' outside of marriage.[54] The court remarked that a child born outside of a non-marital relationship is 'part of that family unit from the moment of his birth and by the very fact of it.'[55] The bond of family life between the child and his parents exists even if the parents' relationship has ended, as it had in Keegan.

In *Schalk and Kopf v Austria* the ECtHR recognised that family life existed between a same sex couple[56] and *Gas and Dubois v France* held that it could include same sex couples with children.[57]

Whilst Ireland is a signatory to the ECHR and its provisions have indirectly been incorporated into Irish law in that they can be invoked through the European Convention on Human Rights Act 2003, this has happened at a sub-constitutional level. This means that the Constitution has priority over the ECHR and the protection of family life in Irish law is confined to the family as defined by the Constitution and its judicial interpretations.

6. Proposals for constitutional reform

A Constitution Review Group, reporting in 1996, recommended removing

52 App. No. 9697/82, (18 December 1986) [75].
53 (1979) 2 EHRR 330.
54 App. No. 16969, (26 May 1994) [44].
55 ibid.
56 App. No. 30141/04 (22 November 2010).
57 App. No. 25951/07, admissibility decision, 31 August 2010.

the link between marriage and constitutional recognition of the family,[58] a stance also reflected in the recommendations of the Citizens' Assembly on Gender Equality ('the Assembly') in 2021.[59] The Assembly recommended constitutional change to extend protection to 'private and family life ... not limited to the family based on marriage.'[60] The Assembly did not offer a specific formulation for a revised Article 41 but the recommendation to protect private and family life suggests the removal of the reference to special protection for the 'Family.' The Oireachtas Joint Committee on Gender Equality tasked with implementing the recommendations of the Assembly proposed more limited constitutional change. It suggested leaving Article 41.1.1⁰ and 41.1.2⁰ unchanged and amending the text of Article 41.3.1⁰ to read 'The State pledges itself to guard with special care the Family, including but not limited to the marital family'[61] Alternatively, it suggested that the existing text could be amended to remove the phrase 'on which the family is founded' thus retaining special protection for the institution of marriage. At the time of going to press, no decision has been made by Government in relation to the wording or precise timing of the proposed constitutional referendum although there is a proposal to hold a referendum in November 2023. A public consultation on the broad proposal to 'amend Article 41 to protect family life, with the protection afforded to the family not limited to the marital family' was held in May 2023.

6.1 Critical thinking point: Should the law extend special protection to the family based on marriage?

Even if a broader interpretation of the constitutional family were to be developed by the courts or inserted into the Constitution by referendum, the legal preference for the family based on marriage will remain unless there is significant legislative reform. Irish law uses the formal status of marriage as a signal of commitment and interdependence. People who marry have taken active steps to achieve a legal status in relation to one another and have an expectation that doing so will mean that their relationship is recognised by the State.[62] Further, relying on marriage to signal family life is administratively efficient in providing a record of who is in a relationship at any given point in time.[63] In contrast, people who cohabit, or live together for other non-contractual reasons have

---

58 *Report of the Constitution Review Group* (Pn 2632, Stationery Office 1996).

59 *Report of the Citizens' Assembly on Gender Equality* (June 2021).

60 ibid 12.

61 Joint Committee on Gender Equality, *Unfinished Democracy: Achieving Gender Equality, Final Report* December 2022 33/GE/03, 39.

62 See Chapter 2.

63 Kathy Griffiths, 'From form to function and back again: a new conceptual basis for developing frameworks for the legal recognition of adult relationships' (2019) 31(3) Child and Family Law Quarterly 227, 231.

made no such commitment; any recognition of their relationship will necessarily be based on what they *do* in their relationship and the levels of commitment and interdependence they demonstrate. As discussed in Chapter 6 in relation to existing legislation providing remedies for former cohabitants, this is necessarily a retrospective exercise requiring evidence of levels of commitment.

In addition to administrative difficulties in identifying who is in a durable relationship, there is a symbolic significance attached to marriage. An important element of the 2015 Marriage Equality referendum was the level of social acceptance and inclusion for LGBTI+ families signaled by the result.[64] Civil Partnership was inferior to marriage and seen as relegating same sex couples to a lesser social category. Equality of legal status through marriage does not eradicate social and cultural inequalities and important inequalities remain for gay and lesbian couples.[65] Nonetheless, continuing the symbolic significance of marriage can marginalise other forms of family life. The regulatory and fiscal advantages conferred on married couples can signal to other families that they are in some way less important and that their familial relationships are less valuable to society.

While marriage is important and valuable, the elevation of marriage in Irish law clearly works to the prejudice of families not based on marriage and arguably disrespects children born to parents who are not married to each other. Constitutional reform appears imminent, but the question regarding the special place of marriage in Irish law will remain, even if the most liberal recommendation of the Oireachtas Joint Committee on Gender Equality is accepted by both Government and the people.

7. Summary

- There are many different ways of thinking about family based on biological connections, formal commitments and bonds of affection. The structure of family life in Ireland has changed very significantly since the foundation of the State as marriage rates have fallen, and more children are born to parents not married to each other.
- The Constitution and its judicial interpretation currently defines the family exclusively as that based on marriage. Although it does recognise the existence of familial connections beyond marriage, for example between a mother and child, these connections do not create a family for constitutional purposes.
- The constitutional primacy afforded to marriage has resulted in

64 Fergus Ryan, 'Unfinished Business? Equality and Family Diversity in the Wake of the Irish Marriage Referendum', [2018] Irish Journal of Family Law 59, 59.

65 ibid 60.

a regulatory framework grounded on the marriage-based family. Whilst limited recognition and regulatory support has been provided to other families, the bulk of family law is focused on ties created by and within marriage.

- The European Court of Human Rights takes a much broader approach to the definition of family, focusing on the quality of family life rather than legal status.
- Legal regulation of family life can be based on a formal legal status such as marriage or civil partnership, or based on a more factual approach, recognising what families do.

8. Further reading

Conor O'Mahony 'Irreconcilable Differences–Article 8 ECHR and Irish Law on Non-Traditional Families' (2012) 26 International Journal of Law, Policy and the Family 31.

Kathy Griffiths, 'From "form" to function and back again: a new conceptual basis for developing frameworks for the legal recognition of family relationships' (2019) 31 Child and Family Law Quarterly 227.

Joint Oireachtas Committee on Gender Equality, *Unfinished Democracy: Achieving Gender Equality Final Report*, (Houses of the Oireachtas 2022)

Fergus Ryan, 'Out of the Shadow of the Constitution: Civil Partnership, Cohabitation and the Constitutional Family' (2012) 48 The Irish Jurist 201.

Fergus Ryan, 'Unfinished Business? Equality and Family Diversity in the Wake of the Irish Marriage Referendum' (2018) Irish Journal of Family Law 59.

Chapter 2

Formation and Validity of Marriage

Deirdre McGowan

LEARNING OBJECTIVES

By the end of the chapter, students will be equipped to:

- Summarise the formalities required for entry into marriage.
- Explain the difference between an impediment to marriage and the grounds upon which a marriage might be declared invalid.
- Distinguish between situations in which a marriage might be declared void and those in which it might be voidable.

CRITICAL THINKING POINTS

- Should the citizenship status of intended spouses affect access to marriage?
- How should the law on nullity of marriage be reformed?

1. Introduction

As discussed in Chapter 1, legal marriage is an important signal of the existence of family life and is the foundation of the constitutional family. The State relies on the formal status of marriage in many contexts to identify commitment and interdependence. This chapter begins by looking at the various rules and procedures that govern the formation of legally valid marriages including factors, known as **impediments**, that will prevent a marriage from going ahead. Sometimes a couple will go through a ceremony of marriage but for a particular legal reason it will later be determined not to have been a legally valid marriage. These reasons are governed by the law on **nullity of marriage**, discussed in the second part of the chapter.

Getting married is the only way that parties to an intimate and committed relationship can have their status automatically recognised by the State. It is important to note at the outset that although some very limited marriage-like obligations can arise between certain cohabiting couples,[1] cohabitants will never be treated as spouses. Only those who have complied with all the necessary formalities will obtain the status, rights and obligations of a married couple.

2. Formalities for Entry into Marriage

Before November 2007, there were different statutory rules governing the solemnisation of religious marriages and civil marriages officiated by a civil registrar.[2] The legal rules for marriage also varied between religions, and the only rules common to all marriages were the need to give notice of marriage to a civil registrar and a registration requirement.[3] Now, Pt 6 of the Civil Registration Act 2004 ('the 2004 Act') contains a single set of rules that apply to all marriages celebrated in Ireland.[4]

To begin, the parties must give three months' notice of marriage, delivered in person to a civil registrar.[5] Both parties must then attend at the registrar's office not less than five days before the ceremony to sign a declaration that there is no impediment to the marriage.[6] Should the parties wish to shorten the notice period, they must make an application for abridgment to the Circuit Court.[7] An abridgment will be granted only where the applicants can demonstrate serious reasons and that an exemption from the notice requirement is in their interests.[8] This provision is mostly used in cases of serious illness. The notice requirement is a substantive requirement for marriage, meaning that if it is not complied with, a subsequently contracted marriage will not be legally valid.[9] Once the notice requirement is satisfied, the registrar will provide the parties with a marriage registration form and the marriage must take place within six months of the date of the form.[10] This form is given to the person solemnising the marriage by the parties and, after the ceremony, is signed by the parties to the marriage, two witnesses and the solemniser. One of the spouses must return it to the registrar within one month for registration.[11]

---

1 Civil Partnership and Certain Rights and Obligations of Cohabitants Act 2010, Pt 15. See Chapter 6.

2 These rules were found in the Marriages (Ireland) Act 1844 as amended.

3 Registration of Marriages (Ireland) Act 1863; Family Law Act 1995, s 32.

4 Pt 6 of the 2004 Act was commenced on 5 November 2007 by the Civil Registration Act 2004 (Commencement) Order 2007, SI 736/2007.

5 Civil Registration Act 2004, s 46(1)(a)(i).

6 ibid, s 46(1)(b).

7 ibid, s 47(1).

8 ibid, s 47(2)(b).

9 ibid, s 46(6).

10 ibid, s 48.

11 ibid, s 49.

Only registered solemnisers, as defined by the 2004 Act, can solemnise marriages,[12] and the ceremonies must take place at a location open to the public, except where otherwise approved by a Superintendent Registrar or an tArd-Chláraitheoir.[13] Both parties to the marriage must be present at the ceremony and the solemniser must satisfy themselves that the parties to the marriage understand the nature of the marriage ceremony and the declarations that they must make.[14] A form of ceremony approved by the an tArd-Chláraitheoir must be used and it must be conducted in the presence of two witnesses over the age of 18. At the ceremony, the parties declare that there are no impediments to the marriage and that they accept each other as husband, wife or spouse.[15] These stipulations are substantive requirements for a valid marriage. Any failure to comply precisely with them will mean that a valid marriage has not taken place and the parties will not be the spouses of each other.[16]

3. Before the Wedding: Impediments to Marriage

Key legislation – s 2(2) of the Civil Registration Act 2004 (impediments to marriage)

(2) For the purposes of this Act there is an impediment to marriage if –

(a) the marriage would be void by virtue of the Marriage Act 1835 as amended by the Marriage (prohibited degrees of relationship) Acts 1907 and 1921,

(b) one of the parties to the marriage is, or both are, already married,

(c) one or both of the parties to the intended marriage will be under the age of 18 years on the date of solemnisation of the intended marriage [....].

(d) one of the parties to the proposed marriage lacks, or both of the parties to the proposed marriage lack, the capacity (within the meaning of the Assisted Decision Making (Capacity) Act 2015) to consent to the marriage.

(f) one of the parties to the marriage is, or, other than where section 2B applies, both are, already party to subsisting civil partnership, or

(g) the marriage would constitute a marriage of convenience.

Parties must confirm to the registrar when giving notice to marry, and again at the marriage ceremony, that there are no impediments to the

---

12 ibid, s 51(1).

13 ibid, s 51(2)(c).

14 ibid, s 51(2)(a), (b).

15 ibid, s 51(4)(b)(iii).

16 ibid, ss 46(4) and 51(5).

marriage. A list of statutory impediments to marriage is set out in s 2(2) of the 2004 Act, as amended.

Section 58 of the 2004 Act provides that a person may at any time before the solemnisation of a marriage lodge an objection in writing to a marriage with any civil registrar. An objection can relate to minor errors in the marriage notification or to the existence of an impediment to marriage. Minor errors are dealt with by the registrar in consultation with the parties. Objections based on alleged impediments are investigated by a Superintendent Registrar and if they are substantiated the marriage cannot proceed. A decision of the Superintendent Registrar regarding an impediment can be appealed to the Circuit Court. The impediments to marriage are dealt with in turn.

3.1 Prohibited degrees of relationship, s 2(2)(a)

Pre-reformation Canon Law prohibited marriage between certain categories of relatives based on legal ties and blood relationships. These rules are ancient but remain largely intact and cover a broad range of relationships. Section 2(a) of the 2004 Act states that there is an impediment to a marriage if it would be rendered void by the Marriage Act 1835 ('the 1835 Act') as amended by the Marriage (Prohibited Degrees of Relationship) Acts 1907 and 1921. The 1835 Act in turn refers to prohibitions set out in three pieces of 16th century legislation based on the Old Testament Book of Leviticus.[17]

The prohibited relationships for marriage are generally divided into two types: blood relations (consanguinity) and legal ties (affinity). In general, an individual cannot marry someone within three degrees of relationship, whether that relationship is created by blood or by marriage. For example, a woman cannot marry her husband's father/mother, nor can she marry her daughter's son/daughter.[18] Some specific exceptions from the three degrees rule have been created to allow a man to marry his deceased or ex-wife's sister and a woman to marry her deceased or ex-husband's brother.[19] The full list of prohibited degrees of relationship is set out in the table below and they apply to both same sex and different sex marriages.[20]

---

17 Marriage Act (No 1) 1537 and Marriage Act (No 2) 1537. The Statute Law Revision Act 2007 confirms that all three Acts remain in force, although elements of them may be constitutionally suspect.

18 Law Reform Commission, *Report on Nullity of Marriage* (LRC 9 – 1984), 46-47.

19 See *O'Shea v Ireland & AG* [2007] 2 IR 313 for a comprehensive overview of the law on this point.

20 Civil Registration Act 2004, s 2A(1).

A person may not marry their:	
grandparent	sibling's child's spouse
grandfather's spouse	spouse's child
spouse's grandmother	child's spouse
parent's sister	sibling
parent's brother	grandchild
parent's brother's spouse	spouse's parent
parent's sister's spouse	child
spouse's parent's sister	spouse's child
spouse's parent's brother	child's spouse
parent	grandchild
step-parent	grandchild's spouse
spouse's parent	spouse's grandchild
child	sibling's child
grandchild's spouse	sibling's child's spouse
spouse's grandchild	spouse's sibling's child
sibling's child	
spouse's sibling's child	

3.2 Already married, s 2(2)(b)

There is an impediment to marriage if either party is either already married to, or in a civil partnership with, a third party.[21] Going through a ceremony of marriage whilst already married also constitutes the criminal offence of bigamy, although prosecutions are now extremely rare.[22] If a couple are already civilly partnered to each other and wish to change their status to married, they can subsequently marry, and their civil partnership will be automatically dissolved.[23] Issues in relation to prior marriages most commonly arise where one of the parties was previously married and has not obtained an Irish divorce or decree of nullity, or where one party has obtained a foreign divorce that is not legally recognised in Ireland (see Chapter 12). The existence of this impediment and the criminal offence of bigamy demonstrate that marriage is understood as a monogamous relationship in Irish Law. Polygamous marriages, involving more than two spouses, cannot be celebrated in Ireland but are legal in other jurisdictions.[24]

---

21 This impediment also applies to parties already married to *each other*, see *Farooq v Superintendent Registrar* [2018] IEHC 261.

22 Offences Against the Person Act 1861, s 57.

23 Civil Partnership and Certain Rights and Obligations of Cohabitants Act 2010, s 109A as inserted by s 11 of the Marriage Act 2015.

24 There is, however, some evidence that polygamous religious marriages are celebrated here. See Susan Leahy and Kathryn O'Sullivan, 'Unrecognised Muslim Marriage in Ireland: Incidence and Implications' (2019) 29(4) Journal of Muslim Minority Affairs 534.

The rules regarding the recognition of foreign divorces are complex and have changed over time.[25] A foreign divorce will generally be recognised in Ireland if one of the parties to the marriage was domiciled in the legal jurisdiction granting it at the time of the divorce.[26] Domicile (discussed further in Chapter 12) involves living in a country with the intention of making it your permanent home and requires more than the residence requirement necessary to obtain a divorce in most countries. An impediment to marriage will therefore exist if one of the parties to a proposed marriage has obtained a foreign divorce that is not recognised in Ireland.

Complexities arising in the recognition of foreign divorces led to a 2019 constitutional referendum that inserted a new Article 41.3.3° into the Constitution allowing provision to be made by law for broader recognition of foreign divorce, but this has to date only been implemented in relation to UK divorces.[27]

3.3 Age, s 2(2)(c)

Since 2018, both parties to a marriage must be over 18 years of age.[28] Previously, marriage between the ages of 16 and 18 was possible, but only where an exemption certificate was obtained from the court.[29]

3.4 Capacity to consent, s 2(2)(d)

Since 2023, there is an impediment to marriage if one or both of the parties lacks capacity to consent within the meaning of the Assisted Decision Making (Capacity) Act 2015 ('the 2015 Act').[30] Parties to an intended marriage will be presumed to have capacity unless the contrary is demonstrated.[31] An objection to the marriage on this ground must be accompanied by an order of the Circuit Court made pursuant to the 2015 Act that one or both parties lack capacity to consent.[32] A determination of capacity involves an assessment of the person's ability to understand the

---

25 The currently applicable rules can be found in the Domicile and Recognition of Foreign Divorces Act 1986 and in respect of divorces granted in other European Union Member States, in Council Regulation 2201/2003 (also known as Brussels II *bis*) and related case law. See Chapter 12.

26 Domicile and Recognition of Foreign Divorces Act 1986, s 5(1).

27 The Withdrawal of the United Kingdom from the European Union (Consequential Provisions) Act 2020, Pt 19.

28 2004 Act, s 2(2) as amended by Domestic Violence Act 2018, s 49.

29 Family Law Act 1995, s 31(1)(a).

30 Assisted Decision-Making (Capacity) Act 2015 (Commencement) (No. 2) Order 2023, SI 193/2023).

31 Assisted Decision Making Capacity Act 2015, s 8(2).

32 ibid, s 58(11).

nature and consequences of a decision at the time the decision is made. The elements of this 'functional test' are set out in s 3 of the 2015 Act.

3.5 Marriage of convenience, s 2(2)(g)

In response to police reports of an increase in the prevalence of 'sham marriages' the Civil Registration (Amendment) Act 2014 amended the 2004 Act to provide that there is an impediment to marriage where the marriage would constitute a marriage of convenience.

Key definition – Marriage of convenience

A **marriage of convenience** is a marriage where at least one of the parties, at the time of marriage, is neither an Irish nor EU citizen and the marriage is contracted solely for the purpose of securing an immigration advantage for one of the parties to the marriage. An immigration advantage is defined as a determination in a person's favour in relation to the grant of a visa, entry into, presence in or removal from the State or any determination of a right to enter or reside in the State in accordance with immigration legislation.[33]

For marriages potentially falling within the definition of marriage of convenience, or where an objection is received on this ground, a Superintendent Registrar will carry out an investigation during which she or he must consider the factors listed in s 58(4C) of the 2004 Act. These include the length of time that the parties have known each other, whether they are familiar with each other's personal details, have lived together and for how long, can communicate in a common language, the existence of a continuing commitment to emotional and financial support, the extent to which they hold themselves out as couple and their immigration status. In practical terms, the investigation involves a review of documentation submitted and a series of interviews with the couple, both together and alone, for the purpose of gathering the information necessary to make a decision on whether the purported marriage would be entered into for the purpose of obtaining an immigration advantage. If the Superintendent Registrar decides that the marriage will be a marriage of convenience, it cannot proceed. The decision of the Superintendent Registrar can be appealed to the Circuit Court.

---

[33] Civil Registration Act 2004, s 2 as amended by Civil Registration (Amendment) Act 2014 and s 58(4A) of the Civil Registration Act 2004, inserted by s 18 of the Civil Registration (Amendment) Act 2014.

3.6 Critical thinking point: Should the citizenship status of intended spouses affect access to marriage?

Allowing proposed marriages to be investigated and prevented on a suspicion that they are for the purpose of immigration advantage is a legislative response to what the government of the day perceived to be the 'persistent problem' of marriages of convenience.[34]

In 2004, an EU Directive extended free movement rights for EU citizens to their non-EU citizen spouses. These spouses are not required to live in the EU before joining their spouse in moving for work to another EU State.[35] The effect of this Directive is to allow non-EU nationals to enter and reside in the EU if they are married to an EU citizen who is exercising their free movement rights by moving for work to another EU Member State.

Although the Directive had anticipated the potential for abuse by allowing Member States to 'adopt the necessary measures to refuse, terminate or withdraw any rights conferred by this Directive in the case of abuse of rights or fraud, such as marriages of convenience'[36] no such measures were initially adopted in Ireland. Irish regulations implementing the Directive took a very naive approach to the risk of immigration fraud. Once a marriage had been celebrated, immigration rights were automatic and there was no discretion to withhold rights on the basis of fraud. A number of court decisions confirmed that a non-EU spouse of an EU citizen had automatic immigration rights and that the State had no power to prevent the celebration of marriages of convenience.[37]

The Irish government created the marriage of convenience impediment because of an increase in marriages between non-Irish EU nationals and non-EU citizens apparently contracted for the purpose of circumventing normal immigration rules. It was suggested by An Garda Síochána that unusual marriage patterns, particularly between Eastern European women and Asian men, indicated criminal behaviour including human trafficking. The intention of the impediment was to provide a legal basis to identify and prevent marriages of convenience before they happen, and consequently to reduce the potential for criminality.

---

34 The Minister for Justice and Equality referred to the difficulty a number of times in reply to parliamentary questions, for example, 16 July 2013, written answers 925; 19 February 2013, written answers 558.

35 Directive 2004/38/EC on the right of citizens of the Union and their family members to move and reside freely within the territory of the Member States (OJ L158/77).

36 art 35.

37 European Communities (Free Movement of Persons) Regulations 2006, SI 656/2006; *Izmailovic v Commissioner of An Garda Síochána* [2011] IEHC 32; *Igunma v Governor of Wheatfield Prison* [2014] IEHC 218.

Immigration regulations were reformed to allow the Minister for Justice to discount marriages of convenience when making determinations on free movement rights.[38] In immigration law, where the Minister has reasonable grounds for believing that a marriage is one of convenience, she or he may request information from the parties who must, within a specific time period, '*satisfy* the Minister that the marriage is not a marriage of convenience'.[39] If information is not received within that time, she or he may deem the marriage to be one of convenience and disregard it in making a determination under immigration law. The information required under the immigration regulations to assess whether a marriage is a marriage of convenience is largely the same as that required under section 58 of the 2004 Act. The effect of this change was to remove automatic immigration rights from non-EU spouses of EU nationals exercising free movement rights. It is therefore questionable whether marriage can confer an immigration advantage in this context.

An tArd-Chláraitheoir, in their 2019 report, noted that measures to prevent marriages of convenience had 'a significant impact on the number of applications to marry received from non-Irish EU citizens wishing to marry non-EU citizens'. In 2015, there were 1,584 notifications of intention to marry by EU (non-Irish) and non-EU citizens, and 860 resulting marriages. In 2019 there were just 369 notifications and 234 resulting marriages. The rules on marriages of convenience are also applied by the Civil Registrar to Irish citizens marrying non-EU citizens. There were 1,518 notifications of such marriages and 1,288 marriage ceremonies in this category in 2015 and 1,363 notifications and 891 ceremonies in 2019. No statistics are offered on the number of objections received by the registrar, but the report notes that '(a)significant element of work relates to dealing with appeals to the courts of decisions made by Superintendent Registrars that a proposed marriage should not proceed because it would constitute a marriage of convenience'.[40]

It is not clear what impact, if any, s 58 has had on combatting immigration fraud or human trafficking given that free movement rights are no longer automatically granted to non-EU spouses upon proof of marriage to an EU national. The marriage of convenience impediment has placed a significant additional administrative burden on non-EU nationals wishing to marry Irish or EU citizens in Ireland. It also creates a significant workload for civil registration offices. Recent news reports have pointed to waiting lists of six months or more for those needing a marriage of convenience interview, in addition to the three-month notice period which applies to

38 European Communities (Free Movement of Persons) Regulations 2015, SI 548/2015.

39 reg 28(2) (emphasis added).

40 Department of Employment Affairs and Social Protection, *Annual Report of An tArd-Chláraitheoir on the operation of the Civil Registration Acts for 2018* (2019), 16.

all couples.[41] Pandemic-related backlogs have exacerbated the difficulties. Media reports indicate that some trans-national couples resident in Ireland are simply travelling to other EU countries with less stringent rules to celebrate their marriages.[42]

4. After the Wedding: Determining the Validity of a Marriage

Once a marriage has been celebrated, its validity can be challenged through an application to the Circuit or High Court pursuant to s 29 of the Family Law Act 1995 ('the 1995 Act'). This provision allows the court to make a determination as to whether a marriage was valid at its inception or whether it existed as a valid marriage at any particular point in time. It also facilitates applications to determine the validity of divorces, judicial separations and annulments obtained in other jurisdictions. Applications under s 29 arise in a variety of contexts, but the focus here is on situations where interpersonal relationships have broken down and one spouse seeks to exit a marriage by claiming that it is invalid.

Key legislation – s 29 of the Family Law Act 1995 (determining the validity of marriage)

(1) The court may, on application to it in that behalf by either of the spouses concerned or by any other person who, in the opinion of the court, has a sufficient interest in the matter, by order make one of the following declarations in relation to a marriage, that is to say:

a. a declaration that the marriage was at its inception a valid marriage,

b. a declaration that the marriage subsisted on a date specified in the application,

c. a declaration that the marriage did not subsist on a date so specified, not being the date of the marriage,

d. a declaration that the validity of a divorce, annulment or legal separation obtained under the civil law of any other country or jurisdiction in respect of the marriage is entitled to recognition in the State,

e. a declaration of the validity of a divorce, annulment or legal separation so obtained in respect of the marriage is not entitled to recognition in the State.

[41] Shamim Malekmian, 'Cross-national couples looking to wed in Ireland can't get the HSE's go-ahead at the moment', *Dublin Inquirer*, 6 October 2021, available at https://www.dublininquirer.com/2021/10/06/cross-national-couples-looking-to-wed-in-ireland-can-t-get-the-hse-s-go-ahead-at-the-moment [last accessed 25 May 2022].

[42] Joanne Hunt, 'Marriage backlog forcing couples to defer or relocate weddings', *The Irish Times*, 19 March 2022, available at https://www.irishtimes.com/life-and-style/people/weddings/marriage-backlog-forcing-couples-to-defer-or-relocate-weddings-1.4828653 [last accessed 25 May 2022].

The body of case law in which judges have made determinations as to the validity of a particular marriage is known as the law of **nullity**. Although applications are now made pursuant to the 1995 Act. The jurisdiction of the courts in nullity applications stretches back to the 19th century and the legal principles upon which decisions are based have their origins in the Ecclesiastical Courts of the Church of Ireland.[43] Nullity applications are not as common now as they were before the introduction of divorce in 1997 when nullity was the only way, except death, to end the legal status of marriage. There was a significant increase in applications for decrees of nullity through the 1980s and 1990s and a corresponding decrease when divorce became available in 1997. In 2020, there were just 4 decrees of nullity granted in the Irish courts, with 11 granted in 2019. In contrast, there were 3,164 divorce decrees in 2020 and 2,545 in 2019.[44] The nullity jurisdiction of the courts nonetheless remains an important way to test the legal validity of purported marriages.

The effect and consequences of a declaration of nullity are quite different to those of an order for divorce. A declaration of nullity means that a valid legal marriage never existed between the parties, that they were never spouses, and as a result have no marital obligations to each other.[45] The parties to a marriage that has been annulled cannot rely on marriage law to claim maintenance or property orders from each other and do not have succession rights to each other's estate. Although the parties' children will technically no longer be children of a marriage, the father will generally retain guardianship of children born before the marriage was voided.[46] Parties to a marriage found to be void may have obligations to each other under Pt 15 of the Civil Partnership and Certain Rights and Obligations of Cohabitants Act 2010 if they have lived together for the periods set out in the Act and can demonstrate the necessary financial dependence.[47]

The case law on nullity can be divided into two main types of claim. The first is where the applicant contends that the marriage is **void** *ab initio* or from the beginning. The claim is that despite a marriage ceremony having taken place, no legal marriage was created, and the parties were never married to each other. Technically, there is no need for a court order confirming invalidity but it is advisable to obtain one, particularly if the parties wish to remarry. Any interested party can apply for a decree of

---

43 Previously the High Court had jurisdiction pursuant to the Matrimonial Causes and Marriage Law (Amendment) Act (Ireland) 1870.

44 Courts Service, *Courts Service Annual Report 2020,* (2021), 56, 59.

45 s 2 of the Family Law Act 1995 provides that a '"decree of nullity" means a decree granted by a court declaring a marriage to be null and void'.

46 Subject to meeting the conditions set out in s 2 of the Guardianship of Infants Act 1964.

47 See Chapter 6.

nullity in respect of a void marriage and can do so even after one or both purported spouses has died. A third party might apply for a decree, for example, where there is a dispute regarding inheritance or ownership of property and the validity or otherwise of a marriage impacts upon the dispute. In the second type of case, the applicant accepts that the marriage was validly celebrated but claims that something came to light after the marriage took place that affects its validity. The marriages in these cases are described as **voidable**, meaning that they remain valid until declared void by the court. Only the parties to the marriage can seek to have the marriage avoided and they can lose their right to do so through acknowledgement that the marriage is valid (approbation) or excessive delay.[48] For both void and voidable marriages, the effect of an order of nullity by the court is the same; *the parties will be considered never to have been the spouses of each other*.

4.1 Void marriages

The Supreme Court recently described modern marriage as:

> the *voluntary* entry into mutual personal and legal commitments on the basis of an equal partnership between two persons, both of whom possess *capacity* to enter into such commitments *in accordance with requirements laid down by law*.[49]

This definition encapsulates the key legal requirements for a valid marriage, the absence of which will render a purported marriage void. To contract a valid marriage, the parties must voluntarily consent to marry each other, have the legal capacity to marry and must, in addition, comply with the legal formalities. The failure of any of these fundamental elements will render a marriage void *ab inito*. We will look at each of these elements in turn beginning with formalities.

---

[48] For an account of the origins of the distinction see the judgment of Costello J in *D v C* [1984] ILRM 173, 190.

[49] O'Malley J in *HAH v SAA* [2017] IESC 40, affirmed by McKechnie J in *MKFS v Minister for Justice* [2020] IESC 48 (emphasis added).

Key distinction – Impediment to marriage v legal basis for nullity

Statutory impediments to marriage sometimes overlap with the legal basis for nullity. The difference between an impediment to marriage and a legal basis for nullity is very important. An impediment is an issue that can prevent a marriage from taking place, whereas a legal basis for nullity is a problem in the formation of marriage that can lead to the marriage being declared legally invalid by the court at a later date, even if the marriage ceremony goes ahead.

Although the existence of any statutory impediment will allow the registrar to prevent a marriage from taking place, not all the impediments listed in the 2004 Act affect capacity to marry. It is possible to object to a marriage taking place on the grounds that it will be a marriage of convenience within the meaning of the 2004 Act, but once celebrated the fact that the marriage was entered into for the sole purpose of securing an immigration advantage is not sufficient grounds for a decree of nullity. In general terms, the reasons why people marry are not the law's concern. As Barrington J noted in *RSJ v JSJ*,[50] people enter marriage for all sorts of reasons, including convenience or self-interest and a marriage will be legally valid even if the parties do not love each other or do not have the capacity to love each other. Arranged marriages were not uncommon in Ireland in the first half of the 20th century and remain an important element of some religious traditions. In simple terms, it is not generally an impediment to marriage that a strong emotional bond does not exist between the parties, it is enough that both parties agree to marry, have capacity, and comply with the formalities.

4.1.1 Non-compliance with formalities under the 2004 Act

The 2004 Act provides that certain formalities are 'substantive requirements for a valid marriage'. This means that if they are not complied with, a valid marriage will not have been celebrated and parties will not be the spouses of each other. These are the rules regarding celebration of the marriage in s 51 and notice of marriage in s 46 as discussed above. The process set out in the 2004 Act has made it much more difficult for doubts to arise in relation to the formalities surrounding marriage and a state marriage certificate is *prima facie* evidence that the required formalities have been complied with. However, if formalities are not complied with, no valid marriage will come into being regardless of the reason for non-compliance. For example, if the formalities are not observed because one or both of the parties is not aware of them, no marriage will come into existence. This can cause difficulties for members

50 [1982] ILRM 263.

of immigrant communities who may not be aware of the need for a civil process and go through religious marriage rituals with the expectation that legal obligations have been created.[51]

4.1.2 Problems with capacity

In addition to complying with formalities, the parties to a marriage must have legal capacity to marry. Capacity in this context refers to the parties being of an appropriate age, not related to each other within the prohibited degrees, not already married, and having the mental capacity to consent. The registrar requires spouses to provide information regarding potential impediments when giving notice to marry and in this way checks some elements of legal capacity, ensuring that the parties are over 18, not married or civilly partnered to someone else and not related within the prohibited degrees. For marriages contracted before the commencement of the 2004 Act, however, the elements of capacity that overlap with impediments to marriage can become the subject of nullity applications. For example, a previously divorced person may discover following remarriage that their foreign divorce was not legally recognised in Ireland. This means that at the time of their remarriage they did not have capacity to marry, and their second marriage is therefore void *ab initio*. In *RB v AS* one of the spouses was previously married and divorced in Germany.[52] The divorce was not recognised in Ireland and the subsequent marriage between the applicant and respondent was therefore void *ab initio*. In *CK v JK* a second marriage was rendered void when it was discovered that a divorce granted in Ohio was not recognised in Ireland.[53] A similar situation can arise where a spouse remarries in a church ceremony following religious annulment of a prior marriage. The Catholic Church, for example, will allow parties to a marriage annulled by church authorities to remarry in the church. Without a civil annulment, however, the first marriage is valid in law, and any subsequent religious marriage will not be recognised by the State.[54]

A further difficulty in relation to prior marriage arises from the practice of **polygamy**, that is the practice or custom of having more than one husband or wife. Polygamy is common in many parts of the world and polygamous marriages may be legally recognised in jurisdictions where the practice is widespread. As a general principle of private international law, a marriage contracted in another country which complies with the laws of that country will be legally valid in Ireland unless it conflicts with

---

51 See Susan Leahy and Kathryn O'Sullivan, 'Unrecognised Muslim Marriage in Ireland: Incidence and Implications', (2019) 29(4) Journal of Muslim Minority Affairs 534.

52 [2002] 2 IR 428.

53 [2004] IESC 21.

54 See for example *FML v An tÁrd-Chláraitheoir* [1984] ILRM 667.

public policy, in particular with regard to the capacity to marry. Because Irish law recognises monogamous marriages only, it will recognise marriages celebrated in countries that allow polygamy so long as there is only one spouse. Where there are two marriages, the second is void under Irish law for lack of capacity, even if it was valid under the legal system where it was celebrated. The issue was given careful consideration by the Supreme Court in determining the validity of a polygamous marriage for immigration purposes in *HAH v SAA & Attorney General*.[55]

4.1.3 Problems with consent

Marriage involves the entry into mutual personal and legal commitments and is a voluntary union between two consenting adults. Each spouse must therefore have the mental capacity to consent, give their consent freely, and be able to base that consent on full information about matters which the law considers fundamental to marriage.

4.1.3.1 Lack of capacity to consent

Applications for nullity based on incapacity to consent traditionally encompassed issues such as intoxication and psychological impairment. There are no modern reported Irish decisions in relation to intoxication, but the 1818 case of *Sullivan v Sullivan* held that where a person is intoxicated to the point that they lack the capacity to consent, the marriage will be void.[56]

As discussed above, lack of mental capacity to consent is now an impediment to marriage, with the determination in relation to capacity made in accordance with the 2015 Act. However, s 138 of the 2015 Act provides that nothing in the legislation will alter the law in relation to capacity to consent to marriage. This means that the common law threshold requiring intending spouses to understand the nature and consequences of the commitment involved at the time of marriage must be met. In *ME v AE,* for example, the husband was experiencing paranoid delusions at the time of marriage and as a result was determined not to have 'capacity to understand the nature of the duties which marriage creates'.[57] It is unclear what impact the 2015 Act will have on assessment of mental capacity to marry for the purpose of nullity law. It seems likely that the functional test and presumption of capacity set out in the 2015 Act will apply for marriages contracted after its commencement in 2023, but the position in relation to older marriages is less clear.

---

55 *HAH v SAA & Attorney General* [2017] IESC 40.

56 (1818) 2 Hag Con 238.

57 Unreported, High Court, O'Hanlon J, 8 July 1985.

4.1.3.2 Absence of freely given consent

A marriage undertaken as a result of force imposed by the other spouse or a third party will not be valid. Indeed, engaging in conduct for the purpose of causing another person to enter a ceremony of marriage can constitute the criminal offence of forced marriage.[58] Historically, for the application of force or duress to render a marriage void it needed to be irresistible pressure, wrongfully applied. In the old case of *Griffith v Griffith,* the husband was threatened with imprisonment if he did not marry a woman whom he was led to believe was expecting his child.[59] He was not, in fact, the father of the child and the marriage was annulled because he was subjected to a threat, wrongfully applied. This implies that if he had been the father, the force would be justified and the marriage valid. The boundaries of what constituted duress softened considerably over time and in *N (orse K) v K* the Supreme Court focused on the need for consent to be free and informed rather than simply unforced.[60] In that case, a 19-year-old pregnant woman, described as shy, passive and highly dependent on her parents, married the father of her child with her parents' encouragement. Her application for a decree of nullity was refused in the High Court, but the Supreme Court granted it noting that:

> if the apparent decision to marry has been caused to such an extent by external pressure or influence, whether falsely or honestly applied, as to lose the character of a fully free act of that person's will, no valid marriage has occurred.[61]

The court emphasised that marriage was more than a private contract, it was the acquisition of a constitutionally-protected status, indissoluble other than by death.[62] Similarly, in *MK v FMcC* parental pressure to marry following an extra marital pregnancy was sufficient to vitiate the applicant spouse's consent.[63] Emotional pressure from a respondent who cried every time the applicant attempted to break off the relationship was enough to undermine the validity of his consent in *O'R v B.*[64] Threats to commit suicide had a similar effect in *PW v AO'C.*[65] Griffin J expressly stated in *N (orse K) v K,* that the test for duress is subjective; it is not whether a reasonable person would have bowed to the pressure but whether the pressure was enough to overbear the will of the particular petitioner.[66] Further, the court confirmed that the source and nature

---

58 Domestic Violence Act 2018, s 38.
59 [1944] IR 35.
60 [1985] IR 733.
61 ibid, *per* Finlay CJ, 742.
62 ibid.
63 [1982] ILRM 277.
64 [1995] 2 ILRM 57.
65 [1992] ILRM 536.
66 [1985] IR 733, 751.

of the duress is not relevant so long as the coercive matters affected a person's mind to the extent that their will was overborne, and they could not be said to have willingly consented.[67]

4.1.3.3 Lack of informed consent

Cases on the ground of lack of informed consent relate to situations in which consent was freely given but based on an untruth or misunderstanding. This could relate to failing to understand the nature of the ceremony, an error as to the identity of the spouse or a fundamental feature of the marriage. In *S v S,* the husband concealed from the wife the fact that he did not intend to engage in sexual intercourse with her during the marriage. Kenny J held that where a person was in error or had been misled as to a fundamental feature of the marriage to the extent that they married in ignorance of an important matter, the marriage would be void.[68] He considered sexual relations to be a fundamental feature of marriage. This ground has been successfully relied upon in situations where one party to a different sex marriage concealed at the time of marriage that they were gay[69] or transgender.[70]

Concealment of a serious psychiatric illness may also be sufficient to vitiate consent. In *MO'M v BO'C* the husband did not tell the wife about his long history of psychiatric treatment prior to the marriage. She sought a decree of nullity on the ground that her consent was not informed because had she known about his illness, she would not have married him. The Supreme Court accepted that mental health or stability is a matter of great importance in deciding whether to marry and applied a subjective test in holding that the wife's consent was not informed because she would not have married him if she had known.[71] Relying on a broad interpretation of the subjective test adopted in *MO'M,* the husband in *PF v GO'M* sought a decree of nullity on the basis of his wife's concealed infidelity, arguing that he would not have married her if he had known about her longstanding affair with a work colleague and her intention to continue it after marriage.[72] The Supreme Court rejected this interpretation, stressing the need for certainty in marriage and drawing a distinction between ignorance of *fundamental characteristics* that might render a marriage void, and concealment of *conduct,* that would not.[73] This distinction was also applied in *LB v TMcC* where the Supreme Court

---

67 ibid, 745, *per* Henchy J.
68 [1976-77] ILRM 156.
69 *F v F* Unreported, High Court, Barron J, 22 June 1988.
70 *SB v FL* [2011] 1 IR 521.
71 [1996] 1 IR 208, *per* Blaney J.
72 [2001] 3 IR 1.
73 ibid, 23, *per* McGuiness J.

held that the husband's deceit regarding the extent of his wealth was not sufficient to vitiate the wife's consent and invalidate the marriage.[74]

Key case – *PF v GO'M* [2001] 3 IR 1

The applicant husband sought a decree of nullity in the High Court on the ground that he did not give his free and informed consent to the marriage. The basis of this claim was that the wife was having an affair before and during the marriage and that had he known about this relationship, he would not have married her. The High Court held that the failure to disclose factual information, such as an affair, was not sufficient to invalidate a marriage. On appeal to the Supreme Court, McGuinness J undertook a thorough review of the law on consent to marriage tracing its development from *S v S*[75] to *M'OM v B'OC*,[76] noting the extent to which legal developments were influenced by the lack of a divorce jurisdiction before 1996.

Historically, she notes, a distinction was made between duress, which vitiated consent and fraud, misrepresentation or mistake which did not. Misrepresentation as to wealth, infidelity, or premarital pregnancy were not sufficient. The older cases explained the reasons for the distinction; a misrepresentation of fact might not be discovered until many years after the marriage when a decree of nullity could produce significant hardship for spouses and children who had for many years relied on its validity.

The applicant in this case referred to *K v K*[77] and *DB v O'R*[78] which dealt with consent in the context of duress and referred to the need for 'informed' consent. McGuinness J pointed out that in these cases, 'informed' referred to information about alternatives to marriage, not information about the character of the purported spouse. The court went on to distinguish *MO'M v BOC* on the basis that the information lacking in that case concerned an unalterable disposition or proclivity rather than a matter of conduct.[79]

74 [2009] IESC 21.
75 [1976-77] ILRM 156.
76 [1996] 1 IR 208.
77 [1985] IR 733.
78 [1991] 1 IR 289.
79 This test was applied in *LB v TMacC* [2009] IESC 21.

In *PF,* McGuinness J emphasises the State's constitutional pledge to protect the institution of marriage and stressed the need for certainty regarding its validity. The extension of the lack of consent ground to include issues of a factual nature would create uncertainty and be undesirable as a matter of public policy and 'contrary to the clear intention of Article 41.3.1'.

McGuinness J acknowledged the significant developments that had occurred in the law of nullity, noting that they were understandable in a context where divorce was not available. She argued however that it was incumbent upon the Oireachtas to produce a clear statutory code setting out the grounds for nullity and its consequences for spouses and children.

4.2 Voidable marriages

In addition to marriages that are void *ab initio,* certain marriage may be **voidable**. This means that the marriage remains valid until one of the parties successfully applies to the court to have it avoided. Unlike void marriages, only the parties to the marriage can make the application. Once the order is made, the marriage will be deemed to be void *ab intio.* The right to avoid a marriage can be lost through excessive **delay** in making the application or by an acknowledgment that the marriage is valid, also known as **approbation**. There are two grounds on which a marriage may be voidable: inability to consummate and inability to enter into and maintain a normal marital relationship.

4.2.1 Inability to consummate the marriage

A marriage will be voidable where either party is incapable of consummating the marriage. Consummation occurs where the spouses, once married, perform a single act of heterosexual sexual intercourse.[80] Where a party relies on impotence, either their own or the other party's, they must demonstrate that it is incurable, at least in respect of their spouse. In *EC v KM* the marriage was avoided as a result of the wife's impotence with respect to the husband only; she went on to have a successful sexual relationship with a third party.[81] Further, the impotence only needs to occur in the context of the marriage, successful sexual intercourse before the marriage will not be a bar to relief.[82] It is unlikely that this ground applies to same sex marriages. Fergus Ryan suggests that the right to avoid on this ground is waived by same sex couples as they

80 For an account of the biological specifics and canonical origins of this ground see *M (orse G) v M* [1986] ILRM 515.

81 [1991] 2 IR 192, see also *LC v BC* [1986] ILRM 618.

82 *R v W* Unreported, High Court, 1 February 1980.

must realise on marriage that they will not be able to consummate the marriage in the manner envisaged by the law.[83] Legislation in England and Wales specifically excludes this ground for nullity in respect of same sex marriages.[84]

4.2.2 Inability to enter into and maintain a normal marital relationship

This ground was first proposed by Barrington J in *RSJ v JSJ* when he observed that the inability to enter into and maintain a normal marital relationship due to psychological incapacity could be a more serious impediment to marriage than impotence.[85] Although *obiter,* that is, not central to the reason for the decision, Barrington J's analogy grounded a number of successful applications for nullity in the High Court over the course of the 1980s. The most notable of these is *D v C* in which the wife argued that the husband's mental ill health at the time of marriage either meant that he was unable to consent, and the marriage was therefore void, or in the alternative that he was incapable of entering into and maintaining a normal marital relationship and the marriage was, as a result, voidable. The court held that despite his illness the husband did have capacity to consent to marriage.[86] However, Costello J building on Barrington J's observations in *RSJ v JSJ,* pointed out that marriage requires an emotional and psychological relationship between the spouses in addition to a physical one and that:

> If the law declares to be null a marriage on the grounds that one spouse is through physical disability incapable of the physical relationship required by marriage, it should do likewise where one spouse is through a psychiatric disability unable to enter into and sustain the normal inter-personal relationship which marriage also requires.[87]

Costello J concluded that the husband's illness at the time of the marriage was so severe as to make him incapable of entering into and maintaining a normal marital relationship. This new ground was affirmed by the Supreme Court in *UF v JC* and extended beyond psychiatric illness by Finlay CJ to cases 'where [the incapacity] arose from some other inherent quality or characteristic of an individual's nature or personality, which

---

83 Fergus Ryan, 'Same-Sex Couples and the Marriage Act 2015: Implications for Practice' Presentation to the Annual Child and Family Law Conference 2015, Law Society of Ireland, 27 November 2015. Available at: https://papers.ssrn.com/sol3/papers.cfm?abstract_id=2700626 [last accessed 2 August 2023].

84 Marriage (Same Sex Couples) Act 2013, Sch 4, Pt 3.

85 [1982] ILRM 263.

86 [1984] ILRM 173.

87 [1984] ILRM 173, 189.

could not be said to be voluntary or self-induced'.[88] In this case, the legal incapacity was the husband's homosexuality, which rendered him incapable of entering into and maintaining a heterosexual marriage.

Severe emotional immaturity or the cumulative effect of a number of psychological factors have also been found to be sufficient to render a marriage voidable on this ground, even without a clinical diagnosis. In *DK v KT* the petitioner's incapacity was the result of the cumulative effect of sexual abuse as a child, troubled family relationships and drug use.[89] O'Higgins J was satisfied that these factors so affected the petitioner's emotional state as to render him incapable of entering into a marriage relationship. Mere incompatibility will, however, not be sufficient. In *RT v VP* the husband's rigid disposition meant that he was unable to provide the wife with the emotional support her more fragile personality required.[90] Although this incompatibility ultimately led to the breakdown of the relationship, it did not amount to an incapacity to enter into and maintain a normal marital relationship for the purpose of a degree of nullity.

4.2.3 Limits to the use of voidable grounds

Voidable grounds are about personal inability to fulfil a common expectation of marriage. When applying for nullity, the applicant can rely on either their own inability, or the respondent's inability. However, they can only base their application for nullity on their own inability where the respondent has in some way indicated that they too do not consider the marriage to be legally valid. This is called '**repudiation**' by the respondent. For example, in *DC v DW* the respondent had made an application for an ecclesiastical annulment of the marriage. This was considered an effective repudiation by the respondent that allowed the applicant to succeed in their claim for nullity.[91] Desertion or other conduct indicating the abandonment of the marriage will also be sufficient.[92]

A person can lose the right to nullity based on a voidable ground where they act in a way that confirms the validity of the marriage. This is called '**approbation**'. This only applies where the person was aware that the marriage was voidable. In *D v C* the petitioner was not aware of her husband's illness, nor that it entitled her to a decree of nullity, until she took legal advice many years after the marriage. Her conduct in cohabiting

88 [1991] 2 IR 330, 356 *per* Finlay CJ.
89 [1998] IEHC 34.
90 Unreported, High Court, 1 January 1990.
91 [1987] ILRM 58.
92 *DK v KT* [1998] IEHC 34.

with the husband and acting as his wife for several years did not amount to approbation because she was not aware of her right to avoid.[93]

The right to annul a marriage based on a voidable ground can also be lost through excessive **delay**. In *O'D v O'D*, the husband sought an annulment of a 32-year marriage on the grounds of his own inability to enter into and maintain a normal marital relationship.[94] O'Hanlon J rejected the application, noting that any question as to the legal status of the parties ought to have been determined as soon as was reasonably possible in all the circumstances of the case.[95] In contrast, delay in making an application will not affect the validity of an otherwise *void* marriage. For example, the applicant in *SB v FL* obtained a decree of nullity after 27 years of marriage on the grounds of lack of informed consent. She did not become aware of her spouse's gender reassignment until after they had issued divorce proceedings.[96] Medical evidence supported a finding that gender dysphoria had existed at the time of the marriage.

4.3 The onus and standard of proof in nullity petitions

Marriage is more than a contract; it confers a status on the parties by mutual consent and has constitutional protection. As a consequence, a ceremony of marriage enjoys a presumption of validity.[97] The burden of proof in an application for nullity therefore rests on the person seeking to invalidate the marriage.[98] Historically, something close to a criminal, 'beyond reasonable doubt' proof was required, but this relaxed somewhat prior to the introduction of divorce.[99] More recently, the courts appear to take a stricter approach to upholding marriage, particularly when there is any delay in seeking to have the marriage annulled. As noted by Reynolds J in *AR v DR,* '[t]he courts require a high standard of proof due to the protection afforded to the institution of marriage and the rarity in the granting of annulments since the introduction of divorce legislation'.[100] The applicant in that case, however, was not able even to prove a *prima facie* case of invalidity. Despite many nullity cases being uncontested, the court must determine whether the marriage is void or voidable based on the evidence presented by the applicant and bearing in mind the presumption of validity. Because there is an obvious potential for spouses to work together to obtain a decree of nullity, the courts retain a discretion to refuse a decree where there is **collusion** between

93 [1984] ILRM 173.
94 Unreported, High Court, 8 May 1992.
95 ibid, 24.
96 [2011] 1 IR 521.
97 *LB v TMcC* [2009] IESC 21, see also *O'R v B* [1995] 2 ILRM 57.
98 *LB v TMcC* [2009] IESC 21.
99 See *N v K* [1986] ILRM 75, 93-94 *per* McCarthy J.
100 [2019] IEHC 246 [64].

the spouses. Collusion in this context means an agreement between the spouses not to present the full facts to the court. The discretion to refuse on this ground applies to applications on both void and voidable grounds because a failure to present the full facts could arise in either type of application. Order 70, r 4 of the Rules of the Superior Courts requires the applicant in a nullity action to confirm on affidavit that there is no 'collusion or connivance' between the parties.[101]

4.4 Consequences of a decree of nullity

Once a decree of nullity has been granted, the marriage is deemed never to have existed and the parties are not the spouses of each other. They do not have succession rights to each other's estate and do not have maintenance or other financial obligations arising from the marriage. An application can be made under s 36 of the 1995 Act for a determination of any question arising between them in relation to the title to, or possession of, property. Such an application would facilitate claims arising under general property law, although there are no reported cases dealing with the section in the context of nullity.

In general terms, where a decree of nullity is granted, both parents will retain guardianship of any children of their relationship. There are some conditions attaching. In the case of voidable marriages, the parents will remain guardians where the decree of nullity is granted during the 10 months before, or at any time after, the birth of the child. For void marriages, the father's guardianship will only be lost if it can be demonstrated that he knew the marriage was invalid either (a) at the time of the ceremony if it took place after the birth of the child, or (b) at sometime within 10 months before the birth if the ceremony took place before the birth.[102]

Where the parties to a marriage that has been annulled have cohabited in an intimate and committed relationship, and can demonstrate financial dependency in the relationship, they may acquire rights and obligations under the Civil Partnership and Certain Rights and Obligations of Cohabitants Act 2010 (see Chapter 6)

---

[101] Rules of the Superior Courts, SI 15/1986, as amended by Rules of Superior Courts (No.1) 1990, SI 97/1990.

[102] Guardianship of Infants Act 1964, s 2(1) and (3).

Table – Void v Voidable Marriages

Void	Voidable
Any interested person can bring an action to invalidate the marriage, during or after the lifetime of the spouses.	Only the spouses can bring an action to invalidate the marriage within their joint lifetime.
Where the ground for nullity is proven the marriage is invalid.	Even where the ground is proven, a nullity can be refused on the basis of approbation, delay or collusion.
Void grounds (should be obvious at the time of the marriage): 1. Non-compliance with formalities. under the Civil Registration Act 2004. 2. Problems with capacity: — Age. — Prohibited Degrees of relationship. — Existence of prior marriage. 3. Problems with consent: — No legal capacity to consent. — Consent was not freely given. — Consent was not informed.	Voidable grounds (may not be obvious until after the marriage has been entered into) 1. Inability to consummate the marriage. 2. Inability to enter into and maintain a normal marital relationship.

4.5 Critical thinking point: How should the law on nullity of marriage be reformed?

Nullity case law indicates the very intrusive and personal nature of the evidence necessary to obtain a decree of nullity. The voidable grounds, in particular, require close examination of the emotional and sexual relationship between the spouses. Older cases can contain very outdated and objectionable views on what constitutes a mental or physical defect sufficient to vitiate consent and some of the cases involve long marriages and shared lives stretching back decades. Whilst the absence of divorce before 1997 explains the development of a flexible nullity jurisdiction, some of the grounds now seem superfluous and unfair.

There have been various calls for reform and codification of the law on nullity in the matrimonial law context. In 1985, Henchy J referred to the nullity jurisdiction of the courts as 'outdated' and called for the enactment of a modern statute setting out clear grounds for the grant of a decree of nullity and its consequences.[103] This sentiment was repeated by McGuinness J in *PF v GO'M.*[104] A 1984 Law Reform Commission Report also recommended significant reforms, making 62 specific proposals.[105] More recently, the Law Society of Ireland's Law Reform Committee compiled a report entitled *Nullity of Marriage: The Case for Reform,*[106] referring to the need for reform as 'urgent,' and hoping that the report would lead to the codification of the law of nullity. The Law Society recommended the abolition of the voidable grounds, a reduction on the number of prohibited degrees of relationship, and the creation of a system of ancillary relief for parties to void marriages.

No steps have been taken toward statutory regulation of nullity of marriage. There is a legislative jurisdiction for nullity of civil partnership in the Civil Partnership and Certain Rights and Obligations of Cohabitants Act 2010.[107] The grounds are lack of age, prior subsisting marriage or civil partnership, non-observance of formalities, parties within prohibited degrees of relationship, and lack of free and informed consent.[108] No provision is made in relation to ancillary relief on grant of a decree of nullity of civil partnership, although claims are possible under the cohabitation provisions of that legislation in certain limited circumstances.[109]

With the availability of divorce on a no-fault basis, the need for a nullity jurisdiction as a remedy for marriage breakdown is questionable, particularly on voidable grounds. Divorce and judicial separation legislation provide a remedy, often without the need to prove fault or incapacity, and in addition make provision for financial settlements between spouses. The impediment provisions of the Civil Registration Act 2004 identify many potential difficulties before marriages are entered into and will, over time, reduce the potential for nullity applications on the void grounds. There may, however, be a continuing need to invalidate a marriage where a person was exploited or coerced into entering into it, as, for example, with forced marriage.

In any event, applications for nullity as a matrimonial remedy are relatively rare. Just 10 nullity applications were made in 2020. This very small number is probably pandemic-related, but only 29 applications were

---

[103] *N v K* [1985] IR 733, 749.
[104] [2001] 3 IR 1.
[105] Law Reform Commission, *Report on Nullity of Marriage* (LRC 9 – 1984).
[106] Law Society, 2001.
[107] s 107.
[108] s 108(a), (b), (c), (d) and (e).
[109] See Chapter 6.

made in 2019 and 20 in 2018.[110] In contrast, there were 5,266 applications for divorce and 636 for judicial separation in 2020.[111] With the reduction in the wait time for divorce from four to two years in 2019,[112] the downward trend in nullity applications is likely to continue.

5. Summary

- How can we be sure that a marriage is valid?
  The Civil Registration Act 2004 sets out rigorous formalities that must be observed to ensure marriages are validly entered into. In addition, the common law requires minimum conditions in relation to consent and capacity to be met.
- What is the difference between an impediment to marriage and a basis for legal nullity?
  Impediments are outlined in the Civil Registration Act 2004 and can be relied on to prevent a marriage from taking place. Nullity applications are brought to prove that a marriage is invalid, sometimes many years after a marriage has taken place.
- How, and in what circumstances can a marriage be declared void or voidable? What is the effect of a declaration of nullity?
  A combination of statutory and common law rules set out the circumstances in which a marriage can be declared void or voidable by the court, although strictly speaking a court order is not necessary in respect of a void marriage. The right to avoid can be lost through approbation or delay, but once a marriage is declared void, it will be void *ab initio* and no legal consequences arise from it.

6. Further Reading

Kathryn O'Sullivan and Susan Leahy, 'Changing Conceptions of Marriage in Ireland: Law and Practice' (2018) 3 Child and Family Law Quarterly 279.

Christine Ryan, 'Commentary on BJM v CM' in Mairead Enright, Julie McCandless and Aoife O'Donoghue (eds) *Northern/Irish Feminist Judgments* (Hart 2017).

Deirdre McGowan 'Impeding Free Movement with Marriage law: The Civil Registration (Amendment) Act 2014' (2016) 19(2) Irish Journal of Family

---

[110] Courts Service Annual Report 2020.

[111] ibid.

[112] Thirty-eighth Amendment of the Constitution (Dissolution of Marriage) Act 2019, Family Law Act 2019, amending s 5 of the Family Law (Divorce) Act 1996.

Law 3. And see *AZ v SS* [2017] IECC 22, for an alternative interpretation of s 58, also applied by the Civil Registrar's office.

Deirdre McGowan, 'Governed by Marriage Law: An Irish Genealogy' (2016) 25(3) Social and Legal Studies 311.

Kieran Walsh, 'Polygamous Marriages and Potentially Polygamous Marriages in Irish Law: A Critical Reappraisal' (2013) 36 Dublin University Law Journal 249.

Maebh Harding, 'The curious incident of the Marriage Act (No 2) 1537 and the Irish statute book' (2012) 32(1) Legal Studies 78.

Maria Luddy, 'Unmarried Mothers in Ireland, 1880-1972' (2011) 20 Women's History Review 109.

Law Society of Ireland, Report on Nullity of Marriage: The Case for Reform (Dublin 2001) available at: https://www.lawsociety.ie/globalassets/documents/committees/lawreform/nullity2.pdf [last accessed 3 August 2023]

Maire Ni Shuilleabhain, 'Accommodating Cultural Diversity under Irish Family Law' (2002) 24 Dublin University Law Journal 175.

Fergus Ryan, '"When Divorce is Away, Nullity's at Play": A New Ground for Annulment, its Dubious Past and its Uncertain Future' (1998) 15(1) Trinity College Law Review 15.

Chapter 3

The End of Marriage – Judicial Separation and Divorce

Deirdre McGowan

LEARNING OBJECTIVES

By the end of the chapter, students will be equipped to:

- Outline the different options for couples seeking legal regulation of marital separation.
- Appreciate the historical context of Irish divorce and judicial separation law.
- Explain the conditions that must be met before an application for judicial separation, divorce or dissolution of a civil partnership can be made.
- Contrast the effect of judicial separation as compared to divorce or dissolution of civil partnership.

CRITICAL THINKING POINT

- Does restrictive divorce law protect marriage?

1. Introduction

When a marriage breaks down, spouses can regulate their separation in a number of ways. They can simply walk away from the relationship and continue their lives independently. This is not uncommon; where spouses can see a clear way to separate without engaging with the law, many will choose to avoid lawyers and the courts. If a couple have difficulty agreeing on specific issues, they may turn to the summary jurisdiction of the District Court to obtain custody of or access to children (Chapter 9), maintenance orders (Chapter 9) and orders protecting them from domestic abuse (Chapter 7). Again, this is a common approach. District Court applications far outnumber applications to the Circuit Court and High Court for more substantive remedies. Couples who own property together or who have more complex issues can make a formal **separation agreement**. This is a legally binding document that typically sets out an agreement to live apart, details of custody, access and residence for children and provisions regarding maintenance and property division (Chapter 5). Individual couples are free to agree as they wish and there is no requirement to obtain legal advice, although it will be necessary if the agreement includes a division of land or buildings. Where spouses cannot agree separation terms, one of them can apply for an order of **judicial separation**. This will result in the terms of the separation being set by the court.

All these approaches can provide practical solutions to marriage breakdown, but they do not dissolve a marriage. Only an order of **divorce** made by the court can dissolve a marriage allowing the spouses to remarry. Civil partners cannot obtain a judicial separation; their only options are a separation agreement or an order for **dissolution** which ends their civil status. This chapter examines the conditions that must be met before an application for judicial separation, divorce or dissolution can be made as well as the historical context within which divorce and judicial separation were introduced. At the end of the chapter, we consider whether, despite a recent change, further reform of the pre-requisites for divorce and dissolution is necessary.

1.1 Options on marital breakdown

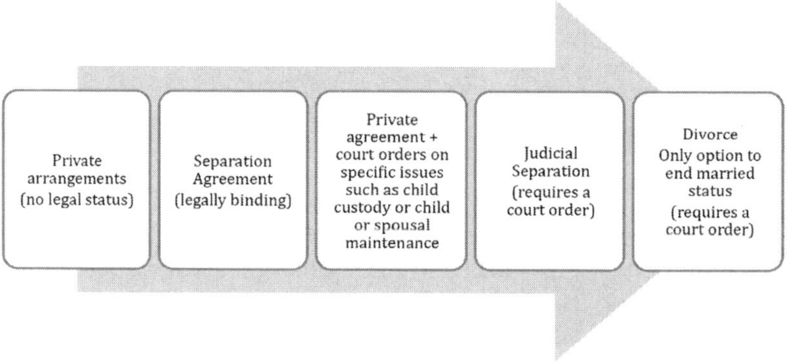

2. Judicial Separation and Divorce – Historical Overview

When the Irish Constitution was adopted in 1937, it contained an absolute prohibition on divorce stating that 'No law shall be enacted providing for the dissolution of marriage'.[1] This provision was seen as a part of the constitutional obligation to 'guard with special care the institution of Marriage, on which the family is founded, and protect it from attack'.[2] The framers of the Constitution believed that a family based

[1] Article 41.3.2° of the Constitution of Ireland as enacted.
[2] This provision remains in force: Article 41.3.1°.

on marriage was essential to the proper functioning of a state. In their view, divorce diminished the value of marriage by making it a temporary rather than lifetime commitment and its availability would destabilise marriage. This attitude to marriage and divorce echoed the doctrine of the majority religion and the text of Article 41 reflected the language of contemporaneous papal encyclicals.[3] Viewing divorce as destructive to society was not unique to Ireland. Debates on divorce reform in the UK during the 1950s and 1960s also emphasised the interest of the state in maintaining the idea of marriage as a lifetime union.[4]

Whilst some people in unhappy marriages found ways to live apart, the socio-economic conditions in twentieth century Ireland made this difficult or impossible for many. The tax and welfare systems were designed around lifetime marriages in which men were breadwinners and wives were dependent homemakers.[5] It was uncommon for married women to work outside the home. Leaving a marriage was economically impossible for most women and when a husband left his family without providing financial support it was often devastating for his wife and children. It was the plight of these 'deserted' married families that provided the impetus for piecemeal reform of family law over the course of the 1970s including a modernised spousal maintenance jurisdiction.[6] Over time, court rulings, social welfare applications and sociological evidence increasingly demonstrated the extent of marriage breakdown and the difficulties encountered by those wishing to enter new relationships. The government began to accept the need for more comprehensive remedies, including the possible introduction of a divorce jurisdiction. In 1986, a constitutional referendum proposed the removal of the ban on divorce, but it was not accompanied by clear solutions to the financial difficulties that dependent wives and children would suffer following divorce. Anti-divorce campaigners pointed out how the form of divorce proposed would shift legal protection from first to second wives. This could leave women who entered marriage in good faith expecting it to last for life without financial protection if their husband remarried. The referendum proposal was defeated by a large majority, but the campaign drew attention to the hopelessly inadequate legal framework governing marriage breakdown. In 1988, the opposition TD and family lawyer, Alan Shatter, introduced a Private Member's Bill proposing comprehensive reform of the law on judicial separation. The government accepted the Bill and it passed into law as the Judicial Separation and Family Law Reform Act 1989. This Act

---

3 Maebh Harding, 'A "catholic" approach to Irish nullity law' in Jane Mair and Esin Örücü (eds), *The Place of Religion in Family Law: A Comparative Search* (Intersentia 2011), 161–185.

4 Alison Diduck and Felicity Kaganas, *Family Law, Gender and the State* (2nd edn, Hart Publishing 2006), 512.

5 Diane Urquhart, *Irish Divorce: A History* (Cambridge University Press 2020), 209.

6 Family Law (Maintenance of Spouses and Children) Act 1976.

established a modern system of judicial separation. Judicial separation is a court order that sets out arrangements for how spouses will live apart. These arrangements are known as ancillary relief. Judicial separation does not end marital status but is a legal acknowledgement that the spouses will live separate lives.

A further referendum on divorce was held in 1995. This time, the government was careful to address the potential vulnerability of dependent spouses and children when a marriage breaks down. Social welfare and pensions legislation was amended to ensure that first spouses would not be excluded from marriage-related benefits and draft divorce legislation was published in advance of the referendum, setting out comprehensive ancillary relief provisions. Obtaining a divorce would not be easy; spouses would need to live apart for four years and ensure proper financial arrangements for both adults and children were in place before a divorce would be granted. Despite these safeguards, people remained concerned that having an option to divorce would lead spouses to take marriage vows less seriously, tempting them to divorce rather than work through relationship difficulties. The referendum passed with a margin of just 9,000 votes.

The Family Law (Divorce) Act 1996 gave effect to draft legislation circulated in advance of the referendum with little further discussion or amendment. The general framework of divorce law has changed very little since. One recent important change is that the living apart period required before an application for divorce can be made was reduced from four to two years in 2019.[7] This change enjoyed cross-party support and an 82% majority in the constitutional referendum that facilitated it.[8] Discussion on this reform mainly centred on the cost and stress caused by the need to live apart for four years before applying for divorce. There was no reconsideration of the assumption that delaying access to divorce encourages spouses to reflect on their decision to separate or that making access to divorce difficult protects or supports marriage. The two-year period was chosen without any substantive consideration of why there should be a living apart requirement and why it should be two years.

3. Judicial Separation – Introduction

Judicial Separation is a court order that suspends the legal obligations of marriage. It is a legal acknowledgement that the interpersonal marital relationship has ended and that, although the spouses are still married, they will lead separate lives. Financial orders, known as **ancillary relief**,

7 Family Law Act 2019.

8 Thirty-eighth Amendment of the Constitution (Dissolution of Marriage) Act 2019.

may be made by the court to facilitate this. A spouse might apply for a judicial separation when their relationship has broken down and the couple cannot agree the terms upon which they will separate.[9] The principal legislation governing this remedy is the Judicial Separation and Family Law Reform Act 1989 ('the 1989 Act').

Judicial separations can be granted by both the Circuit Court and the High Court. Where the value of assets in respect of which an order might be made exceeds €3m, judicial separation proceedings must be brought in the High Court.[10] Like most other family law cases, hearings take place in private and in special family law sittings on different days to the ordinary business of the court. Proceedings are as informal as practicable with no wigs or gowns worn by lawyers or judges.[11]

The applicant must satisfy the court that one or more of the grounds entitling them to an order for judicial separation exists. Where the facts are proven on the balance of probabilities, the court may grant a decree of judicial separation only if it is satisfied that provision exists or will be made for the welfare of dependent children of the family.[12] In addition to the order for judicial separation, the court may, in the same proceedings, make orders under the Guardianship of Infants Act 1964, the Family Home Protection Act 1976, the Domestic Violence Act 2018 as well as a range of financial and property orders, also known ancillary relief orders.[13] The rules governing ancillary relief are largely the same for judicial separation and divorce and are dealt with in detail in Chapter 4. Section 8(1) of the 1989 Act sets out the effect of an order for judicial separation: 'Where the court grants a decree of judicial separation it shall no longer be obligatory for the spouses who were the parties to such proceedings to cohabit'. This means that an order of judicial separation is an acknowledgement that the spouses will now live separate lives even though they remain legally married.

---

9 Pension assets cannot be divided by agreement, any division of pensions requires a pension adjustment order made the court. See Chapter 4.

10 Judicial Separation and Family Law Reform Act 1989, s 31.

11 s 34 provides that 'Proceedings under this Act shall be held otherwise than in public'.

12 1989 Act, s 3(1).

13 Family Law Act 1995, ss 6–14 and 16.

3.1 Judicial separation – grounds

> **Key legislation – Judicial Separation and Family Law Reform Act 1989**
>
> Section 2 (1): An application by a spouse for a decree of judicial separation from the other spouse may be made to the court having jurisdiction to hear and determine proceedings under *Part III* of this Act on one or more of the following grounds:
>
> (a) that the respondent has committed adultery;
>
> (b) that the respondent has behaved in such a way that the applicant cannot reasonably be expected to live with the respondent;
>
> (c) Subject to *subsection (2)* of this section, that there has been desertion by the respondent of the applicant for a continuous period of at least one year immediately preceding the date of the application;
>
> (d) Subject to *subsection (2)* of this section, that the spouses have lived apart from one another for a continuous period of at least one year immediately preceding the date of the application
>
> (e) [repealed]
>
> (f) That the marriage has broken down to the extent that a normal marital relationship has not existed for a period of at least one year immediately preceding the date of the application.

The grounds upon which a judicial separation order can be granted are set out in s 2 of the 1989 Act. Of course, relationships can break down for all sorts of reasons but for judicial separation the applicant spouse must demonstrate that one or more of the grounds set out in the 1989 Act exists at the time the application is made. It is not enough for one spouse to believe that the relationship is over; the legislation requires proof of an objective reason for the application. Each of the grounds on which judicial separation may be granted is dealt with in turn.

3.1.1 Adultery – s 2(1)(a) of the 1989 Act

Section 2(1)(a) of the 1989 Act provides that one spouse (the applicant) can apply for judicial separation if the other spouse (the respondent) has committed adultery. An applicant cannot rely on their own adultery. Adultery is not defined in the legislation, but it generally means that one spouse has had a sexual relationship with a person other than their spouse. There is no Irish case law on what specifically constitutes adultery under the 1989 Act, but the common law understanding involves some element of penile-vaginal penetration.[14] This different sex requirement effectively rules out this ground for same sex couples. There is no

14 *Dennis v Dennis* [1955] 2 All ER 51.

minimum period of marriage or separation required before an application can be made, but if the spouses live together for more than a year after the applicant spouse discovers the act of adultery, it can no longer be relied upon. Adultery can, however, contribute to an application under the next ground, unreasonable behaviour.[15] An extra marital relationship that does not fall within the narrow legal definition of adultery could also contribute to unreasonable behaviour. Cases seldom require actual proof of adultery; it is generally admitted once alleged.[16]

3.1.2 Behaviour – s 2(1)(b)

The second ground for judicial separation is that the respondent has behaved in such a way that the applicant cannot reasonably be expected to live with them. The type of behaviour sufficient for this purpose is a matter for the court but something more than a decision by one party to end the marriage is needed. The case law suggests that sustained physical and verbal abuse meets the required threshold, but as seen in *RS v PS* (2009) requesting a divorce and prolonged absence from the family may also be sufficient.[17] An applicant will not succeed on this ground if they continue to cohabit with the respondent spouse for a period of, or periods amounting to, six months after the date of the last incident which the applicant alleges makes it impossible to live with the respondent.[18]

3.1.3 Desertion – s 2(1)(c)

A judicial separation can be granted where the respondent has deserted the applicant for a continuous period of at least one year immediately preceding the date of application. Desertion means intentionally leaving the home where the spouses normally live together with the intent to abandon the marriage. Working away from home, a prolonged holiday or being unable to return due to legal or situational reasons will not be sufficient. 'Desertion' for this purpose includes 'conduct on the part of one spouse that results in the other spouse, with just cause, leaving and living apart from that other spouse'.[19] This means that if one spouse had to leave the home due to the actions of the other spouse, they can rely on desertion despite being the person who left.

3.1.4 Living apart – s 2(1)(d)

The first three grounds rely on some element of fault; one spouse has

---

15 1989 Act, s 4(1).

16 For example, in *PD v RD* [2015] IEHC 174, the husband admitted instances of adultery alleged by the wife.

17 *RS v PS* [2009] IEHC 579.

18 1989 Act, s 4(2).

19 1989 Act, s 2(3)(b).

actively done something to rupture what the law considers an essential element of the marital relationship. The remaining grounds do not require proof of fault. The courts will generally attempt to make an order for judicial separation on one of these no-fault grounds rather than make a finding of fault against one of the spouses. The first no fault ground is a simple living apart requirement: a judicial separation can be granted where the spouses have lived apart for a continuous period of one year immediately before the date of the application. This time period was reduced from three years by the Family Law Act 2019 ('the 2019 Act'), which also reduced the living apart period for divorce. In addition, the 2019 Act clarified the statutory definition of 'living apart'. Spouses who live in the same dwelling will be considered to be 'living apart' if the court is satisfied that they are not living together as a couple in an intimate and committed relationship. The legislation also provides that a relationship does not cease to be intimate because it is no longer sexual. There is no further definition of what intimacy or commitment means in this context, but the same phrase is used in the Civil Partnership and Certain Rights and Obligations of Cohabitants Act 2010 ('the 2010 Act') with statutory guidance on what it means. The 2010 Act and its judicial interpretation is considered in detail in Chapter 6. The issue has not yet been considered in the context of judicial separation or divorce, but it seems likely that the factors listed in the 2010 Act will be instructive. In general terms, a sexual relationship between spouses equates to intimacy, but the lack of a sexual relationship does not always mean no intimacy. Intimacy can exist where the parties share important aspects of their lives and provide mutual care and support. For practical purposes, the definition is intended to allow spouses to apply for judicial separation on the living apart ground in situations where, due to lack of alternative accommodation or other circumstances, the spouses continue to share a home despite the breakdown of their relationship.[20]

3.1.5 No normal marital relationship – s 2(1)(f)

The final ground has been the most common ground upon which judicial separation is granted, although this may change with the reduction in the living apart requirement from three years to one year. A judicial separation can be granted where the marriage has broken down to the extent that the court is satisfied that no normal marital relationship has existed between the spouses for a period of one year before the date of the application. The courts will accept the withdrawal of consent by one party to continuation of the marriage during the one-year period as enough to satisfy this ground. In *TF v Ireland,* Murphy J expressed the view that the opposition of one spouse to the continuation of the

[20] 1989 Act, s 2(3)(a).

marriage 'must destroy the fundamental relationship'.[21] Although the lack of sexual activity between the parties will not necessarily indicate the lack of a normal marital relationship, any consensual sexual activity between the spouses in the year prior to the application will mean that a judicial separation will not be granted on this ground. In *PD v RD* (2015) the court expressed a preference for granting the judicial separation on the s 2(f) ground rather than one of the fault-based grounds, but because there was evidence of a sexual relationship between the spouses within the year before the application, this was not possible, and the order was granted on the adultery ground.[22]

3.2 Safeguards – legislative attempts to discourage Judicial Separation

The constitutional imperative to protect marriage and the related political assumption that facilitating marriage breakdown in some why harmed the institution of marriage led to the inclusion of several mechanisms intended to encourage reconciliation or separation by agreement in the 1989 Act.

3.2.1 Calculation of time periods – s 2(2)

For the purpose of the desertion and living apart grounds, s 2(2) provides that the one-year period does not need to be continuous. It can be made up of an accumulation of periods punctuated with periods of cohabitation not exceeding 6 months. These periods of cohabitation will not, however, count towards the one-year period. The purpose of this provision is to avoid discouraging spouses from attempts to reconcile.

3.2.2 Providing information – ss 5(1) and 6 (1)

Any solicitor engaged to act for an applicant or respondent in judicial separation proceedings must, before the application is made or a defence entered, discuss with the applicant or respondent, as applicable, the possibility of reconciliation. They must in addition provide the names and address of people qualified to assist the spouses with effecting a reconciliation. In practical terms this means that solicitors must provide literature relating to marriage counselling to spouses who consult them about a judicial separation. Solicitors must also discuss the possibility of engaging in mediation for the purpose of agreeing the terms of a separation agreement and provide details of qualified mediators. In addition, there is a requirement to discuss the possibility of effecting a settlement by negotiation and separation agreement. Each solicitor acting for an applicant or respondent in judicial separation proceedings

---

21 *TF v Ireland* [1995] 1 IR 321, 330.

22 *PD v RD* [2015] IEHC 174.

must file an affidavit in the court confirming that they have provided this information to their client.

3.2.3 Adjourning proceedings

Attempts toward reconciliation are expected to continue even after the court proceedings have begun. Section 7 provides that the court 'shall give consideration to the possibility of a reconciliation of the spouses' and may adjourn the proceeding at any time to allow the spouses to consider it. Should the spouses resume living together during an adjournment 'no account will be taking of that fact for the purpose of those proceedings'. The aim of this section is to ensure that parties are not discouraged from attempting to reconcile. Any communication between the spouses and a third party for the purpose of seeking assistance in reconciliation or in reaching the terms of a settlement agreement is not admissible as evidence in the judicial separation proceedings.

3.2.4 Reconciliation after order of judicial separation

Even after the court makes an order of judicial separation, s 8 allows the spouses to apply to the court to have the order set aside. It will be set aside if the court is satisfied that the spouses have reconciled and have already resumed or wish to resume cohabiting. The court can also vary any ancillary orders made. There is no evidence that any applications have been made under s 8 since the legislation was enacted. As discussed below there is little evidence that couples successfully reconcile after commencing formal legal proceeding to end their marriage.

4. Divorce

Key Constitutional provision – Article 41.3.2°

A Court designated by law may grant a dissolution of marriage where, but only where, it is satisfied that –

i. there is no reasonable prospect of a reconciliation between the spouses,
ii. such provision as the Court considers proper having regard to the circumstances exists or will be made for the spouses, any children of either or both of them and any other person prescribed by law, and
iii. any further conditions prescribed by law are complied with.

The key difference between judicial separation and divorce is that only divorce will legally end a marriage. Although it is possible to separate by agreement, only a court can grant a divorce. All applications for divorce therefore require an application to the court and at least one court appearance. The general conditions for the grant of a decree of divorce are set out in Article 41.3 of the Constitution. It provides that a court may dissolve a marriage where there is no prospect of reconciliation, provision considered proper by the court is made for spouses and dependent family members, and any further conditions proscribed by law are complied with. These provisions are given legislative shape by the Family Law (Divorce) Act 1996 ('the 1996 Act'). Section 5(1) provides that the court may grant a divorce where (a) the spouses have lived apart from one another for a period of, or periods amounting to at least two years during the previous three years (b) there is no reasonable prospect of reconciliation between the spouses and (c) such provision as the court considers proper in the circumstances exists for each of the spouses and any dependent members of the family. The meaning of the 'living apart' condition had been the subject of a number of court decisions but has been clarified in the Family Law Act 2019 which provides that spouses living in the same dwelling can be considered to be living apart if they, whilst living in the same dwelling, do not live together in an intimate and committed relationship.[23] As discussed above in relation to judicial separation, an ongoing sexual relationship is not an essential part of an intimate and committed relationship, but consensual sexual activity between the parties will be taken to indicate the existence of an intimate relationship. If a couple remain living in the same dwelling after the breakdown of their relationship, they can be considered to be living apart if their relationship is no longer intimate and committed. However, even if they physically live apart, the presence of a consensual sexual relationship at any time during the two years prior to an application for divorce will likely make them ineligible for divorce.

Ireland has a fully **'no fault' divorce regime** in the sense that it is not necessary to prove that there has been any misconduct or wrongdoing by either party in order to obtain a divorce. The court will require evidence of living apart, although an uncontested statement by the applicant is generally sufficient. There has been little judicial engagement with the 'no prospect of reconciliation' requirement, suggesting that the issue of divorce proceedings following the required wait period is sufficient proof of relationship breakdown. The final precondition is that provision which the court considers proper exists or will be made for spouses and dependents. The couple can agree terms which they believe to be proper and submit their agreement to the court for approval. Alternatively, the court will decide what it considers proper provision based on submissions made by the parties and make relevant ancillary relief orders. These orders can redistribute property and income between the spouses and make provision of for the care and financial support of children. The

[23] Family Law (Divorce) Act 1986, s 5.

types of provision and factors to be taken into account in making orders are largely the same for divorce as for judicial separation and are dealt with in Chapter 5.

A divorce can be granted by both the Circuit Court and the High Court. Where the value of assets in respect of which an order might be made exceeds €3m, divorce proceedings must be brought in the High Court.[24] Like most other family law cases, hearings take place in private and in special family law sittings on different days to the ordinary business of the court.[25] The 1996 Act also provides that the proceedings shall be as informal as practicable with no wigs or gowns worn by lawyers or judges.

4.1 Safeguards – Legislative attempts to discourage divorce

The Constitution, as well as making provision for divorce, requires the State to protect marriage. This has been interpreted as placing an obligation on the legislature to both protect the institution of marriage *and* individual marriages. As we have seen in the case of judicial separation, this requirement led to the inclusion of provisions focused on reconciliation and separation by agreement in the governing legislation. And the same is true for divorce. Despite the longer wait period, divorce legislation is also concerned with encouraging reconciliation. A solicitor acting for an applicant or respondent in a divorce is obliged to discuss the possibility of reconciliation with their client and provide details of marriage counsellors. Additionally, they must provide details of mediators who can assist with reaching a negotiated settlement. And finally, despite the client engaging the solicitor for the purpose of obtaining a divorce, the solicitor must also discuss the possibility of effecting a *separation* by agreement and ensure that they are aware of judicial separation as an alternative to divorce.[26]

The court is also required to consider the possibility of reconciliation and to adjourn proceedings to facilitate attempts at reconciliation where it appears to the court that reconciliation may be possible.[27] As with judicial separation, communications in relation to attempted reconciliation or agreement on terms of separation or divorce are not admissible as evidence in the divorce action.[28]

---

24 1996 Act, s 31.

25 1996 Act, s 34 provides that 'Proceedings under this Act shall be held otherwise than in public'.

26 1996 Act, ss 6 and 7.

27 1996 Act, s 8.

28 1996 Act, s 10.

Effect of decree of divorce – Key legislation

Family Law (Divorce) Act 1996
Section 10

> (1) where the court grants a decree of divorce, the marriage, the subject of the decree, is thereby dissolved and a party to that marriage may marry again.
>
> (2) for the avoidance of doubt, it is hereby declared that the grant of a decree of divorce shall not affect the rights of the father and the mother of an infant, under section 6 of the Act of 1964, to be guardians of the infant jointly.

4.2 Effect of a divorce decree

Once a decree of divorce has been granted, the spouses are no longer married. They have no legal obligations to each other beyond those specifically set out in the divorce decree, or variations thereof. In addition, they have no default entitlements arising from the marriage. For example, divorced spouses do not have automatic rights to one another's property on death, rights under pension or tax legislation or a default obligation to maintain each other. Any obligations that arise will be mandated by a court and specifically set out in the court order. A divorce does not change the parental rights of former spouses.

5. Dissolution of Civil Partnership

Civil partnership was available for same sex couples between 1 January 2010 and the commencement of the Marriage Act 2015 on 16 November that year. There is no equivalent to judicial separation for civil partners, although they can enter into separation agreements. Same sex marriages are subject to divorce law in the same way as different sex marriages, but for civil partners who wish to end their relationship, the relevant rules are set out in Civil Partnership and Certain Rights and Obligations of Cohabitants Act 2010 ('the 2010 Act'). Where civil partners decide to marry each other, their civil partnership is automatically dissolved on marriage;[29] they will then require a divorce in accordance with the 1996 Act should they wish to dissolve the marriage.

The preconditions for a dissolution of a civil partnership are that the civil partners have lived apart for a period of, or periods amounting to, two years during the previous three years and that provision that the court considers proper exists or will be made for the civil partners.[30] The court can make this provision through the use of ancillary relief orders,

---

29 Civil Partnership and Certain Rights and Obligations of Cohabitants Act 2010, s 109A.
30 2010 Act, s 110.

discussed further in Chapter 4. A dissolution order dissolves the civil partnership and the parties may marry other people. There is provision in the legislation for the court to adjourn proceedings to facilitate reconciliation or agreement on the terms of the proposed dissolution,[31] but there is no obligation on solicitors acting on behalf of the civil partners to provide information on mediation or counselling before initiating or defending proceedings.

6. Jurisdiction

For dissolution, divorce and judicial separation, a court can only make an order if at least one of the spouses is either domiciled (living with the intention to remain) or ordinarily resident for a period of one year in the State at the date of commencement of proceedings.[32]

7. Critical thinking point: does restrictive divorce law protect marriage?

Irish law governing the breakdown of marriage reflects a political assumption that making it difficult to divorce will somehow prevent marriage breakdown. A restrictive divorce jurisdiction is also assumed to make people think more carefully about marriage and to protect marriage as a lifetime social institution. The original four year wait period was envisaged as a period of reflection and adjustment that would prevent spouses from rushing to end their marriages and give them time to think about the terms upon which they might live apart. It was also expected to prevent the development of a 'divorce culture' in which divorce and remarriage became common place.[33]

Sociological research has demonstrated that long wait periods between relationship breakdown and divorce exacerbate tensions within relationships and that the consequent uncertainty can be harmful to children.[34] A recent prolonged divorce reform process in England and Wales focused primarily on the removal of fault-based grounds in divorce, but also demonstrated the unreality of political expectations that creating barriers to divorce makes people more likely to either reconcile or reach amicable settlements. Divorce by mutual agreement was available in that jurisdiction following a two-year wait period, but most couples chose to manufacture a fault ground to obtain earlier resolution. The reformed law

---

31 s 111.

32 1989 Act, s 32(4); 1996 Act, s 27(1); 2010 Act, s 140(3).

33 Frank Martin, 'The Changing Face of Family Law in Ireland' (2005) 5(1) Judicial Studies Institute Journal 16.

34 See for example, Helena Moore, 'Delaying Divorce: Pitfalls of Restrictive Divorce Requirements' (2016) 37(16) Journal of Family Issues 2265, 2271.

now requires a wait period of six months between the date of application for divorce and the grant of the final decree, but other than a restriction on application during the first year of marriage, application can be made for divorce with no living apart requirement and grounded on a simple statement by one of the spouses that the marriage has broken down irretrievably.[35]

In Ireland, the recent reduction in the living apart requirement for divorce from four years to two years was represented as a compassionate step which would assist people in moving on with their lives,[36] but no explanation was offered as to why a two-year period was appropriate. At the same time, the wait period for a non-consensual, no-fault judicial separation was also reduced from three years to one year on the basis that it should be more difficult to get a divorce than a judicial separation. Because there are still different living apart requirements for judicial separation and divorce, this approach retained the much-criticised two-step pathway to divorce; those in most urgent need of court-based adjudication for marital difficulties must first apply for a judicial separation and then, once the two-year period has elapsed, return to court for a divorce. This is an expensive and stressful process particularly when ancillary relief rules mean that a financial settlement reached on judicial separation will not necessarily apply on divorce.[37] Therefore, although the recent reform makes getting a divorce easier, it also indicates that assumptions about the role of divorce law in protecting marriage remain politically influential.

Ireland has one of the lowest divorce rates in the EU.[38] This is at least partially the result of restrictive divorce law, but not because marriages are saved by limited access to divorce. The 2016 census recorded almost as many separated as divorced people, indicating that easier access to divorce could double the divorce rate, bringing us closer to European norms. Indeed, court service data suggest that divorce will become more common with the reduction in the wait time from four to two years; applications for divorce increased by 31% between 2019 and 2021.[39]

---

35 For an account of the UK reform process and rules on divorce see Edwina Higgins and Kathryn Newton, 'Seeking a Divorce' in Ruth Lamont (ed), *Family Law* (2nd edn, Oxford University Press 2022), Chapter 3.

36 Minister for Justice and Equality on introducing the second stage of the Thirty-eight Amendment of the Constitution (Dissolution of Marriage) Bill 2016 to the Oireachtas, 9 April 2019, Vol 264, No 15.

37 See Chapter 4.

38 Eurostat data extract – Marriage and Divorce Statistics, May 2022, available at https://ec.europa.eu/eurostat/statistics-explained/index.php?title=Marriage_and_divorce_statistics#Fewer_marriages.2C_fewer_divorces [last accessed 7 September 2022].

39 Courts Service, *Annual Report 2021* (Courts Service 2022), 60 available at https://www.courts.ie/acc/alfresco/24bce47c-3cc6-4e86-b647-04cdc64c2445/Courts_Service_Annual_Report_2021.pdf/pdf#view=fitH [last accessed 7 September 2022].

Further, factors other than the law have a significant impact on divorce rates. The Law Commission in England and Wales pointed to demographic, socio-economic and attitudinal changes in that jurisdiction that led to increases in divorce over the course of the late twentieth and early twenty first century. It is likely that many of these changes also apply in the Irish context including:

> Changing expectations from marriage. People now expect more emotional happiness in marriage than in the past.
>
> Longer life expectancies. People live longer creating longer marriages and more opportunities for forming second relationships.
>
> The changing position of women in society. Women may have more social and economic freedom to walk away from marriage and are no longer expected to accept poor behaviour from their husbands.
>
> Reduction in stigma. As divorce becomes more common, it is more socially acceptable to divorce.[40]

Irish law is prepared to recognise in judicial separation legislation that a marriage has broken down after one year of living apart but nonetheless requires an additional one year wait before the marriage can be dissolved. The experience in England and Wales demonstrates that couples want and need access to divorce and will make allegations of fault, even were none exists, to obtain it. In Ireland, barriers to divorce have resulted in a low headline divorce rate but have not prevented an increase in relationship breakdown similar to that of other western European countries. Divorce law can protect marriage only to the extent that it stops people divorcing, but this type of protection may come the expense of allowing people to decide for themselves when their relationship is over.

8. Summary

- Couples seeking legal regulation of marital separation may opt for a separation agreement, judicial separation or divorce.
- Divorce was introduced by the Family Law Act 1996 after two divisive constitutional referendums on the issue. Divorce is regulated at constitutional level in Article 41.

---

[40] Law Commission, *Facing the Future: A Discussion Paper on the Ground for Divorce* (HC 479, Law Com No. 170, 1988), para 2.17.

- Judicial separation can only be granted where one of the following five grounds is satisfied: adultery of the respondent, behaviour of the respondent, desertion for a period of at least one year, the spouses have lived apart for at least one year or where no normal marital relationship has existed for at least one year.
- Divorce can only be granted where there is no reasonable prospect of a reconciliation between the spouses, provision that the court considers proper has been made for the spouses and any children, and the spouses have lived apart for at least two years.
- Dissolution of civil partnership can by granted where the civil partners have lived apart for a period of at least two years and provision that the court considers proper has been made for the partners and any dependent children.
- Judicial separation does not end marital status, the couple remain married to each other. The decree is an acknowledgment that the couple are now leading separate lives and is an opportunity to make financial arrangements. In contrast, a decree of divorce or a dissolution of civil partnership ends the status of marriage or civil partnership and allows the couple to remarry.

9. Further reading

Lisa Keenan, 'The Divorce Referendum 2019' (2020) 35(1) Irish Political Studies 80.

Laura Cahillane, 'Revisiting Article 41.2' (2017) 40(2) Dublin University Law Journal 107.

Catriona Beaumont, 'Women, Citizenship and Catholicism in the Irish Free State, 1922–1948' (1997) 6(4) Women's History Review 563.

Deirdre McGowan, 'Governed by Marriage Law: An Irish Genealogy' (2016) 25(3) Social and Legal Studies 311.

Deirdre McGowan, 'Class Criminality and Marriage Breakdown' in Niamh Howlin and Kevin Costello (eds), *Law and the Family in Ireland 1800–1950* (Palgrave 2017).

Louise Crowley, 'Irish divorce law in a social policy vacuum – from the unspoken to the unknown' (2011) 33(3) Journal of Social Welfare and Family Law 227.

Carmel Hannan and Brendan Halpin, 'The Influence of Family Structure on Child Outcomes: Evidence for Ireland' (2014) 45(1) Economic and Social Review 1.

Ezra Hasson, 'Setting a Standard or Reflecting Reality? The 'Role' of Divorce Law, and the Case of the Family Law Act 1996' (2003) 17 International Journal of Law, Policy and the Family 338.

Chapter 4

Financial Consequences of Ending Marriage – Court ordered proper provision

Kathryn O'Sullivan

LEARNING OBJECTIVES

By the end of the chapter, students will be equipped to:

- Assess the ways in which courts can make financial provision for spouses and redistribute assets on marital breakdown.
- Identify the type of assets that might be redistributed by the courts on marital breakdown.
- Critique the level of discretion given to the courts in regulating the financial consequences of marital breakdown.

CRITICAL THINKING POINTS

- How predictable is the Irish approach to ancillary relief provision on marital breakdown?
- Why does Ireland adopt such a highly discretionary approach to ancillary relief provision on marital breakdown?
- What kind of reforms could Ireland introduce to improve the ancillary relief scheme on marital breakdown?

1. Introduction

Irish law has a discretionary approach to financial provision and the division of assets on marital breakdown. While we are all familiar with storylines in films and television series' centring on the equal sharing of property on marital breakdown, that is not the approach adopted in Ireland. Instead, the courts have broad powers to transfer property and money from one spouse to the other on divorce as they see fit. This is cumulatively known as ancillary relief. There are no strict rules dictating the equal division of assets nor is there any formula applied to calculate maintenance. The courts have wide discretion to determine what, if any, assets ought to be subject to sharing as well as the amount and duration of any maintenance ordered for the benefit of a financially weaker spouse or children. In deciding what orders to make, the courts are often guided by the broad idea of fairness and different factors can affect what is considered fair in the circumstances of each case. Even where spouses reach a settlement through private ordering as discussed in Chapter 5, it remains within the power of the court to adjust the provision agreed to ensure 'proper provision' is made for the spouses and any dependent members of the family.

This chapter sets out the legal framework for ancillary relief provision on marital breakdown in Ireland. It considers the extent of judicial discretion and draws on recent case law to analyse each of the statutory factors to which the court must have regard in determining the nature and extent of the provision ordered. It highlights the types of orders available to the court in making proper provision before turning to consider how predictable the Irish system is and how it might be reformed.

2. The legislative framework for ancillary relief provision

2.1 The meaning of 'proper provision'

Part II of the Family Law Act 1995 ('the 1995 Act') and Pt III of the Family Law (Divorce) Act 1996 ('the 1996 Act') provide the courts with extensive redistributive powers to order such 'provision as the court considers proper', commonly known as 'proper provision'. The requirement to make 'proper provision' is both legislative and constitutional in nature and a pre-condition to the award of a decree of divorce.[1] The 1996 Act states the court 'shall ensure' that 'such provision as the court considers proper having regard to the circumstances exists or will be made for the spouses and any dependent member of the family concerned',[2] thereby mandating the court to achieve this end. A slightly less definitive approach is adopted by the 1995 Act which states the court 'shall *endeavour* to ensure' (emphasis added) such provision is made for each spouse and for any dependent member of the family.[3] Despite the different wording, in practice, the courts take the same approach to proper provision on both judicial separation and divorce.

The word 'proper' in the context of financial provision has proven tricky to define. As Hardiman J observed in *WA v MA*, the term is not defined in the statute and has many meanings. As a result, he noted that it is 'in fact a word of peculiar difficulty'.[4] Having considered the various definitions, he concluded, that it would not be 'proper, that is "fit, apt or suitable",

1 See Article 41.3.2° Constitution of Ireland.
2 1996 Act, s 20(1).
3 1995 Act, s 16(1).
4 [2005] 1 IR 1, [2005] 1 ILRM 517.

much less "correct or in conformity with rule"' to make any order against the husband in the circumstances of the case.[5]

2.2 The statutory factors

Key legislation – The statutory factors

Section 20(2) of the Family Law (Divorce) Act 1996 provides:

> ...in deciding whether to make ... an order ... and in determining the provisions of such an order, the court shall, in particular, have regard to the following matters:
> (a) the income, earning capacity, property and other financial resources which each of the spouses concerned has or is likely to have in the foreseeable future,
> (b) the financial needs, obligations and responsibilities which each of the spouses has or is likely to have in the foreseeable future (whether in the case of the remarriage or registration in a civil partnership of the spouse or otherwise),
> (c) the standard of living enjoyed by the family concerned before the proceedings were instituted or before the spouses commenced to live apart from one another, as the case may be,
> (d) the age of each of the spouses, the duration of their marriage and the length of time during which the spouses lived with one another,
> (e) any physical or mental disability of either of the spouses,
> (f) the contributions which each of the spouses has made or is likely in the foreseeable future to make to the welfare of the family, including any contribution made by each of them to the income, earning capacity, property and financial resources of the other spouse and any contribution made by either of them by looking after the home or caring for the family,
> (g) the effect on the earning capacity of each of the spouses of the marital responsibilities assumed by each during the period when they lived with one another and, in particular, the degree to which the future earning capacity of a spouse is impaired by reason of that spouse having relinquished or foregone the opportunity of remunerative activity in order to look after the home or care for the family,

5 [2005] 1 IR 1, [2005] 1 ILRM 517.

(h) any income or benefits to which either of the spouses is entitled by or under statute,
(i) the conduct of each of the spouses, if that conduct is such that in the opinion of the court it would in all the circumstances of the case be unjust to disregard it,
(j) the accommodation needs of either of the spouses,
(k) the value to each of the spouses of any benefit (for example, a benefit under a pension scheme) which by reason of the decree of divorce concerned, that spouse will forfeit the opportunity or possibility of acquiring,
(l) the rights of any person other than the spouses but including a person to whom either spouse is remarried.'[6]

Although the judiciary are afforded wide power in deciding whether or not to order ancillary relief in favour of a spouse, or what shape any such order might take, s 16(2) of the 1995 Act and s 20(2) of the 1996 Act include a list of factors to be considered by the court.[7] Each factor will now be considered in turn:

2.2.1 The income, earning capacity, property and other financial resources of the spouses.

The court must consider all the wealth and available resources of the spouses, irrespective of when or how they were acquired or inherited. While many jurisdictions have clearly defined rules regarding which assets should be shared ('family/marital' assets) and which may be exempted from sharing ('non-family/marital' assets), Irish law applies no such categorisation. Although the origin of an asset *may* be taken into consideration depending on the circumstances – with recent cases appearing to show a greater willingness to have regard to how an asset was acquired[8] – *all* the assets of both spouses are technically available for redistribution.[9]

As the Court of Appeal explained in *NO v PQ,* when trying to be fair to

6 See also s 16(2) of the 1995 Act which largely reflects this list on judicial separation.
7 The importance of trial judges referring to these factors in their judgments has been repeatedly emphasised, see *MD v ND* [2015] IESC 16 [4.14]. See also s 16(4)(a)–(g) of the 1995 Act and s 20(4)(a)–(g) of the 1996 Act which list factors to be considered by the court when deciding whether to make any ancillary orders in favour of dependent members of the family other than the spouse.
8 In *G v G* [2011] IESC 40 [22] the Supreme Court noted: 'Assets which are inherited will not be treated as assets obtained by both parties in a marriage. The distinction in the event of separation or divorce will all depend on the circumstances.' In *PB v AB* [2012] IEHC 616, the court observed that it should be wary of redistributing inherited assets once basic needs are met.
9 Assets and financial resources are valued at the date of the divorce or judicial separation. See *T v T* [2002] IESC 68.

spouses in how property is divided, the court should take account of the fact that a farm may have been in a family for generations and may have been inherited by one of the spouses with the expectation that it would be kept intact and passed on to future generations.[10] However, at the same time, the court reiterated that there are no strict rules for farming cases and how a farm is dealt with in any given case will depend on the circumstances of the case.

The Supreme Court noted in *MD v ND* that before it decides what order to make for 'proper provision', an 'important starting point' must be determining and valuing all the relevant resources so that the court has a definite overall picture of the wealth of both spouses.[11] To this end, parties are required as part of pre-trial procedure to specify their assets and other resources in an Affidavit of Means (Form 37A) provided for in the Circuit Court Rules.[12] To further assist the court, a basic schedule of assets was devised in *MD v ND* wherein each spouse lists of all the assets which they believe should be considered by the court in its overall assessment of proper provision.[13]

Where one party does not make a full disclosure of all his/her resources, the court is likely to take a dim view.[14] In *AN v KN* the court refused the husband's application for divorce because he had not disclosed his assets in full.[15] The wife's application for judicial separation was, however, granted with provision based on the court's *estimate* of his wealth.[16] Moreover, s 35 of the 1995 Act and s 37 of the 1996 Act empower the court to review and to make an order preventing a proposed disposal of an asset, or set aside a disposal already completed, where it is intended to prevent or reduce relief to an applicant spouse.[17]

Section 20(2)(a) also requires the court to evaluate the future earning

---

10 *NO v PQ* [2021] IECA 177 [78].

11 *MD v ND* [2015] IESC 16 [4.4].

12 Circuit Court Rules (Case Progression in Family Law Proceedings) 2008, SI 358/2008.

13 ibid, sched 4.

14 In *T v K* [2022] IEHC 529, the respondent husband was ordered to pay €160,000.00 to the applicant wife for her legal costs since his failure to make full and frank financial disclosure caused conflict and protracted the case.

15 [2022] IEHC 528. The court held at [83] 'that the respondent [had] deliberately failed to disclose his true means' by presenting 'unreliable, misleading and incomplete evidence to the court concerning his means and the true financial picture'. It concluded at [109] that 'the evidence and information deficit here concerning the respondent's means is truly grotesque.'

16 The wife was opposed to a divorce being granted prior to proper provision being made for herself and the children since a divorce would put her outside a trust set up by the husband's father and she was 'anxious' that any provision awarded by the court would be complied with before any decree of divorce. See [87].

17 See Lucy-Ann Buckley, 'The Conveyancing Conundrum: Reviewable Dispositions and the In Camera Rule' (2003) 6(3) Irish Journal of Family Law 13.

capacity of both spouses. In *NO v PQ*, the Court of Appeal offered an in-depth consideration of this task which it noted can be particularly difficult for the trial judge.[18] It reiterated the need for convincing evidence of established earning capacity, warning against hypothetical speculation,[19] and confirmed that in a long marriage it is not enough, for example, to rely on work experience from before the marriage or the birth of children in determining future earning capacity.[20] Setting out a quite stringent test to determine earning capacity, it stated that a court must be satisfied that there is a real prospect of stable work within a reasonable distance of the dependent spouse's home before determining that a spouse is self-sufficient and consequently reducing or denying spousal maintenance payments.[21]

2.2.2 The financial needs, obligations, and responsibilities of the spouses

A broad spectrum of needs, obligations and responsibilities may be considered under this heading, beyond the basic needs of spouses to ensure, for example, that they have secure accommodation and income going forward. Again, to give the court a clear picture, in completing their affidavit of means (Form 37), parties are required to provide details of their debts, liabilities and expenses. Where one or both spouses suffer from any medical ailments or conditions, this will be captured as will any responsibility either spouse has towards their children.[22] The responsibility of parents towards their adult children who, although no longer legally dependant, continue to live with them and are in full time education, are unemployed or are in the formative stages of their career will also be considered.[23]

Similarly, where there is a business or a family farm, the needs of the owning spouse to retain enough money to maintain the business or farm as a viable income-generating enterprise will be relevant.[24] In this regard, the Supreme Court explained in *MD v ND*, that although in some circumstances it might not be appropriate to sell or divide a business,

18 *NO v PQ* [2021] IECA 177 [73].
19 ibid [76]
20 ibid [75].
21 ibid [76] (emphasis added). See below for more.
22 In *AN v KN* [2022] IEHC 528 [86] the court noted 'The applicant has significant financial needs with three children entering an expensive stage of their young lives.'
23 See *SB v RB* [1996] IFLR 220 (CC), [1997] 3 Fam LJ 66. In *NO v PQ* [2021] IECA 177 the obligations of a mother to an adult child with Asperger's Syndrome was noted.
24 See *JD v DD* [1997] 3 IR 64 where the need for considerable working capital to remain in the husband's business was accepted by the court. See also Lucy-Ann Buckley, 'Matrimonial Property and Irish Law: A Case for Community' (2002) 53 Northern Ireland Law Quarterly 39, 60.

it might be possible to order a lump sum payment in favour of the dependent spouse instead.[25]

2.2.3 The standard of living enjoyed by the family

Notwithstanding that marital breakdown and the division of a family into two separate households almost invariably results in a fall in the standard of living for family members, the standard enjoyed by the family at the point when the marriage ended is a factor considered by the court. Consequently, as Hogan J explained in *C v C,* 'where it is financially possible to do so, the wife is entitled to receive maintenance as will endeavour to match the standard of living which she previously enjoyed prior to the separation'.[26] However, the 'inevitable reality' that financial needs may be different post-divorce/separation, thereby affecting the standard of living 'that can realistically be expected to be enjoyed', was recently acknowledged in the Court of Appeal in *NO v PQ.*[27] Therefore, while it may be suggested that the 'standard of living' factor can act as a cap on provision where there are ample resources, in the majority of cases there will be insufficient assets to maintain the marital standard of living in two households with the focus instead on meeting basic needs.

2.2.4 The age of the spouses, the duration of their marriage[28] and the length of time they lived together

The age of a couple and the length of time they were in a relationship together can play an important role in a court's determination of proper provision although this may not be explicitly acknowledged. In short, a long marriage is more likely to result in the transfer of property between spouses than a short one. For example, while in *NO v PQ* the Court of Appeal emphasised the significant contribution of the wife to the successful dairy farm during the 23 years of the marriage in increasing her provision,[29] O' Donovan J in *CO'R v MO'R* referenced the short duration of the marriage in justifying why greater provision was not made for the wife in that case.[30]

---

25 *MD v ND* [2015] IESC 16 [4.3]. See also *T v K* [2022] IEHC 529 [138].

26 *C v C* [2016] IECA 410 [37]. See also *QR v ST* [2016] IECA 421 [106] per Irvine J and *G v G* [2011] IESC 40.

27 [2021] IECA 177 [103]. See also *A v A* [2022] IEHC 340 [7].

28 The duration of the marriage is *not* included in the criteria to which the court must have regard on judicial separation.

29 In *NO v PQ* [2021] IECA 177 [93], the Court of Appeal noted 'The trial judge fell into error in failing, notwithstanding clear evidence of same, to properly value the significant contribution the work of the appellant made to the successful dairy enterprise on the farm *during the 23 years of the marriage*...' (emphasis added).

30 [2000] IEHC 66.

2.2.5 Any physical or mental disability of the spouses

A physical or mental illness may create additional financial need. In *RS v IS*, the High Court adjusted a Circuit Court award to better take into account the additional health needs of a spouse.[31]

2.2.6 The contributions which the spouses have made or are likely to make to the welfare of the family, including to the income, earning capacity, property and financial resources of the other spouse and any contribution made by looking after the home or family

The requirement to consider spousal contributions, including non-financial contributions was regarded as a 'major development in family law' when originally included in s 20(2) of the Judicial Separation and Law Reform Act 1989.[32] However, to what extent sufficient recognition continues to be given to such contributions is open to question. On one hand, McGuinness J argued in *MK v JP (Orse SK)* that Irish courts do offer 'full credit' to work provided in the home.[33] Recent judgments have also emphasised the need to consider such contributions. The court referred to the 'unstinting dedication' of the mother to the family and home in *AN v KN*[34] while in *NO v PQ* the Court of Appeal held that the trial judge made a mistake in failing to properly value 'the significant contribution' the appellant made to the family farm.[35]

On the other hand, questions have been raised as to whether such recognition ultimately translates into increased provision. In 2007, Elena Moore conducted a study aimed at assessing whether women were adequately compensated for domestic contributions.[36] On the basis of her analysis, she concluded that the courts place greater value on financial contributions and work outside the home while at the same time undervaluing domestic contributions and caring.[37]

---

31 [2015] IEHC 837 [11].

32 Geoffrey Shannon, *Divorce Law and Practice* (Round Hall 2007), 85. Through the inclusion of this factor, the legislature sought to consolidate the constitutional protection afforded to housewives by Article 41.2.1° of the Constitution. For a recent critique of this Article, see Louise Crowley, 'Sheltering the Homemaker in Irish Family Law: Ireland's Failure to Evolve with the Shifting Social and Family Norms' in Margaret Brinig (ed) International Survey of Family Law (Intersentia 2018). For a summary of the applicable principles under this heading, see *M v S* [2020] IEHC 562 [58].

33 [2001] IESC 87; [2001] 3 IR 371; [2003] 1 IR 326.

34 [2022] IEHC 528 [86]. The court also expressly recognised that the applicant wife's contributions 'enabled the respondent to be a successful businessman' having 'moulded [her life] around a joint decision which was made having regard to his career and business interests'.

35 [2021] IECA 177 [93].

36 Elena Moore, 'The Significance of "Home-maker" Contributions upon Divorce' (2007) 10(1) Irish Journal of Family Law 15.

37 ibid, 17.

2.2.7 The effect on the earning capacity of the spouses of the marital responsibilities assumed when they lived together and, in particular, the degree to which the future earning capacity of a spouse is impaired by having relinquished or foregone the opportunity of remunerative activity to look after the home or family

This factor requires the court to consider whether one or both spouses' earning potential has diminished by virtue of the responsibilities assumed during the marriage, particularly where one has taken primary care of the family and home. Thus, while factor (a) discussed above mandates a consideration of future earning capacity, factor (g) involves the court investigating *why* a spouse may have a reduced capacity and whether that links to the responsibilities assumed in looking after the home or family.

Insofar as this factor links to earning capacity, the career which is sacrificed will be relevant in how the court addresses a finding that reduced earning capacity was the result of contributions made in the home and for the family. For example, in *SD v BD* one of the reasons why the applicant wife received a lump sum in the region of 25% of the net disposable assets as compared to the lump sum worth 37% of the net disposable assets provided to the applicant wife in *T v T,* was the 'greater sacrifice of career prospects' of the doctor wife in *T v T* than the wife in *SD v BD* who held a secretarial qualification.[38]

Moreover, this factor does not merely relate to those who have given up a career nor is it solely an assessment of future earning prospects. Even where a spouse did not withdraw entirely from the workforce, the extent to which the adoption of greater responsibilities in the home impacted on their ability to contribute to a private or social welfare pension, thereby creating 'an income handicap' in the future, may also be considered by the court.[39]

Whether the courts place enough weight on this factor in deciding how much provision to make for financially weaker spouses, usually women, on divorce is debatable. The amount of property or maintenance that is awarded to women who have sacrificed their career, earning capacity and pension contributions to look after the family and perhaps work in a family business seems in many cases to be quite small. While it is typically (although not always) the case that husbands are financially stronger and enjoy a higher earning capacity at the breakdown of a marriage, divorce has long been identified internationally as a major risk factor for women, in particular, to fall into poverty.[40] This lack of equality of outcome,

---

38 [2007] IEHC 492.

39 See *RS v IS* [2015] IEHC 837.

40 Lenore Weitzman and Mavis Maclean (eds) *Economic Consequences or Divorce* (Oxford University Press 1992).

stemming from an apparent under-valuing of a) domestic contributions and b) the significant impact these contributions can have on career prospects and earning capacity therefore continues to create problems.

Key case – *NO v PQ* [2021] IECA 177 – Spousal maintenance

In *NO v PQ* the Court of Appeal considered the judicial separation of a couple who had been together for 23 years and were parents to three children, two of whom had disabilities.[41] Although the case involved an application for judicial separation, the court confirmed that the jurisprudence arising from s 20 the of the Family Law (Divorce) Act 1996 was relevant.

The family farm where the family lived was valued at €1.1million and was held in the sole name of the husband. The husband's annual income was estimated at more than €100,000 before tax. The wife was the primary caregiver for the family, did all the housework and made a 'significant contribution' on the farm.

Before the case reached the Court of Appeal, the wife had received two lump sum payments worth €320,000 in total and her husband's pension, worth approximately €55,000, was transferred to her. While the children remained dependent (meaning under 18 or in full time education or suffering a disability to such extent that it is not reasonably possible for them to maintain themselves fully), the High Court had ordered child maintenance of €1,200/month. Spousal maintenance of €800/month was ordered by the High Court for a period of four years.

In the Court of Appeal, the wife successfully argued that the High Court had failed to make proper provision for her in both the amount and duration of the spousal maintenance ordered. Her appeal was successful.

The Court of Appeal held that the High Court had 'significantly' overestimated the likelihood of the wife earning an income in the future. It found the High Court had not valued her unpaid work in the home and on the farm enough or recognised sufficiently the fact that her 'negligible earning capacity' was a direct result of the marriage and 'the parties' *joint* decision' that she should give her life to being a wife and a mother, working in the home and on the farm.

As a result, the Court of Appeal doubled the spousal maintenance ordered to €1,600/month. Importantly, although the High Court had ordered that spousal maintenance should stop after four years, the Court of Appeal removed this limitation. Instead, it ordered that spousal maintenance should continue to be paid into the future and should only be reduced when she became entitled to pension payments.

---

41 *NO v PQ* [2021] IECA 177.

2.2.8 Any income or benefits to which either of the spouses is entitled by or under statute

The court may consider social welfare or other payments to which either spouse may be entitled, such as social welfare pension, child benefit, widow's pension (if previously married), carer's allowance *et cetera*.

2.2.9 The conduct of the spouses if it would be unjust to disregard it

Generally, the courts enjoy broad discretion to determine the relevance or otherwise of each of the statutory factors. However, when it comes to the conduct of the parties, the legislature has specified the threshold which it must meet to be considered: if it would be 'unjust to disregard it'. In *QR v ST*, the Court of Appeal reflected on the standard:

> The wording ... would suggest ... a *strong* presumption in favour of discounting conduct as immaterial to the issue of proper provision and that *something relatively exceptional* in terms of conduct would be required before the court would reflect that conduct in the manner in which it made proper provision for the parties.[42]

Moreover, the court noted, any such conduct is to be considered having regard to 'all the circumstances' and 'it is only if it would be unjust to ignore the conduct in that context that it should be taken into account'.[43] Indeed, reflecting the high threshold of misconduct required by the courts, in *T v T* Keane J endorsed the approach of Denning MR in the English case of *Wachtel v Wachtel*:

> There will no doubt be a residue of cases where the conduct of one of the parties is ... 'both obvious and gross', so much so that to order one party to support another whose conduct falls into this category is repugnant to anyone's sense of justice ... But short of cases falling into this category, the court should not reduce its order for financial provision merely because of what was formerly regarded as guilt or blame.[44]

Ultimately, as the Court of Appeal explained in *QR v ST*, except perhaps in 'quite special and unusual cases', issues of personal fault and misconduct during a marriage will rarely be relevant in deciding proper provision.[45]

---

42 *QR v ST* [2016] IECA 421 [49] (emphasis added).

43 ibid.

44 *T v T* [2002] IESC 68 [3]–[40] citing *Wachtel v Wachtel* [1973] EWCA Civ 10, [1973] Fam 72.

45 [2016] IECA 421 [53]

Despite this general reluctance to engage in an assessment of conduct, caselaw has crystallised around three core categories of misconduct. First, as regards personal misconduct, the courts have held that while infidelity will rarely amount to conduct that is so obvious and gross such that it would be unjust to ignore, where there has been domestic violence or alcoholism which caused serious financial consequences for the family, this may be taken into consideration.[46] Secondly, where conduct caused a reduction in the assets available for consideration in making proper provision, this may amount to financial misconduct.[47] Thirdly, where a spouse does not fully comply with their disclosure obligations in relation to divorce or judicial separation proceedings, this may constitute litigation misconduct. However, as confirmed in *QR v ST*, the court will not consider litigation misconduct in deciding the amount of provision to make for a financially weaker spouse unless the court was convinced that the other spouse had deliberately lied and tried to mislead the court.[48]

Finally, where the threshold for misconduct is met, the courts have reiterated that this 'does not mean that a person against whom such a finding is made has no rights' but rather that 'it is another factor for the court to have regard to, in determining what, in the circumstances, is adequate and reasonable provision under the section'.[49]

2.2.10 The accommodation needs of either of the spouses

The courts adopt a pragmatic approach in the consideration of this factor and the need to ensure stability for dependent children is often an overriding consideration. For instance, the Supreme Court noted in *MD v ND*, 'If other means are available, then the sale of a family home while children are at a delicate stage in their education may properly be avoided'.[50] However, this does not mean that the presence of dependent children will always be determinative in deciding the outcome. In *RS v IS*, the High Court recognised that the family home provided 'more [than] what [was] needed having regard to the present budget of the

46 See *QR v ST* [2016] IECA 421 [55]–[58]. See also Inge Clissmann and Ciara McLoughlin, 'Beginning or the end?' (2022) (Aug/Sept) Law Society Gazette 20.

47 See *QR v ST* [2016] IECA 421 [59]–[60].

48 *QR v ST* [2016] IECA 421 [64]. See also *T v K* [2022] IEHC 529 [138] where although the respondent husband was found guilty of litigation misconduct for having 'sought to mislead the applicant and the court as to the true worth of the matrimonial assets and as to his income', the court concluded 'that it would not be unjust to disregard' it. Interestingly, in *AN v KN* [2022] IEHC 528 the court noted at [86] that while it 'could hold the respondent to account for gross and obvious misconduct in not disclosing his means' it would not do so given that it was 'not in a position to quantify what is being concealed'. Instead the court decided to 'make proper provision in light of its finding that the respondent [was] much wealthier' than he pretended.

49 *R v R* [2006] 2 ILRM 267, per McMahon J.

50 [2015] IESC 16 [4.3].

family'.[51] Conscious that the husband was living in rented accommodation which was 'probably too expensive', the court concluded that the accommodation needs of the family would be better met if the home was sold and the family traded down. In order to balance such an order with the needs of the children, however, the court postponed the order for sale for five years until the youngest child would be 16.[52]

2.2.11 The value to each of the spouses of any benefit which by reason of the decree of judicial separation/divorce concerned, that spouse will forfeit the opportunity or possibility of acquiring

The court may consider benefits arising under a prior separation agreement or under statute with this factor frequently arising in the context of pension benefits.

2.2.12 The rights of any person other than the spouses but including a person to whom either spouse is remarried

Finally, the court must consider the rights of third parties such as mortgagees and creditors.[53] Although it is not uncommon for the court to consider liabilities of spouses' to their siblings/parents, the need to consider the rights of persons to whom either spouse is remarried will only arise where there is an application to vary an order for ancillary relief where a divorce has previously been granted.[54]

The 1996 Act does not attach any particular weight to any of the factors listed, instead allowing the judiciary the freedom to determine the importance or otherwise of each. Neither is the list exhaustive; other factors deemed relevant by the court may be considered beyond those set out in s 16 of the 1995 Act and s 20 of the 1996 Act. In this context, the importance of the statutory list of factors in guiding the court might be questioned. Indeed, until relatively recent times many judgments did not explain how the court had applied the various factors, simply stating they had been considered. However, more and more judgments do now look at each factor individually[55] and it appears significant weight is attached to the list by at least some members of the judiciary. As Barr J in *JBB v SMB* recently noted: 'This statutory obligation [in s 20 of the 1996 Act], in my view, provides an invaluable guide or check list without which a trial

---

51 [2015] IEHC 837 [11].

52 Note, the court of first instance had ordered the postponement of the sale of the family home until the youngest child was 23.

53 See also s 15(5) of the 1995 Act and s 19(5) of the 1996 Act.

54 See below for the courts powers to vary orders made.

55 This is especially true since the Supreme Court reiterated the need for courts to make specific reference to the factors in their judgments in *MD v ND* [2015] IESC 16 [4.14] per Clarke and MacMenamin JJ (joint judgment).

judge might easily omit to consider matters of fundamental or critical importance to a just and fair result in terms of proper provision'.[56]

Beyond these factors, although few judicially developed principles have emerged, it does appear that notions of fairness play an especially important role. As the Court of Appeal explained in *NO v PQ*: 'the clear objective is to provide a *fair* outcome, bespoke to the individual and specific circumstances of each case ... with the overarching aim of achieving *fairness* and justice between the parties'.[57] There is, however, no real guidance as to what fairness means in practice.

2.3 Other influences on the court

In the context of divorce, s 20(3) of the Family Law (Divorce) Act 1996 provides that the court must consider the terms of any separation agreement which has been entered into by the spouses and is still in force as discussed in Chapter 5. However, notwithstanding that the court 'shall' have regard to arrangements agreed by the spouses, it is open to the court to vary, or indeed disregard, some or all of the provisions of a prior agreement. Similarly, although regard may be had to their terms in determining what proper provision is in the circumstances, pre-nuptial agreements are not enforceable in Irish law.[58]

Finally, pursuant to s 16(5) of the 1995 Act and s 20(5) of the 1996 Act, the court is prohibited from making any order for an applicant spouse unless 'it would be in the interests of justice to do so'. This measure operates as a final check on the appropriateness of the order, but it is so broad that it is unclear what further protection it provides.

2.4 Types of orders available to the courts

The Irish courts enjoy broad redistributive powers to make proper provision for spouses and children. The three most important orders at the disposal of the courts are:

---

56 [2018] IEHC 146 [48].

57 [2021] IECA 177 at [60] (emphasis added).

58 The Law Society of Ireland, *Divorce in Ireland: The case for reform* (2019) noted at 47: 'In the absence of legislation and case law, the prudent view would be to assume that pre-nuptial agreements are recognisable in Irish law, although not necessarily enforceable per se'. See also Louise Crowley, 'Ireland' in Jens M. Scherpe (ed) *Marital Agreements and Private Autonomy in Comparative Perspective* (Hart Publishing 2012) and Department of Justice, Equality and Law Reform, *Report of the Study Group on Pre-nuptial Agreements* (April 2007).

2.4.1 Periodic payments and lump sum orders

Section 8 of the 1995 Act and s 13 of the 1996 Act provide for periodic payments and lump sum orders, whether for the benefit of a spouse or dependent children. When granting a decree of divorce or at any time thereafter, the court may make a periodic payments order,[59] a secured periodic payments order[60] or an order that either of the spouses shall make to the other spouse a lump sum payment(s) of such amount(s) and at such time(s) as may be specified.[61] Although not expressly named as such, these provisions are commonly referred to as the 'maintenance' provisions of the Acts.

2.4.2 Orders to adjust the ownership of property (property adjustment orders)

When making a property adjustment order, the court may use provisions in ss 9 and 10 of the Family Law Act 1995 and ss 14 and 15 of the Family Law (Divorce) Act 1996. The court is empowered to order the settlement of property to which either spouse is entitled[62] or order the transfer of a proprietary interest to which one spouse is entitled.[63]

In relation to the family home,[64] the courts must specify which spouse gains exclusive occupation if there is no outright transfer of the property ordered.[65] In addition, specific provisions empower the court to make an order for the sale of the family home and the division of the proceeds.[66] The court may not make orders after divorce affecting a home in which one of the spouses lives with a new spouse.

2.4.3 Orders to adjust pensions (pension adjustment orders)

As noted in *MD v ND*, '[t]he precise role which pension orders may properly play in an assessment of proper provision can often be a

---

59 1995 Act, s 8(1)(a) and 1996 Act, s 13(1)(a).

60 1995 Act, s 8(1)(b) and 1996 Act, s 13(1)(b).

61 1995 Act, s 8(1)(c) and 1996 Act, s 13(1)(c). Lump sum payments may be made as a 'lump sum' or may be made by instalments.

62 This order may be made for a spouse and/or any dependent member of the family.

63 Or the transfer could be made to any dependent member of the family or other specified person for the benefit of the dependent.

64 'Family home' for the purposes of the 1995 and 1996 Acts is that defined in s 2(1) of the Family Home Protection Act 1976: 'primarily a dwelling in which a married couple ordinarily reside. The expression comprises, in addition, a dwelling in which a spouse whose protection is in issue ordinarily resides, or if that spouse has left the other spouse ordinarily resided before so leaving.' See *National Irish Bank v Graham* [1995] 2 IR 244.

65 See 1995 Act, s 10(1)(a)(i) and 1996 Act, s 15(1)(a)(i).

66 1995 Act, s 10(1)(a)(ii) and 1996 Act, s 15(1)(a)(ii).

difficult and complex task'.[67] In fact, although pensions may be the most valuable asset that a spouse owns – and despite the reality that many women, in particular, may not have built up an equivalent pension pot to their breadwinner husbands for various reasons linked to the division of responsibilities in relation to childcare and the family – pension adjustment orders may only be used as a last resort. Section 17(23)(b) requires a court to consider whether proper provision can be made for the spouse concerned or the dependent member of the family with other orders of the court, such as property adjustment or maintenance orders.

Where a pension adjustment order is being granted, s 12 of the 1995 Act and s 17 of the 1996 Act empower the court to make two main types of orders. First, in a process known as earmarking, the court may make an order stating that a percentage of the whole or part of a benefit ought to be paid directly to the other spouse (or to another person for the benefit of a dependent member of the family). Secondly, it may make an order for pension splitting whereby a percentage of a retirement benefit which has been earmarked for the other spouse is valued and is then used to provide a separate pension for that spouse.[68]

2.5 Absence of a 'clean break' principle

The 1995 and 1996 Acts do not adopt a policy of 'clean break' whereby financial ties between former spouses end definitively at a certain specified point. Instead, either spouse may apply for ancillary relief, not only at the application for a decree of judicial separation or divorce but anytime thereafter[69] provided the applicant has not remarried.[70] An application for variation may be made, not only by either of the spouses concerned, but in the case of the death of either of the spouses, by any other person who has, in the opinion of the court, a sufficient interest in the matter or by a person on behalf of a dependent member of the family concerned.[71]

There are pros and cons to having such an open-ended approach. On one hand, it means the courts have greater flexibility to address the consequences of divorce for financially weaker spouses, both at the time of divorce and thereafter. On the other hand, it adds even more

67 *MD v ND* [2015] IESC 16 [6.6].

68 Note, pension splitting is only available in relation to 'retirement benefits'.

69 See 1995 Act, s 18(2) and 1996 Act, s 22(2).

70 1995 Act, s 9(3) and 1996 Act, s 14(3).

71 1995 Act, s 18(2) and 1996 Act, s 22(2). In addition, s 22(2)(c) of the 1996 Act provides that in the case of the remarriage of either of the spouses, his or her spouse may make an application. However, note also the availability of 'blocking orders' under s 15A(10) of the 1995 Act and s 18(10) of the 1996 Act.

uncertainty into the scheme and could prevent former spouses from fully moving on from their past relationship.

The appropriateness of this approach has been questioned, and although the Supreme Court acknowledged that clean break is a legitimate aspiration,[72] the importance of ensuring open-ended ties and ongoing provision is frequently highlighted. Therefore, although divorce ends a marriage, proper provision can result in ongoing financial ties to a former spouse ending only on the death of the receiving spouse.

Key case – *A v A* [2022] IEHC 340 – No clean break

In the 2022 case of *A v A*, the High Court rejected a husband's claim for clean break.[73] The court highlighted the ongoing need to recognise the contribution of the wife to the husband's career, explaining that if the husband worked after retirement age, he would continue to earn an income based on the professional experience that he was, in part, able to gain thanks to his wife's work in the home. While the court accepted that the husband had worked hard at his career also, it reiterated the unfairness that it would create if he could 'cash in' on his career, even though that career had been facilitated by his wife's contributions.[74]

In many other contexts, ongoing maintenance and the absence of clean break are justified by the court's desire to ensure the needs of the financially weaker spouse are met going forward, thus highlighting the depth of the marital obligations owed.[75]

3. Critical thinking points

3.1 Critical thinking point: How predictable is ancillary relief provision on marital breakdown?

Few, if any, jurisdictions apply an ancillary relief system incorporating such a high degree of judicial discretion as that adopted in Ireland. Across the common law world, most jurisdictions have approaches involving rules or presumptions for the division of assets while civil law jurisdictions are characterised by the adoption of community of property regimes,

---

72 *G v G* [2011] IESC 40 [22]. If, for example, there is a short marriage or there are ample assets, a clean break approach may be more likely to be considered appropriate.

73 *A v A* [2022] IEHC 340.

74 ibid [39].

75 See Louise Crowley, 'Sheltering the Homemaker in Irish Family Law: Ireland's Failure to Evolve with the Shifting Social and Family Norms' in Margaret Brinig (ed) *International Survey of Family Law* (Intersentia 2018)

whether immediate (with assets shared on marriage) or deferred (with assets shared at the point of divorce).[76]

A system based on judicial discretion has the advantage of flexibility. With few constraints, it allows the court to create a bespoke package of provisions, ensuring individualised justice for each divorcing couple. However, the specific ancillary relief scheme in the Family Law Acts 1995 and 1996 has significant shortcomings. The Law Society of Ireland recently noted 'criticisms are often levelled at the entirely subjective nature' of the system 'which leaves considerable scope for a variety of outcomes and diverging judicial discretion'.[77] Reflecting the challenges faced in practice, it explained: 'The "proper provision" requirement causes difficulties in some cases because it is interpreted and defined by different judges in different ways allowing the unfettered exercise of judicial discretion'.[78]

The lack of predictability has particularly serious implications for the vast majority of spouses who seek to reach a settlement out of court. These couples, who should be able to bargain within clear parameters set by the courts, are often left with little foreseeability as to what the outcome might be if they pursued legal action. Of particular concern are financially vulnerable spouses, often women, who may be in a weak bargaining position in the absence of an entitlement to anything in particular. As Scherpe has highlighted in England and Wales, where there are no rules in place, and the provision that is made depends entirely on the discretion of the court, a financially weaker spouse bears the full weight of having to argue for sharing, for compensation and for their needs to be met. While such a flexible approach may work well where spouses are financial equals and thus bargaining on equal terms, the reality is that this is rarely the case with the 'male breadwinner model' continuing to dominate Irish family arrangements.[79]

3.2 Critical thinking point: Why does Ireland adopt such a highly discretionary scheme?

The origins of the Irish scheme can be traced to the ban on divorce which applied in Ireland until 1996 as discussed in Chapter 3. Given that the introduction of divorce required a constitutional referendum, the issue of how property, in particular, would be divided in the event of marital breakdown became a politically charged topic. The potential impact of

---

[76] See Katharina Boele-Woelki, Joanna K. Miles and Jens M. Scherpe (eds) *The Future of Family Property in Europe* (Intersentia 2020).

[77] The Law Society of Ireland, *Divorce in Ireland: The case for reform* (2019) 3.

[78] ibid, 8.

[79] Jens Scherpe, 'Marital agreements and private autonomy in comparative perspective' in Jens Scherpe (ed), *Marital Agreements and Private Autonomy in Comparative Perspective* (Hart Publishing 2012), 476.

divorce on farm holdings was especially contentious. It was noted of the divorce referendum in 1986, for example,

> The anti-divorce lobby argued that the introduction of divorce would ultimately threaten the integrity of the family farm as the courts would inevitably be given power to distribute property as they saw fit. The image of the disintegration of holdings which have passed intact through generations proved to be quite an emotive one.[80]

Fears that financially dependent wives would be left in a precarious financial position on marital breakdown also abounded. In this context, as a means of appeasing both sides of the argument in advance of an inevitable second constitutional referendum on the issue of divorce, a flexible approach based on equitable redistribution was adopted in the Judicial Separation and Family Law Reform Act 1989 ('the 1989 Act'). By giving responsibility to the judiciary to determine how assets should be shared and what provision should be made for spouses on marital breakdown, the government side-stepped difficult political decisions. Landowners were somewhat relieved that farms would not be divided automatically while advocacy groups representing women were reassured that significant provision could be made for those left vulnerable on marital breakdown.

The ancillary relief provisions of the 1989 Act were later repealed with almost identical provisions subsequently replicated through the Family Law Acts 1995 and 1996. In the intervening 28 years, few meaningful amendments of the overarching system have been attempted with the discretionary system introduced in 1989 remaining almost entirely as originally enacted.

3.3 Critical thinking point: What kind of reforms could Ireland introduce to improve the ancillary relief scheme on marital breakdown?

Given the uncertainty produced by the highly discretionary approach to ancillary relief provision, it is perhaps unsurprising that the need for reform has been highlighted. A wide variety of stakeholders including the Law Society of Ireland[81] and numerous academics working in the area have called for action and it appears that reform may now be on the horizon. The Law Reform Commission of Ireland's *Fifth Programme of Law Reform* will consider what further guidance may be provided to ensure 'a consistency in the approach taken to the exercise of ... judicial

[80] Peter Ward, *Divorce in Ireland, Who should bear the cost?* (Cork University Press 1993) 26–27.

[81] The Law Society of Ireland, *Divorce in Ireland: The case for reform* (2019).

discretion' in determining proper provision on divorce, 'in particular to assist spouses to reach settlements'.[82]

What direction this guidance will take remains to be seen. It is unlikely that the Law Reform Commission will recommend any major shift in policy towards the adoption of a more rule-based regime like that applied in civil law jurisdictions. Such reform would be beyond the scope of the Law Reform Commission's project and would, in any event, be unlikely to make it past the legislature. In reality, this kind of a change in approach would likely seem too sharp for both politicians and the public. A rule based regime would sacrifice important flexibility to respond to the nuances of different family contexts.

Thankfully, there are many different points on the spectrum between the current highly discretionary approach and such rule-based schemes. Many common law jurisdictions adopt starting points or presumptions of equal sharing over defined categories of assets. These schemes typically give the courts residual discretion to depart from the starting point or presumption in certain defined circumstances and clearly set out the objectives or principles guiding the exercise of judicial discretion.[83] Such an approach would have a lot to recommend it. However, even if presumptions or starting points are not favoured, 'mandatory guidelines', as advocated for by the Law Society of Ireland, could still be utilised to better direct the discretion of the courts.[84]

There are a huge range of possible reforms which could be considered as a means of bringing much needed foreseeability and certainty to the Irish ancillary relief system. As much as it will be important to see what recommendations are ultimately advanced by the Law Reform Commission, it will count for little unless some steps are taken, on a legislative or non-legislative basis, to address the shortcomings of the system as it currently stands.

4. Summary

- The requirement to make 'proper provision' is both legislative and

---

82 Law Reform Commission of Ireland, *Fifth Programme of Law Reform* (2019), 16 available at https://www.lawreform.ie/news/fifth-programme-of-law-reform.857.html [last accessed 2 June 2021]. Although the Commission refers to 'divorce', any recommendations made will likely apply to the assessment of proper provision on judicial separation also.

83 See, for example, s 9 of the Family Law (Scotland) Act 1985 which sets out key guiding principles or the Property (Relationships) Act 1976 in New Zealand. See also the Family Law Act 2011 in British Columbia, Canada.

84 The Law Society of Ireland, *Divorce in Ireland: The case for reform* (2019), 8.

constitutional in nature and a pre-condition to the grant of a decree of divorce.

- Wide discretion is given to the judiciary to decide the nature and amount of all provision made for spouses on marital breakdown.
- There is no legislative policy of 'clean break' with spouses able to return to court for further provision potentially many years post-divorce/separation.
- The court must consider *all* wealth both earned and received and all the available assets of the spouses may be subject to redistribution: assets are not categorized into 'family/marital' and 'non-family/ marital assets'.
- The level of discretion given to the courts in regulating the financial consequences of marital breakdown is very high. This means that the courts can be flexible to reflect the circumstances of the parties. However, it also means that awards are difficult to predict which makes it difficult for parties to come up with settlements.

5. Further Reading

5.1 Irish scholarship

Kathryn O'Sullivan, 'Spousal maintenance in Ireland: past, present and future' (2022) 44(1) Journal of Social Welfare and Family Law 63.

Law Society of Ireland, *Divorce in Ireland: The case for reform* (2019) available at https://www.lawsociety.ie/globalassets/documents/ submissions/divorce-in-ireland-april-2019.pdf.

Kathryn O'Sullivan, 'Pensions on divorce in Ireland: law, practice and a way forward?' (2019) 70(3) Northern Ireland Legal Quarterly 311.

Louise Crowley, 'Sheltering the Homemaker in Irish Family Law: Ireland's Failure to Evolve with the Shifting Social and Family Norms' in Margaret Brinig (ed) *International Survey of Family Law* (Intersentia 2018).

Kathryn O'Sullivan, 'Rethinking Ancillary Relief on Divorce in Ireland: The Challenges and Opportunities' (2016) 36(1) Legal Studies 111.

Louise Crowley, 'Dividing the Spoils on divorce: rule-based regulation versus discretionary-based decision' (2012) International Family Law 388.

Lucy Ann Buckley, 'Matrimonial Property and Irish Law: A Case for Community' (2002) 53 Northern Ireland Legal Quarterly 39.

5.2 International scholarship

Emma Hitchings and Joanna Miles, 'Rules Versus Discretion in Financial Remedies on Divorce' (2019) 33(1) International Journal of Law, Policy and the Family 24.

New Zealand Law Commission, *Review of the Property (Relationships) Act 1976* (Report 143–2019).

New Zealand Law Commission, *Dividing relationship property – time for change?* (Issue Paper 41 – 2017).

Chapter 5

Financial Consequences of Ending Marriage – Private Ordering

Connie Healy

LEARNING OUTCOMES

By the end of the chapter, students will be equipped to

- Compare the main methods of resolving the financial consequences of relationship breakdown outside of the courts' process.
- Evaluate each process as a means of less adversarial dispute resolution.
- Outline the legal effect of private settlement and the importance of court approval in ensuring proper provision.

CRITICAL THINKING POINTS

- Are the rights of all parties protected within alternative methods of dispute resolution?
- To what extent, if any, is the voice of the child heard within private dispute resolution processes?

1. Introduction

The constitutional provisions protecting the institution of marriage in Ireland mean that when marriages end the courts have ultimate responsibility for ensuring substantive and procedural fairness. As examined in Chapter 4, fairness is based on ensuring proper provision, loosely framed on an established set of factors, but with wide judicial discretion in each case.[1] Access to justice is provided through an adversarial hearing in the courts or, if appropriate, by upholding agreements reached by the parties through a variety of autonomous decision-making processes.

This chapter will explore the options available for couples who wish to reach agreements to divide assets, make arrangements for children and provide for the end of a relationship without recourse to the courts. Prior

1 Article 41.3.2°.iii of the Constitution; s 20 of the Family Law (Divorce) Act 1996.

to entering a marriage or civil partnership, the parties may opt to draw up a **Pre-nuptial Agreement.** The extent to which these agreements are recognised in Ireland is discussed. Less adversarial options are also available for parties who have entered a marriage or civil partnership, and who wish to terminate the relationship, including drafting a **separation agreement,** which is signed by the parties noting the terms agreed and incorporated into a formal **deed of separation** by lawyers.[2]

In reaching an agreement, the parties also have several **process options**. **Mediation** and **collaborative practice** (collaborative law) are voluntary consensual methods of dispute resolution leading to an agreement that can be recorded in a deed of separation (or ruled as a **consent order** for judicial separation or divorce), and **arbitration**, during which the parties agree to hand the decision as to how matters are to be resolved to a neutral arbitrator with experience of dealing with family law matters. Mediation and collaborative law are 'interest-based' methods of dispute resolution. They allow the parties to focus on what is of importance to them and give them freedom to work together to craft a resolution to their dispute, rather than have a decision imposed upon them by a court. Arbitration, in contrast, is similar to the courts in that the parties present their arguments, orally or in writing, and an arbitrator decides on the issues in dispute.

These alternative processes can provide a less adversarial, less expensive, and more timely resolution of the issues at hand. However, settlements reached through any of these processes will require court approval in accordance with the legislative and constitutional requirements to ensure that proper provision has been made for any dependent spouse or children.[3] Once court approval has been obtained, any agreements reached can form part of a court order with the consent of the parties or be incorporated into a deed of separation. This chapter will examine how these processes work and their effectiveness. It will focus on whether they provide merely a means of settlement or conflict resolution enabling a more holistic solution for all the family. Further, it will assess the extent to which the aims of substantive and procedural justice are upheld in alternative dispute resolution.

---

2 A deed of separation is a legally binding document which records the terms upon which the parties have agreed to separate. It is usually drafted by solicitors and signed by both parties.

3 See Chapter 4.

Key legislation
Mediation Act 2017 Judicial Separation and Family Law Reform Act 1989 Family Law (Divorce) Act 1996

2. Pre-nuptial agreements

A pre-nuptial agreement is an agreement made between two parties in contemplation of marriage or civil partnership. These agreements are framed to ensure the protection and allocation of property in a manner that opts out of the provisions of marriage law and excludes the jurisdiction of the court. Pre-nuptial agreements are not recognised as legally binding agreements. Traditionally this was because they were considered contrary to the constitutional requirement to respect and protect the institution of marriage.[4] Concerns were also raised as to whether marriages might, in some instances, become conditional upon the execution of pre-nuptial agreements, overtly or covertly placing parties under duress to agree to specific terms. The extent to which agreements entered into before marriage could sufficiently accommodate changing family circumstances including the arrival of children or changes in the financial position of either of the parties was also of concern.[5]

More recently, some sectors of society have argued that agreements entered into pre-marriage should be legally enforceable, particularly in situations where there is a family business or farm. In 2007, a study group was established by the Department of Justice, Equality and Law Reform.[6] It recommended that pre-nuptial agreements should be recognised and enforceable when there is full disclosure of all relevant financial information, each party has obtained independent legal advice, the agreement is in writing, signed by both parties, witnessed and made at least 28 days before the marriage.[7] In 2019, the Law Society of Ireland also undertook a review of the law on this issue.[8] They concluded

4 Lucy-Ann Buckley, 'Autonomy and Prenuptial Agreements in Ireland: A Relational Analysis' (2018) 38 Legal Studies 164.

5 The only concession in relation to pre-marital or pre-civil partnership arrangements is under s 113 and 113A of the Succession Act 1965, where a future spouse or civil partner can renounce their legal right share.

6 Department of Justice, Equality and Law Reform, *Report of the Study Group on Pre-nuptial Agreements*, (2007) available at https://jobs.justice.ie/en/JELR/PrenupRpt.pdf/Files/PrenupRpt.pdf [last accessed 5 December 2022]. The Study Group recommends that express statutory provision be made for pre-nuptial agreements by way of introducing a new s 16(2)A of the Family Law Act 1995 and a new s 20(3)A of the Family Law (Divorce) Act 1996. To date the Report has not be actioned and the position remains somewhat uncertain.

7 *Report of the Study Group on Pre-nuptial Agreements* (n 6) 84.

8 Law Society of Ireland, *Divorce in Ireland – The case for reform* (2019) available at

that 'the prudent view' at present is that 'pre-nuptial agreements are recognisable in Irish law, although not necessarily enforceable *per se*'.[9] Similar to the earlier study, the Law Society recommended that the law should acknowledge that 'a court may take pre-nuptial agreements into account when deciding "proper provision"', provided 'that they are valid and enforceable to the extent that they support and foster the interests of children and spouses'. This recommendation was made with the usual caveat that 'the judiciary should retain a wide discretion to vary their terms'.[10] It was not anticipated that pre-nuptial agreements would have the same weight as a post-nuptial separation agreement but rather that oversight by the judiciary would continue to ensure that a balance is struck between allowing party autonomy and ensuing that the constitutional protections are upheld.[11]

In England and Wales pre-nuptial agreements are given effect by a divorce court if it can be shown that the parties understood the nature of the agreement, that it was freely entered into, and that it was fair in the circumstances. The legal effect of pre-nuptial agreements in England and Wales was considered by the UK Supreme Court in 2010 in the case of *Radmacher (Formerly Granatino) v Granatino.*[12] The majority of the court decided that:

> The court should give effect to a nuptial agreement that is freely entered into by each party with a full appreciation of its implications unless in the circumstances prevailing it would not be fair to hold the parties to their agreement.[13]

Lady Hale in her dissent highlighted that a distinction needs to be made between agreements reached before marriage (pre-nuptial) and afterwards (post nuptial). She raised concerns that that pre-nuptial agreements can often be used to 'deny the economically weaker spouse the provision to which [they] would be otherwise entitled' and called for a full review of the law.[14]

2.1 What is the legal effect of a prenuptial agreement?

In Ireland, pre-nuptial agreements have no legal standing. There is no

---

https://www.lawsociety.ie/globalassets/documents/submissions/divorce-in-ireland-april-2019.pdf [last accessed 2 August 2023]

9 Law Society of Ireland (n 8), 47. There is no statutory framework in Ireland, at present, to provide for these agreements.

10 Law Society of Ireland (n 8), 11.

11 To date the report has not be actioned and the position remains somewhat uncertain.

12 *Radmacher (Formerly Granatino) v Granatino* [2010] UKSC 42.

13 [2010] UKSC 42 [75].

14 [2010] UKSC 42 [137].

requirement in law that judges *must* consider the terms of a pre-nuptial agreement when deciding proper provision but judges *may* accept evidence from the parties as to terms agreed and this, along with other factors, may influence a decision as to whether proper provision has been made. The Law Society has provided recommendations as set out above. It is likely that pressure from interest groups may lead to these, or similar, recommendations being considered in the future.

3. Separation Agreements

Resolving matters by entering into a separation agreement, given legal effect through a deed of separation, can be a less costly and less adversarial way of finalising issues arising out of the breakdown of a relationship post-marriage or civil partnership. The terms can be agreed between the parties themselves, often termed 'kitchen table divorce', negotiated by their solicitors, or by way of mediation or collaborative practice. The agreement will normally address custody and access arrangements for children, the division of assets including the family home and any other property, and maintenance for dependants. By signing a separation agreement, the parties agree to live separate and apart and they can elect for the separation agreement to be considered 'full and final settlement' of the issues between them. In effect, therefore, a separation agreement is a contract and any breach of the agreement would give rise to a contractual dispute.

Factors that need to be considered in opting for a deed of separation are first, that doing so may preclude the parties from seeking a decree of judicial separation. The courts have held that once the parties agree to live separately and apart, there are no grounds for granting a judicial separation. Being ineligible for a judicial separation precludes the granting of the many court orders that are only available as ancillary relief (see Chapter 4) including property adjustment orders, orders for occupation of the family home and pension adjustment orders.[15] A further important consideration is that agreement cannot be reached by the parties themselves regarding the allocation of pension benefits.[16] As pension funds are managed by trustees, it is necessary to seek the trustees' consent prior to any application for splitting of a fund and a court order is required to give legal effect to any reallocation of assets within a fund.

---

15 Note that maintenance and child custody orders are available as standalone issues from the District Court, see Chapter 9.

16 A pension is a long-term savings plan achieved through regular or lump sum payments to provide for funds for retirement and can be a valuable asset depending on the number of years accrued. The monies, once invested, are managed by the trustees of the fund. Pension terms cannot be varied by the parties without the approval of the trustees.

What happens then if there is a validly executed separation agreement and the parties wish to apply for a divorce? As discussed in Chapter 4, only a decree of divorce will permit spouses to remarry; separation agreements manage arrangements for the spouses to live apart. A separation agreement is not a bar to seeking a decree of divorce.

An important issue for separating couples is whether the terms of a prior separation agreement will be taken into consideration by the court in making any final financial orders on the granting of a divorce. In *YG v NG*, Denham CJ noted that a

> separation agreement is an extant legal document, entered into with consent of both parties, and it should be given significant weight. It will, therefore, be one of the factors considered by the court when determining proper provision. This is so, especially if the separation agreement was intended to be a full and final settlement of all matters arising.[17]

In assessing proper provision under s 20 of the Divorce Act 1996, a deed of separation stated to be in full and final settlement is therefore a significant factor. The longer the agreement has been in place, the more weight will be given to the autonomous wishes of the parties. Evidence may be provided if there is a significant change in circumstances for one of the parties. Matters considered significant include serious health issues or changes to employment status.

3.1 What is the legal effect of a separation agreement?

A separation agreement once incorporated into a deed of separation is a legally binding document and is a bar to an application for judicial separation. However, a separation agreement is not a bar to applying for a divorce. The terms agreed by the parties in a prior separation agreement will be taken into consideration by the court and in practice, if the court is satisfied that proper provision has been made, may influence the court's decision. However, the court retains discretion under the law and Constitution to make the final decision.

4. Mediation

Mediation is defined in the Mediation Act 2017 as:

> a confidential, facilitative, and voluntary process in which parties

---

17 *YG v NG* [2011] IESC 40 [22] (Denham CJ).

> to a dispute, with the assistance of a mediator, attempt to reach a mutually acceptable agreement to resolve the dispute.[18]

Viewed as an appropriate and less adversarial way to resolve conflict in family law matters, there is a statutory obligation for lawyers acting on behalf of separating parties to advise of the availability and possible benefits of mediation. Solicitors are obliged to provide this information under both the Judicial Separation and Family Law Reform Act 1989[19] and the Family Law (Divorce) Act 1996.[20]

Key words in the definition of mediation include confidential, facilitative, and voluntary. Parties seeking to resolve the issues arising from their relationship breakdown must agree to the use of mediation as a dispute resolution mechanism. They therefore enter the process *voluntarily* and can choose to leave the process at any time, without the need for explanation. If the parties agree to mediation, they sign an agreement to mediate.[21] As part of that agreement, they undertake to negotiate in good faith and to work with a neutral mediator, an independent third party, who *facilitates* discussion and helps them to reach a solution. And finally, all discussions that take place within the mediation process are *confidential* and cannot be discussed outside of the process. Negotiations are undertaken on a 'without prejudice' basis. This means that any proposals or offers made during the mediation process cannot be referred to in any subsequent court proceedings. Within the mediation process, nothing is considered agreed until everything is agreed and the agreement is reduced to writing by the mediator and signed by the parties.

The mediator as a neutral facilitator of the agreement has a key role to play in assessing the suitability of the parties for the process and in managing how the discussions proceed. Central to this is screening at the outset to ensure, in so far as it is possible to ascertain, that there are no impediments to either party's ability to negotiate freely within the process. Key issues that a mediator will screen for include any past or ongoing issues of domestic violence, drug, or alcohol abuse. Mediation may be, and generally is, deemed unsuitable where there is any fear or undue influence affecting either party's ability to negotiate.[22] This is particularly important because there is generally no one other than the parties present during mediation sessions. Mediation sessions are

---

18 Mediation Act 2017, s 2.

19 Judicial Separation and Family Law Reform Act 1989, ss 5 and 6.

20 Family Law (Divorce) Act 1996, ss 6 and 7.

21 Mediation Act 2017, s 7.

22 Women's Aid, *Submission to the Family Courts Bill General Scheme*, February 2021 available at https://www.womensaid.ie/assets/files/pdf/submission_to_the_court_bill_general_scheme_february_2021.pdf [last accessed 16 September 2023].

arranged a time that suits the parties and matters can often be resolved more quickly rather than having to wait for a court hearing.

The mediator's role is to manage the process and he or she ensures that equal time is given to each party to express their views and to negotiate freely. As such it can be argued that mediation provides access to justice in that the parties have an opportunity to discuss issues that a judge might not be willing to entertain in a court hearing. Agreements reached can be more creative and can be tailored to meet the needs of that family, rather than what may be perceived as binary choices made by a judge within the adversarial process. Some mediators, with the consent of the parties, may hold a family session at the end of the process where the custody and access arrangements or other issues are discussed with the children of the relationship.

While there are many advantages to mediation as a dispute resolution process, it also has disadvantages. Parties can leave the process at any time, without explanation. Agreements may be reached within the process but may not be adhered to, meaning that court intervention may be required. Feminist scholarship on the process, while initially favourable, viewing mediation as a less patriarchal system than the courts, has more recently raised concern about the extent to which the non-earning partner can have the requisite autonomy to make decisions, particularly if they are also trying to achieve a solution in the best interests of any dependent children and the family.[23] This can impact the extent to which justice is truly achieved within the process.

4.1 Mediation Act 2017

The Mediation Act 2017 ('the 2017 Act') was a long-awaited piece of legislation which it was hoped would provide for greater transparency around the mediation process and the qualifications required for mediators in this jurisdiction. The 2017 Act provided some structure for the process and raised mediation's prominence as a dispute resolution mechanism. Statutory obligations for lawyers to inform potential litigants about mediation were extended beyond the family law sphere and accompanied by cost sanctions in situations where parties were deemed by the court to have 'unreasonably refused' to meditate.[24]

The 2017 Act does not establish a regulating body with set requirements in terms of accreditation and experience for mediators. Instead, it provides for the establishment of a Mediation Council to oversee the

---

23 June R Carbone, 'A Feminist Perspective on Divorce: The Future of Children' (2004) 4 (1) Children and Divorce 183, 192.

24 Mediation Act 2017, s 21.

practice of meditation in Ireland. Although enacted on 1 January 2018, to date, no council has been established. Another criticism is that the 2017 Act does not provide specific privilege for negotiations that take place during the mediation process. While discussions are confidential and without prejudice, privilege over the matters discussed must be claimed rather than provided for by legislation.[25] This makes litigation arising after the breakdown of the mediation process or as a result of a failure to adhere to the agreement reached more cumbersome. Finally, while the draft Heads of the Mediation Bill published in 2012, included Head 18, specifically acknowledging the need to hear the child, this was not carried through to the 2017 Act. Head 18, although limited in that consultation with children had to be with the consent of the parents and agreement of the mediator, at least provided some formal recognition. Reasons for the failure to include this in the 2017 Act may include the financial resources required in providing specific training in child-inclusive methods for all mediators or a general cultural reluctance to speak to and recognise the importance for children of being considered and included as part of the family.

4.2 What is the legal effect of a mediated agreement?

A mediated agreement is not legally binding on the parties. While the Mediation Act 2017 provides that parties may seek legal advice at any time during the mediation process, agreements are often reached without the benefit of legal advice.[26] Most mediators are not lawyers, and it is not their role to provide legal advice. If the parties wish to incorporate the terms of a mediated agreement into a legally binding agreement, they can consult a solicitor who will provide advice and draft the necessary documentation. As always, a court will not approve any settlement reached unless it is satisfied that proper provision has been made for the dependent spouse and any dependent children.[27]

5. Collaborative practice

Collaborative practice has been described by the Irish Law Reform Commission as 'an emerging method of dispute resolution'.[28] Originating in the United States in the early 1990s, the aim of the process is to resolve

---

[25] Providing specific privilege for mediation by statute would provide greater reassurance for parties that matters referred to in the process would not be relied upon in future court proceedings.

[26] Mediation Act 2017, s 4(c).

[27] Deirdre McGowan, 'Reframing the mediation debate in Irish all-issues divorce disputes: from mediation vs. litigation to mediation and litigation' (2018) 40 Journal of Social Welfare and Family Law 181.

[28] Law Reform Commission, *Alternative Dispute Resolution: Mediation and Conciliation* (LRC 98 2010), 121.

family law matters outside of the adversarial courts' process, but with the support and assurance of each party having a lawyer with them as they negotiate.

To participate, both separating parties must be represented by a lawyer trained in the process. Like mediation, the lawyers must screen clients as to their suitability to engage in the process assessing any issues of power imbalance, history of domestic abuse and commitment to resolving the issues in a non-adversarial manner. At the outset, the parties sign a participation agreement through which they agree to negotiate in good faith, be honest and open in their dealings with each other and, where there are children of the relationship, to keep the best interests of their children front and centre during the negotiations. Like mediation, the separating parties have more input and control over the negotiations, taking an 'interests-based' rather than positional approach. They decide on the agenda for, and scheduling of, meetings, whether they wish to continue in the process and the ultimate terms of any settlement.

Aside from the requirement to have a lawyer, the other distinctive features of collaborative practice include the fact that lawyers also sign the participation agreement, not as parties to the agreement, but to confirm their representation of their clients and their agreement with the terms of the disqualification clause.[29] Secondly, this is the first process that specifically provides an established framework within which separating parties may select to take a more holistic, inter-disciplinary approach to conflict resolution. Some of these elements of the process have been controversial.[30]

The disqualification clause provides that if settlement cannot be reached within the process, that the lawyers acting for both parties are disqualified from acting for them in any subsequent court proceedings. Stuart Webb, the founder of the collaborative practice, has described the disqualification clause as the glue that holds the process together by focusing all parties on reaching settlement rather than abandoning the negotiations and going to court.[31] If they leave the process, the parties incur the legal costs and impact of having to begin the separation process

---

29 Stuart Webb, 'Collaborative Law: A Practitioner's Perspective on its History and Current Practice' (2008) 21 Journal of the American Academy of Matrimonial Lawyers 155–169, 160.

30 Pauline Tesler and Peggy Thompson, *Collaborative Divorce: The Revolutionary New Way to Restructure your Family, Resolve Legal Issues, and Move on with Your Life* (Harper Collins 2007), 91; John Lande, 'The Promise and Perils of Collaborative Law' (2005–2006) 12 Dispute Resolution Magazine 29.

31 Stuart Webb and Ron Ousky, *The Collaborative Way to Divorce: The Revolutionary Method that Results in Less Stress, Lower Costs, and Happier Kids- Without Going to Court* (Penguin 2007).

anew. For the lawyers, they lose a client and the associated potential fee income. To avoid situations where one lawyer in a firm may simply hand the file over to another lawyer in the same firm, there is also an 'imputed disqualification' provision, which disqualifies all lawyers within that firm in relation to the particular issue set out in the participation agreement. Much debate has ensued as to whether the disqualification provision puts extra pressure on the parties to remain in the process beyond the point at which they may have decided that it was not working for them and whether this is a positive as opined by Webb or indeed a flaw.[32] It highlights the importance of screening and of ensuring that clients are fully informed prior to choosing the process so that they do not unwittingly engage in a process that they then find difficult to leave.

Further, while the original model of collaborative law was a lawyer only model, over time it has developed into what has been described as collaborative practice or collaborative divorce. This model broadens the approach to conflict resolution in family law cases by providing a structure whereby the parties can engage experts from other disciplines to assist with the emotional and financial issues involved. All experts are trained in the collaborative method and understand and appreciate the importance of working together as a team for the benefit of the family as a whole. Rather than both parties, for example, employing accountants, an independent accountant is appointed to review the financial affairs of the parties and assist in dealing with issues such as the family home, maintenance, and the division of other assets. Research around divorce and separation has indicated that 80% of the issues between the parties are emotional in nature rather than legal. By having counsellors assist with issues such as how to communicate effectively, the parties are removed from what Pauline Tesler calls the 'shadow state' where their judgment at this important juncture is clouded by conflict.[33] Another important aspect of the process is that a trained child specialist can be engaged to speak to children and give them an opportunity to have their voices heard. The child specialist brings the children's views to the parents at a joint meeting. No formal reports are written, removing the possibility of polarising the parties. Instead the focus is on finding a resolution that meets the needs of the entire family.

The question therefore arises as to how effective the process is in the actual resolution of conflict in family law cases. Research has been undertaken in the US, Canada and in England and Wales.[34] All of the

---

32 John Lande, 'The Promise and Perils of Collaborative Law' (2005–2006) 12 Dispute Resolution Magazine 29.

33 Pauline Tesler, *Collaborative Law: Achieving Effective Resolution in Divorce without Litigation* (2nd edn, American Bar Association 2008) 30.

34 Julie Macfarlane, 'The Emerging Phenomenon of Collaborative Family Law (CFL): A Qualitative Case Study' (Department of Justice Canada 2005) available at

studies broadly concur that client satisfaction with the process is high and that up to 80% of cases settle within the process. In Ireland, the findings were similar. In a study conducted in 2012,[35] the terms of settlements reached through collaborate practice were not significantly different to those achieved through negotiation within the courts' process thus providing little evidence of what Ronalda Murphy referred to as the couple becoming a 'unit of law-making'.[36] What was different, however, was the level of preparation undertaken by lawyers in discussing the family's needs and the time given to the parties to explore options that suited their specific interests.[37]As was evident throughout the research internationally, the main motivation for Irish participants in choosing the process was that they could deal with separation in a less acrimonious manner. One participant commented that their 'main goal would be that I would be able to separate without any major stress or hassle, that we would still be able to talk and that the kids wouldn't be affected'.[38] Those interviewed expressed a sense of commitment to the process and though aware of the implications of the disqualification provision, were satisfied to use it. Comments made included:

> I was clear at the outset that that would happen and, at one point it looked like we weren't going to get the information we needed, but I always wanted to keep in the collaborative process. I never wanted to go away from that.[39]

Two out of the ten participants interviewed left the process and proceeded to court. For one, they felt the collaborative process was only for 'the long-term separated who had an arrangement that they wanted to legalise, if it is a mutual decision'.[40] For the other, they were disappointed that settlement could not be reached as 'what was agreed within the process was foundation of what we took into court two years later'.[41]

---

www.justice.gc.ca; International Academy of Collaborative Professionals (www.collaborativepractice.com); Mark Sefton, 'Collaborative Family Law: A report for Resolution', Association of Family Lawyers in the UK. (Resolution 2009).

35 For key findings of this research see Connie Healy, *Collaborative Practice: An International Perspective* (Routledge 2017), 109–143.

36 Ronalda Murphy, 'Is the turn toward collaborative law a turn away from justice?' (2004) 42(3) Family Court Review 460–470, 466.

37 Connie Healy, *Resolution of Conflict in family law matters: An alternative and child-inclusive approach*, Unpublished PhD Thesis, University of Galway, 2014.

38 ibid, 288.

39 ibid, 288.

40 Connie Healy, *Collaborative Practice: An International Perspective* (Routledge 2017) 109–143, 128.

41 Healy (n 40), 289.

5.1 What is the legal effect of collaborative practice?

Agreements reached during the collaborative process can be incorporated into a Deed of Separation or ruled on consent before the court. As with all other settlement mechanisms, the court must be satisfied that proper provision has been achieved. Compared to mediation, however, the parties and the court have the assurance that agreements were concluded with the benefit of legal advice. Those who opted to use the interdisciplinary model may also have succeeded in dealing with some of the emotional issues surrounding the family break-down and may as a result be better equipped to co-parent children. It is hoped that as collaborative practice becomes more familiar that more separating couples will see the benefit of engaging a child specialist so that they can understand what the separation has been like for their children.

6. Arbitration

Arbitration is a more formal process whereby separating couples refer their dispute to an individual, the arbitrator. The arbitrator will generally be an expert in the subject matter of the dispute and the parties agree to accept the arbitrator's decision as final and binding. Initially used as a means of resolving international or commercial disputes where each of the parties would be of somewhat equal bargaining power, more recently it has been used in the resolution of family law disputes.

To-date the process has not been used extensively in family law cases in Ireland. Advantages of arbitration are arguably that it is more expedient, private, and less costly. Like mediation or collaborative practice, an arbitration can be held at a time and date that is convenient to the parties.

The grounds upon which an arbitrator's decision can be challenged are quite limited.[42] In a family law context therefore, the question arises as to whether a decision made by an arbitrator, though technically accurate, can be challenged on the grounds of 'fairness'. This has not been addressed by the Irish courts, as yet. A recent decision of the Court of Appeal in England and Wales in *Haley v Haley*,[43] however, may provide some guidance. The Haleys were allocated a hearing date for their case before the High Court. Shortly before the hearing they were advised that there was no judge available and were given the option of having the matter determined by an arbitrator. The parties consented to arbitration. Mr Haley was unhappy with the arbitrator's award and sought to challenge it before the courts. While several grounds were cited in the appeal, the main issue for consideration was whether the award

---

42 Arbitration Act 2010, s 11.

43 *Haley v Haley* [2020] EWCA Civ 1369.

made by the arbitrator was governed by English arbitration legislation[44] or whether the decision of the arbitrator could be subject to appeal under the Matrimonial Causes Act.[45] If determined under the Arbitration Act 2010 the grounds of appeal are quite limited and '[f]airness as a concept has no place in a challenge to an arbitral award; arbitration being a procedure designed to provide certainty across the international commercial world'.[46] Previous case-law had, however, stressed the importance of fairness in family law cases, for example, *White v White*[47] and *Miller v Miller*[48] which the Court of Appeal noted established that:

> ... the overriding criterion to be applied in ancillary relief proceedings is that of fairness and identify the three strands of need, compensation and sharing that are relevant to the question of what is fair.[49]

Judges have been keen to stress that the English divorce courts' role is not to act as a 'bloodhound' or 'ferret' in examining settlement proposals reached nor is it their role to merely rubber stamp them.[50] Similarly, caution has been expressed about treating family law matters differently to other areas of law before the courts.[51] The UK Court of Appeal has noted that the often-used description of a decision to arbitrate as being 'the right to buy the wrong decision' cannot be applied in family law cases or permit a judge to 'shrug his or her shoulders' and refuse to examine the award.[52] A distinction was also made that while respecting autonomy is appropriate where parties have reached their own agreements in a consensual manner, often with the benefit of advice, in exercising autonomy to use the arbitration process the parties do not have any input into the arbitrators award. The court was keen to stress the importance of arbitration as a dispute resolution mechanism in family law matters. It noted the necessity of ensuring that people entering the process are not deterred because the outcome is not sufficiently certain. Nonetheless, is also important for separating parties to have the assurance that there is a remedy if the outcome is unjust. It held that arbitration awards, like agreements based on consent, can be scrutinised by the court. Referring to previous decision of Munby J, *S v S* (Arbitral Award: Approval)[53] which held that a court would only interfere with an arbitral award when the

44 Arbitration Act 1976.
45 Matrimonial Causes Act 1973.
46 *Haley v Haley* [2020] EWCA Civ 1369 [14].
47 *White v White* [2001] 1 AC 596.
48 *Miller v Miller* [2006] UKHL 24.
49 *Haley v Haley* [2020] EWCA Civ 1369 [43].
50 *L v L* [2006] EWHC 956 (Fam); [2008] 1 FLR 26 [73].
51 *Prest v Petrodel Resources Ltd & Others* [2013] UKSC 34.
52 *Haley v Haley* [2020] EWCA Civ 1369 [91].
53 *S v S* (Arbitral Award: Approval) [2014] EWHC 7 (Fam) [21].

error 'leapt off the page', the Court of Appeal ruled instead that an award can be overturned:

> if the judge decides that the arbitrator's award was wrong; not seriously or obviously wrong, or so wrong that it leaps off the page, but just wrong.[54]

This decision has therefore clarified that fairness is to remain the overriding factor in family law cases and that it is for the court to determine, in any given set of circumstances, what may be considered fair. The outcome of this case has been much discussed and debated. Some view it as providing clarity and giving assurance to parties choosing arbitration that they will not be unduly prejudiced in using the process, and that they can appeal to the court. Others see it as the death knell for family law arbitration.[55]

6.1 What is the legal effect of arbitration?

Parties enter the arbitration process on the basis that they will accept the decision of the arbitrator as final and binding. It is unclear what would happen if the parties were not satisfied with a family law decision. Under the Irish Arbitration Act 2010, there are very limited grounds on which an arbitration award can be appealed. However, the approach taken in *Haley* indicates that principles of fairness in family law legislation may carry over to consideration of arbitral awards. In a divorce dispute in Ireland, any arbitral award will need to be ruled by the court, as only the court can grant a decree of divorce. The court has a constitutional and statutory obligation to ensure proper provision prior to granting a divorce. Should one party be unhappy with the decision of the arbitrator, it seems likely that the court would examine the award to ensure that it represents proper provision in all of the circumstances and that any property or other orders required to give effect to the decision of the arbitrator would be 'in the interests of justice'.[56]

7. Critical thinking points

7.1 Critical thinking point: Are the rights of all parties protected within alternative methods of dispute resolution?

Justice requires both substantive and procedural fairness. Post-*Haley*[57] concerns have been raised by scholars as to whether agreements reached

---

54 *Haley v Haley* [2020] EWCA Civ 1369 [74].

55 Anna Heenan, 'Haley v Haley: Family Law Arbitration and the New Frontier of Private Ordering' (2021) 84(6) Modern Law Review 1385–1398.

56 As required by s 20 of the Family Law (Divorce) Act 1996.

57 *Haley v Haley* [2020] EWCA Civ 1369.

in alternative methods of dispute resolution may also be, on occasion, tainted by unfairness.[58] Can we be sure that decisions are made with full autonomy and are gender-neutral in terms of the outcome? Under Irish law, all agreements must reach a threshold of ensuring proper provision for dependent spouses and children. Arguably, in theory at least, this provides some assurance. In practice, however, with extensive court lists and other pressures on court time, the extent to which the judiciary can truly scrutinise each case may be limited. Where parties are represented by lawyers, one can assume that they have been adequately advised. For self-represented litigants, it may be more challenging.

It also needs to be recognised that interests-based processes like mediation and collaborative practice are not necessarily easier options for parties in dispute. Negotiating face to face post separation is difficult no matter how amicable the relationship break down may have been. On the other hand, parties who cannot afford to pay for private dispute resolution are left with no option but to proceed through the adversarial courts' process. These are some of the critical debates under discussion by the Family Justice Oversight Group, tasked with designing a new family court structure in Ireland.[59]

7.2 Critical thinking point: To what extent, if any, is the voice of the child heard within private dispute resolution processes?

The underlying assumption in most cases is that at a time of family transition parents will act in the best interests of their children. The difficulty is that parents often determine what their best interests are without any consultation with the children themselves. Can parents truly act in the best interests of their children if they have not spoken to them about the family transition? How does this impact on the rights of children?[60]

It is arguable that private dispute resolution processes like mediation and collaborative practice provide an opportunity for a more holistic approach. Research, however, indicates that while there are benefits to consulting with children, this is not often done. It tends to be at best child-focused, rather than child-inclusive.[61] Failure of the legislature to provide

---

58 Anna Heenan, 'Haley v Haley: Family Law Arbitration and the New Frontier of Private Ordering' (2021) 84(6) Modern Law Review 1385–1398.

59 Department of Justice, *Family Justice Strategy 2022–2025*, (2022) available at https://www.gov.ie/en/collection/4790f-family-justice-strategy/[last accessed 2 August 2023].

60 Connie Healy, '"Still my parent's child": Breaking through the barriers of determining best interests and voice of the child post-separation and divorce' (2021) 33 Child and Family Law Quarterly 237.

61 Simone McCaughren, Stephanie Holt, Aisling Parkes, Soma Gregory, 'Research report on guidance on contact time for infants and young children in separated families',

for the inclusion of the voice of the child in the Mediation Act 2017 was a missed opportunity. Likewise, even within the collaborative process, arguably designed to be more holistic, children are rarely consulted.

Research internationally[62] and recently undertaken by Ann O'Kelly in this jurisdiction points to the benefits of hearing the voice of the child within the mediation process.[63] Children in O'Kelly's research spoke about how important it had been for them to consult with the mediator. O'Kelly reports: 'For Amy, even though the change she desired did not occur, her involvement in the mediation process re-assured her that her concerns were taken seriously':

> I wanted to spend more time at my Mam's house. My Mam tried to sort it out, but I'd have to get up extra early for the school bus. It helped me though that I'd be listened to if I needed to change anything.

Michael, similarly, was happy that his views were considered:

> I met the mediator; it was helpful talking to someone outside the family. And they took note of my message; the one thing I really wanted was to have them both together at Christmas time which did happen. This was a huge relief cos that would have been one thing I'd have missed a lot.

A third participant, Kate, while she found the meeting with the mediator helpful, felt that one meeting was not enough:

> It was a lot better afterwards, I was clearer on what I thought, I don't think I realised what was bothering me until I said it out loud.....and I was able to talk to them [parents] and it made it easier than just accepting things....[the meeting] made Mam and Dad more conscious of how we were feeling and to include

---

Trinity College Dublin and UCC, (December 2022) available at https://cora.ucc.ie/server/api/core/bitstreams/c9f80caf-e3c0-4b2e-b054-a7273edb7db2/content [last accessed 2 August 2023].

62 Jennifer McIntosh, Yvonne Wells and Caroline Long, 'Child-Focused and Child-Inclusive Family Law Dispute Resolution: One-year findings from a prospective study of outcomes' (2007) 13 Journal of Family Studies 8; Jill Goldson, 'Hello, I'm Voice, Let me Talk: Child-Inclusive Mediation in Family Separation' (Families Commission, Innovative Practice Report No1/06 December 2006) available at http://www.jillgoldson.co.nz/ [last accessed 2 August 2023].

63 Ann O Kelly, 'How do children and young people in Ireland experience the process of their parents' separation and divorce and subsequent changed family life? Giving recognition to children's experiences', Unpublished PhD thesis, (University of Galway, 2017) available at https://aran.library.nuigalway.ie/bitstream/handle/10379/6498/E%20Thesis%20Ann%20O%27Kelly.pdf?sequence=1&isAllowed=y [last accessed 2 August 2023].

> us….I think it helped everyone… [however, she continued] just meeting someone once is not enough.

Despite the research showing the benefits of including the voice of the child, this seldom occurs in practice. Even within the collaborative process which provides a structured approach to holistic resolution of family law disputes, the evidence suggests that the voice of the child is not always heard or considered. In an Irish context, this may be because the process is relatively new and therefore less developed than in other jurisdictions. There may not be a body of appropriately trained child specialists. Additional factors may be the costs involved in engaging such experts.

Studies undertaken in England and Wales, also raise concerns about the extent to which the voice of the child is heard in family dispute resolution whether through negotiation by lawyers, mediation or collaborative practice.[64] Barlow et al note that throughout family law dispute resolution it was interesting to note 'how easy it was for the focus on the child to be lost and for children's interests to recede into the background. Moreover, the voice of the child – direct attention to children's wishes and preferences from their own perspective – was notably absent… '.[65] This is a concern and an ongoing issue that needs to be addressed. The message from children themselves however is clear. As noted by Morrison, 'children repeatedly tell researchers they need', a 'system of child advocacy that ensures independent advice, ongoing support and trusting relationships'.[66]

The consequences of things said, and actions taken during a tumultuous time in peoples' lives can have intergenerational impacts for them and their children. It is important that separating couples and their families are adequately supported and guided through the transition and respected in the decisions they decide to take. There are advantages and disadvantages to all dispute resolution methods. It is important that all parties are offered a full range of options and that decisions on any particular process are made with fully informed consent rather than any form of coercion from the opposing party, the system (relieving the burdens on the courts) or the State (less costly for the taxpayer). Handing a file over to a lawyer and being able to take an arm's length approach is arguably easier. However, as one participant in my research commented:

> I suppose, nobody wants to go into court to decide how you

64 Anne Barlow, 'Mapping Paths to Family Justice: a national picture of findings on out of court family dispute resolution' (2013) Family Law 306.
65 ibid.
66 Fiona Morrison, E Kay M Tisdall, Jane EM Callaghan, 'Manipulation and Domestic Abuse in Contested Contact–Threats to Children's Participation' (2020) 58 (2) Family Court Review 403–416, 413.

> are going to live the rest of your life, kind of, so if there is an alternative it is the better route to go.[67]

8. Summary

- For separating couples who wish to avoid taking the resolution of issues arising from the relationship breakdown through the courts, there are a number of alternatives.
    - Those who are able to work together to reach a solution without assistance from a third party can agree terms and have a solicitor incorporate those terms into a deed of separation or a court order for judicial separation or divorce on consent.
    - For those that require more assistance, it may be beneficial to engage the services of a mediator, a neutral person that will facilitate discussion between the parties and assist them to reach their own agreement. Mediation works best when both parties are able to negotiate well and freely and there are no underlying concerns regarding power balance within the relationship.
    - If the parties wish to settle outside of the courts' process but feel like they need to be accompanied by their lawyers, collaborative practice may be the best solution. This also allows for a multidisciplinary approach by engaging a team to address the legal, financial, and emotional issues and to ensure that the voice of the child is heard in a protected way during the process.
    - Another option, more common in the UK, is through family law arbitration. Here, the parties submit the dispute to a neutral arbitrator, generally an expert in family law who is not a judge of the court. Awards made by an arbitrator are final and binding, but following the Court of Appeal decision in *Haley,* this no longer the position in family law cases in England and Wales if the court is of the view that the award is 'wrong' and thereby arguably, unfair.
- The Irish courts are constitutionally required to ensure that proper provision exists before granting a divorce degree. This means that no private settlement can be truly final because it may be revisited by the court in divorce proceedings.

[67] Healy (n 40).

9. Further reading

Law Society of Ireland, *Divorce in Ireland – The case for reform* (2019) available at https://www.lawsociety.ie/globalassets/documents/submissions/divorce-in-ireland-april-2019.pdf.

Deirdre McGowan, 'Reframing the mediation debate in Irish all-issues divorce disputes: from mediation vs. litigation to mediation and litigation' (2018) 40 Journal of Social Welfare and Family Law 181.

Connie Healy, *Collaborative Practice: An International Perspective* (Routledge 2017).

Connie Healy, '"Still my parent's child": Breaking through the barriers of determining best interests and voice of the child post-separation and divorce' (2021) 33 Child and Family Law Quarterly 237.

Chapter 6

Cohabitation

Maebh Harding

LEARNING OBJECTIVES

By the end of this chapter, students will be equipped to:

- Compare the financial vulnerability of cohabiting couples to that of married couples.
- Outline the operation and limits of the financial redress scheme available to cohabiting couples under the Civil Partnership and Certain Rights and Obligations of Cohabitants Act 2010.
- Analyse the extent to which cohabitants can make their own agreements to regulate their finances and property.

CRITICAL THINKING POINTS

- Is legal protection of cohabitants compatible with the Irish State's duty to protect marriage?
- How should law measure adult commitment?
- Should there be an entirely unregulated space for intimate relationships?

1. Introduction

Cohabitation can mean different things to different people. Students living in a shared house might be described as cohabiting. Older siblings living together on a family farm might also consider themselves to be cohabiting because they live under the same roof. The housing crisis in Ireland means that different types of households are formed out of financial necessity with adult friends sharing flats for long periods or even buying property together. However, for family law purposes, cohabitation means more than just the fact of living together. It refers to a type of inter-dependent relationship between adults where two people in an intimate relationship live together without making a formal legal commitment like civil partnership or marriage. Due to the informality of cohabiting relationships, it can be difficult to tell when they start, or the level of commitment involved. For example, a couple might start out living in separate houses but spend most nights together. Their decision to move in together might not be a clear deliberate one. It might be a gradual transition or result from one of the partners having to leave rental accommodation. The uncertainty of cohabitation and the variety of cohabiting couples makes it a tricky area of family life to regulate. 'One size' does not fit all.

Cohabitation is the fastest growing form of family life in Ireland. Home sharing by cohabiting couples increased by 125% between 1996–2002 giving rise to calls for legal change to protect this type of family. Since that time, the number of cohabiting couples in Ireland has again doubled. According to the 2016 census there are 152,302 cohabiting couples living in Ireland. 5,196 of these couples are same sex couples. 75,587 cohabiting couples are living with children (409 of these are cohabiting same sex couples). Families based on marriage still outnumber families based on cohabitation by more than 5:1.[1]

Irish law does not treat cohabiting couples as a family. As discussed in Chapter 1, constitutional case law defines the family as based on marriage.[2] The protections of Article 41 of the Constitution simply do not extend to non-marital families.

Article 8 of the European Convention on Human Rights (ECHR) protects families from unlawful state interference and illegal discrimination by granting everyone the right to respect for their private and family life. In contrast to the Irish constitutional approach, where family life is based on the formal status of marriage, proving family life for the purposes of art 8 does not require marriage or formal commitment but is a question of fact, based on the practice of close family ties.[3] The European Court of Human Rights (ECtHR) will look at factors such as whether applicants live together,[4] the length of the relationship and the presence of children.[5] Irish statute law that interferes with art 8 rights to family life can be challenged as being incompatible with Ireland's obligations under the ECHR.[6] But the existence of family rights under art 8 does not give rise to formal legal status as a family in Irish law.[7] Even within the jurisprudence of the ECtHR, mere cohabitation does not result in recognition of family life, the quality of the relationship will be subject to scrutiny.[8]

1 Based on the 2016 Census, there are 847,251 married couples living in Ireland.
2 See eg, *Murray v Ireland* [1985] IR 532, 536; *O'B v S* [1984] IR 316, 536.
3 *Paradiso and Campanelli v Italy* App no 25358/12 (ECtHR Grand Chamber, 24 January 2017) [140].
4 *Johnston and Others v Ireland* App no 9697/82 (ECtHR, 18 December 1986) [56].
5 *X, Y and Z v the United Kingdom* App no 21830/93 (ECtHR, 22 April 1997) [36].
6 European Convention on Human Rights Act 2003, s 5.
7 *J McD v PL* [2009] IESC 81.
8 *Evers v Germany* App no 17895/14 (ECtHR, 28/05/2020) [52].

Lack of automatic legal recognition can leave cohabitants in a vulnerable financial position where their relationship breaks down or where one of them dies. Today, Pt 15 the Civil Partnership and Certain Rights and Obligations of Cohabitants Act 2010 ('the 2010 Act') allows certain cohabitants to apply to court for financial redress if their relationship has broken down or when one of the cohabitants has died without making financial provision for the other. While the 2010 Act can be viewed as progressive in giving some statutory recognition to cohabiting families, the redress scheme provides only a limited safety-net and can be difficult to access. Cohabitants still have no automatic legal rights or status under Irish law.

1.1 'Cohabitant' as a legal term across Irish family law

The term 'cohabitant' as defined in s 172(1) of the 2010 Act is used across Irish law to refer to adults who are both living together *and* in an intimate relationship.

Key definition – Civil Partnership and Certain Rights and Obligations of Cohabitants Act 2010, s 172(1)
A cohabitant is one of two adults (whether of the same or the opposite sex) who live together as a couple in an intimate and committed relationship and who are not related to each other within the prohibited degrees of relationship or married to each other or civil partners of each other.

This definition applies in adoption law[9] where cohabiting couples are eligible to adopt jointly,[10] and is used in the statutory rules[11] determining parentage following donor assisted human reproduction.[12] The same definition of cohabitant is also used in the Guardianship of Infants Act 1964,[13] and across the Social Welfare Code.[14] The definition is extended for the purposes of child maintenance to include former cohabitants as well as current cohabitants.[15] Domestic violence legislation does not

---

9 Adoption Act 2010, s 3.

10 Adoption Act 2010, s 33(1)(a)(ib) as amended by the Adoption (Amendment) Act 2017.

11 Guardianship of Infants Act 1964, s 2(4A); see discussion in Chapter 6.

12 See eg, s 5(1) of the Children and Family Relationships Act 2015 where the cohabitant of a mother undergoing donor assisted human reproduction can be considered to be the second legal parent of a donor-conceived child.

13 Guardianship of Infants Act 1964, s 2.

14 Social Welfare Consolidation Act 2005, s 2 as inserted by the Social Welfare and Pensions Act 2010, s 15. See Social Welfare Consolidation Act 2005 (running consolidation) which is maintained by the Department of Social Protection available at https://www.gov.ie/en/policy-information/81fdaa-social-welfare-consolidation-act-2005/ [last accessed 2 August 2023].

15 Family Law (Maintenance of Spouses and Children) Act 1976, s 3.

use the term cohabitant but instead separates the issue of whether an intimate relationship exists between applicant and respondent[16] from the question of their living situation and property rights.[17]

Even when the status of cohabitant is relevant in an area of family law it does not necessarily create automatic rights. For example, the right to apply for financial redress under the 2010 Act is limited to **qualified cohabitants** who satisfy a strict list of conditions (see discussion below). Single fathers who cohabit with the mother of their children are not entitled to automatic guardianship. Instead, they must have lived with the mother for a period of not less than one year including at least three months of living together after the birth of the child.[18] Cohabitants can be obliged to pay child maintenance for their partner's dependent child, where they are not that child's parent, but only where they have been appointed legal guardian of that child.[19]

In most legislative situations, the court will decide whether or not a person is a cohabitant based on the ordinary and natural meaning of s 172(1) of the 2010 Act. However, where a cohabitant is seeking financial redress under the 2010 Act or establishing an entitlement under the social welfare code, their status as cohabitant will be scrutinised. The Department of Social Protection have published the criteria they use to determine whether cohabitation exists.[20] The approach taken by the court to determining eligibility under the 2010 Act is examined below.

1.2 The financial vulnerability of cohabitants as compared to spouses

Unlike married couples, cohabitants have no automatic legal rights or duties to financial support from their partner. Cohabitants can therefore be left in a vulnerable financial position where their relationship breaks down or where one of the cohabitants dies.

As examined in Chapter 3, where married couples want to legally end their marriage, they must go to court for a decree of divorce. A divorce may only be granted if the court considers that 'proper provision' for spouses and children has been made. The court has powers to redistribute property on divorce, taking it from one spouse and giving it to the other spouse where appropriate.

In contrast, when cohabitants break up, there is no requirement to go

---

16 See eg, Domestic Violence Act 2018, s 6.
17 For discussion see Chapter 7.
18 Guardianship of Infants Act 1964, s 6B(2).
19 Family Law (Maintenance of Spouses and Children) Act 1976, ss 5B and 5C.
20 Department of Social Protection, *Cohabitation* (2019) available at https://www.gov.ie/en/publication/d258d8-cohabitation/ [last accessed 2 August 2023].

to court and the courts have no general powers to redistribute property outside of the narrow confines of the redress scheme set out in the 2010 Act. Each cohabitant keeps what they own, however unfair this may be. Sometimes cohabitants will go to court to determine who owns what, particularly when it comes to their shared home.[21] Cohabitants do not have any rights in their shared home under the Family Home Protection Act 1976. This means that if they do not own a share in the home, they are vulnerable to eviction by the home-owning cohabitant.

Married couples are also in a more protected position where one spouse dies. Under Irish law a spouse is entitled to a legal share in their deceased spouse's estate even where a will has been made leaving them nothing. The spouse's statutory share under s 111 of the Succession Act 1965 ensures that one spouse cannot write the other spouse out of their will entirely. Where no provision is made in a will, the surviving spouse is entitled to one half of the deceased's estate where there are no children and one third of the estate where there are children.[22] Where the deceased has not made a will, a surviving spouse is entitled to everything if there are no children and two thirds of the deceased's estate where there are children.[23] Spouses pay no inheritance tax on inheritances from each other.

Cohabitants are in a much weaker situation than spouses on death. They may be entitled to nothing unless they can make an application under the 2010 Act for provision from their deceased cohabitant's estate. They have no intestacy rights. They can be written out of their partner's will entirely, and if they do inherit are liable for inheritance tax at the rate of 33% on amounts over the relevant tax-free threshold.[24]

The relative financial vulnerability of cohabitants can be justified on the basis that they have made an informed choice not to marry. However, anecdotal evidence from Irish solicitors suggests that many cohabitants are unaware that they do not enjoy the same rights as married couples. They only realise their mistake when the relationship comes to an end. Research carried out in England suggests that many cohabitants believe in the myth of common law marriage; a fiction that after living together for a long time, a couple enjoy the same rights as a married couple.[25] This sort of marriage has never been part of the law in Ireland or England.

---

21 See eg, *C(M) v S(B)* [2010] 1 IR 107; *McGrane v O'Foghlu* [2020] IECC 1.

22 Succession Act 1965, s 111.

23 Succession Act 1965, s 67.

24 For further details see Revenue, Gift and Inheritance Tax (Capital Acquisitions Tax – Cat) available at https://www.revenue.ie/en/gains-gifts-and-inheritance/gift-and-inheritance-tax-cat/index.aspx [last accessed 2 August 2023].

25 Rebecca Probert, 'The evolution of the common-law marriage myth' (2011) Family Law 283.

Whatever the reason for this misunderstanding as to legal rights by Irish cohabitants, it leaves financially dependent cohabitants in a vulnerable position when the relationship ends.

This financial vulnerability was a key driver of Irish law reform efforts to provide a legal safety net for cohabiting couples.[26]

1.3 The background to the Civil Partnership and Certain Rights and Obligations of Cohabitants Act 2010

Several very different pressures came together to drive a programme of law reform to recognise and safeguard cohabiting couples in Ireland. In the early 2000s, cohabitation was a rapidly growing family form and for many couples, a prelude to marriage. Legal protection was required for couples who seemed to have opted out of marriage. For same sex couples, who were legally precluded from marrying until 2015, there was simply no legal option for recognition of their commitment or to protect them from financial vulnerability resulting from cohabitation.

In 2006, the Department of Justice and Law Reform presented an *Options Paper*[27] outlining different ways in which the State might regulate to safeguard cohabitants. At the same time, the Law Reform Commission issued its final report on the *Rights and Duties of Cohabitants* recommending a safety-net system to protect the most vulnerable cohabitants from the economic vulnerability of their family relationship alongside measures encouraging cohabitants to come to their own financial arrangements.[28]

1.4 Critical thinking point: Is legal protection of cohabitants compatible with the Irish State's duty to protect marriage?

Debates over how best to legislate to protect the rights of cohabitants have been complicated by a legal argument that legal protection for cohabiting couples could constitute an unconstitutional 'attack on marriage'. This argument is rooted in a statement by Henchy J in the 1966 case of *State Nicolau v An Bórd Uchtálá*[29] that awarding equal constitutional protection to a family founded on an 'extra marital' union would disregard the state's pledge in Article 41.3.1⁰ to guard with special care the institution of marriage. *Nicolau* was a case in which an unmarried father's attempts to prevent the adoption of his child were unsuccessful as he was not recognised as being part of the constitutional family under

---

26 Law Reform Commission, *Consultation Series: Rights and Duties of Cohabitees* (LRC 32-2004), 24-27.

27 Working Group on Domestic Partnership, *Options Paper* (Department of Justice2006).

28 Law Reform Commission, *Report: Rights and Duties of Cohabitants* (LRC 82-2006).

29 [1966] IR 567.

Article 41 and so had no constitutional rights of parental authority or any equivalent legal rights. Adoption law has subsequently been reformed (see Chapter 11).

Henchy J's statement supported arguments that giving legal recognition to cohabiting couples would undermine marriage either by favouring unmarried couples or by discouraging people from getting married. The issue arose again in *Ennis v Butterly*[30] (discussed below).

The 1996 Constitution Review Group recommended revisions to Article 41 itself to retain the pledge to protect marriage, but to make it clear that the Oireachtas could provide protection for families based on a relationship other than marriage.[31] However, in 2004, the Law Reform Commission took the more pragmatic view that legislating to protect cohabitants would not violate the obligations of Article 41 unless it granted cohabitants greater rights than those enjoyed by married couples.[32] They recommended that any redress scheme must also protect the rights of spouses and cannot apply to a cohabitant who is married to a third party.

The redress scheme in the 2010 Act protects spouses and recognises cohabitation as a lower level of adult commitment than marriage. The redress scheme does not automatically recognise cohabitation as an alternative form of family life. It merely provides a mechanism for avoiding the worst effects of financial vulnerability arising as a result of cohabitation. The financial rights of any spouses or former spouses of the cohabitant are protected throughout the scheme and are preferred to the claims of cohabitants.

2. Civil Partnership and Certain Rights and Obligations of Cohabitants Act 2010

The Civil Partnership and Certain Rights and Obligations of Cohabitants Act 2010 came into force on 1 January 2011. The 2010 Act introduced civil partnership as an alternative to marriage for same sex couples (see Chapter 1). It also creates a redress scheme for qualifying cohabiting couples. This redress scheme provides a limited safety net for financially dependent cohabitants if a long-term cohabiting relationship ends through death or separation. In successful applications, the court has a broad discretion to make financial orders requiring one cohabitant to

---

30 [1996] 1 IR 426.

31 Constitution Review Group, *Report of the Constitution Review Group* (Stationery Office 1996), 332.

32 Law Reform Commission, *Consultation Series: Rights and Duties of Cohabitees* (LRC 32-2004), 7-11.

provide the other with financial support,[33] or the court may order the adjustment of property ownership in a shared home,[34] or make a pension adjustment order.[35] Where one cohabitant has died, the court may make an order for financial provision out of the deceased's estate.[36]

The redress scheme is not automatic, cohabitants must litigate by bringing their claims to court. This can be a protracted and upsetting process, particularly where one cohabitant has died and the application is challenged by the deceased cohabitant's extended family. The legislation creates several barriers for cohabitants applying to court. Even where an application is successful, the discretionary nature of the scheme means that the **quantum of relief** (i.e. the amount that a successful cohabitant can expect to receive) is uncertain.

The 2010 Act originally made no provision for children of cohabitants and was focussed solely on adult commitment. Today,[37] the court may make a child maintenance order under ss 5A or 5B of the Family Law (Maintenance of Spouses and Children) Act 1976. Such orders are used to require a cohabitant to pay maintenance to their ex-cohabiting partner to support their own biological children, their children conceived through donor-assisted human reproduction (DAHR), or any non-biological children to whom they are recognised as legal guardian (see Chapter 9).

Key legislation – Navigating the 2010 Act

- Introduced Civil Partnership as an alternative to marriage for same sex couples.
- Creates a redress scheme for qualifying cohabiting couples.
- All the provisions relating to cohabitants are found in Pt 15 of the 2010 Act.
- There are two statutory checklists that the court must consider when exercising its discretion:
    - s 172(2) when considering if a cohabiting relationship exists.
    - s 173(3) when deciding what is fair and equitable to award.

2.1 Eligibility to apply for financial redress

Cohabitants seeking financial redress from the courts must overcome several different barriers to their application.

---

[33] s 175.

[34] s 174.

[35] s 187.

[36] s 194.

[37] Following changes made by the Children and Family Relationships Act 2015.

1. They must prove that they are a **qualified cohabitant**.[38]
2. They must apply within two years of relationship breakdown,[39] or six months of a grant of probate where the other cohabitant has died.[40]
3. Cohabitants seeking redress from a cohabitant who is still alive must also prove financial dependency.[41]

2.1.1 Who counts as a qualified cohabitant under the 2010 Act?

Not all cohabitants are permitted to apply for redress. In order to fall into the definition of cohabitant under the 2010 Act, the claimant must prove that the couple lived together in an intimate and committed relationship.[42]

To be considered a 'qualified' cohabitant, the couple must have lived together for a defined period of time immediately before the relationship ended. The period of time that must be proven differs depending on whether or not the couple have a child together. Where there are no dependent children, the couple must have lived together for at least five years before the relationship ended. Where both cohabitants are parents of one of more dependent children, a duration of two years must be proven.[43] The requirements relating to the quality of the relationship and the duration of the relationship have been considered by the High Court in recent case law which is examined below.

Section 172(6) of the 2010 Act[44] precludes someone from being considered a qualified cohabitant if the other cohabitant is married to someone else and at the time the cohabiting relationship ended, their spouse is not eligible to bring divorce proceedings because the 'living apart' requirement for divorce is not satisfied. This protects the rights of spouses by ensuring that cohabitants do not get a time advantage over a spouse in bringing their financial claim. When the 2010 Act came into force, divorce was only obtainable after living apart for four out of five years whereas it was possible for a cohabitant to bring a claim immediately after two years of living together if the couples had a dependent child. This section is less relevant now that the living apart requirement for divorce has been reduced to two out of the previous three years.[45]

---

38 s 172.
39 s 195.
40 s 194(1).
41 s 173.
42 s 172(1).
43 s 172(2).
44 As amended by Family Law Act 2019, s 4(2).
45 See further Chapter 3.

In *Z v Y*,[46] the court considered the definition of living together where Mr X was married to Mrs Y but had an intimate relationship with Ms Z in the five years before he died. Ms Z sought a declaration that she was a qualified cohabitant within the meaning of the 2010 Act claiming that Mr X had lived with her in a shared rented house for the six years before he died. Mrs Y accepted that an intimate relationship with Ms Z had taken place but claimed that Mr X continued to live with her in the marital home during this time, although the couple kept separate bedrooms. Barrett J found that Mr X had spent many evenings with Ms Z during this time but that he had returned to sleep in his marital home every day between 1–2am, telling Ms Z that he was working night shifts as a private security guard. He concluded that Mr X and Ms Z were not 'living together' in the manner contemplated by s 172(1) but were spending time together and enjoying occasional intimate relations. He held that Ms Z was not a qualified cohabitant within the meaning of the 2010 Act.

2.1.1.1 'Intimate and committed' relationships

Key legislation – s 172(2) Civil Partnership and Certain Rights and Obligations of Cohabitants Act 2010 (determining if a couple are intimate and committed)

2) In determining whether or not 2 adults are cohabitants, the court shall take into account all the circumstances of the relationship and in particular shall have regard to the following:

(a) the duration of the relationship;
(b) the basis on which the couple live together;
(c) the degree of financial dependence of either adult on the other and any agreements in respect of their finances;
(d) the degree and nature of any financial arrangements between the adults including any joint purchase of an estate or interest in land or joint acquisition of personal property;
(e) whether there are one or more dependent children;
(f) whether one of the adults cares for and supports the children of the other; and
(g) the degree to which the adults present themselves to others as a couple.

The 2010 Act defines cohabitation as an 'intimate and committed relationship' between two adults. The 2010 Act does not expressly state that the couple must have a sexual relationship, but it is clear from the legislation that this is what is intended. A couple are not considered to be cohabiting if they are excluded by law from marrying. Close relatives

[46] [2022] IEHC 583.

are expressly excluded and s 173(2) states that a relationship does not cease to be intimate where it is no longer sexual in nature.

The determination of whether a relationship is 'intimate and committed' is a matter for the court. Section 172(2) outlines a list of seven factors that the court should consider when making its determination, including the degree of financial interdependence and how the couple present themselves to the world. This examination of the couple's relationship can be very intrusive, particularly where one cohabitant has died and their extended family is disputing the nature of the relationship.

The correct approach to assessing whether a relationship is 'intimate and committed' was explored by Baker J in *DR v DC*.[47] In this case, a 64-year-old male cohabitant applied for an order for provision out of his deceased cohabitant's estate. The couple had been together for nearly 20 years and had moved in together in 2004. The female cohabitant died in 2014 from cancer leaving an estate valued at €1.41 million. She had not made a will so her entire estate went to her surviving brothers under the rules of intestacy. The brothers challenged the claim on the basis that the couple had merely been friends and that no committed and intimate relationship existed.

Baker J held that more than friendship is required. The relationship must involve sexual intimacy at some point.[48] Applying the s 172(2) checklist she found that the couple had led shared lives, there had been sexual intimacy, they presented themselves to society as a couple and the degree of financial dependence that evolved between them suggested a relationship of shared commitment.

The case demonstrates how intrusive a retrospective examination of an intimate relationship can be. The applicant testified that the couple had shared a double bed until his partner had become very ill, thereafter they had single beds in one room until she entered a hospice. He produced birthday, Christmas and Valentine's cards for the court. Ten witnesses described the relationship as close and supportive. The court accepted that the couple had attended over 40 weddings together as a couple.

The need to prove the intimate nature of a cohabiting relationship arose again in *GR v Niamh Regan*[49] where a female cohabitant applied for provision out of her deceased cohabitant's estate. She had lived with her partner for 32 years and given up her job as a cook to care for him in the last six years of his life after he developed vascular dementia. The

---

47 [2015] IEHC 309.

48 [2015] IEHC 309 [21].

49 [2020] IEHC 89.

man's surviving siblings claimed that the woman was the deceased's housekeeper and carer. Here the evidence of intimacy was not as clear cut as in *DR v DC*.[50] Applying the s 172(2) factors, Allen J found the couple were in an intimate and committed relationship. He attached significance to the fact that the woman had given up a job of 15 years to care for her partner and that they had been treated as a couple by doctors, bank managers and the deceased's brother.

2.1.2 Living together for a required duration

As well as assessing the level of intimacy in the relationship, the court must also establish that the couple have lived together for a minimum period of five years immediately before the breakdown of the relationship or, where the couple are parents of dependent children, for two years. This requirement is intended to ensure that only relationships that have endured for a significant period of time can form the basis of a claim for financial redress. However, the wording of the provisions has given rise to some interpretive challenges where the couple have had an 'on again/ off again' relationship or where the breakup has been drawn out, with periods of reconciliation. Case law has examined two questions: How do we measure the required period of living together? What does 'living together' actually mean?

In *MW v DC*[51] the Court of Appeal considered the situation of a couple who had lived together since 1996 but separated for a period in 2010 before reconciling and finally splitting up in February 2011. They had two dependent children. The timing of the end of the relationship was very important in this case as the 2010 Act only came into force on 1 January 2011. MW claimed that the relationship had ended in February 2011 which would allow her to access the redress scheme. DC claimed that the relationship had ended in 2010, before the 2010 Act came into force.

Finlay-Geoghegan J held that in order to qualify for redress, the relationship must have lasted for a single continuous period of at least two years before it ended. The minimum period under the 2010 Act cannot be satisfied by aggregating broken periods of cohabitation.[52] This means that a cohabiting relationship is deemed to end whenever the first person moves out. If a couple reconcile or attempt to reconcile after a breakup, the clock on the required period of cohabitation restarts. For *MW v DC* this meant that their 14-year relationship had ended in 2010 and so MW was ineligible for redress under the 2010 Act. In newer cases,

50 [2015] IEHC 309.
51 [2017] IECA 255.
52 ibid [23].

the effect of the rule is not so harsh because a couple have two years to bring proceedings after the end of a cohabiting relationship.

The Court of Appeal also held that a cohabiting couple is not required to physically share the same residence at all times during the required period of time.[53] The trial judge must decide on the facts if the couple continue to live together as a couple where they are not physically living together in the same residence.

The High Court revisited the question of what 'living together' means in *XY v ZW*.[54] Here a female cohabitant applied for a property adjustment order, periodic payments and a pension adjustment order from her ex-partner following the breakdown of the relationship. The length of the relationship was disputed. The female partner said that relationship commenced in 2007 and ended in 2016. While the couple had spent time apart during this period, she claimed that they remained in an intimate and committed relationship throughout. The male cohabitant argued that while the relationship had finally ended in 2016, between 2007-2016 the couple had broken up three times and lived separately and so the required duration of five years of living together immediately before the relationship ended had not been satisfied.

The case centred on whether the couple had been living together for one entire period of five years even though they had spent time living apart. There was extensive cross examination in this case about where the female cohabitant had stayed on different nights. Friends and relatives were also called to give evidence. Binchy J held that the relationship had broken down during each of the three periods of living apart. While couples do not have to live in the same house at all times to be considered as 'living together', in this case, he found that the separations had nothing to do with illness or holidays or work. The couple separated on each occasion because their relationship had broken down and they had no intention of reconciling, although they later changed their minds.[55] The relationship was not continuous throughout a five-year period but was made up of three separate shorter periods which could not be aggregated. The parties were not qualified cohabitants within the meaning of s 172(5) and the woman was not eligible to apply for financial redress.

In *GR v Niamh Regan*[56] the relationship had lasted from 1982–2013 but the couple had not lived in the same house for all that time. The couple had lived together in England from 1982–1987 when the female

53 ibid [29].
54 [2019] IEHC 257.
55 ibid [94].
56 [2020] IEHC 89.

cohabitant returned to Dublin to care for her father who was terminally ill. Although the couple moved into a house in South Dublin in 1998, the male cohabitant had difficulty finding a job in Ireland and commuted back and forth to Scotland and Germany for work between 1998–2005. He then developed vascular dementia and died in 2013.

Mr Justice Allen found that the couple had lived together from 1982–1987 and again from 1998–2013. The fact that the deceased cohabitant often stayed away from home for work between 1998–2005 did not mean that the couple were not 'living together' during that time.[57]

2.2 Critical thinking point: how should the law measure adult commitment?

Where couples marry, the law assumes that they make a certain type of commitment to each other. Irish law looks only at the form of commitment and does not generally look behind the status of marriage to the functional level of commitment in a marriage except in an immigration context.[58] Article 41 of the Constitution protects the married family as a private space. However, when it comes to cohabitants, a 'one-size-fits-all' level of commitment cannot be assumed in the same way. While some cohabitants may clearly express their financial commitment to each other in the terms of a cohabitation agreement, most cohabitants will have entered their relationship in a much less formal way.

Assessing commitment is challenging for the courts because their task is retrospective. Instead of measuring the commitment from the most optimistic point of the relationship, they must assess it after the relationship has ended and the evidence is in dispute.

Kathy Griffiths[59] argues that function-based ways of recognising adult relationships are always administratively messy and intrusive but that this is the price of having a flexible case by case system. Formal commitments such as marriage are simpler and will always appeal to couples who want to make an 'up-front' symbolic commitment. The law needs both systems to properly recognise the range of adult commitments.

---

57 ibid [54].

58 Where a person seeks permission to come to Ireland to live with a spouse who is already legally resident in Ireland (a process called family reunification) they must prove the genuineness of their marital relationship. INIS, *Policy Document on Non-EEA Family Reunification* (December 2016) available at https://www.irishimmigration.ie/wp-content/uploads/2021/04/Policy-document-on-Non-EEA-family-reunification.pdf [last accessed 8 June 2022].

59 Kathy Griffiths, 'From "form" to function and back again: a new conceptual basis for developing frameworks for the legal recognition of family relationships' (2019) Child and Family Law Quarterly 227.

However, Robert Leckey[60] warns that marriage remains such a dominant way of measuring adult commitment that judges tend to compare cohabiting relationships to marriage when assessing the commitment rather than understanding different types of adult commitment on their own terms.

2.2.1 Proving financial dependency

Where a cohabitant seeks financial support from a former cohabitant who is still alive, s 173(2) requires the qualified cohabitant to prove that he or she is financially dependent on the other cohabitant *and* that the financial dependency arises from the relationship or from the ending of the relationship. This provision is designed to ensure that the redress scheme is limited to addressing economic hardship that is caused by the cohabiting relationship itself. For example, where a cohabitant gives up paid employment to care for their partner through an illness and has no other source of financial support. As John Mee points out, this means that the scheme does not address all situations of financial unfairness caused by a cohabiting relationship but only ones in which a cohabitant is left 'in need of financial support'. This suggests that where the court considers a cohabitant to have alternative means to support themselves, such as family support or savings, they may not qualify to access the redress scheme.[61] Mee argues that this is unfair because cohabitants who have suffered large financial losses as a result of sacrifices made during a cohabiting relationship are deserving of a remedy against their partner, regardless of their overall level of wealth. Brian Tobin disagrees, arguing that the redress scheme is fairly limited to cases of significant hardship because cohabitants have not made an up-front legal commitment. For the redress scheme to address all situations of relationship generated financial hardship would, for Tobin, interfere with the autonomy of cohabitants.[62]

There is, as yet, no reported case which considers whether or not this standard of financial dependence has been satisfied. It remains to be seen if the court will consider the cohabitant's standard of living before the financial loss caused by the cohabiting relationship to be relevant or whether the requirement to be 'in need of financial support' will be set at a much lower subsistence level.

There is no need to prove financial dependency to *apply* for provision from

---

60 Robert Leckey, 'Judging in Marriage's Shadow' (2018) 26 Feminist Legal Studies 25.

61 John Mee, 'Cohabitation Law Reform in Ireland' (2011) 23 Child and Family Law Quarterly 333.

62 Brian Tobin, 'The regulation of cohabitation in Ireland: achieving equilibrium between protection and paternalism?' (2013) 35 Journal of Social Welfare and Family Law 283.

a deceased cohabitant's estate. In such situations, applicants will often introduce evidence of financial dependence on their deceased partner because this is taken into account by the court in deciding whether the relationship is intimate and committed and also when deciding what level of financial award to make. However, evidence of financial dependency in these cases is not required for access to the redress scheme.

2.3 Determining how much to award in successful applications

The 2010 Act gives considerable discretion to the court to determine what level of financial award is appropriate in cohabitant cases. However, the rights of any spouse or former spouse are preferred to the needs of the cohabitant.[63] The court simply cannot make an order that would affect any right of a spouse or former spouse. Where the dispute is between two living cohabitants, financial awards cannot affect existing maintenance obligations to a spouse or former spouse. Similarly, no award to a cohabitant can affect a bequest made to a surviving spouse under a will, a surviving spouse's statutory share under the Succession Act 1965 or a surviving spouse's rights on intestacy as outlined above.

Where provision is sought from the estate of a deceased cohabitant, the court's discretion is additionally limited by three specific considerations.

1. The court must be satisfied that '**proper provision**' has not already been made for the applicant during the lifetime of the deceased.[64] This is a flexible limitation as the nature of 'proper provision' will depend on the court's assessment of the circumstances and the quality of the cohabiting relationship. In *DR v DC*[65] the court suggested that there could be no rule of thumb in relation to the nature of 'proper provision' in this context. Proper provision means whatever provision the court considers to be appropriate in the circumstances of the surviving cohabitant.[66] It is permissible for cohabitants to have some separate financial resources. Similarly in *GR* v *Niamh Regan*,[67] Allen J held that proper provision would differ depending on the nature and duration of the cohabiting relationship.[68]

2. The court must also take into account the rights of any other persons having an interest in the matter.[69] This will include

---

[63] ss 173(5) and 194(10).
[64] s 194(3).
[65] [2015] IEHC 309.
[66] ibid [124].
[67] [2020] IEHC 89.
[68] ibid [59].
[69] s 194(3).

anyone who would otherwise inherit under the deceased cohabitant's will or on intestacy. By making an award to the surviving cohabitant the financial interests of these people are displaced. In reported cases, the court has considered the rights of the deceased's surviving siblings who would have inherited everything under the rules of intestacy if it had not been for the surviving cohabitant's claim. The weight given to these rights when calculating the award for the cohabitant depends on both the practical circumstances of the relatives and their closeness to the deceased.

For example, in *DR v DC*[70] where a female cohabitant died intestate, the court sought to balance the needs of the surviving cohabitant against the needs of the surviving siblings who would otherwise have inherited everything. The court noted that the siblings were not in any financial need and had a similar level of wealth to the deceased cohabitant because of family inheritance.[71]

In *GR v Niamh Regan*[72] Allen J notes that the court is also entitled to take into account the closeness of the relationship between the deceased and those with inheritance rights suggesting that the court would give less weight to the rights of a cousin in Australia who had never met the deceased as compared to a sibling who had lived with the deceased.[73]

3. The need to prioritise marriage over cohabitation is also seen in a **legislative ceiling** which is placed on the amount that a cohabitant applicant can be awarded. The award made by the court cannot be greater than the share the cohabitant would have been entitled to if they had been a spouse of the deceased cohabitant.[74] In *DR v DC*[75] the court held that this provision effectively placed no ceiling on awards where the deceased cohabitant had no children. In such cases a spouse would inherit everything on intestacy and half the estate under the statutory share where a will was made, so in practical terms, the ceiling is set at 100% where there is no will. The court did note that an upper limit would come into effect if the deceased cohabitant had children.

In all situations, the court will make an award that is 'just and equitable' in all the circumstances and must consider a checklist outlined by s 173(3).

---

70 [2015] IEHC 309.
71 ibid [123].
72 [2020] IEHC 89.
73 ibid [67].
74 s 194(7).
75 [2015] IEHC 309 [131].

Key legislation – s 173(3) Civil Partnership and Certain Rights and Obligations of Cohabitants Act 2010 (determining what is 'just and equitable')

(3) In determining whether or not it is just and equitable to make an order in all the circumstances, the court shall have regard to—

(a) the financial circumstances, needs and obligations of each qualified cohabitant existing as at the date of the application or which are likely to arise in the future,

(b) subject to subsection (5), the rights and entitlements of any spouse or former spouse,

(c) the rights and entitlements of any civil partner or former civil partner,

(d) the rights and entitlements of any dependent child or of any child of a previous relationship of either cohabitant,

(e) the duration of the parties' relationship, the basis on which the parties entered into the relationship and the degree of commitment of the parties to one another,

(f) the contributions that each of the cohabitants made or is likely to make in the foreseeable future to the welfare of the cohabitants or either of them including any contribution made by each of them to the income, earning capacity or property and financial resources of the other,

(g) any contributions made by either of them in looking after the home,

(h) the effect on the earning capacity of each of the cohabitants of the responsibilities assumed by each of them during the period they lived together as a couple and the degree to which the future earning capacity of a qualified cohabitant is impaired by reason of that qualified cohabitant having relinquished or foregone the opportunity of remunerative activity in order to look after the home,

(i) any physical or mental disability of the qualified cohabitant, and

(j) the conduct of each of the cohabitants, if the conduct is such that, in the opinion of the court, it would be unjust to disregard it.

The court is directed to consider the financial circumstances of both cohabitants at the time of the case and into the future. The court is expressly directed to consider the rights and also the entitlements of any spouse or former spouse or any dependent children and how they might be affected by the award. In deciding how much to award, the court is again required to consider the nature of the cohabiting relationship including the duration of the relationship, the degree of commitment of the parties to each other and any understandings between the parties about the basis on which they entered into the relationship. The court must also consider any physical or mental disability of the qualified cohabitant and the conduct of each of the cohabitants.

Where both cohabitants are still alive, the court has the power to make orders that transfer money from one spouse to the other,[76] (such as orders for periodic payments or lump sum payments), pension adjustment orders[77] (orders which ensure that a cohabitant receives some payment from the other cohabitant's pension scheme) and property adjustment orders[78] which transfer interests in real property (such as a house or piece of land) from one cohabitant to another. The legislation requires the court to prioritise the use of orders transferring money or pension interests over orders for the transfer of interests in real property where practical. This means that the court should try to come up with a solution without changing the property interests of the economically stronger cohabitant.[79]

2.3.1 How much have cohabitants been awarded?

There is considerable variation in the level of financial awards made by the courts in reported cohabitant cases. The court seems to prioritise the housing needs of the dependent cohabitant.

In *MO'S v EC,*[80] following the break up of a 25-year relationship, a financially dependent female cohabitant was awarded two properties with a combined value of €1.5 million, a lump sum of €850,000, maintenance of €70,000 per annum for her alongside €10,000 per annum in maintenance for a dependent child. This award represented about 10% of her former cohabitant's total assets which were valued at €26 million. Unfortunately, Horgan J's reasoning for this award is not reported. This award was imposed on a living cohabitant and so cannot be meaningfully compared with awards made from the estate of deceased cohabitants.

In *DR v DC,*[81] the deceased cohabitant's estate was valued at €1.41M. The surviving cohabitant was awarded two residential properties and their contents amounting to about 45% of the overall estate. Baker J was at pains to point out that this was not an attempt to suggest a particular percentage share for cohabitants. She justified the award on the basis that the couple had been together for 20 years in a marriage-like relationship but had chosen to keep their assets separate and the

---

76 s 175.
77 s 187.
78 s 174.
79 s 174(2).
80 Unreported, Circuit Court, Horgan J. The facts are outlined in Justin Spain, 'Live with me', Law Society Gazette, 26 December 2015.
81 [2015] IEHC 309.

deceased had chosen not to make a will. The surviving male cohabitant had a source of income and a farm of his own but had become dependent on his cohabiting partner for accommodation needs. The court also took into account the fact that the property had been inherited by the deceased cohabitant. There was significant financial disparity between the cohabitants but the court felt that the man's needs were modest. He had made a considerable contribution to the mental and emotional welfare of his partner by caring for her during years of illness.

In *GR v Niamh Regan*,[82] the surviving female cohabitant was awarded a house worth €490k which made up 85% of the deceased cohabitant's estate. Remaining bank deposits of €82k were distributed to the deceased's three surviving siblings. The reasoning of the court was expressly based on housing need, but the court also noted that the deceased had suffered sudden and rapidly declining health which had prevented him from making a will to provide for his cohabiting partner. The court considered the huge contribution that the surviving cohabitant had made to the welfare of her partner by caring for him and giving up her job to do so.

2.4 Cohabitation agreements and opting out of the 2010 Act

The 2010 Act encourages cohabitants to exercise their legal autonomy and make their own bespoke agreements to organise their financial affairs. Section 202 clarifies Irish law surrounding the enforceability of such agreements between cohabitants.

2.4.1 The historical legal problem with cohabitation agreements

In *Ennis v Butterly*[83] Kelly J found 'agreements to cohabit' to be unenforceable under the law of contract because they were against public policy. In this case, both cohabitants were married to other people. No divorce law was then in force in Ireland. The couple had promised each other that they would marry as soon as divorce was introduced and, in the meantime, would live together as 'man and wife'. A written agreement stated that the female cohabitant would be 'loved, honoured and cherished by the defendant as his wife and he would be loyal and faithful to her and that she would be emotionally and financially secure for life'.[84] In reliance on this agreement, the woman gave up her successful fashion business and became a full-time homemaker. The man left her and returned to his wife after nine years of cohabitation.

[82] [2020] IEHC 89.
[83] [1996] 1 IR 426.
[84] ibid, 433.

The woman sued for contractual remedies for breach of the cohabitation contract. Kelly J found the agreement to cohabit to unenforceable in Irish law because it was against public policy.

English contract law from the 19th century[85] was cited in the case where such contracts were held to be unenforceable and immoral because the consideration within the contract was 'wifely services ... rendered on the part of a mistress'. In other words, the 19th century English court considered such agreements to be illegal contracts for sex. Kelly J held that Article 41 of the Constitution as interpreted in *Nicolau* bolstered the argument that agreements to cohabit were against Irish public policy. He held that to enforce such a contract would give it a similar status in law as a marriage contract and this was in conflict with the state's constitutional duty to protect marriage.[86] He was influenced by the lack of Irish legislation conferring rights on cohabitants.

2.4.2 The legal solution

Following *Ennis v Butterly* there was concern that the case meant that cohabitation contracts could never be enforceable in Irish law.[87] In their 2004 consultation, the Law Reform Commission separated out the idea of a contract to engage in sexual relations outside marriage from an agreement which was limited to sorting out financial and property arrangements at the end of a relationship. They suggested that the contract in *Ennis v Butterly* was exceptional because it had tried to do both; it was a substitute commitment for both parties because they could not marry *and* it made financial arrangements in the event that the relationship ended. They suggested that there was no contractual or public policy barrier to recognising an agreement which is limited to regulating financial and property arrangements and does not make cohabitation or sexual relations a condition of the contract.

Section 202 now makes this position clear in Irish law stating that cohabitants may enter into 'a cohabitants agreement to provide for financial matters during their relationship or when their relationship ends'. Section 202(2) sets out formal requirements for such agreement to be given contractual force. The cohabitants must have received appropriate legal advice, the agreement must be in writing and signed by both cohabitants and the general law of contract must be complied with. Such agreements do not, however, have the full force of contract

---

85 *Beaumount v Reeve* (1846) 8 QB 483.

86 ibid, 439.

87 Law Reform Commission, *Consultation Series: Rights and Duties of Cohabitees* (LRC 32-2004), 39-42.

as they can be set aside or varied in exceptional circumstances where the court considers enforcement to cause serious injustice.[88]

2.4.3 Opting out of the statutory redress scheme

Section 202(3) allows cohabitants to opt out of the statutory redress scheme as part of a cohabitants agreement. Both cohabitants can agree that neither will apply to court after the end of the relationship for redress, regardless of the economic circumstances. This 'opt -out' must be expressed in a written agreement and signed by both parties following appropriate financial advice. However, such opt-outs are subject to the protection of s 202(4). This allows the court to set aside the opt- out and allow a qualifying cohabitant to apply to court for redress where the enforceability of the opt-out would cause serious injustice.

2.5 Critical thinking point: Should there be an entirely unregulated space for adult relationships?

The Irish redress scheme means that qualified cohabitants cannot entirely avoid state regulation of their relationship if extreme financial hardship is caused by the relationship and the circumstances are exceptional. However, for most couples, an opt-out will allow them to avoid the redress scheme.

The Law Reform Commission felt that this opt-out balances the right of autonomy of an adult couple (to opt out of state regulation and make their own decisions about their finances) against the need for protection against the economic hardship caused by such relationships in certain circumstances. This unfairness is a gendered issue which particularly affects women who take on caring responsibilities which affect their long-term earning capacity and make them dependent on a earning partner. The scheme encourages autonomy and private regulation but allows a judge to meet the justice of a particular case in exceptional circumstances.[89]

This compromise might not be enough for some academic commentators such as Ruth Deech who give more importance to the right of individual autonomy to avoid state regulation. Deech has argued that 'there ought to be a corner of freedom for such couples to which they can escape and avoid family law'.[90] This argument assumes that cohabitants have deliberately chosen to opt out of the protection afforded by marriage

---

[88] s 202(4).

[89] Law Reform Commission, *Consultation Series: Rights and Duties of Cohabitees* (LRC 32-2004), 20-28.

[90] Ruth Deech, 'The Case against Legal Recognition of Cohabitation' (1980) 29 International and Comparative Law Quarterly 480, 483.

and made a mutual decision not to assume the financial responsibilities imposed by marriage. However, people cohabit for a variety of different reasons and cannot be treated as a block.

Where cohabitants choose to make provision for their partners, individual legal solutions are available to them. Cohabitants have always been able to make wills. Couples are encouraged to make their own arrangement in relation to finances. The problem is that many cohabitants will not take these actions and it is never clear if that is deliberate choice or simply a failure to take action. Perhaps there is never a good moment to have a conversation about death. A couple might be intending to marry but never get around to it. And in the most vulnerable relationship the power dynamic is not equal. It may be impossible for an economically dependent partner to convince their cohabitant to put financial commitments in writing. A default redress scheme allows such situations to be considered by the courts.

3. Summary

- Cohabiting partners are more vulnerable than spouses where their relationship ends due to breakdown or death. Unlike spouses they have no automatic entitlement to financial provision from their partner.
- The Civil Partnership and Certain Rights and Obligations of Cohabitants Act 2010 provides a redress scheme which allows cohabitants to apply to court for financial support. The redress scheme is limited in operation. Cohabitants must satisfy onerous eligibility requirements and even in the event of a successful claim, the amount that they will receive is very uncertain.
- The Civil Partnership and Certain Rights and Obligations of Cohabitants Act 2010 now makes it clear that cohabitants may come to their own agreements about appropriate financial arrangements if their relationship breaks down. These agreements will only be enforceable as contracts if certain formalities have been complied with. But such agreements can also be set aside by the court in cases of serious injustice.

4. Further Reading

Academic commentary on Irish cohabitation law

John Mee, 'Cohabitation Law Reform in Ireland' (2011) 23 Child and Family Law Quarterly 323.

Brian Tobin, 'The regulation of cohabitation in Ireland: achieving equilibrium between protection and paternalism?' (2013) 35 Journal of Social Welfare and Family Law 279.

Niamh Rodgers, '"Should have put a Ring on it?" A comparative analysis of the law of cohabitation in Ireland, Scotland and England and Wales' (2012) 11 Hibernian Law Journal 122.

Law Reform Commission, *Report on the Rights and Duties of Cohabitants* (LRC 82-2006) available at https://publications.lawreform.ie/Portal/External/en-GB/RecordView/Index/36049.

Law Reform Commission, *Consultation Paper on the Rights and Duties of Cohabitees* (LRC CP 32-2004) available at https://publications.lawreform.ie/Portal/External/en-GB/RecordView/Index/34996.

Options Paper presented by the Working Group on Domestic Partnership (2006) https://www.justice.ie/en/JELR/OptionsPaper.pdf/Files/OptionsPaper.pdf (sometimes known as the Colley Report).

International articles which look at concepts within the law of cohabitation in other legal systems

Kathy Griffiths, 'From "form" to function and back again: a new conceptual basis for developing frameworks for the legal recognition of family relationships' (2019) Child and Family Law Quarterly 227.

Robert Leckey, 'Judging in Marriage's Shadow' (2018) 26 Feminist Legal Studies 25.

Ruth Deech, 'The Case against Legal Recognition of Cohabitation' (1980) 29 International and Comparative Law Quarterly 480.

Chapter 7

Protection from Domestic Abuse

Susan Leahy

LEARNING OBJECTIVES

After reading this chapter, students will be equipped to:

- Outline the different civil protection orders available for victims of domestic abuse in the Domestic Violence Act 2018.
- Contrast the eligibility criteria which apply to the different civil protection orders in the Domestic Violence Act 2018.
- Analyse the grounds on which the civil orders under the Domestic Violence Act 2018 are granted.
- Discuss the procedure for applying for these orders (including the protections available for applicants during the application process).
- Assess the consequences for breach of civil orders under the Domestic Violence Act 2018.
- Evaluate the adequacy of criminal liability for domestic abuse in Ireland.

CRITICAL THINKING POINTS

- How should domestic abuse be defined?
- Does current Irish legislation and policy achieve an appropriate balance between civil and criminal law responses to domestic abuse?

1. Introduction

Domestic abuse is an unfortunate reality in many Irish families. Research conducted by Watson and Parsons with a nationally representative sample of 3,077 adults in Ireland in 2003 found that 15% of women had experienced severely abusive behaviour of a physical, sexual or emotional nature from a partner at some time in their lives.[1] Statistics from Irish organisations that support victims of domestic abuse persistently reveal

[1] Dorothy Watson and Sara Parsons, *Domestic Abuse of Women and Men in Ireland: Report on the National Study of Domestic Abuse* (National Crime Council 2005) 53.

significant levels of domestic abuse. For example, Women's Aid's Annual Impact Report 2021 reported 33,831 disclosures of domestic abuse against women and children.[2] The categories of abuse against women included: emotional abuse (19,902 incidents); physical abuse (4,707 incidents); sexual abuse (1,104 incidents), and economic abuse (2,383 incidents).[3] While statistics consistently demonstrate that the majority of victims of domestic abuse are women and children, men can also be victims. Statistics on men's experiences of domestic abuse in Ireland are limited. However, Watson and Parson's study mentioned above showed that 6% of men had experienced severe abuse from an intimate partner.[4]

The Domestic Violence Act 2018 ('DVA 2018') was commenced on 1 January 2019, reforming and consolidating the pre-existing legislation in this area. A key driving force for the new legislation was to support the State in meeting its obligations under the Council of Europe Convention on preventing and combatting violence against women and domestic violence ('the Istanbul Convention'),[5] which Ireland ratified in March 2019.[6] The Istanbul Convention is an international human rights treaty which creates binding obligations on Member States regarding preventing and responding to violence against women. The provisions of the Convention centre on four key areas of action, which are sometimes referred to as 'the four Ps': *preventing* violence against women; *protecting* victims; *prosecuting* perpetrators, and; implementing comprehensive and co-ordinated *policies* in this area.[7] Similar to previous legislation such as the Domestic Violence Act 1996, the DVA 2018 provides for civil protection orders which prohibit individuals from engaging in

---

2 There were 28,096 disclosures of domestic abuse against women and 5,736 disclosures of abuse against children: Women's Aid, *Annual Impact Report 2021* (Women's Aid 2022) 7.

3 Women's Aid, *Annual Impact Report 2021* (Women's Aid 2022) 16.

4 Dorothy Watson and Sara Parsons, *Domestic Abuse of Women and Men in Ireland: Report on the National Study of Domestic Abuse* (National Crime Council 2005) 53. The charity, Men's Aid, provides support for male victims of domestic abuse in Ireland: see www.mensaid.ie.

5 Speaking about the commencement of the DVA 2018, then Minister for Justice, Charlie Flanagan, remarked that the legislation 'completes a major step towards Ireland's ratification of the [Istanbul Convention]': Department of Justice, 'Press Release: Minister Flanagan brings landmark Domestic Violence Act into operation', 2 January 2019 available at: https://www.gov.ie/en/press-release/e6d5da-minister-flanagan-brings-landmark-domestic-violence-act-into-operati/ [last accessed 25 July 2022].

6 'Press Release: Minister Flanagan announces ratification of the Istanbul Convention by Ireland on International Women's Day' available at: https://www.gov.ie/en/press-release/ca853a-minister-flanagan-announces-ratification-of-the-istanbul-convention-/?referrer=http://www.justice.ie/en/JELR/Pages/PR19000066#:~:text=The%20Convention%20entered%20into%20force,once%20it%20enters%20into%20force [last accessed 18 October 2022].

7 To learn more about the Istanbul Convention, see: Council of Europe, *Key Facts about the Istanbul Convention* available at: https://www.coe.int/en/web/istanbul-convention/key-facts [last accessed 2 August 2023].

abusive behaviours, including in some instances excluding them from their home. Breach of such orders is a criminal offence. However, unlike older legislation, the DVA 2018 also addresses direct criminal liability for domestic abuse, most notably with the introduction of the offence of coercive control. Both the civil and criminal law aspects of the legislation are addressed in this chapter.

2. What is domestic abuse?

Before discussing the provisions of the DVA 2018, it is worth exploring the types of harm which are, or should be, encompassed within societal and legal understandings of domestic abuse.

2.1 Critical thinking point: How should domestic abuse be defined?

There are a variety of ways in which abuse within the home can be described, including 'domestic violence', 'domestic abuse' and 'intimate partner violence'. Although the DVA 2018 refers to 'domestic violence,' the more appropriate terminology 'domestic abuse' is used throughout this chapter. *Domestic* abuse is appropriate and inclusive terminology to adopt in this context because it includes all relationship types, not just intimate partners. The term thereby includes all categories of victims (eg, intimate partners, children, parents of adult children, relatives). Further, while references to domestic *violence* tend to create a focus on physical forms of abuse and injury, domestic *abuse* more appropriately reflects the reality that domestic abuse victims experience many other types of harm such as emotional, psychological or financial abuse. Thus, it would have been better if the DVA 2018 had adopted the terminology of 'domestic abuse', rather than 'domestic violence'.

This shortcoming in the terminology adopted by the legislation is further compounded by the anomalous situation whereby the legislation does not provide a definition of domestic abuse or domestic violence and thus does not define the harms which it is intended to address. Given developments in our understanding of the nuances and complexities of domestic abuse, it is regrettable that the legislature did not take the opportunity to provide a clear definition of the forms of harm that are the focus of the DVA 2018's provisions. At present, An Garda Síochána's *Domestic Abuse Intervention Policy* provides the primary official Irish guidance on what constitutes domestic abuse, defining it as: 'the physical, sexual, financial, emotional or psychological abuse of one person against another who is a family member or is or has been an intimate partner, regardless of...gender or sexuality'.[8]

---

8 An Garda Síochána, *Domestic Abuse Intervention Policy 2017*, 1.

A statutory definition of domestic abuse would serve an important educative function, clearly defining what it is that society needs to tackle[9] in responding effectively to domestic abuse.

Article 3(b) of the Istanbul Convention defines domestic violence as: 'all acts of physical, sexual, psychological or economic violence that occur within the family or domestic unit or between former or current spouses or partners, whether or not the perpetrator shares or has shared the same residence with the victim'. This definition is referred to and adopted in the Irish national strategy on responding to domestic, sexual and gender-based violence.[10]

The English Domestic Abuse Act 2021 also contains a useful definition of domestic abuse. Section 1(2) of that Act provides that '[b]ehaviour of a person ("A") towards another person ("B") is "domestic abuse" if: (a) A and B are each aged 16 or over and are personally connected to each other, and (b) the behaviour is abusive.' Section 1(3) sets out that behaviour is "abusive" if it consists of any of the following:

> (a) physical or sexual abuse;
> (b) violent or threatening behaviour;
> (c) controlling or coercive behaviour;
> (d) economic abuse (i.e. any behaviour that has a substantial adverse effect on B's ability to: (a)acquire, use or maintain money or other property, or (b)obtain goods or services);[11]
> (e) psychological, emotional or other abuse;
>
> and it does not matter whether the behaviour consists of a single incident or a course of conduct.[12]

Importantly, the definition of 'personally connected' in the English Act makes clear that domestic abuse can occur in a variety of relationships, including spouses, civil partners, persons in intimate relationships, persons with a parental relationship in relation to the same child and relatives.[13]

The English definition of domestic abuse is comprehensive and nuanced, reflecting both the diversity of harms which victims may experience and

---

9 Stephanie Holt and John Devaney, 'Understanding domestic abuse and sexual violence: Prevalence, policy and practice' in Deirdre Healy et al (eds), *The Routledge Handbook of Irish Criminology* (Routledge 2016) 71.

10 Government of Ireland, *Zero Tolerance: Third National Strategy on Third National Strategy on Domestic, Sexual & Gender-Based Violence 2022-2026* (Stationery Office 2022) 9.

11 Domestic Abuse Act 2021, s 1(4) (England and Wales).

12 ibid s 1(3).

13 ibid s 2(1).

the variety of relationships in which such abuse may occur. Adopting the terminology 'domestic abuse' and introducing a similar definition would represent a significant improvement to Irish law and policy in this area.

3. Civil protection orders available in the Domestic Violence Act 2018

There are five types of orders available in the DVA 2018. Two of these orders prohibit the use or threat of violent and abusive behaviour: safety orders and protection orders. The other three orders operate to exclude the respondent from a property: barring orders, interim barring orders, and emergency barring orders. Each order is explained below, including an overview of eligibility requirements and the effect and duration of each order. The DVA 2018 provides protection to a wide variety of domestic and personal relationships, including not only the traditional categories of spouses and cohabitants but also, for example, the parents of adult children and parents who share a child but are no longer in an intimate relationship. However, there are restrictions on who can apply for protection under the legislation. In particular, the orders which exclude an individual from the home have stricter eligibility criteria, and an applicant for a barring order or interim barring order must hold sufficient ownership rights in that property.

The primary benefit of the DVA 2018 orders is that their breach is a criminal offence. Thus, they place an onus on individuals to comply and to desist from abusive behaviour. Furthermore, often the greatest protection to victims who obtain these orders is that An Garda Síochána (AGS) have the power to arrest without warrant where it is suspected that such an order has been breached. This offers protection to victims in situations of immediate danger, allowing for immediate removal of an individual who is engaging in abusive or threatening behaviour.

3.1 Judicial decision-making criteria when determining applications for orders

The explanation of each of the orders available under the DVA 2018 sets out the legal test which an applicant must satisfy to obtain an order. These tests are not very detailed and judges retain significant discretion in deciding whether or not to grant an order. To support judicial decision-making in this area, s 5(2) provides a detailed list of 'factors or circumstances' which the court should consider when determining applications for orders. This is a significant innovation which was not present in the previous legislation and encourages consistent decision-making which recognises the complexities of domestic abuse. The factors, listed in s 5(2), are as follows:

a. any history of violence inflicted by the respondent on the applicant or a dependent person;
b. any conviction of the respondent for an offence under the Criminal Justice (Theft and Fraud Offences) Act 2001 that involves loss to, or is to the prejudice of, the applicant or a dependent person;
c. any conviction of the respondent for an offence that involves violence or the threat of violence to any person;
d. whether any violence inflicted by the respondent on the applicant or a dependent person is increasing, or has increased, in severity or frequency over time;
e. any exposure of any dependent person to violence inflicted by the respondent on the applicant or any other dependent person;
f. any previous order under this Act or the Act of 1996 made against the respondent with regard to any person;
g. any history of animal cruelty by the respondent;
h. any destruction or damage caused by the respondent to: (i) the personal property of the applicant, the respondent or a dependent person, or (ii) any place where the applicant or a dependent person resides;
i. any action of the respondent, not being a criminal offence, which puts the applicant or a dependent person in fear for his or her own safety or welfare;
j. any recent separation between the applicant and the respondent;
k. substance abuse, including abuse of alcohol, by the respondent, the applicant or a dependent person;
l. access to weapons by the respondent, the applicant or a dependent person;
m. the applicant's perception of the risk to his or her own safety or welfare due to the behaviour of the respondent;
n. the age and state of health (including pregnancy) of the applicant or any dependent person;
o. any evidence of deterioration in the physical, psychological or emotional welfare of the applicant or a dependent person which is caused directly by fear of the behaviour of the respondent;
p. whether the applicant is economically dependent on the respondent;
q. any matter required to be considered by the court regarding a respondent's engagement with a programme or service in relation to his/her abusive behaviour;[14]

[14] This specifically relates to s 29 of the DVA 2018 which provides that when making a safety order, barring order or emergency barring order, a court can recommend

r. any other matter which appears to the court to be relevant to the safety or welfare of the applicant and any dependent person.

The comprehensive list of factors provided serves an important educative function in drawing judges' attention to the features of domestic abuse that must be considered when deciding whether to make an order under the DVA 2018. For example, it is important to thoroughly consider the respondent's history of and propensity for abusive behaviour in the relationship[15] but also in his/her previous relationships by considering previous orders made against the respondent in relation to *any* person[16] and any convictions for violence or threats of violence.[17] The list of factors also highlights circumstances which may heighten the risk posed to an applicant and necessitate a more interventionist approach. An important example may be found in s 5(2)(n) which draws attention to the state of health of the applicant, specifically referencing pregnancy. Unfortunately, research indicates that domestic abuse can commence or escalate during pregnancy. Women's Aid's Annual Impact Report for 2020 reported that 148 women who used their services had been abused while pregnant. These statistics also demonstrate the significant consequences of domestic abuse in pregnancy, with 28 women reporting suffering a miscarriage because of the abuse.[18]

Other significant risk factors highlighted by s 5 include separation,[19] which is also associated with an increased risk of harm for victims and, accessibility of weapons,[20] a factor which naturally greatly increases the likelihood of serious harm or even death. Finally, references to animal cruelty acknowledge that animal abuse can be a precursor to abuse of humans but also that harming or threatening to harm animals can be a factor in psychological abuse or coercive control. For example, 'animal maltreatment may be used to show victims what might happen to them if they attempt to act independently'.[21]

---

that a respondent engage with certain programmes or services that may assist in addressing the behaviour which contributed to the application for the order being made. This includes perpetrator programmes, addiction, counselling, psychotherapy or financial planning services. Section 29(2) provides that a court may consider the respondent's engagement with such services in subsequent proceedings relating to the aforementioned orders under the Act. The court will also have regard to the view of the applicant on that engagement and its effect on the respondent's behaviour: s 29(3).

15 s (2)(a) and (d).

16 s 5(2)(f).

17 s 5(2)(c).

18 Women's Aid, *Annual Impact Report 2020* (Women's Aid 2021) 19.

19 s 5(2)(j)

20 s 5(2)(l).

21 Amy J Fitzgerald et al, 'Domestic Violence and Animal Abuse' in John Devaney et al (eds), *The Routledge International Handbook of Domestic Violence and Abuse* (Routledge 2021) 327.

3.2 Orders which prohibit the use or threat of violence and abusive behaviour

The DVA 2018 provides for safety orders and protection orders which prohibit the use or threat of violent or abusive behaviour but do not exclude a respondent from a property. They can provide protection to victims who either do not wish to have an individual excluded from their home or who cannot satisfy the eligibility criteria for the barring orders discussed below. Safety orders and protection orders offer the same protections and are available to the same applicants. The key difference is that the protection order is an interim order which provides protection on a short-term basis while an applicant awaits the determination of an application for a safety or barring order.

3.2.1 Safety Orders

Section 6 of the DVA 2018 provides for safety orders, which do not exclude a respondent from a property but prohibit him/her from engaging in certain threatening or intimidating behaviours.

3.2.1.1 Eligibility

The following persons are eligible to apply for safety orders:[22]

- Spouses and civil partners;
- an individual who was in an intimate relationship with the respondent prior to the application for the safety order;
- the parent of a respondent where the respondent is an adult and not a 'dependent person';
- an individual who resides with the respondent in a relationship the basis of which is not primarily contractual; or
- the parent of a child whose other parent is the respondent.

The first two categories of applicants are self-explanatory: spouses, civil partners and those within intimate relationships (including cohabitants who are not married) are perhaps the typical applicants one might instinctively think of when considering applications for protection from domestic abuse. The remaining categories require some further explanation. The parent of a respondent who is not a 'dependent person' refers to the situation where a parent may require protection from an adult child. For the purposes of the legislation, a 'dependent person' is any child (i.e. individual who is under the age of eighteen):

a) of the applicant and the respondent or in respect of whom both of them are in *loco parentis*;

[22] s 6(1)(a).

b) of the applicant or in respect of whom the applicant is in *loco parentis*, or

c) of the respondent or in respect of whom the respondent is in loco parentis and (i) where the child is a child of the respondent, the applicant is in *loco parentis* to that child, or (ii) where the respondent is in *loco parentis* to the child, the child is a child of the applicant.[23]

Notably, if an individual has reached the age of eighteen but 'is suffering from a mental or physical disability to such an extent that it is not reasonably possible for him or her to live independently of the applicant', then s/he will continue to be a 'dependent person' for the purposes of the legislation.[24]

The category of applicants which requires greatest explanation are those who live with the respondent 'in a relationship the basis of which is not primarily contractual'. In deciding whether the relevant relationship exists, the court must have regard to:

(i) the length of time those persons are residing together,

(ii) the nature of any duties performed by either person for the other person or any kindred[25] person of that other person,

(iii) the absence of any profit or of any significant profit made by either person from any monetary or other consideration given by the other person in respect of residing at the place concerned, and

(iv) any other matters the court considers appropriate in the circumstances.[26]

Although seemingly complicated, this category of applicants can be understood as referring to individuals who live together other than on the basis of an underlying contract such as a lease (ie landlord/tenant relationship) or a contract of employment (eg a professional live-in carer). An example of a potential applicant in this category is an individual who lives with a relative but is not paying rent or receiving a wage.

The final category of applicant is an individual who shares a child with the respondent, irrespective of whether they live together or have ever lived together. This provides important protection to parents who may be experiencing abusive or threatening behaviour in the context of the

---

23 s 2(1).

24 s 2(1).

25 '"Kindred" in relation to two or more persons, means the relationship of each of those persons to the other person or to the rest of those persons by blood, adoption, marriage or civil partnership': s 6(1)(a).

26 s 6(1)(b).

parenting relationship, for example, where one parent is being exposed to threats or abuse when meeting the other parent to fulfil obligations in relation to access or custody arrangements.

3.2.1.2 Legal test for granting Safety Orders

A safety order may be granted where the court is of the opinion that there are reasonable grounds for believing that the safety or welfare[27] of an applicant or a dependent person so requires.

3.2.1.3 Effect of Safety Orders

A safety order prohibits the respondent from doing one or more of the following[28]:

(a) using or threatening to use violence against, molesting or putting in fear the applicant or the dependent person;
(b) if s/he is residing at a place other than the place where the applicant or the dependent person resides, watching or besetting a place where the applicant/dependent person resides;
(c) following or communicating (including by electronic means) with the applicant or the dependent person.[29]

'Molest' is not defined in the legislation, despite this type of behaviour being prohibited by all of the orders. Case-law from England and Wales (where the term molest is also undefined in legislation), indicates that 'molestation' does not require that violence or threats of violence are made. It may be understood as any deliberate conduct which creates a high degree of harassment justifying intervention by the court.[30] Commenting on the Domestic Violence Act 1996, which also used the term 'molest' without providing a definition, the Law Reform Commission commented that examples of molestation might include 'rifling through a partner's handbag, shouting obscenities, sending abusive letters and giving the press pictures of a former partner'.[31]

A safety order will be subject to such exceptions and conditions as the

---

[27] References to 'welfare' in the DVA 2018 include both physical and psychological welfare: s 2(1).

[28] It should be noted that when deciding whether to make orders under the DVA 2018, the court must have regard to the power available to it under s 12 of the DVA 2018 to make a child protection order under the Child Care Act 1991. This is discussed below in paragraph 3.6 below.

[29] s 6(2).

[30] *Horner v Horner* [1982] EWCA Civ J0218-1.

[31] Law Reform Commission, *Report on Aspects of Domestic Violence* (LRC 111- 2013) 20–21.

court may specify.[32] Safety orders have a maximum duration of five years[33] and may be renewed for a further period of up to five years.[34]

Notably, a court cannot, on an application for a barring order, make a safety order unless there is also an application for a safety order before the court concerning the same matter.[35] The same rule applies for applications for safety orders, that is, a court cannot make an order for a barring order on an application for a safety order, unless there is also an application for a barring order before the court.[36] Consequently, if there is doubt about which order may be most appropriate, it would seem prudent to apply for both, thereby allowing the court to grant the order which it deems most suitable.

3.2.2 Protection Orders

Section 10 of the DVA 2018 provides for protection orders, which provide similar protection to safety orders, on an interim basis. A protection order does not exclude a respondent from a property. Protection orders may be sought on application for a safety order or a barring order or between the making of such an application and its determination.[37]

3.2.2.1 Eligibility

The following persons are eligible to apply for protection orders:[38]

- Spouses and civil partners;
- an individual who was in an intimate relationship with the respondent prior to the application for the order;
- the parent of a respondent where the respondent is an adult and not a 'dependent person';
- an individual who resides with the respondent in a relationship the basis of which is not primarily contractual; or
- the parent of a child whose other parent is the respondent.

3.2.2.2 Legal test for granting a protection order

A protection order may be granted where there are reasonable grounds

32 s 6(3).
33 s 6(4).
34 s 6(5).
35 s 6(7).
36 s 7(11).
37 s 10(1).
38 s 10 does not contain a list of individuals who may apply for protection orders but since these orders may only be sought by applicants for safety or barring orders, those who are eligible for these orders may also apply for protection orders.

for believing that the safety or welfare of the applicant or a dependent person requires it.

3.2.2.3 Effect of Protection Orders

Protection orders have the same effect as safety orders, prohibiting the respondent from doing one or more of the following:

(a) using or threatening to use violence against, molesting or putting in fear, the applicant or the dependent person;
(b) if he or she is residing at a place other than the place where the applicant or the dependent person resides, watching or besetting the place where the applicant or the dependent person resides;
(c) following or communicating (including by electronic means) with the applicant or the dependent person.

A protection order may be subject to such exceptions and conditions as the court may specify.[39] As with the other interim orders, a protection order may be made ex parte where 'having regard to the circumstances of the particular case, the court considers it necessary or expedient to do so in the interests of justice'.[40] The same requirements apply as for other ex parte applications under the DVA 2018, that is, the application must be grounded on an affidavit or information sworn by the applicant[41] and, if an order is granted, this must be provided to the respondent, along with a note of evidence[42] and a copy of the order as soon as is practicable.[43] A protection order ceases to have effect once the court has determined the application for the safety or barring order.[44] Unlike the situation with interim barring orders and emergency barring orders, there are no special time limits which apply where a protection order is made ex parte. This is due to the more limited nature of this order, which does not impact on a respondent's access to property.

3.3 Orders which exclude an individual from a property

The three orders which operate to exclude an individual from a property are barring orders, interim barring orders and emergency barring orders.

---

39 s 10(2).
40 s 10(7).
41 s 10(8).
42 As with the other interim orders, a note of evidence given by the applicant must be prepared by the judge, the applicant or his/her solicitor or as otherwise directed by the judge: s 10(9)(a).
43 s 10(9)(b).
44 s 10(10).

3.3.1 Barring Orders

Section 7 of the DVA 2018 provides for barring orders which exclude a respondent from a property, as well as prohibiting him/her from engaging in violent or abusive behaviour towards the applicant.

3.3.1.1 Eligibility

The following individuals may apply for a barring order:[45]
• Spouses and civil partners; • an individual who lived with the respondent in an intimate relationship prior to the application for the barring order (i.e. cohabitants);[46] or • the parent of a respondent where the respondent is an adult and not a 'dependent person'.[47]

While spouses and civil partners are automatically entitled to apply for barring orders, the other two categories of applicants (ie cohabitants and parents of adult children) must satisfy additional criteria related to property rights.

Section 7(6) provides that the court shall not make a barring order in respect of the place where the applicant or dependent person resides where the respondent has a legal or beneficial interest in the property and: (i) the applicant has no legal or beneficial interest, or (ii) the applicant's legal or beneficial interest is, in the opinion of the court, less than that of the respondent. This means that where a cohabitant or the parent of an adult child does not have an equal or greater legal or beneficial interest in the relevant property, s/he does not qualify for a barring order.

3.3.1.2 Legal test for granting a barring order

A court may issue a barring order where there are reasonable grounds for believing that the safety or welfare of the applicant or a dependent person requires it.

3.3.1.3 Effect of barring orders

The effect of a barring order is to:

---

45 s 7(1).

46 These applicants must satisfy ownership requirements in the relevant property to be eligible.

47 These applicants must satisfy ownership requirements in the relevant property to be eligible.

(i) direct the respondent, if residing at a place where the applicant or the dependent person resides, to leave the place, and
(ii) whether the respondent is or is not residing at a place where the applicant or the dependent person resides, prohibit the respondent from entering the place until further order of the court or until such other time as the court shall specify.[48]

When making a barring order, the court may also, if it considers it appropriate, prohibit the respondent from doing one or more of the following:

(a) using/threatening to use violence against, molesting or putting in fear, the applicant or the dependent person;
(b) attending at or in the vicinity of, or watching or besetting, a place where the applicant or the dependent person resides;
(c) following or communicating (including by electronic means) with the applicant or the dependent person.[49]

A barring order may be subject to such exceptions and conditions as the court may specify.[50] These orders may last for a maximum period of three years and may be renewed for a period of up to three years.[51]

3.3.2 Interim Barring Orders

Section 8 of the DVA 2018 provides for interim barring orders (IBOs) which provide the same protection as barring orders but on a temporary basis. Applicants may apply for such orders when applying for a barring order or between the making of such an application and its determination.[52]

[48] s 7(2)(a). It is noteworthy that '[i]n deciding whether to make a barring order the court shall have regard to the safety and welfare of any dependent person in respect of whom the respondent is a parent or in loco parentis, where the dependent person is residing at the place to which the order, if made, would relate': s 7(2)(b). The court must also take account of any order made or to be made under the Child Care Act 1991 or in relation to an application for its direction on any question relating to the welfare of a child that is being made by a child's guardian under s 11 of the Guardianship of Infants Act 1964: s 7(2)(a) (read in conjunction with s 15(2) (a) and (d)).
[49] s 7(3).
[50] s 7(5).
[51] s 7(8)-(10).
[52] s 8(1).

3.3.2.1 Eligibility

The following individuals may apply for an IBO:[53]
• Spouses and civil partners; • cohabitants;[54] or • parents of adult children.[55]

As with barring orders, the court cannot issue an IBO for cohabitants or the parents of adult children unless their legal or beneficial interest in the property is greater than or equal to that of the respondent.[56]

3.3.2.2 Legal test for granting Interim Barring Orders

An IBO may be granted where the court is of the opinion that there are reasonable grounds for believing that (a) there is an immediate risk of significant harm to the applicant or a dependent person, and (b) the making of a protection order would not be sufficient to protect the applicant or a dependent person.[57]

In *X v Y*,[58] an unsuccessful appeal against the grant of an IBO, Barrett J offered some clarity on these criteria. Notably, it is the *risk* of significant harm which must be immediate, not the actual harm itself.[59] The requirement of immediacy will be interpreted broadly.[60] Barrett J also noted that the requirement of 'significant harm' served only to exclude harms that would be so 'trivial and/or contrived in nature or substance that a reasonable-minded person would conclude that in truth no harm has been suffered at all'.[61] In this context, 'a court should ever be mindful that the scale of a harm is not just measured by a discrete act complained of but rather is informed by all the behaviours and circumstances that surround and inform that act, as well as the fear of future reoccurrences of same'.[62] Consequently, 'once any harm is established...in practice there

53 The persons who may apply for an IBO are not listed in s 8. However, as the application for an IBO may be made on an application for a barring order or between the making of an application and its determination, it follows that the same applicants may apply for both orders.

54 This category of applicants must satisfy ownership requirements in the relevant property to be eligible to apply.

55 This category of applicants must satisfy ownership requirements in the relevant property to be eligible to apply.

56 s 8(5).

57 s 8(1).

58 *X v Y* [2020] IEHC 525.

59 ibid [40].

60 ibid.

61 ibid [41].

62 ibid.

will be few if any real-life circumstances in which such harm is found not to be a "significant harm"'.[63]

3.3.2.3 Effect of Interim Barring Orders:

The IBO has the same effect as a barring order, that is to:

(i) direct the respondent, if residing at a place where the applicant or the dependent person resides, to leave that place, and
(ii) whether the respondent is or is not residing at a place where the applicant or the dependent person resides, prohibit the respondent from entering the place until further order of the court or until such time as the court may specify.[64]

Also, as with barring orders, where appropriate, an IBO may also prohibit the respondent from doing one or more of the following:

(a) using/threatening to use violence against, molesting or putting in fear, the applicant or the dependent person;
(b) attending at or in the vicinity of, or watching or besetting, a place where the applicant or the dependent person resides; or
(c) following or communicating (including by electronic means) with the applicant or the dependent person.[65]

An IBO may be subject to such exceptions and conditions as the court may specify.[66]

An application for an IBO may be made ex parte where, in the circumstances of the particular case, the court considers it 'necessary or expedient to do so in the interests of justice'.[67] Where an application is made ex parte, it must be grounded on an affidavit or information sworn by the applicant.[68] If an IBO is made ex parte, a note of the evidence must be prepared.[69] This must be provided to the respondent 'as soon as practicable' along with a copy of the IBO and the affidavit or information

---

63 ibid.
64 s 8(1).
65 s 8(2).
66 s 8(3). An example of the type of detail which may be included in an IBO can be seen in the judgment of *X v Y* [2020] IEHC 525 [44].
67 s 8(10).
68 s 8(11). This must state whether the property from which it is sought to bar the respondent is also a place of business of the respondent or includes or abuts a place of business of the respondent: s 8(12).
69 This can be prepared by: (i) the judge; (ii) the applicant and his/her solicitor and approved by the judge, or; (iii) as otherwise directed by the judge: s 8(13)(a).

sworn by the applicant.[70] Given the significant consequences of an IBO (ie excluding an individual from a property), where the order is granted ex parte and the respondent has not been afforded an opportunity to be heard, the order has a maximum duration of eight working days.[71] However, the order may be confirmed by the court in a subsequent hearing on notice to the respondent.[72] An IBO which has been made on notice to the respondent will remain in place until the court determines the application for the barring order.[73]

3.3.3 Emergency Barring Orders (EBOs)

The EBO was introduced for the first time by s 9 of the DVA 2018 and makes protection similar to an IBO available to cohabitants and parents of adult children who do not satisfy the ownership requirements to obtain an IBO. The EBO is a stand-alone order, that is, there is no requirement that the applicant is also applying for a barring order.

3.3.3.1 Eligibility

The following persons may apply for an EBO:
• Cohabitants; or • parents of adult children.

The key requirement of eligibility for an EBO is that the property is the applicant's home and (a) the respondent has a legal or beneficial interest in the place but the applicant has *no* such interest, or (b) the applicant's legal or beneficial interest is, in the opinion of the court, *less than* that of the respondent.[74] The order is intended to give emergency, limited duration protection to applicants living in a property fully or mostly owned by the respondent. These applicants are ineligible to apply for a barring order or interim barring order.

3.3.3.2 Legal Test for Granting an EBO

An EBO may be granted where the court 'is of the opinion that there are reasonable grounds for believing that there is an immediate risk of significant harm to the applicant or a dependent person if an order is not made immediately'.[75]

[70] s 8(13)(b).
[71] s 8(14).
[72] s 8(14).
[73] s 8(16).
[74] s 9(2).
[75] s 9(3).

3.3.3.3 Effect of EBOs

The effect of the EBO is to:

(a) direct the respondent, if residing at the place where the applicant or dependent person resides, to leave that place, and
(b) whether the respondent is or is not residing at the place where the applicant or dependent person resides, prohibit the respondent from entering that place for such period, **not exceeding 8 working days**, as is specified in the order.[76]

If the court deems it appropriate, an EBO may also prohibit the respondent from doing one or more of the following:

(a) using or threatening to use violence against, molesting or putting in fear, the applicant or the dependent person;
(b) attending at or in the vicinity of, or watching or besetting, a place where the applicant or the dependent person resides; or
(c) following or communicating (including by electronic means) with the applicant or the dependent person.[77]

An EBO may also be subject to such exceptions and conditions as the court may specify.[78]

Similar to IBOs, an application for an EBO may be heard ex parte where 'the court considers it necessary or expedient to do so in the interests of justice'.[79] These applications must also be grounded on an affidavit or information sworn by the applicant[80] and where an EBO is granted ex parte, a note of the evidence and a copy of the order and the affidavit or information must be served on the respondent as soon as practicable.[81] Where an EBO is made ex parte, it shall have effect for a maximum period of eight working days.[82] Further, where an EBO has been made against a respondent, a further such order cannot be granted against that respondent by or on behalf of the same applicant for at least one month after the expiration of the first order unless there are exceptional circumstances which justify the making of a further order.[83]

---

76 s 9(3).
77 s 9(4).
78 s 9(5).
79 s 9(11).
80 s 9(12).
81 s 9(14)(b).
82 s 8(15).
83 s 9(16).

3.3.3.4 Analysis of EBOs

The EBO is an important order which provides protection to victims who do not hold a sufficient legal or beneficial interest in their home to have an abuser barred from a property, even temporarily, under the other orders. In this sense, the EBO may be seen as extending the availability of the IBO. While this is welcome, using the name 'emergency barring order' is potentially problematic because this tends to suggest that it provides for the immediate removal of a respondent from a property by police. However, as an application to court is required, there will inevitably be a time delay before a person can be removed and protection cannot thus be provided immediately. Consequently, 'the phraseology "emergency barring order" is...somewhat misleading and masks a gap in the current protection afforded to victims of domestic abuse in Ireland'.[84]

Article 52 of the Istanbul Convention requires signatory states to:

> ... take the necessary legislative or other measures to ensure that the competent authorities are granted the power to order, in situations of immediate danger, a perpetrator of domestic violence to vacate the residence of the victim or person at risk for a sufficient period of time and to prohibit the perpetrator from entering the residence of or contacting the victim or person at risk.

The EBO provided for in the DVA 2018 arguably does not offer the optimum level of compliance with art 52 of the Istanbul Convention as it requires a court application and thus does not allow for sufficiently immediate removal of a respondent.[85]

To provide comprehensive protection to victims of domestic abuse in emergency situations, Irish domestic abuse law should include an emergency order which permits AGS to remove a perpetrator of domestic abuse from a property and exclude him/her for a short period of time (eg 48 hours). This would provide victims with immediate protection in emergency situations and allow for breathing space to apply for more long-term orders and to make plans for securing their safety going forward.

---

84 Susan Leahy, 'What Is Next for Irish Law and Policy on Domestic Abuse?: Lessons from our Neighbours' (2022) 25(4) Irish Journal of Family Law 65, 66.

85 As noted below, s 24 of the DVA 2018 provides for out of hours access to the courts to facilitate applications for orders. However, this would still involve a time-lapse preventing an immediate response in an emergency situation.

3.4 Power of the Child and Family Agency to apply for orders

In general, individuals will apply for the orders available under the DVA 2018 on their own behalf and/or on behalf of a dependent person. However, s 11 of the DVA 2018 also provides that in appropriate circumstances, Tusla, the Child and Family Agency[86] (i.e. the state agency responsible for child protection and family support) may apply for an order on behalf of an 'aggrieved person'.[87] In practice, Tusla would make such an application where it is working with a family and becomes aware of domestic abuse occurring which is directed towards the children or where they are affected by domestic abuse which is directed towards their parents or guardians. Tusla can apply for orders on behalf of a child or on behalf of an adult where it is felt that the adult is not in a position to make an application on his/her own behalf, for example, where they are too afraid to do so.[88]

An application under s 11 may be made where Tulsa:

(a) becomes aware of an alleged incident or series of incidents which in its opinion puts into doubt the safety or welfare of an aggrieved person; and
(b) has reasonable cause to believe that the aggrieved person has been subjected to molestation, violence or threatened violence or otherwise put in fear of his/her safety or welfare; and
(c) is of the opinion that there are reasonable grounds for believing that, where appropriate in the circumstances, a person would be deterred or prevented as a consequence of molestation, violence or threatened violence by the respondent or fear of the respondent from pursuing an application for a safety order, a barring order or an emergency barring order on his/her own behalf, or on behalf of a dependent person, and
(d) considers, having ascertained as far as is reasonably practicable the wishes of the aggrieved person or where the aggrieved person is a dependent person, of the person who would apply on their behalf if they were not likely being deterred or prevented from doing so, that it is appropriate

---

86 References in the DVA 2018 to 'the Agency' are to be understood as references to the Child and Family Agency: s 2(1).

87 This power was also available under the previous legislation, the Domestic Violence Act 1996.

88 An example of s 11 in use can be found in a recent report from the Child Law Project: 'CFA seeks interim barring order to protect children already under care order', Child Law Project, Case Reports 2022, Volume 2, available at: https://www.childlawproject.ie/publications/cfa-seeks-interim-barring-order-to-protect-children-already-under-care-order/ [last accessed 8 February 2023].

in all the circumstances to apply for a safety order, a barring order or an emergency barring order on behalf of the aggrieved person.

The requirements must all be satisfied if Tusla is to apply for an order. Tusla may apply to court for a safety order, a barring order[89] or an EBO where the aggrieved person would be entitled to apply for the order on their own behalf, or on behalf of a dependent person[90] (ie the eligibility criteria in the relevant legislative provisions, including ownership requirements, must be complied with). When deciding whether to grant the order, the court must have regard to any wishes expressed by the aggrieved person(s) on whose behalf the order is sought.[91]

Where the application relates to an aggrieved person who is a dependent person, the first and second requirements listed above need not be complied with if the court is of the opinion that: (a) the dependent person has been or is being assaulted, ill-treated, sexually abused or seriously neglected, or; (b) the dependent person's health, development or welfare has been, is being or is likely to be avoidably impaired or seriously neglected, and if that order is made the likelihood of harm to that dependent person will not arise or will be materially diminished.[92]

Where a barring order, IBO or EBO is being sought on behalf of an aggrieved person who is a dependent person, Tusla must satisfy the court that the person who would otherwise have applied on behalf of that dependent person is willing and able to provide reasonable care for that dependent person.[93] This requirement ensures that there will be someone in a position to care for a child if their parent is removed from the family home.

3.5 Applying for orders: Procedures and protections available for applicants

Both the District Court and Circuit Court can hear applications for orders under the DVA 2018.[94] Applications for these orders may take place as

---

89 By implication, given that the Agency can apply for a safety or barring order, it should follow that applications for related interim orders (i.e. interim barring orders and protection orders) are also possible. Indeed, ss 6 to 10 inclusive of the DVA 2018 are expressly referenced when referring to the court's functions under s 11: see s 11(3). Moreover, the Agency is specifically identified as a potential applicant for a variation of all of the relevant orders: see ss 6(8), 7(12), 8(7), 9(8), 10(4).

90 s 11(2).

91 s 11(3). Where the aggrieved person is a dependent person, the court will have regard to his/her wishes where this is considered appropriate: s 11(3)(b).

92 s 11(4).

93 s 11(5).

94 s 22(1). Although the High Court is not mentioned in this section, it too has jurisdiction

standalone proceedings or may arise in the context of other family law proceedings such as applications for judicial separation or divorce.[95] As with all family law proceedings, hearings are conducted *in camera*.[96] Proceedings should be 'as informal as is practicable and consistent with the administration of justice'.[97] Section 24 of the DVA 2018 allows for out of hours access to the courts. A member of AGS, not below the rank of sergeant, may request the Courts Service to arrange a special sitting of the District Court where a person has informed the member that s/he wishes to make an application for an order, and at the time, there is no District Court sitting in the relevant district.[98] This is an important provision, maximising victims' access to the courts, which may be particularly important in an emergency where the victim finds him/herself in immediate need of protection.

The DVA 2018 includes a number of measures designed to minimise the challenges faced by individuals participating in court applications for orders. Section 16 provides that, unless the interests of justice require otherwise, the applicant or respondent should be prohibited from personally cross-examining a child who is giving evidence in such applications.[99] The section also provides that where an applicant, respondent or dependent person over the age of eighteen is giving evidence, the court has discretion to prohibit either the respondent or the applicant from personally conducting the cross-examination.[100] Where an applicant or respondent is prohibited from conducting the cross-examination personally, a lawyer may be appointed for this purpose.[101] Section 25 also provides for the giving of evidence by television link by a person, other than the respondent. Where the person giving evidence is a child, evidence may be given in this way 'unless the court sees

---

to grant an order under the Act during divorce and judicial separation proceedings heard before it.

95 Two recent reported judgments provide examples of domestic abuse orders being sought as part of divorce and judicial separation proceedings: *A v B* [2020] IEHC 610; *Y v Z* [2020] IEHC 611. These cases provide an insight into the reality of domestic abuse, particularly how family law proceedings can exacerbate domestic abuse and contribute to further traumatisation of victims.

96 s 23(1). This is subject to s 40 of the Civil Liability and Courts Act 2004 which permits certain individuals such as bona fide researchers or journalists to attend hearings. However, where this occurs any resultant publications relating to proceedings must not identify the parties involved.

97 s 22(3) (District Court) and s 22(4) (read in conjunction with ss 32 and 33 of the Judicial Separation and Family Law Reform Act 1989 (Circuit Court).

98 s 24(1).

99 s 16(1).

100 s 16(2).

101 The affected applicant or respondent can appoint their own legal representative (s 16(3)). If they decline to do so and the court is of the view that cross-examination is necessary, the court may appoint a lawyer to conduct it: s 16(4)-(5).

good reason to the contrary'.[102] For adults, the court may give leave for evidence to be given in this way. Finally, in addition to having a legal representative, an applicant is also entitled to be accompanied in court by a person (including a support worker[103]) of his/her choice.[104] The court can, however, refuse to allow an applicant to be accompanied by a particular person at any stage in proceedings if it 'considers that it would not be in the interests of justice for the individual concerned to accompany, or continue to accompany, the applicant'.[105] Where such refusal occurs, the court must give reasons for it.[106]

A final procedural point of note is that the judge is required to give reasons for his/her decision to grant or refuse an order or, where applicable, any decision to make an order subject to exceptions or conditions or to vary such exceptions or conditions.[107] This encourages consistency and increases transparency in decision-making regarding orders.

3.6 The Impact of domestic abuse on children

Domestic abuse has a profound effect on children, regardless of whether the abuse is directly targeted at them or not. Witnessing domestic abuse in the home is traumatic for children and significantly disrupts their lives. Further, the impact of domestic abuse on a child's caregiver can have significant knock-on effects on parenting capacity. For example, Kertesz et al suggest that children are profoundly affected when their mothers' ability to be available to children and to care for their physical and emotional well-being is interfered with by violence and abuse.[108] Growing up in an abusive home environment can critically jeopardise the developmental progress and personal ability of children.[109] Consequently, it is essential that children's needs and, where appropriate, their views, are taken into account when making decisions about orders. The DVA 2018 recognises and responds to the impact of domestic abuse on children in the following ways.

Section 27 provides that where an order is sought on behalf of a child,

---

[102] s 25(1)(a)

[103] 'Support worker' 'means a volunteer of, or an individual employed...by an organisation which provides support to victims of domestic violence'. s 26(3).

[104] s 26(1).

[105] s 26(2).

[106] s 26(2).

[107] s 17.

[108] Margaret Kertesz, Larissa Fogden and Cathy Humphreys, 'Domestic Violence and the Impact on Children' in John Devaney et al (eds), *The Routledge International Handbook of Domestic Violence and Abuse* (Routledge 2021) 129.

[109] Stephanie Holt and John Devaney, 'Understanding domestic abuse and sexual violence: Prevalence, policy and practice' in Deirdre Healy et al (eds), *The Routledge Handbook of Irish Criminology* (Routledge 2016) 74-75.

the court *may*, having regard to his/her age and maturity, ascertain the child's views prior to deciding whether or not to make the order in so far as that order relates to that child.[110] This is a weaker protection than in most areas of child law (discussed in Chapters 8, 9 and 10) where the views of a child must be ascertained if the child is capable of expressing them. Moreover this provision does not apply where the application is for an interim order.[111] Where the court exercises its discretion to determine a child's views, an expert[112] may be appointed to assist with this.[113] In determining whether to appoint an expert, the court must consider the following: (a) the child's age and maturity; (b) any previous report under s 27 in respect of the child; (c) whether appointment of an expert will assist the child in expressing his/her views, and; (d) the child's best interests.[114] Once appointed, an expert must ascertain the child's maturity[115] and, where requested by the court, determine whether the child is capable of forming his/her views on the matters which are the subject of the proceedings and report to the court on that determination.[116] Where the expert determines that the child is capable of forming his/her own views, those views should be ascertained and a report should be furnished to the court.[117] An expert may be called as a witness in the proceedings.[118] The expert's fees and expenses must be paid by the parties to the proceedings in 'such proportions, as the court may specify'.[119]

Section 12 of the DVA 2018 also recognises the importance of protecting children living in situations of domestic abuse, empowering the court to adjourn proceedings under the DVA 2018 where it appears that it may be appropriate for a care or supervision order to be made in relation to a child.[120] In the event of such adjournment, the court can direct Tusla to investigate the child's circumstances. The court's power to make safety

---

110 s 27(1).
111 s 27(1).
112 The required qualifications for an expert appointed under s 27 are those set out in the Guardianship of Infants Act (Child's Views Expert) Regulations 2018 (SI 587/2018), see s 27(6). Article 3(1) of the Regulations provides that the following persons may act as an expert: (a) a psychiatrist who has practised child and adolescent psychiatry for a relevant period; (b) a psychologist who has practised child and adolescent clinical psychology for a relevant period; (c) a social care worker who has practised in the area of provision of social care services to children, for a relevant period; (d) a social worker who has practised in the area of provision of social work services to children, for a relevant period; (e) a registered teacher who has taught children for a relevant period. The 'relevant period' is a minimum of five years within the ten years immediately preceding the appointment: art 3(2)(a).
113 s 27(2).
114 s 27(3).
115 s 27(4)(a).
116 s 27(4)(b).
117 s 27(4)(c).
118 s 27(5).
119 s 27(7).
120 s 12(1).

orders,[121] barring orders,[122] IBOs[123] and EBOs[124] are all subject to the court's powers under s 12 (ie the court must consider the use of s 12 when deciding whether or not to make these orders). This is an important provision which recognises that, in some instances, protecting children who are living in a home affected by domestic abuse may require external support in the form of state intervention.

3.7 When do orders take effect?

An order under the DVA 2018 does not take effect until the respondent is notified of it.[125] Oral communication, along with providing a copy of the relevant order, will satisfy the notification requirements.[126] Moreover, where the respondent is present at the hearing, s/he will be taken to have been notified of the order.[127] It is also possible for the court to order that an order be served on a respondent by a member of AGS where: (a) there are reasonable grounds for believing that the respondent may evade service of the order, or (b) there is any other good and sufficient reason to so direct.[128] Effective notification of orders is vital to ensure that they are enforceable. This was emphasised in the judgment in *DPP v RK*.[129] Simons J held that:

> it is an essential proof in a prosecution for an alleged breach of a barring order to establish that the accused person had been given notification of the making of the barring order. It would not be sufficient that the accused person had been merely notified of the fact that a barring order has been made, rather he or she must have been furnished with a copy of the barring order. The only exception to this is where the accused person has been present at a sitting of the court at which the barring order was made.[130]

There is some flexibility[131] as to the means by which a barring order is provided to a respondent. This includes, prepaid post, personal service effected by the applicant or members of AGS, as well as in urgent cases at least, 'by way of email or as an attachment to a text message'.[132] The

---

121 s 6(2).
122 s 7(2).
123 s 8(1).
124 s 9(3).
125 s 18(1).
126 s 18(2).
127 s 18(3).
128 s 18(4).
129 *DPP (At the Suit of Garda Graham Doolin) v RK* [2019] IEHC 852.
130 ibid [54].
131 ibid [55].
132 ibid [55].

onus is on the prosecutor to prove that the order has been appropriately furnished to the respondent.[133]

Section 19 also provides that where an order under the DVA 2018 is made, varied or discharged, a copy of the relevant order must be provided to specified individuals, including the applicant, respondent, AGS or the Tusla (if applicable).

3.8 Appeals and applications for variation or discharge

Section 20 provides that a decision to grant an order under the DVA 2018 may be appealed. An appeal from a safety or barring order shall, if the court determines (but not otherwise), stay the operation of the order on such terms (if any) as may be imposed by the court.[134] However, an appeal from a protection order, IBO or EBO will not stay their operation.[135]

An applicant or respondent or, if applicable, Tusla, may apply for variation of an order while it is in force.[136] The court may, upon hearing the application for variation, make such order for variation as it considers appropriate in the circumstances.[137] An applicant, respondent or, if applicable, Tusla may apply to have an order discharged. The court will discharge the order if it is of the opinion that the safety and welfare of the applicant or the dependent person for whose protection the order was made does not require that the order should continue in force.[138]

3.9 Consequences for breaches of orders

Contravention of any of the orders in the DVA 2018 is a criminal offence, punishable on summary conviction with a class B fine or imprisonment for a term not exceeding 12 months, or both.[139] Importantly, where a member of AGS has reasonable cause for believing that an order is being or has been contravened, the member may, on complaint being made to him/her by or on behalf of the applicant, arrest the respondent without warrant.[140] For the purposes of arrest, 'a member of [AGS] may enter, if need be by force, and search a place where the member, with reasonable cause, suspects the respondent to be'.[141]

---

133 ibid [57].
134 s 20(1).
135 s 20(2).
136 ss 6(8), 7(12), 8(7), 9(8), 10(4).
137 ss 6(9), 7(13), 8(8), 9(9), 10(5).
138 s 20(2). An order may also be discharged in the course of other family law proceedings, such as proceedings relating to marriage separation: s 20(3).
139 s 33(1).
140 s 35(1).
141 s 35(2).

4. Criminal liability for domestic abuse

Criminal liability arising from domestic abuse has been discussed above with reference to the consequences for breach of civil protection orders. In this context, an individual is prosecuted for breaching the relevant order, not directly for the abusive behaviour which s/he has engaged in. However, abusive behaviour may in itself be criminal, constituting offences under the Non-Fatal Offences against the Person Act 1997 (eg assault offences,[142] harassment,[143] threats to kill[144] or false imprisonment[145]), or sexual offences or offences under the Harassment, Harmful Communications and Related Offences Act 2020 (ie offences relating to non-consensual distribution of intimate images[146]). While domestic abuse often involves the commission of criminal offences, legal responses are typically civil in nature, with victims seeking the protection of the family law courts via the orders available under the DVA 2018, rather than the instigation of criminal prosecutions for the behaviour itself.

This tendency to focus on civil, family law responses to domestic abuse can be linked to the history of domestic abuse, which was once seen as a private matter in which the law and society should not intervene. Indeed, this attitude towards domestic abuse persisted until the 1970s in Ireland, creating a situation where there was little, if any, protection or support available for domestic abuse victims. As Stephanie Holt and John Devaney note the first refuges opened in the 1970s and the first piece of legislation to help abused women, the Family Law (Maintenance of Spouses and Children) Act 1976, came into force in 1976.[147] Although the 1976 Act was limited, providing only for the barring of spouses from the family home, it represented 'one of the first legislative encroachments in the private sphere of the family'.[148] Fortunately, in the intervening years, there have been significant advancements in the protection available to victims, including strengthening legislative responses (culminating in the DVA 2018), an increased societal awareness of the realities of domestic abuse and the provision of supports for victims such as refuges and access

---

[142] That is, assault (s 2), assault causing harm (s 3), and assault causing serious harm (s 4).

[143] s 10.

[144] s 5.

[145] s 15.

[146] Offences under the 2020 Act include: distributing, publishing or threatening to distribute or publish intimate image without consent (s 2); recording, distributing or publishing an intimate image without consent (s 3), and; distributing, publishing or sending threatening or grossly offensive communication (s 4).

[147] Stephanie Holt and John Devaney, 'Understanding domestic abuse and sexual violence: Prevalence, policy and practice' in Deirdre Healy et al (eds), *The Routledge Handbook of Irish Criminology* (Routledge 2016) 80.

[148] Louise Crowley, 'Domestic Violence Law' in Lynsey Black and Peter Dunne, *Law and Gender in Modern Ireland: Critique and Reform* (Hart Publishing, 2019) 146.

to services including therapy and assistance with engaging with the legal process. Recent years have also seen increased efforts to develop criminal justice system responses to domestic abuse. The DVA 2018 represents significant progress in this area, most notably by criminalising coercive control. The DVA 2018 also provides guidance for sentencing for certain offences relating to domestic abuse. However, as discussed in the second critical thinking point at the end of this chapter, questions remain about the extent to which the Irish legal system is achieving the correct balance between civil and criminal justice system responses in this area.

4.1 Coercive control

Section 39(1) of the DVA 2018 provides that:

> A person commits an offence where he or she knowingly and persistently engages in behaviour that:
> (a) is controlling or coercive,
> (b) has a serious effect on a relevant person,[149] and
> (c) a reasonable person would consider likely to have a serious effect on a relevant person.

A person's behaviour 'has a serious effect on a relevant person' if it causes him/her (a) to fear that violence will be used against him or her, or (b) causes serious alarm or distress that has a substantial adverse impact on his or her usual day-to-day activities.[150] The punishment for this offence is: (a) on summary conviction, a class A fine or imprisonment for a term not exceeding 12 months, or both, or; (b) on conviction on indictment, a fine or imprisonment for a term not exceeding 5 years, or both.[151]

The criminalisation of coercive control is a key development in the Irish criminal justice system response to domestic abuse, recognising a form of psychological abuse which had heretofore not been punishable. The offence reflects the enhanced understanding of domestic abuse as involving much more than physical violence, recognising the significant harms inflicted by controlling and coercive behaviours. However, recognition of coercive control as a crime in legislation is just the first step in effectively tackling this form of domestic abuse. Given the complexity of coercive control, much work is required to ensure that the offence is appropriately investigated and prosecuted, not least because AGS are required to investigate the totality of a relationship in order to

---

149 A 'relevant person' is: (a) the spouse or civil partner of that other person, or (b) not the spouse or civil partner of that other person and is not related to that other person within a prohibited degree of relationship but is or was in an intimate relationship with that other person: s 39(4).

150 s 39(2).

151 s 39(3).

gather sufficient evidence to prosecute. Investigating the presence of controlling behaviour within a relationship is much more challenging than investigating a violent incident like an assault.

Irish domestic abuse service providers interviewed by Stephanie Thompson et al highlighted that the dynamics of coercive control must be fully understood if cases are to be effectively investigated, stressing that coercive control is '"not a single incident crime" and that the "cumulative impact" on the victim needs to be recognised'.[152] Interviewees also recognised the potential for evidential difficulties in practice, emphasising that evidence must be gathered effectively from a variety of sources to ensure that there is sufficient evidence to support the prosecution and that the sole evidence is not the victim's testimony.[153] Consequently, training and awareness-raising about the dynamics and signs of coercive control are vital for all criminal justice system stakeholders involved in the investigation, prosecution and trial of coercive control offences. Further, appropriate resourcing is essential to allow for effective evidence-gathering and investigation of this complex crime.

4.2 Sentencing for offences related to domestic abuse

Section 40 of the DVA 2018 provides that the relationship between the defendant and the victim should be an aggravating factor when sentencing for certain offences. The relationships covered by this provision are those between current and former spouses and civil partners[154] and persons who are or were in an intimate relationship.[155] This is a significant development as historically offences committed within intimate relationships were often trivialised because they occurred in a private context between individuals who were known to each other. The offences covered by s 40 include:

(a) an offence under sections 2 to 15 of the Non-Fatal Offences against the Person Act 1997 (i.e. assault offences, syringe offences, coercion, harassment, demands for payment of debt causing alarm, poisoning, endangerment, endangering traffic and false imprisonment);

---

152 Stephanie Thompson et al, '"A welcome change . . . but early days": Irish Service Provider Perspectives on Domestic Abuse and the Domestic Violence Act 2018' (2022) Criminology and Criminal Justice https://doi.org/10.1177/17488958211067912 ,4 [last accessed 2 August 2023].

153 ibid.

154 s 40 refers to spouses and civil partners but for the purposes of the DVA 2018, this includes former spouses and civil partners: see s 2(1).

155 s 40(6).

(aa) an offence under section 2 or 3 of the Harassment, Harmful Communications and Related Offences Act 2020;[156]
(b) any offence which involves violence or the threat of violence to a person other than an offence in the Non-Fatal Offences against the Person Act 1997 or coercive control;
(c) rape;
(d) rape under section 4 of the Criminal Law (Rape)(Amendment) Act 1990;
(e) sexual assault;
(f) aggravated sexual assault, or;
(g) any offence of attempting or conspiring to commit, or aiding or abetting, counselling or procuring or inciting the commission of the foregoing offences.

Section 40 requires a court to impose a sentence which is greater than that which would have been imposed if the defendant was not a current or former spouse, civil partner or intimate partner of the victim.[157] This applies unless the court considers that there are exceptional circumstances justifying a different approach.[158] However, the sentence cannot be greater than the maximum sentence permissible for the relevant offence.[159] Section 40 recognises that the commission of an offence in the context of domestic abuse is especially harmful because of the abuse of trust within which it occurs, as well as the likelihood that such offences have taken place in the context of a pattern of abuse, harassment and intimidation which may have occurred over a sustained period.

5. Critical Thinking Point: Does Current Irish Legislation and Policy Achieve an Appropriate Balance Between Civil and Criminal Law Responses to Domestic Abuse?

In 21st century Ireland, it can no longer be said that domestic abuse is viewed as a private problem occurring behind closed doors. However, as noted above, domestic abuse still tends to be dealt with as a private matter because the predominant legal response remains centred on victims seeking protection in the civil family law courts via applications for orders under the DVA 2018. The criminal law developments in the DVA 2018 outlined above, particularly the criminalisation of coercive control, mark a shift towards greater recognition of the importance of appropriate criminal justice system responses to domestic abuse. However, it is

[156] As inserted by s 11 of the Harassment, Harmful Communications and Related Offences Act 2020.
[157] s 40(2).
[158] s 40(3).
[159] s 40(4).

questionable whether Irish legislation and policy is currently achieving an appropriate balance between civil and criminal law responses in this area.

Due to the very specific features of domestic abuse, strengthening criminal justice system responses is complicated. Perhaps most notably because many victims have complex reasons for not wanting to support a criminal prosecution of their partners, former partners or relatives. For example, they may feel that it is a private family matter, which they would prefer to deal with in the family law courts, or they may not want to see a partner, former partner or relative imprisoned. For victims who consider making a formal complaint and supporting a criminal prosecution, the fact that this necessitates engaging with the criminal justice system in addition to pursuing protection via the family law courts may act as a disincentive, requiring them to navigate two court systems at a time of significant trauma and disruption in their personal lives.[160] Ultimately, the primary concern for victims is seeking protection and many will understandably focus their efforts on this, rather than on supporting a criminal prosecution of their abuser.

There are also broader policy reasons why, despite recent developments in the DVA 2018, Irish criminal law offers a somewhat blunt response to domestic abuse. Existing criminal legislation such as the Non-Fatal Offences against the Person Act 1997 was introduced 'to deal with problems of stranger violence and public order and is based on physical violence that is typically committed in public by one man against another'.[161] Thus, it is not necessarily suited to the prosecution of domestic abuse, which occurs in private spaces, is committed by individuals who are or were in intimate relationships with or related to their victims and usually involves a pattern of behaviour over a period of time, rather than a single incident such as in a typical prosecution for a criminal offence. In domestic abuse cases, this can raise issues for the presentation of evidence as the use of traditional offence categories requires the prosecution of single incidents of, for example, assault or sexual assault. This approach obscures 'the nuances and complexity of domestic abuse' and does not allow 'courts ... to "see" the systematic nature of abuse'.[162] This fails to accurately represent the reality of domestic abuse and may in turn ultimately impact on the likely success of the prosecution.

---

160 Nuala Egan and Ellen O'Malley Dunlop, *A Report on the Intersection of the Criminal Justice, Private Family Law and Public Law Child Care Processes in Relation to Domestic and Sexual Violence* (2023) available https://www.nwci.ie/images/uploads/NWC_DoJ_DSV_Justice_Report.pdf [last accessed 2 August 2023]. Chapter 3.

161 Charlotte Bishop, 'Domestic Violence: The Limitations of a Legal Response' in Sarah Hilder and Vanessa Bettinson, eds, *Domestic Violence: Interdisciplinary Perspectives on Protection, Prevention and Intervention* (Palgrave MacMillan 2016), 65.

162 Victor Tadros, 'The Distinctiveness of Domestic Abuse: A Freedom Based Account' (2005) 65(3) Louisiana Law Review 989, 996.

Appropriate balancing of civil and criminal law responses to domestic abuse is not straightforward and there is more work to be done in this area in Ireland. Victims must have the protection of civil orders and for many this will be the only legal intervention they seek. However, it is important in order to continue to develop the criminal law response to domestic abuse, to maximise the potential for victims who wish to pursue formal complaints and criminal prosecution for the harm they have experienced to feel empowered to do so.

One way of achieving this would be to introduce a specific offence of domestic abuse rather than coercive control, which would encompasses all the forms of abuse which victims experience, allowing for prosecution of the totality of the harm to be prosecuted within one offence.[163] The creation of such an offence would serve an important symbolic function, signalling clearly that domestic abuse in all forms is a crime which is taken seriously by the State. It would also overcome some of the challenges encountered when using existing offence categories which are not suited to the complexities of domestic abuse and create obstacles to effective prosecutions. In addition to legislative change, procedural and practical improvements within the legal system may also assist those victims who wish to engage with the criminal justice system. The optimum way to achieve this would be reforming court procedures so that victims could pursue both protection and prosecution within one system, for example, by the creation of unified/specialist domestic abuse courts. Admittedly, the development of such a system would not be straightforward and is necessarily a long-term objective. However, in the mean-time, there are many ways in which victims who wish to engage with the criminal justice system may be supported and empowered to do so, for example, by ensuring that victims always have access to appropriate advice and support from both AGS and relevant support organisations.

6. Summary

- The DVA 2018 provides a range of five types of civil orders which offer protection to victims of domestic abuse: protection orders, safety orders, barring orders, interim barring orders and emergency barring orders.
- The eligibility criteria for safety orders and protection orders are broad encompassing a diverse approach to family life. The criteria for barring orders and interim barring orders are narrower and moreover, the court cannot issue an interim barring order for

[163] For a discussion of the introduction of an offence of domestic abuse in Ireland, see: Susan Leahy, 'What Is Next for Irish Law and Policy on Domestic Abuse?: Lessons from our Neighbours' (2022) 25(4) Irish Journal of Family Law 65, 69-70.

cohabitants or the parents of adult children unless their legal or beneficial interest in the property is greater than or equal to that of the respondent.

- The emergency barring order provides temporary protection to victims who do not hold a sufficient legal or beneficial interest in their home to have an abuser barred from a property.
- Safety, protection and barring orders under the DVA 2018 are granted where there is reasonable cause to believe that the safety or welfare of the applicant requires such an order to be made. For interim or emergency barring orders immediate risk of significant harm must be shown.
- Breach of a civil order made under the DVA 2018 gives rise to criminal liability. Further, AGS have the power to arrest without warrant where it is suspected that an order has been breached. This provides important protection for victims who are in situations of immediate danger.
- Applicants for domestic abuse orders are entitled to certain supports and protections during applications for civil orders. These include prohibiting respondents from personally cross-examining the applicant and permitting the applicant to give evidence by television link where this is necessary. Applicants are also entitled to be accompanied by a support person of their choice during proceedings.
- The offence of coercive control, for the first time in Irish law, imposes specific criminal liability for the harms encompassed in domestic abuse. The DVA 2018 also addresses sentencing for offences relating to domestic abuse.

7. Further reading

Government of Ireland, *Zero Tolerance: Third National Strategy on Domestic, Sexual & Gender-Based Violence 2022-2026* (Government of Ireland 2022).

Susan Leahy, 'What Is Next for Irish Law and Policy on Domestic Abuse?: Lessons from our Neighbours' (2022) 25(4) Irish Journal of Family Law 65.

Susan Leahy, 'Still a Private Matter? Evaluating the Irish State's Response to Domestic Abuse' (2023) 37(1) International Journal of Law, Policy and the Family, https://doi.org/10.1093/lawfam/ebad008.

Stephanie Thompson et al, '"A welcome change . . . but early days": Irish Service Provider Perspectives on Domestic Abuse and the Domestic Violence Act 2018' (2022) Criminology and Criminal Justice https://doi.org/10.1177/17488958211067912 [last accessed 2 August 2023].

Cassandra Weiner, 'Seeing What is 'Invisible in Plain Sight': Policing Coercive Control' (2017) 56(4) Howard Journal of Crime and Justice 500-515.

Nuala Egan and Ellen O'Malley Dunlop, *A Report on the Intersection of the Criminal Justice, Private Family Law and Public Law Child Care Processes in Relation to Domestic and Sexual Violence* (2023) available https://www.nwci.ie/images/uploads/NWC_DoJ_DSV_Justice_Report.pdf.

Chapter 8

Children's Rights within Family Law

Lydia Bracken

LEARNING OBJECTIVES

By the end of this chapter, students will be equipped to:

- Identify the sources of children's rights in international and national law.
- Examine whether the United Nations Convention on the Rights of the Child adequately protects children's rights.
- Evaluate the significance of Article 42A of the Irish Constitution.

CRITICAL THINKING POINTS

- (How) can 'protection' and 'participation' be reconciled in children's rights?
- Has Article 42A.2.1° of the Irish Constitution changed the threshold for state intervention in family decision-making?

1. Introduction

Children's rights are the range of civil, political, social, economic and cultural rights that apply to children. Children's rights are part of the broader human rights framework but are regarded as a distinct category of rights,[1] which acknowledges that children are differently situated to adults and therefore the recognition of children as rights holders raises unique considerations. In this chapter, these considerations are unpacked through an examination of the protection of children's rights at international level in the United Nations Convention on the Rights of the Child (UNCRC), at European level in the European Convention on Human Rights (ECHR), at national level in the Irish Constitution, particularly Article 42A, and in legislation. It will be shown that these instruments protect both the individual rights of children and the rights of children as a group within society.

The chapter involves consideration of two international instruments:

[1] Jaap E Doek, 'The Human Rights of Children: An Introduction' in Ursula Kilkelly and Ton Liefaard (eds), *International Human Rights of Children* (Springer 2019) 25.

the UNCRC and the ECHR. At the outset, therefore, it is important to note that when a State ratifies (formally consents to) an international treaty or convention, it agrees to be legally bound by its terms. However, under Ireland's dualist system of international law,[2] an international treaty or convention does not automatically become part of Irish law upon ratification. Instead, the international treaty or convention must be specifically incorporated into Irish law by the Oireachtas in order for it to have legal effect in domestic law. Although Ireland has ratified the UNCRC, that Convention has not been incorporated into Irish law and so its provisions are not directly enforceable in Ireland. The UNCRC has, however, influenced the development of Irish domestic law in many ways as detailed in this chapter. In contrast to the UNCRC, the ECHR has been specifically incorporated into Irish law at a sub-constitutional level by the European Convention on Human Rights Act 2003.

2. United Nations Convention on the Rights of the Child

The United Nations Convention on the Rights of the Child (UNCRC) was adopted by the United Nations General Assembly on 20 November 1989. Ireland ratified the UNCRC on 21 September 1992. The UNCRC has become the most widely ratified human rights treaty in the world; the only country that has not ratified it is the United States of America.[3]

The UNCRC was not the first international instrument to protect the rights of the child,[4] but it is more wide-ranging than those that had come before. The earlier treaties had focused on the child's need for care and protection without recognising that children themselves are rights holders. The UNCRC thus brought about a new perspective that centralises the rights of the child and recognises their evolving capacity to exercise their rights. For the purpose of the UNCRC a child is defined as a person under the age of 18 years unless the law applicable to the child recognises them as an adult at an earlier age.[5]

The rights protected by the UNCRC are comprehensive and relate to all aspects of the child's life. Often, the rights protected by the UNCRC are described as covering 'the three Ps' of provision, protection, and

---

2 For discussion of international law in Ireland, see Raymond Byrne, Paul McCutcheon, Laura Cahillane and Emma Roche-Cagney, *Byrne and McCutcheon on the Irish Legal System* (7th edn, Bloomsbury Professional 2020) 939–945.

3 UN Treaty Body Database, 'Ratification Status for CRC–Convention on the Rights of the Child' < https://tbinternet.ohchr.org/_layouts/15/TreatyBodyExternal/Treaty.aspx?Treaty=CRC&Lang=en> [last accessed 17 November 2022].

4 The UNCRC was preceded by the Geneva Declaration on the Rights of the Child 1924; the Declaration on the Rights of the Child 1948; and the Declaration of the Rights of the Child 1959.

5 UNCRC, art 1. This article does not specify when childhood begins.

participation,[6] although this categorisation has been criticised for depicting children's rights as something very different to the human rights of adults.[7] The UNCRC recognises children as rights holders, but it does not present children's rights as existing in a vacuum, nor does it disregard the important role played by parents and the family. In fact, the Preamble to the UNCRC recognises the family 'as the fundamental group of society and the natural environment for the growth and well-being of all its members and particularly children'[8] and various articles recognise the rights of parents[9] and the importance of family to children and to the protection of their rights.[10]

The UNCRC is overseen by the Committee on the Rights of the Child, a group of 18 independent experts.[11] The Committee monitors States' compliance with the UNCRC through a reporting process, which is detailed in art 44 of the UNCRC. States are required to submit an initial report within two years of ratifying the UNCRC, and thereafter to submit a report every five years. The reports detail the State's progress on implementing UNCRC rights. Following consideration of the State report, the Committee issues recommendations to the State in the form of 'concluding observations'. The Committee can also issue 'general comments', which contain general guidance for States on the interpretation and implementation of UNCRC rights. Often, these general comments are published following consideration of a particular matter at a 'day of general discussion' (DGD).[12]

2.1 Guiding principles

Implementation of the rights provided for in the UNCRC is guided by four **guiding principles** that support the interpretation of the other provisions. The guiding principles are also free-standing rights. The four guiding principles are: non-discrimination (art 2); the best interests of the child (art 3); life, survival and development (art 6); and the voice of the child (art 12).

---

6 Thomas Hammarberg, 'The UN Convention on the Rights of the Child—And How to Make it Work' (1990) 12 Human Rights Quarterly 97. For discussion of different categorisations of children's rights, see Jane Fortin, *Children's Rights and the Developing Law* (Cambridge University Press 2009) 15–17.

7 Ann Quennerstedt, 'Children, but not really humans? Critical reflections on the hampering effect of the "3 p's"' (2010) 18(4) The International Journal of Children's Rights 619, 630.

8 UNCRC, Preamble.

9 See, for example, UNCRC, arts 5, 14, 18.

10 See, for example, UNCRC, arts 7, 8, 9, 10, 16, 20, 29.

11 UNCRC, art 43.

12 For more information on the role of the Committee on the Rights of the Child, see United Nations, 'Committee on the Rights of the Child' available at https://www.ohchr.org/en/treaty-bodies/crc [last accessed 2 August 2023].

2.1.1 Article 2 of the UNCRC

Key provision – Article 2 of the UNCRC

1. States Parties shall respect and ensure the rights set forth in the present Convention to each child within their jurisdiction without discrimination of any kind, irrespective of the child's or his or her parent's or legal guardian's race, colour, sex, language, religion, political or other opinion, national, ethnic or social origin, property, disability, birth or other status.

2. States Parties shall take all appropriate measures to ensure that the child is protected against all forms of discrimination or punishment on the basis of the status, activities, expressed opinions, or beliefs of the child's parents, legal guardians, or family members.

Article 2 of the UNCRC prohibits discrimination against children across specified areas and incudes a final catch all proviso that prohibits discrimination on any 'other status'. The article places a positive obligation on States to take steps to protect children from discrimination that is based on any of these statuses or arises because of the status, activities, expressed opinions, or beliefs of the child's parents, legal guardians, or family members.

2.1.2 Article 3 of the UNCRC

Key provision – Article 3 of the UNCRC

1. In all actions concerning children, whether undertaken by public or private social welfare institutions, courts of law, administrative authorities or legislative bodies, the best interests of the child shall be a primary consideration.

2. States Parties undertake to ensure the child such protection and care as is necessary for his or her well-being, taking into account the rights and duties of his or her parents, legal guardians, or other individuals legally responsible for him or her, and, to this end, shall take all appropriate legislative and administrative measures.

3. States Parties shall ensure that the institutions, services and facilities responsible for the care or protection of children shall conform with the standards established by competent authorities, particularly in the areas of safety, health, in the number and suitability of their staff, as well as competent supervision.

Article 3 of the UNCRC requires that the best interests of the child are **a primary consideration** in all actions concerning them. By applying to 'all actions concerning children', the remit of the best interests principle is expansive, but as a primary consideration, it is but one factor to be taken into account in determining the outcome of a decision.[13] There are other mentions of the best interests of children elsewhere in the UNCRC where greater weight is afforded to the principle. For example, in the specific context of adoption, art 21 of the UNCRC requires that the best interests of the child are 'the paramount consideration'. This stronger formulation is justified on the basis that art 21 of the UNCRC is limited to the specific area of adoption, whereas art 3 of the UNCRC has broader application.

According to the Committee on the Rights of the Child, the body that monitors implementation of the UNCRC, the best interests principle is a threefold concept: it is a substantive right; a fundamental interpretative legal principle; and a rule of procedure.[14] There is no fixed definition of best interests, instead the principle is a dynamic concept that requires individualised consideration of the specific circumstances of each child or group of children.[15] To guide the application of the principle, the Committee suggests that the following elements could be included in a best-interests assessment: the child's views; the child's identity; preservation of the family environment and maintaining relations; care, protection and safety of the child; situation of vulnerability; the child's right to health; and the child's right to education. Other factors should also be considered where relevant.[16]

The best interests principle is often criticised for being a vague and indeterminate standard that leaves considerable discretion to the decision-maker to determine what is best for the child.[17] The threefold construction of the principle proposed by the Committee adds a layer of transparency to the decision-making process and the proposed list of factors helps to guide the decision-making, thereby reducing (but not eliminating) the subjectivity of the best interests assessment. At the same time, it should be noted that some authors regard the unfixed nature of the best interests principle as its main strength since the absence of a strict definition permits flexibility and individualised decision-making in respect of children.[18]

---

[13] Committee on the Rights of the Child, *General comment No. 14 (2013) on the right of the child to have his or her best interests taken as a primary consideration (art. 3, para. 1)* CRC/C/GC/14, [38].

[14] ibid [6].

[15] ibid [48].

[16] ibid [53]–[79].

[17] Robert Mnookin, 'Child-Custody Adjudication: Judicial functions in the face of Indeterminacy' (1975) 39 Law and Contemporary Problems 226; Helen Reece, 'The Paramountcy Principle: Consensus or Construct?' (1996) 49 Current Legal Problems 267.

[18] Elaine E. Sutherland, 'Article 3 of the United Nations Convention on the Rights of the Child: The Challenges of Vagueness and Priorities' in Elaine E. Sutherland and

2.1.3 Article 6 of the UNCRC

Key provision – Article 6 of the UNCRC

1. States Parties recognize that every child has the inherent right to life.

2. States Parties shall ensure to the maximum extent possible the survival and development of the child.

Article 6 of the UNCRC encompasses three separate rights: the right to life, the right to survival and the right to development. It has been noted that while there is no hierarchy among the four guiding principles of the UNCRC, none of the other rights could be exercised without the right to life.[19] Protection of the right to life gives rise to both negative obligations (the State cannot unlawfully take away life) and positive obligations (the State must take action to protect life).

The rights of survival and development do not appear in other UN human rights treaties and are, therefore, unique to children's rights.[20] These aspects are interpreted broadly to encompass a holistic understanding of the 'physical, mental, moral, spiritual and social dimensions' of children's development.[21]

2.1.4 Article 12 of the UNCRC

Key provision – Article 12 of the UNCRC

1. States Parties shall assure to the child who is capable of forming his or her own views the right to express those views freely in all matters affecting the child, the views of the child being given due weight in accordance with the age and maturity of the child.

2. For this purpose, the child shall in particular be provided the opportunity to be heard in any judicial and administrative proceedings affecting the child, either directly, or through a representative or an appropriate body, in a manner consistent with the procedural rules of national law.

Lesley-Anne Barnes Macfarlane (eds), *Implementing Article 3 of the United Nations Convention on the Rights of the Child* (Cambridge University Press 2016) 36; Lydia Bracken, *Same-Sex Parenting and the Best Interests Principle* (Cambridge University Press 2020) 28.

19 Ursula Kilkelly, *Children's Rights in Ireland: Law, Policy and Practice* (Tottel Publishing 2008) 27.

20 Noam Peleg, 'International Children's Rights Law: General Principles' in Kilkelly and Liefaard (n 1) 146.

21 Committee on the Rights of the Child, *General comment No 15 (2013) on the right of the child to the enjoyment of the highest attainable standard of health (art. 24)* CRC/C/GC/15, [16].

Article 12 of the UNCRC gives rise to two related rights: the right of every child who is capable of expressing a view to do so in any matter that affects them and the subsequent right for those views to be given due weight in line with the child's age and maturity.[22] The provision recognises that children have important perspectives that should be considered in decision-making and in the creation of law and policy.[23]

Article 12 of the UNCRC refers to children who are *capable* of forming their own views. There is an obligation on States to assess the capacity of the child in this area and States are encouraged to start from a presumption that the child has capacity to express their views.[24] States should not set a minimum age at which children are deemed capable of forming their own views; capacity should be assessed on a case-by-case basis. This recognises that children can form and express views at a very young age and that expression may take non-verbal forms such as play or body language.

After the child has expressed their view, Article 12 of the UNCRC requires that the decision-maker gives that view due weight in line with the child's age and maturity. The assessment of age and maturity must take place on a case-by-case basis and age alone should not be determinative of the weight afforded to the child's views. Instead, the decision-maker should focus on whether the child is able to understand the implications of a particular matter.[25]

2.2 Critical thinking point: (How) can protection and participation be reconciled in children's rights?

There is a tension within children's rights between the need to protect children and the need to promote their capacity for self-determination. It is sometimes said that it is paternalistic for adults to decide what is best for children under the best interests principle, in particular where the adult determination conflicts with the child's own views.[26] Yet, this paternalism may be considered necessary or indeed inevitable by some authors in light of children's legal and political status.[27]

The Committee on the Rights of the Child has made it clear that the best

---

[22] Committee on the Rights of the Child, *General Comment No. 12 (2009) The right of the child to be heard CRC/C/GC/12,* [15].

[23] ibid [12].

[24] ibid [20].

[25] ibid [30].

[26] Jane Fortin, *Children's Rights and the Developing Law* (Cambridge University Press 2009) 19; Aoife Daly, *Children, autonomy and the courts: Beyond the right to be heard* (Brill 2017) 7.

[27] Fortin, ibid 19–22.

interests of the child cannot be ascertained without first hearing the child's views. In this way, it could be argued that the right to participate in Article 12 of the UNCRC mitigates against the alleged paternalism of the best interests principle by giving children a voice in the decision about their best interests.[28] There is a tension, however, between the laudable goal of participation and its realisation in practice. Article 12 of the UNCRC is based on the premise that children do not have full autonomy.[29] While ideas of participation acknowledge that children's autonomy increases as they grow up (in line with the concept of evolving capacities[30]), participation does not equate to autonomy, nor does it give children the ability to determine the outcome of the decision that is being made about them. Instead, vindication of the right to participate remains highly contingent on the adult decision-maker who retains the power.[31]

Under Article 12 of the UNCRC, not only do the adults decide which children are capable of expressing a view (albeit they are encouraged to start from a presumption of capacity), they also decide how much weight to give those views when they are expressed. There is a concern that the right to participate may be rendered tokenistic in this approach, particularly where the child's views are overridden.[32] The Lundy Model of Participation is widely regarded as an advantageous approach for facilitating children's participation that addresses some of these concerns. This model is based on four inter-related elements: space, voice, audience and influence.[33] The model is endorsed within Irish policy[34] and has been adopted by Ireland's Child and Family Agency (Tusla) as a core practice model.[35]

2.3 Optional protocols

The text of the UNCRC is supplemented by three Optional Protocols that add to the obligations contained in the Convention: the Optional Protocol to the Convention on the Rights of the Child on the involvement of children in armed conflict (OPAC); the Optional Protocol to the Convention on the Rights of the Child on the sale of children, child prostitution and

---

28 Peleg (n 20) 148.
29 Committee on the Rights of the Child (n 22) [1].
30 UNCRC, art 5.
31 Peleg (n 20), 149; Daly (n 26) 2.
32 Roger A Hart, *Children's Participation: From Tokenism to Citizenship* (Innocenti Essay No 4, UNICEF 1992).
33 Laura Lundy, '"Voice" is not enough: conceptualising Article 12 of the United Nations Convention on the Rights of the Child' (2007) 33 British Educational Research Journal 927.
34 National Strategy on Children and Young People's Participation in Decision-Making, 2015–2020.
35 Tusla, *Child and Youth Participation Strategy 2019–2023* (Child and Family Agency 2019) 7.

child pornography (OPSC); and the Optional Protocol to the Convention on the Rights of the Child on a communications procedure. The latter protocol created a complaints procedure in respect of alleged violations of children's rights under the UNCRC or under the first two Optional Protocols. The complaints, which are heard by the Committee on the Rights of the Child, can be submitted by or on behalf of individual children or groups of children (individual communications) or they can be made by a State against another State (inter-State communications). The Committee on the Rights of the Child can also initiate its own inquiry.[36] At the time of writing (June 2023), Ireland has ratified OPAC and the Optional Protocol on a communications procedure but has not yet ratified OPSC.

3. European Convention on Human Rights

The European Convention on Human Rights (ECHR) is a treaty of the Council of Europe that was adopted on 4 November 1950 and entered into force on 3 September 1953. The ECHR protects a range of civil and political rights, which are set out in the Convention itself and in its Protocols. The Convention is overseen by the European Court of Human Rights (ECtHR), which hears individual or state applications alleging violations of the rights set out in the ECHR.

Ireland ratified the ECHR in 1953. Since then, Ireland has been a respondent in a number of significant cases pertaining to family life including *Johnston v Ireland*,[37] which concerned the rights of non-marital children and *Keegan v Ireland*,[38] which concerned the rights of a non-marital father in respect of the adoption of his child. The ECHR was incorporated into Irish domestic law at a sub-constitutional level by the European Convention on Human Rights Act 2003. This Act requires the Irish courts to interpret and apply laws in a manner compatible with the ECHR and allows for the provisions of the ECHR to be argued before the Irish courts. As the incorporation of the ECHR took place at a sub-constitutional level, the Irish Constitution retains primacy over the ECHR such that if there is any conflict between the provisions of the two instruments, the Constitution takes precedence.

The ECHR does not contain any child-specific rights but since art 1 of the Convention affords rights to everyone, children benefit from the same ECHR rights as adults. This section focuses on art 8 of the ECHR, which protects the right to respect for private and family life, home and correspondence. Many cases concerning children's rights in family law

---

[36] Third Optional Protocol to the Convention on the Rights of the Child on a communications procedure, art 13.

[37] *Johnston v Ireland* App no 9697/92 (ECtHR, 18 December 1986).

[38] *Keegan v Ireland* App no 6969/90 (ECtHR, 26 May 1994).

arise under this article but it should be noted that all other ECHR rights are also relevant to children.[39]

Key provision – Article 8 of the ECHR

1. Everyone has the right to respect for his private and family life, his home and his correspondence.

2. There shall be no interference by a public authority with the exercise of this right except such as is in accordance with the law and is necessary in a democratic society in the interests of national security, public safety or the economic wellbeing of the country, for the prevention of disorder or crime, for the protection of health or morals, or for the protection of the rights and freedoms of others.

Article 8 of the ECHR primarily gives rise to a negative obligation whereby the State must refrain from arbitrarily interfering with private life, family life, home and correspondence, but it may also give rise to positive obligations where the State must take steps to protect the rights set out in the Article. It is important to note that not all interferences with private life, family life, home and correspondence will result in a violation of art 8 of the ECHR. In accordance with art 8(2) of the ECHR, interferences are permitted where these are in accordance with law and *necessary* to achieve one of the legitimate aims specified. In considering what is necessary in a particular case, the ECtHR will consider the proportionality of the response by balancing the interests of the State with the rights of the applicant. The ECtHR will also take into account the **margin of appreciation** that gives States a measure of discretion in their implementation of ECHR rights. The extent of the margin of appreciation to be afforded to the State will vary depending on the nature of the issues involved in a particular case. Usually, the margin will be wide where there is no European consensus on a particular matter or where the matter is found to concern a sensitive issue, such as the regulation of surrogacy[40] or the legal recognition of same sex relationships.[41]

Many cases concerning children's rights in family law are taken under the family life limb of art 8 of the ECHR, although the earlier case law tended to focus on the rights of the parents rather than the rights of the child.[42]

39 For an examination of the jurisprudence of the European Court of Human Rights in relation to children, see Claire Fenton-Glynn, *Children and the European Court of Human Rights* (Oxford University Press 2021).

40 See, for example, *Paradiso and Campanelli v Italy* App No 25358/12 (ECtHR, 24 January 2017).

41 See, for example, *Gas and Dubois v France* App No 25951/07 (ECtHR, 15 March 2012).

42 Lydia Bracken and Conor O'Mahony, 'The Child's Right to Family Life: Shifting Sands and Social Science' in Philip Czech, Lisa Heschi, Karin Lukas Manfred Nowak and Gerd Oberleitner (eds), *European Yearbook on Human Rights 2020* (Intersentia 2020) 82–83.

More recently, the ECtHR has shown a greater willingness to focus on the rights of the child, which is helped in many cases by the addition of the child as an applicant to the proceedings.

Family life for the purpose of art 8 of the ECHR is a question of fact that depends on the existence of close personal ties. It encompasses marital, non-marital and cohabiting relationships between adults and focuses on the quality and duration of the relationship rather than simply whether a marriage has occurred.[43] Family life under art 8 of the ECHR has been found to exist between parents and their children regardless of the marital status of the parents[44] and whether or not there is a genetic relationship between the parents and child.[45] Family life can also extend to relationships between children and extended family members.[46] In this way, the concept of family life under art 8 of the ECHR is much broader than the Irish constitutional definition of the 'Family' as discussed in Chapter 1.

4. Irish Constitution

Article 42A of the Irish Constitution provides express protection for the rights of the child. This Article was inserted into the Irish Constitution in 2015 following the so-called 'children's rights referendum' that took place in 2012.[47] In some areas, the language adopted in Article 42A is similar to that used in provisions of the UNCRC but it should be noted that Article 42A does not make the UNCRC part of Ireland's domestic law – in line with Ireland's dualist approach to international law, the UNCRC would need to be specifically incorporated into Irish law in order for this to occur.

---

43 *Marckx v Belgium* App No 6833/74 (ECtHR, 13 June 1979); *Johnston v Ireland* App No 9697/92 (ECtHR, 18 December 1986).

44 *Marckx v Belgium* App No 6833/74 (ECtHR, 13 June 1979).

45 *Valdís Fjölnisdóttir and Others v Iceland* App No 71552/17 (ECtHR, 18 May 2021).

46 *Boyle v United Kingdom* App No 16580/90 (ECtHR, 28 February 1994).

47 The result of the referendum was subsequently (unsuccessfully) challenged in the case of *Jordan v Minister for Children and Youth Affairs* [2015] IESC 33, which delayed insertion of Article 42A into the Constitution.

Key provision – Article 42A of the Constitution

1 The State recognises and affirms the natural and imprescriptible rights of all children and shall, as far as practicable, by its laws protect and vindicate those rights.

2 1° In exceptional cases, where the parents, regardless of their marital status, fail in their duty towards their children to such extent that the safety or welfare of any of their children is likely to be prejudicially affected, the State as guardian of the common good shall, by proportionate means as provided by law, endeavour to supply the place of the parents, but always with due regard for the natural and imprescriptible rights of the child.

2° Provision shall be made by law for the adoption of any child where the parents have failed for such a period of time as may be prescribed by law in their duty towards the child and where the best interests of the child so require.

3 Provision shall be made by law for the voluntary placement for adoption and the adoption of any child.

4 1° Provision shall be made by law that in the resolution of all proceedings—

i brought by the State, as guardian of the common good, for the purpose of preventing the safety and welfare of any child from being prejudicially affected, or

ii concerning the adoption, guardianship or custody of, or access to, any child,

the best interests of the child shall be the paramount consideration.

2° Provision shall be made by law for securing, as far as practicable, that in all proceedings referred to in subsection 1° of this section in respect of any child who is capable of forming his or her own views, the views of the child shall be ascertained and given due weight having regard to the age and maturity of the child.

In the case of *In the Matter of JJ*, the Supreme Court noted that the objective of the new Article 42A 'was not a single clear-cut reversal of the direction of the law … but rather a more wide-ranging, though subtle, change to the posture of the Constitution in relation to child and family matters'.[48] The subtlety of the change is impacted by the fact

[48] *In the Matter of JJ* [2021] IESC 1 [130] [hereinafter '*JJ*'].

that Article 42A does not stand alone and must be read in line with the existing Articles 41 and 42 of the Constitution, which give a preference to the marital family as discussed in Chapter 1.

The following sections explain the main features of each subsection of Article 42A.

4.1 The natural and imprescriptible rights of all children

The recognition of children as rights-holders is not a new concept under the Irish Constitution. Under Article 42, children have always benefitted from rights pertaining to education and under the older Article 42.5 (which was deleted from the Constitution upon the insertion of Article 42A), there was a reference to 'the natural and imprescriptible rights of the child' thereby providing an express acknowledgement of children's rights in the text of the Constitution. This provision, however, only applied in the context of state intervention in the family and thus the reference to the rights of the child in this Article was limited in application.

Children also benefited (and continue to benefit) from certain unenumerated (unwritten) rights under Article 40.3 of the Constitution, the personal rights guarantee. For example, in *G v An Bord Uchtála* O'Higgins CJ found that:

> The child also has natural rights ... [he or she] has the right to be fed and to live, to be reared and educated, to have the opportunity of working and of realising his or her full personality and dignity as a human being.[49]

In addition, a marital child benefits from the rights associated with membership of a constitutional family under Article 41 of the Constitution.[50]

In this way, the recognition of the natural and imprescriptible rights of all children in Article 42A.1 has not radically altered Irish law, but the reference to *all* children is notable because it clarifies that, notwithstanding the protection afforded to the marital family in Articles 41 and 42, the State is obliged to protect the rights of *all* children regardless of whether their parents are married or unmarried. Article 42A.1 does not, however, specify what exactly the natural and imprescriptible rights of the child are.

---

[49] *G v An Bord Uchtála* [1980] IR 32, 55. See also *DG v Eastern Health Board* [1997] 3 IR 511, 537; *North Western Health Board v HW* [2001] 3 IR 622, 727 where the courts expanded upon this list of unenumerated rights.

[50] *In Re JH* [1985] IR 375; *N v Health Service Executive* [2006] 4 IR 374.

4.2 Exceptional cases where parents fail in their duty towards their children

In general, parents have broad autonomy to make decisions in respect of their children. However, in the exceptional cases detailed in Article 42A.2.1°, the State is required to supply the place of the parents. For example, a child may need to be removed from the family and taken into state care where their safety or welfare so requires. When the State 'suppl[ies] the place of parents', it takes on 'not only the parental duty to educate but also the parental duty to cater for the other personal rights of the child'.[51]

Article 42A.2.1° replaced the older Article 42.5, which has now been deleted from the Constitution. There are some clear textual differences between the two Articles, but an on-going discussion point is whether the *threshold* for state intervention has changed under the new Article.

4.3 Critical thinking point: Has Article 42A.2.1° of the Irish Constitution changed the threshold for state intervention in family decision-making?

Much of the impetus for Ireland's children's rights referendum emerged from concerns that the threshold for state intervention in the family as originally provided for in Article 42.5 of the Constitution was too high and created situations where the State was not able to intervene in order to protect children's welfare.[52] In particular, criticism was directed at cases concerning the marital family where the case law established a constitutional presumption that the welfare of the child is met by his or her married parents with a high threshold required to rebut that presumption.[53]

From the outset, scholars have been divided on whether Article 42A.2.1° alters the threshold for state intervention in family decision making when compared to the older Article 42.5.[54] The now-deleted Article 42.5 provided:

> In exceptional cases, where the parents for physical or moral

---

51 *In Re Article 26 of the Constitution and the Adoption (No. 2) Bill, 1987* [1989] IR 656, 663.

52 Conor O'Mahony, 'The Same, but Different? Article 42A and the Threshold for State Intervention in Family Life: In Re JJ' (2022) 4 Irish Supreme Court Review 141, 141.

53 Lydia Bracken, *Child Law in Ireland* (Clarus Press 2018) 36.

54 See for example the differing views of Oran Doyle and David Kenny, 'Constitutional Change and Interest Group Politics: Ireland's Children's Rights Referendum' in Richard Albert, Xenephon Contiades and Alkmene Fotiadou (eds), *The Foundations and Traditions of Constitutional Amendment* (Hart Publishing 2017) 199–218 and Maria Corbett, 'The Children's Referendum is a Game-Changer for Children's Rights in Ireland' (2012) 15(4) Irish Journal of Family Law 95, 97.

> reasons fail in their duty towards their children, the State as guardian of the common good, by appropriate means shall endeavour to supply the place of the parents, but always with due regard for the natural and imprescriptible rights of the child.

Article 42A.2.1° now provides:

> In exceptional cases, where the parents, **regardless of their marital status**, fail in their duty towards their children **to such extent that the safety or welfare of any of their children is likely to be prejudicially affected**, the State as guardian of the common good shall, **by proportionate means as provided by law**, endeavour to supply the place of the parents, but always with due regard for the natural and imprescriptible rights of the child.

There are three main textual differences between Article 42A.2.1° and Article 42.5 highlighted in bold text above. First, Article 42A.2.1° makes it clear that it applies irrespective of the marital status of the parents and so the same test is to be applied to intervention in the decisions of marital and non-marital families. There is some disagreement in the literature as to whether the older Article 42.5 applied to non-marital families,[55] but regardless of the older position, Article 42A.2.1° clarifies the current approach, that is that the same test applies irrespective of the parents' marital status. It should be noted, however, that this provision does not affect the constitutional presumption as to the welfare of the child being met within the marital family: since Article 42A must continue to be read alongside Articles 41 and 42, it is likely that this constitutional presumption will continue to apply to marital families only.

Second, Article 42A.2.1° makes reference to 'proportionality' whereas Article 42.5 contained the word 'appropriate'. These words are generally understood to relate to the same requirement, that is that the restriction on the rights of the family brought about by state intervention must not go beyond that required to achieve the aim of protecting the rights of the child.

Third, in the context of parental failure, Article 42A.2.1° removes the words 'for physical or moral reasons' that had been included in Article 42.5 and adds a requirement that the failure of parental duty must be 'to such extent that the safety or welfare of any of their children is likely to be prejudicially affected'. In *JJ,* the Supreme Court considered that these changes of wording resulted in a 'significant change of focus from the *cause* of parental failure to its *effect*' such that blameworthiness is no

---

[55] See, for example, the differing views of Geoffrey Shannon, *Child and Family Law* (3rd edn, Round Hall 2020), 19 and O'Mahony (n 52) 146.

longer a feature of the test for state intervention.[56] Instead, the question of parental failure is to be judged by reference to the consequence of any decision on the safety or welfare of the child.[57] Moreover, since the 'touchstone for state intervention' is prejudicial effect on the safety or welfare of a child, the Court was satisfied that the failure under Article 42A.2.1° can relate to a single incident or decision and need not be a 'persistent failure' of parental duty.[58]

Thus, the Supreme Court in *JJ* observed a different, arguably more child-centred approach for intervention under Article 42A.2.1° when compared to Article 42.5. However, the Court also acknowledged that 'the fact that parental failure is now specified as being of such an extent as to have an effect on safety or welfare...[describes] more clearly the type of failure which *would always have triggered State involvement*'.[59] If the type of failure specified in Article 42A.2.1° would have always allowed for state intervention under Article 42.5, it implies that the threshold for intervention has not in fact changed.[60]

Following *JJ*, commentators continue to advance different interpretations on whether the threshold for state intervention has changed as a result of Article 42A.2.1.[61] Future case law will therefore be instructive in clarifying whether the threshold has in fact changed under Article 42A.2.1°. It also remains to be seen whether the older compelling reasons test[62] for state intervention has survived the enactment of Article 42A.2.1° as a separate basis for intervention in family decision-making – in *JJ*, the Supreme Court felt it unnecessary to consider this point.[63] Hence, it is unclear whether intervention for reasons other than parental failure is possible following the insertion of Article 42A into the Constitution. For all of these reasons, it is necessary to approach the older case law decided under Article 42.5 'with some caution not just because of the distinctions between the facts in such cases, but also because of the changes made to the Constitution'.[64]

4.4 Adoption where the parents fail in their duty

Article 42A.2.2° makes provision for the adoption of any child where the parents have failed in their duty towards them. This provision is relevant

56 *In the Matter of JJ* [2021] IESC 1 [134].
57 ibid [153].
58 ibid [135].
59 ibid [134] [emphasis added].
60 O'Mahony (n 52), 153.
61 See, for example Finn Keyes, 'Children's Rights and End of Life Decision-Making: In the Matter of JJ' (2021) 5(1) Irish Judicial Studies Journal 58, 70; O'Mahony (n 52).
62 This test had been referred to in older cases such as *Re JH* [1985] IR 375; *North Western Health Board v Health Service Executive* [2006] 4 IR 374.
63 *In the Matter of JJ* [2021] IESC 1 [176].
64 ibid [137].

to non-voluntary adoptions where the parents do not consent but where the adoption is deemed necessary due to the parental failure of duty. The reference to 'any child' in the Article indicates that the law must provide for the non-voluntary adoptions of both marital and non-marital children in situations of parental failure. Previously, a very high threshold was set for the adoption of marital children (that did not apply to non-marital children) due to the fact that the rights and duties of married parents are described as inalienable under Articles 41 and 42 of the Constitution.[65]

Article 42A.2.2° was introduced to make 'it somewhat easier to permit the adoption of children of a marital family'.[66] The Article specifies that '[p]rovision shall be made by law' for such adoptions, and that the failure of parental duty must take place for a defined period of time 'as may be prescribed by law' before the adoption can take place. These words indicate that the Article is to be given effect through legislation. Section 54(2A) of the Adoption Act 2010 gives effect to the provision by specifying the criteria and time periods that must be met in order for the High Court to dispense with the parents' consent to an adoption order in cases of parental failure.[67] The topic of adoption is addressed in Chapter 11.

4.5 Voluntary placement for adoption

Article 42A.3 makes provision for the voluntary placement for adoption of 'any child'. This clarifies that both marital and non-marital children may be voluntarily placed for adoption. Prior to the insertion of this Article, only non-marital children could be voluntarily placed for adoption since marital children could only be adopted in cases of parental failure as described above. Article 42A.3 requires that '[p]rovision shall be made by law' to give effect to it. The provision is given legislative effect by s 23 of the Adoption Act 2010, as amended, which allows for the adoption of any child who resides in the State and who is under the age of 18 years.[68]

4.6 Best interests of the child

Article 42A.4.1° requires that provision is made by law to ensure that the **best interests of the child** are the **paramount consideration** in specified legal proceedings, namely child care proceedings, adoption, guardianship, custody and access. While it is encouraging to see a reference to the best interests of the child in the Article, it is notable that it is not enshrined

---

65 Adoption of a marital child was possible but only in accordance with the strict criteria specified in s 54(2) of the Adoption Act 2010.

66 *In the Matter of JJ* [2021] IESC 1 [127].

67 Adoption Act 2010, s 54(2A), as inserted by Adoption (Amendment) Act 2017, s 24.

68 Adoption Act 2010, s 23(1), as substituted by Adoption (Amendment) Act 2017, s 12.

as a constitutional right – it merely requires that legislation is enacted to give effect to the provision.

Pre-existing statutes had recognised the 'welfare' of the child as the first and paramount consideration[69] in each of the areas covered by Article 42A.4.1°. As a result of the Article, amendments have been made to the statutes in each area to provide that the 'best interests of the child' shall be the 'paramount consideration' in the relevant proceedings, and to include a list of factors (sometimes referred to as 'best interests checklists') that should be taken into account by a court when determining the best interests of the child in the context of guardianship, custody and access;[70] adoption;[71] and care proceedings.[72]

4.7 Views of the child

Article 42A.4.2° requires that legislation is enacted to allow children to express their views in specified legal proceedings, namely child care, adoption, guardianship, custody and access proceedings and for those views to be given due weight in accordance with age and maturity. The wording of this provision is similar to the wording adopted in art 12 of the UNCRC but, like the best interests principle discussed above, Article 42A.4.2° does not enshrine the expression of the views of the child as a constitutional right; it simply requires that legislation is enacted to give effect to such expression.

Legislative provisions have been introduced to enable children to express their views in the different areas[73] and it is notable that in each of the best interests checklists that have been introduced to guide the determination of the best interests of the child, the views of the child are specifically mentioned.[74] This aligns with the approach of the Committee on the Rights of the Child, which has stated that '[a]ssessment of a child's best interests must include respect for the child's right to express his or her

---

69 For example: Guardianship of Infants Act 1964, s 3; Adoption Act 2010, s 19; Child Care Act 1991, s 24.

70 Guardianship of Infants Act 1964, s 31, as inserted by Children and Family Relationships Act 2015, s 63.

71 Adoption Act 2010, s 19(2), as substituted by Adoption (Amendment) Act 2017, s 9.

72 Child Care Act 1991, s 24(2), as substituted by Child Care (Amendment) Act 2022, s. 4.

73 Child Care Act 1991, s 24A, as inserted by Child Care (Amendment) Act 2022, s 5; Adoption Act 2010, s 19(3), as substituted by Adoption (Amendment) Act 2017, s 9; Guardianship of Infants Act 1964, s 25, as inserted by Children Act 1997, s 11.

74 Child Care Act 1991, s 24(2)(c), as substituted by Child Care (Amendment) Act 2022, s 4; Adoption Act 2010, s 19(2)(d), as substituted by Adoption (Amendment) Act 2017, s 9; Guardianship of Infants Act 1964, s 31(2)(b), as inserted by Children and Family Relationships Act 2015, s 63.

views freely and due weight given to said views in all matters affecting the child'.[75]

5. Summary

- Children's rights are protected at international level in the United Nations Convention on the Rights of the Child (UNCRC), at European level in the European Convention on Human Rights (ECHR) and at national level in the Irish Constitution, most notably Article 42A, and in legislation.
- The UNCRC is a comprehensive international treaty that protects a wide range of children's rights and places obligations on States to uphold children's rights.
- Article 42A provides express protection for the rights of the child in the Irish Constitution. The Supreme Court has described the impact of Article 42A as a 'wide-ranging, though subtle, change to the posture of the Constitution in relation to child and family matters'.[76] In the area of adoption, Article 42A has significantly altered Irish law, particularly as regards the adoption of marital children. In other areas, however, there is some debate as to the practical significance of the changes introduced by the Article.

6. Further reading

Lydia Bracken 'Assessing the best interests of the child in cases of cross-border surrogacy: inconsistency in the Strasbourg approach?' (2017) 39 Journal of Social Welfare and Family Law 368.

Aoife Daly, 'The Right of Children to be Heard and the Emerging Law of the European Convention on Human Rights' (2011) 15(3) The International Journal of Human Rights 441.

Michael Freeman, 'What's Right with Rights for Children' (2006) 2 International Journal of Law in Context 89.

Ursula Kilkelly and Conor O'Mahony, 'The Proposed Children's Rights Amendment: Running to Stand Still?' (2007) 10 Irish Journal of Family Law 19.

---

[75] Committee on the Rights of the Child (n 13) [43].

[76] *In the Matter of JJ* [2021] IESC 1 [130].

Laura Lundy, '"Voice" is not enough: conceptualising Article 12 of the United Nations Convention on the Rights of the Child' (2007) 33 British Educational Research Journal 927.

Conor O'Mahony, 'The Same, but Different? Article 42A and the Threshold for State Intervention in Family Life: In Re JJ' (2022) 4 Irish Supreme Court Review 141.

Chapter 9

Children and Parents

Maebh Harding and Brian Tobin

LEARNING OBJECTIVES

By the end of this chapter, students will be equipped to:

- Outline the different ways in which the law determines a child's legal parents.
- Evaluate the limitations of legal regulation of parentage following the use of assisted reproductive technology.
- Distinguish between the concepts of guardianship, custody and access.
- Examine how the best interests principle is applied by the court in private child law disputes.
- Analyse to what extent the voice of the child is heard in private child law disputes.
- Appraise the effectiveness of child maintenance orders.

CRITICAL THINKING POINTS

- How should the law recognise the parentage of surrogate-born children?
- Should all parents have equal rights of guardianship?

1. Introduction

This chapter explores how disputes between parents/guardians about the upbringing of their children are resolved. This area of law is known as private child law because it concerns disputes brought to court by private individuals. The different legal statuses of parents and guardians and their associated legal rights to care for children shape the way in which these disputes come to court.

The chapter begins by examining **legal parentage,** explaining how the law determines who a child's legal parents are. Parentage is an important legal status, recognising a lifelong connection between parent and child. Different legal rules apply to determine legal parentage depending on how a child is conceived. A special statutory regime now applies to determine the parentage of children who are conceived through a very specific type of Donor Assisted Human Reproduction (DAHR) as outlined in the Children and Family Relationships Act 2015.[1] Common law-based rules apply to determine the parentage of children conceived through sexual intercourse and all other forms of assisted reproduction not covered by the 2015 Act.

The second part of the chapter looks at **guardianship** which gives an adult rights, responsibilities, and decision-making powers in respect of children. Some legal parents have automatic guardianship rights by operation of law while others must take specific steps to acquire them. Non-parents who are caring for children can also acquire guardianship rights in certain circumstances. This section also examines how decision-making disputes between guardians are resolved by the courts.

The third section of this chapter discusses **custody and access** disputes which commonly occur between separated parents. Custody refers to an adult's right to exercise physical day-to-day care and control over a child who lives with them.[2] In contrast, access is viewed as a right of the child,[3] allowing them to maintain contact with their parents, siblings and other persons involved in their care and upbringing.[4]

The terms 'guardianship', 'custody' and 'access' used across Irish legislation have been criticised by the Law Reform Commission as emphasising parents' authority rather than their legal responsibility towards children.[5] Although more child-focussed language was recommended by the Law Reform Commission, Article 42A of the Constitution now enshrines the historical terms, guardianship, custody and access, in the Constitution. These terms have been retained in the Children and Family Relationships Act 2015.[6]

As discussed in Chapter 8, Article 42A mandated legislative change to centre **the best interests of the child as the paramount consideration** in guardianship, custody and access proceedings.[7] Section 3 of the Guardianship of Infants Act 1964 ('the 1964 Act') now expressly requires the court to regard the best interests of the child as the paramount consideration in resolving disputes. The court must make an individualised

---

1 s 4.
2 *RC v IS* [2003] 4 IR 431, 439.
3 art 9(3) UNCRC; *MM v GM* [2015] IECA 29.
4 *MD v GD* [1992] FLJ 34 1992 WJSC-HC 3403, [1992] 7 JIC 3002.
5 Law Reform Commission, *Report on the Legal Aspects of Family Relationships* (LRC 101–2010) 8-11.
6 See Explanatory Note for Head 31 of the General Scheme of the Children and Family Relationships Bill 2014.
7 Article 42A.4.1°, Constitution of Ireland.

assessment of what outcome would further the best interests of the child in the circumstances before it. In doing so, the court must consider the list of factors set out in s 31 of the 1964 Act. This best interests 'checklist' is discussed in further detail later in the chapter.

Article 42A also required legislative change to ensure that, as far as practicable, **the views of a child** who is capable of forming their own views, **shall be ascertained and given due weight**, having regard to the age and maturity of the child.[8] The court is expressly required to consider such views as part of the best interests checklist.[9] When obtaining the views of the child, the court shall facilitate free expression by the child and may make an order for those views to be ascertained by an expert and presented to the court in the form of a report.[10] The strength of these statutory changes in ensuring that the views of children are heard in private law proceedings is assessed in this chapter.

The final section of this chapter analyses **maintenance** disputes, where a parent or guardian comes to court to enforce a legal duty to financially support dependent children. These disputes are mostly resolved using the Family Law (Maintenance of Spouses and Children) Act 1976. In contrast to other disputes involving the upbringing of children, there is no constitutional imperative for the rights of children to be given legislative recognition in this area of law. The best interests of the child is not paramount in maintenance disputes, nor is there special statutory provision for the views of children to be heard in such disputes.

Most private child law cases take place in the District Court or Circuit Court and are not routinely reported. This means that although private law disputes relating to children are commonplace,[11] published judicial consideration of the best interests principle and the need to consider the ascertainable views of the child is very limited.

2. Legal parentage

Legal parentage is a concept used to determine who is recognised in law as a child's parent. Legal parentage is an important factor relevant to establishing a right to family life under art 8 of the European Convention on Human Rights (ECHR). Legal recognition of the parent-

---

8 ibid, Article 42A.4.2°.

9 Guardianship of Infants Act 1964, s 31(2)(b).

10 ibid, s 32; Family Law Act 1995, s 47.

11 8,667 applications in relation to guardianship, custody and access were resolved by the District Court in 2021 and 1,412 orders related to the guardianship, custody and access were made by the Circuit Court as part of judicial separation, divorce and dissolution proceedings. Courts Service, *Annual Report 2021*, 64

child link also brings with it automatic legal consequences relating to inheritance,[12] citizenship[13] and immigration rights, the prohibited degrees of relationship for marriage, and tax law. Legal parents are liable to pay child maintenance.[14] However, as explored in the next section, not all legal parents have the same rights in relation to their child at the time of birth.

Different legal rules apply to determine a child's legal parents depending on how the child was conceived. Where a child is conceived through Donor Assisted Human Reproduction (DAHR) as defined in the Children and Family Relationships Act 2015, the rules of that Act will determine who has the status of legal parent. For all other children, older legal rules based on principles of common law apply. These 'standard rules' are now found in the Status of Children Act 1987. The rules were developed to support a presumption of legitimacy for children who were born to married mothers. Illegitimacy was a very real legal stigma affecting the lives of mothers and children.[15] Although illegitimacy was legally abolished by the Status of Children Act 1987,[16] the standard rules preserve legal presumptions based on the marital status of a child's mother. These rules reflect traditional assumptions about family life and do not reflect the social realities of modern family life.

Irish law has no specific legal rules to determine the legal parentage of children born following surrogacy agreements. Legislative reform has been proposed to address this issue and will be discussed below.

2.1 The standard rules of legal parentage

The rules of parentage outlined in the Status of Children Act 1987 were developed for children conceived through heterosexual sexual intercourse, but they also apply to any children who do not fall within the narrow statutory regime applying to children conceived through DAHR.[17]

The **woman who gives birth** to a child, is recognised in Irish law as the child's **legal mother**.[18]

The **father** of a child is the man who is the child's **genetic father**. In *A B & C v Ireland,* Murray J held that this genetic-based understanding is the

---

12 Succession Act 1965, s 4A (as amended by the Children and Family Relationships Act 2015).

13 Irish Nationality and Citizenship Act 1956, s 7(1); *A, B & C v Minister for Foreign Affairs and Trade* [2023] IESC 10.

14 Liability for maintenance is discussed later in this chapter.

15 See Chapter 11.

16 Status of Children Act 1987, s 44.

17 Brian Tobin, 'Assisted Reproductive Techniques and Irish Law: No Child Left Behind?' (2020) 64 Irish Jurist 138 for discussion on reciprocal IVF.

18 *MR v An tArd Chláraitheoir* [2014] 3 IR 533.

correct interpretation of 'father' where the term appears in legislation unless a more specific meaning is given in a particular statute.[19]

The Status of Children Act 1987 preserves two pragmatic legal presumptions about who the child's genetic father is.

1. Where a child's mother is married to a man at the time of birth, her husband is presumed to be the child's legal father.[20] No such legal presumption applies where the mother is married to another woman.[21]
2. Where a man is named on a birth certificate as the child's father, he is presumed to be the child's legal father and this presumption takes priority over the presumption in favour of a mother's husband.[22] There is a legal requirement to register the birth of all children.[23] While there is no legal requirement to register a child's father's details if he is not married to the child's mother,[24] it is an offence under the Civil Registration Act to register information which is known to be false.[25]

Both legal presumptions can be rebutted on the *balance of probabilities*.[26]

Legal parentage can also be established by applying to court for a declaration of parentage under s 35 of the Status of Children Act 1987. This allows the genetic father of a child to establish legal parentage by proving, on the balance of probabilities,[27] that a biological link exists between father and child. The court may make a direction for the use of DNA tests to determine legal parentage.[28] Where an adult does not consent to the taking of a DNA sample, the court may draw such inferences from this refusal as appear proper in the circumstances.[29] Taking a DNA sample from a child requires the consent of the person with care or control over the child.[30]

---

19 *A, B & C v Minister for Foreign Affairs and Trade* [2023] IESC 10 [75].
20 Status of Children Act 1987, s 46(1). Unless she has lived apart from her husband for more than ten months before the birth of the child.
21 See discussion Lydia Bracken, 'Challenging normative constructions of parentage in Ireland' (2017) 39 Journal of Social Welfare and Family Law 316.
22 Status of Children Act 1987, s 46(3).
23 Civil Registration Act 2004, s 19.
24 ibid, s 22.
25 ibid, s 69(3).
26 Status of Children Act 1987, s 46.
27 *GN v KK* [1998] IEHC 15.
28 Status of Children Act 1987, s 38
29 ibid, s 42.
30 ibid, s 39.

DNA testing is sometimes used in immigration cases[31] to establish a genetic link between mother and child. In cases where no assisted reproductive technology has been used in the conception of the child this will be good evidence to establish legal motherhood. In such cases, the genetic mother and the gestational mother are known to be one and the same person. However, the legal rule is clear that gestation, rather than genetics determine legal motherhood.[32]

The standard rules of legal parentage do not always reflect adult intentions about parenting roles. This can cause particular difficulty for same sex couples who wish to co-parent a child.

Key case – *JMcD v PL* [2010] 2 IR 199

In *JMcD v PL*,[33] (explored in greater detail later in the chapter) a female couple wanted to become parents. A man agreed to donate his sperm to create the child using assisted reproductive technology outside a clinical setting. It was agreed that the man's role would be to act as a 'favourite uncle' and not as a father and that he would recognise the couple as the child's primary parents.[34] Following the birth of the child, a dispute arose between the couple and the man about the role he would play in the child's life. The standard rules of legal parentage gave no effect to the expressed adult intentions about parenting roles. The woman who gave birth to the child was recognised as his legal mother. The man who had donated his sperm was recognised as the child's legal father and the mother's partner had no status as a legal parent.

Same sex female couples, like the couple in *JMcD*, can be recognised as legal parents from the birth of their child if they comply with the statutory scheme set out in the Children and Family Relationships Act 2015 for DAHR. In *JMcD* the child was born before the scheme became available, but there is still no way for both intended parents in this situation to be recognised as legal parents other than through adoption (see Chapter 11).

2.2 Parentage following donor-assisted human reproduction

The Children and Family Relationships Act 2015[35] ('the 2015 Act') determines the legal parentage of children conceived in Ireland following

[31] *MH and SH v Minister for Justice and Equality* [2020] IEHC 360; and *FB v Minister for Justice and Equality* [2020] IECA 89.

[32] *MR v An tArd Chláraitheoir* [2014] 3 IR 533.

[33] [2010] 2 IR 199.

[34] ibid, 211.

[35] See Pts 2 and 3 of the Children and Family Relationships Act 2015. On 4 November 2019, the then Minister for Health, Simon Harris, signed the Children and Family Relationships Act 2015 (Pts 2 and 3) (Commencement) Order 2019, which commenced Pts 2 and 3 on 4 May 2020.

a donor assisted human reproduction (DAHR) procedure. The 2015 Act applies to children conceived after 4 May 2020 when the Act came into force.

A DAHR procedure is a tightly defined form of assisted reproduction. The procedure must take place in Ireland at a clinical facility. It must involve a donated embryo or donor gamete(s)[36] and result in the implantation of an embryo in the womb of the woman who requests the procedure.[37] The embryo or gametes used must have been donated according to the terms of the 2015 Act. Donors are required to give detailed written consent and must also make a declaration that they understand that they will not become a legal parent as a result of the DAHR procedure.[38] The 2015 Act is very clear that such donors are not legal parents and do not have any rights or duties in respect of the child.[39]

Section 5 of the 2015 Act provides that the **legal mother** of a child born following a DAHR procedure is the **woman who gave birth to the child.**

The spouse, civil partner or cohabitant of the mother will be recognised as the second legal parent of the child under s 5 if the appropriate consents and declarations have been made. The woman giving birth to the child must have consented to being the legal mother and made appropriate declarations,[40] and she must also have consented to the recognition of her spouse, civil partner or cohabitant as a second legal parent.[41] The second legal parent must also have consented to becoming a legal parent and made the required declarations.[42] A legal obligation is placed on the DAHR facility to ensure that all appropriate consents and declarations are given before a DAHR procedure is carried out.[43]

The 2015 Act allows different-sex couples and female same-sex couples to be recognised as legal parents of children with whom they may have no genetic connection, as long as they have complied with all the relevant provisions of the Act. However, the scope of the 2015 Act is very narrow[44] and does not apply to the parentage of children conceived through assisted reproductive techniques that take place outside of a DAHR facility. Irish law does not allow a child to have two male parents other

---

36 Sperm and/or eggs.
37 Children and Family Relationships Act 2015 s 4.
38 Children and Family Relationships Act 2015, ss 6, 14,16.
39 ibid, s 5(5)-(7).
40 ibid, s 9.
41 ibid, s 9.
42 ibid, s 11.
43 ibid, ss 25 and 26.
44 Department of Health, *Children and Family Relationships Act 2015 Publication*, 2 March 2020, available at: https://www.gov.ie/en/publication/e2bd0a-children-and-family-relationships-act-2015/ [last accessed 5 May 2023].

than via adoption.[45] A recent survey by Bracken of 99 LGBTI+ families, found that in 53% of families, all the children of the family did not have a legally recognised relationship with both their parents.[46]

2.3 Protection of the child's right to know their genetic identity following DAHR

The 2015 Act protects the child's right to know their genetic identity by requiring the use of identifiable donors and placing express legal obligations on DAHR facilities to collect identifying information to be recorded on the newly-established National Donor-Conceived Person Register.[47] Information relating to the child, the intended parents, and any donor(s) is recorded and once a child reaches the age of 18, they can request identifying and/or non-identifying information about their donor(s).[48]

If the child requests identifying information about their donor such as their name, date of birth and contact details, the Minister for Health is required to inform the donor that such a request has been made. The information will be released to the child after 12 weeks unless the donor makes representations to the Minister explaining why the safety of the donor, the donor-conceived child, or both, requires the information to be withheld. Based on these representations, the Minister may decide that the donor's identifying information should be withheld from the child, but there is a right of appeal to the Circuit Court.[49]

A child who has reached the age of 18 may have their identifying information added to the Register and may consent to the release of such information if it is requested by their donor(s) or other persons conceived with the same donor(s).[50] This facility enables donor-conceived adults with the same donor(s) to request identifying information about one another. Nonetheless, the Minister will still notify the donor-conceived adult if such a request is received, and they may object to the release of their identifying information. No right of appeal to the courts exists in this situation.[51]

The National Donor-Conceived Person Register is linked to the Register

---

[45] Adoption Act 2010, s 33 as amended by Adoption (Amendment) Act 2017, s 16.

[46] Lydia Bracken, *LGBTI+ Parent Families in Ireland: Legal Recognition of Parent-Child Relationships,* University of Limerick, 2021, 24, available at https://lgbt.ie/wp-content/uploads/2021/11/LGBTI-Parent-Families-Report.pdf [last accessed 8 March 2022] .

[47] Children and Family Relationships Act 2015, s 33.

[48] ibid, s 34.

[49] ibid, s 35.

[50] ibid, ss 36 and 37.

[51] ibid.

of Births. Once an entry is made in the National Donor-Conceived Person Register, the Minister must notify an tArd Chláraitheoir, who will make a note in the child's entry in the Register of Births that the child is donor-conceived and that additional information is available from the National Donor-Conceived Person Register.[52] When a donor-conceived child who is over the age of 18 years applies for a copy of their birth certificate they will be informed by the Registrar that further information relating to them is available from the National Donor-Conceived Person Register.[53] This measure is designed to ensure that donor-conceived children will have access to the information, even where they did not know that they were donor conceived. It remains to be seen how effective this measure will be.

2.4 Retrospective recognition of parentage under the Children and Family Relationships Act 2015

The 2015 Act provides transitional measures to allow for the retrospective recognition of legal parentage for children conceived through assisted reproductive techniques before 4 May 2020.[54] The legal mother and the second intended parent can apply to court for a declaration that the second intended parent is a legal parent of the child.[55] The process cannot be used if a second parent has already been recorded as the other parent of the child on the Irish Register of Births.[56]

The court may make the declaration where the child was conceived through anonymous or identifiable gamete donation either within Ireland or outside Ireland. No declaration can be made where a 'known donor' was used, where assisted reproduction occurred in a non-clinical setting,[57] or where the child was born outside Ireland.

The court must be satisfied that the declaration is in the best interests of the child.[58] This is the only situation in Irish law in which the best interests of the child can determine legal parentage. The court must also, to the extent possible given their age and understanding, give the child the opportunity to make their views on the matter known, and the court shall have regard to those views.[59]

These transitional measures were intended to facilitate all families who

---

52 ibid, s 39.

53 ibid.

54 ibid, s 20.

55 ibid, s 23.

56 ibid, s 20(1)(f).

57 Brian Tobin, 'Regulating Non-Clinical Donor-Assisted Human Reproduction in Ireland' (2018) 60 Irish Jurist (NS) 179.

58 Children and Family Relationships Act 2015, s 21(9)(b).

59 ibid, ss 21(8) and 22(4).

had used assisted reproductive techniques to have children before the 2015 Act. However, Bracken's study on LGBTI+ families suggests that the eligibility requirements are too narrow. 18% of respondents to the survey who conceived children using assisted reproduction techniques before 4 May 2020 were not eligible to apply for a retrospective declaration of parentage either because they had used a known donor, had not used a clinical setting or because the child was born outside Ireland.[60]

2.5 Parentage following surrogacy

Surrogacy takes place when a woman,[61] known as the surrogate, agrees to become pregnant and give birth to a child on behalf of another person or couple known as the intended parent(s). There is no specific Irish legislation to regulate surrogacy or legal parentage following surrogacy. Surrogacy is regulated in other jurisdictions and Irish parents make use of international surrogacy services. In 2018, a survey carried out by Families through Surrogacy (now Growing Families) estimated that up to 68% of all surrogacies for Irish couples have taken place in Ukraine.[62] However, Irish rules apply to the question of parentage when they return to Ireland and this is discussed further in Chapter 12.[63] The application of the standard rules to a surrogacy situation will not give effect to adult intentions about intended parentage.

Key case – *MR v An tArd Chláraitheoir* [2014] 3 IR 533

In this case a women agreed to act as a surrogate for her sister (the intended mother) and her sister's husband (the intended father). The intended mother's eggs were fertilised with the intended father's sperm and placed in the surrogate's womb. The surrogate mother gave birth to twins. The intended father was registered on the children's birth certificates and was recognised as their legal father. However, the Supreme Court held that Irish law recognised the gestational mother as the legal mother. It was not possible for the intended mother to be registered on the children's birth certificates or recognised as the children's legal mother.

Following *MR*, an intended mother cannot be recognised as the legal

---

60 Lydia Bracken, *LGBTI+ Parent Families in Ireland: Legal Recognition of Parent-Child Relationships*, University of Limerick, 2021, 24, available at https://lgbt.ie/wp-content/uploads/2021/11/LGBTI-Parent-Families-Report.pdf [last accessed 2 August 2023].

61 A transgender person who is legally recognised or self-identifies as male can also potentially act as a surrogate.

62 See Brian Tobin, 'Long-Awaited Surrogacy Laws still won't Recognise many Parents', *TheJournal.ie*, 4 March 2019, available at *https://www.thejournal.ie/readme/opinion-long-awaited-surrogacy-laws-still-wont-recognise-many-parents-4513551-Mar2019/* [last accessed 29 September 2022].

63 e.g. *EP (an Infant) v Attorney General* [2013] IEHC 300.

mother of her genetic child where surrogacy is used. Where two men enter into a surrogacy arrangement, the genetic father can be recognised as the legal father, but the other intended parent cannot.

Step-parent adoption is a possible legal option to grant legal parentage to intended parents.[64] This applies to both married and cohabiting couples. The child must have lived with the step-parent and the birth parent for a continuous period of two years before an adoption order can be made.[65] The couple must otherwise be eligible and suitable for adoption (See Chapter 11). Nonetheless, Bracken's recent study, suggests that adoption has not been used to date in such circumstances.[66] A freedom of information response seen by RTE in 2021 indicated that the Adoption Authority of Ireland is reluctant to process adoption applications relating to surrogacy and other forms of assisted human reproduction outside the scheme of the 2015 Act.[67] The recent Supreme Court decision in *AAI v C&D,*[68] held that foreign step-parent adoption orders made in surrogacy situations were not contrary to public policy and should be recognised if they were otherwise in compliance with legal requirements. This decision may result in a change of approach from the Adoption Authority.

Intended parents can, in any event, apply for legal guardianship under s 6C of the Guardianship of Infants Act 1964. This is discussed below.

2.6 Critical thinking point: How should the law recognise the parentage of surrogate-born children?

The failure to give any effect at all to intended parental arrangements following surrogacy agreements may violate the art 8 of the ECHR rights of the intended parents and the child.[69] However, the ECtHR leaves a lot of discretion to the states on how they should recognise the relationship between a child born through surrogacy and their intended parents. A failure to recognise intended parents as the child's *legal parents* does not violate art 8 unless the non-recognition prevents the family from enjoying their private and family life together. For example, in *Valdís*

---

64 Adoption Act 2010, s 33.

65 ibid, s 37(5)(b). Conor O'Mahony, *A Review of Children's Rights and Best Interests in the Context of Donor-Assisted Human Reproduction and Surrogacy in Irish Law* (Department of Children Equality, Disability, Integration and Youth 2020) 13.

66 Lydia Bracken, *LGBTI+ Parent Families in Ireland: Legal Recognition of Parent-Child Relationships,* University of Limerick, 2021, 32, available at https://lgbt.ie/wp-content/uploads/2021/11/LGBTI-Parent-Families-Report.pdf [last accessed 2 August 2023].

67 AilbheConneely, 'Legal Rights Call for Children Born Through Surrogacy', *The Irish Times*, 10 June 2021, available at https://www.rte.ie/news/ireland/2021/0610/1227220-surrogacy/ [last accessed 2 August 2023].

68 [2023] IESC 6. See also *Re A and B minor, A v Adoption Authority of Ireland* [2021] IEHC 784.

69 E.g. *Mennesson v France* App No 65192/11 (ECHR, 26 June 2014).

Fjölnisdóttir and others v Iceland[70] the court found that treating the parenting arrangement as a permanent fostering arrangement was adequate with regard to respect for family life and the child's right to private life. Requiring the intended parents to adopt the child is also rights compatible.[71] Conor O'Mahony argues that the current legal situation in Ireland is rights compatible because intended parents can apply for adoption or guardianship.[72] However, Brian Tobin believes that the two-year waiting period that applies before an intended parent can apply for adoption or guardianship may be contrary to the child's rights under Article 8 ECHR.[73]

Draft legislation to regulate surrogacy agreements and to grant intended parents the status of legal parents is currently before the Oireachtas. The Health (Assisted Human Reproduction) Bill 2022 contains proposals to regulate surrogacy arrangements that are carried out *in Ireland*. Whereas the Oireachtas Joint Committee on International Surrogacy published a report in 2022 containing recommendations as to how *international surrogacy arrangements* might be regulated.[74] The 2022 Bill may be amended to contain proposals to regulate international surrogacy arrangements that are consistent with the recommendations contained in the report of the Oireachtas Joint Committee on International Surrogacy.

A central dispute in the regulation of parentage following surrogacy is whether parentage should be accorded to the intended parents before or after the child is born. The 'standard rules' accord parentage to the surrogate mother. Should this be transferred to the intending parents after birth or should pre-birth authorisation ensure that the intended parents have legal status immediately on birth? Legislative proposals must balance the competing interests of intending parents, children and surrogates and be international human rights compliant. In cases of dispute between the surrogate and the intended parents, the people with the status of legal parent will be in a stronger legal position.

---

70 App No 71552/17 (ECHR, 18 May 2021).

71 *Advisory Opinion requested by the French Court of Cassation* (P16-2018-001, 10 April 2019) Grand Chamber.

72 Conor O' Mahony, *A Review of Children's Rights and Best Interests in the Context of Donor-Assisted Human Reproduction and Surrogacy in Irish Law* (Department of Children, Equality, Disability, Integration and Youth 2021) 39.

73 Brian Tobin, *The Legal Recognition of Same-Sex Relationships: Emerging Families in Ireland and Beyond* (Hart 2023) 116.

74 Joint Committee on International Surrogacy, *Final Report of the Joint Committee on International Surrogacy* (Joint Committee on International Surrogacy 2022), available at https://data.oireachtas.ie/ie/oireachtas/committee/dail/33/joint_committee_on_international_surrogacy/reports/2022/2022-07-06_final-report-of-the-joint-committee-on-international-surrogacy_en.pdf [last accessed 2 August 2023].

Irish academics such as Tobin,[75] O'Mahony[76] and Bracken[77] argue in favour of a pre-birth legal order. This is more certain for the intended parents and ensures that surrogate mothers cannot be left with responsibility for the baby. They argue that if Irish law provided such certainty, intended parents would be encouraged to enter into surrogacy arrangements in Ireland rather than going abroad for such services and this would discourage use of unregulated international surrogacy services that can be exploitative of women. Such models give a surrogate a post-birth right to confirm or revoke her consent and challenge the legal parentage of the intended parents. This means that post-birth legal proceedings are possible but only necessary in disputed cases. The English Law Commission and the Scottish Law Commission have recently recommended a similar model.[78]

As initiated, the Health (Assisted Human Reproduction) Bill 2022 is limited to domestic surrogacy agreements. It proposes pre-birth authorisation by the Assisted Human Reproduction Regulatory Authority (AHRRA) followed by a post-birth court order transferring parentage from the surrogate to the intended parents. Intended parents must ensure that they and their surrogate comply with various pre-conception safeguards (independent legal advice, AHR counselling, etc) before their agreement can be approved by the AHRRA. The child must have a genetic link to at least one of the intending parents[79] and the arrangement must not be commercial.[80] The surrogate will be the child's legal mother at birth and the intended parents must apply for a post-birth parental order from the courts. At the time of the order, the child must live with the intended parents, the surrogate must consent, and the order must be in the best interests of the child. There is no option for the court to dispense with the surrogate mother's consent, even where it is unreasonably withheld. In such cases, the court would use guardianship, custody and access orders to come up with a solution that is in the best interests of the child.

A third model, suggested by McCandless and Sheldon[81] is to give the

75 Brian Tobin, 'An appraisal of Ireland's current legislative proposals for regulating domestic surrogacy arrangements' (2019) 41 Journal of Social Welfare and Family law 205.

76 Conor O' Mahony, *A Review of Children's Rights and Best Interests in the Context of Donor-Assisted Human Reproduction and Surrogacy in Irish Law* (Department of Children, Equality, Disability, Integration and Youth 2021).

77 Lydia Bracken, 'The Position of the Surrogate in the Health (Assisted Human Reproduction) Bill 2022' (2022) 25(3) Irish Journal of Family Law 45..

78 Law Commission of England and Wales and Scottish Law Commission *Building families through surrogacy: a new law* (2023), available at https://www.lawcom.gov.uk/project/surrogacy/ [last accessed 2 August 2023].

79 Health (Assisted Human Reproduction) Bill 2022, s 53.

80 ibid, s 54.

81 Julie McCandless and Sally Sheldon, 'The Human Fertilisation and Embryology Act (2008) and the Tenacity of the Sexual Family Form' (2010) 73(2) Modern Law Review 175.

intended parents and the surrogate equivalent legal status at the time of the child's birth. This model would allow the surrogate to cede her rights by declaration if everything goes smoothly but places everyone on the same legal footing in case of a dispute about who should care for the child.

3. What is guardianship?

Guardianship gives an adult rights, responsibilities, and decision-making powers in respect of children. Guardianship is not defined in Irish legislation but some of the rights and responsibilities of guardianship are outlined by the Guardianship of Infants Act 1964 (GIA). Section 10(2)(a) grants guardians a right of custody over a child as against non-guardians and entitles a guardian to take proceedings for the return of a child to their custody. Section 6C(11) outlines a list of rights and responsibilities enjoyed by court appointed guardians:

(a) to decide on the child's place of residence;
(b) to make decisions regarding the child's religious, spiritual, cultural and linguistic upbringing;
(c) to decide with whom the child is to live;
(d) to consent to medical, dental and other health related treatment for the child, in respect of which a guardian's consent is required;
(e) under an enactment specified in subsection (12);[82]
(f) to place the child for adoption, and consent to the adoption of the child, under the Adoption Act 2010.

A key aspect of guardianship is the responsibility for making decisions about the most significant aspects of a child's welfare and upbringing. Where more than one guardian exists, guardianship rights can be exercised separately unless a specific statutory provision requires all guardians to agree. However, in *RC v IS*, Finlay Geoghegan J suggested that guardianship also includes the right to be consulted on important matters affecting the welfare of the child[83] such as in what country a child should reside and how they should be educated.

Guardianship rights are not unlimited. For example, parents are required to ensure that their children receive a minimum standard of education,[84]

---

82 The specified enactments are: s 2A(2) of the Firearms Act 1925; s 5 of the Protection of Young Persons (Employment) Act 1996; ss 50 and 50A of the International Criminal Court Act 1996; ss 79, 79A and 79B of the Criminal Justice (Mutual Assistance) Act 2008; s 14 of the Passports Act 2008; and the Criminal Justice (Forensic Evidence and DNA Database System) Act 2014.

83 *RC v IS* [2003] 4 IR 431, 440.

84 Education (Welfare) Act 2000, s 17.

and all forms of physical punishment of children are illegal in Ireland.[85] Although Article 42 of the Irish constitution gives great autonomy to parents over their children, as discussed in Chapter 8, the State can interfere with parental decisions where they violate the rights of children or where parents fail in their duties towards the child.

Guardianship comes to an end when the child reaches the age of 18.[86]

3.1 Who has guardianship rights?

Guardianship is a different concept to legal parenthood. Not all parents have equal legal rights at birth in relation to their children. Some parents have automatic guardianship rights at the time of birth while others must take steps to acquire them. Non-parents can also acquire guardianship rights, but it is easier to get guardianship rights if you have the status of legal parent.

3.2 Legal parents with automatic guardianship rights

All legal mothers have automatic legal guardianship of their children from birth.[87] This is a personal right of the mother recognised under Article 40.3 of the Constitution.[88] In contrast, not all legal fathers enjoy automatic constitutional or statutory rights of guardianship. The relationship of a child's second legal parent to their legal mother is key to understanding the rules of automatic guardianship. Marital status remains very important in this area of law. Legal fathers who are married to their child's legal mother have automatic guardianship rights.[89] This includes legal fathers to a child born following DAHR. The female spouse of a woman who gives birth following a DAHR procedure and who is recognised as a legal parent also has automatic guardianship rights.[90]

Where a couple jointly adopt, both parents will be joint guardians of their adoptive child, regardless of their marital status.[91]

Legal fathers who are not married to the child's mother do not have automatic guardianship rights[92] and must take steps to acquire

---

85 Children First Act 2015, s 28.

86 Guardianship of Infants Act 1964, s 8A.

87 ibid, s 6(1) and (4).

88 *State (Nicolaou) v An Bord Uchtála* [1966] IR 567.

89 Guardianship of Infants Act 1964, s 6(1)(1).

90 ibid, s 6B(1)

91 ibid, s 6(1A); Adoption Act 2010, s 58.

92 The definition of 'father' in s 2 of the 1964 Act does not include the natural father of a child born outside of marriage. Therefore, such a father cannot have automatic guardianship rights under Guardianship of Infants Act 1964, s 6(1).

guardianship rights.[93] The same is true for women recognised in law as second legal parents who are not married to the child's mother.[94]

3.3 Acquiring guardianship rights as a legal parent

Legal fathers and second female parents who do not have automatic guardianship rights can acquire guardianship after the birth of a child in one of four ways:

1. Through marriage to the mother.[95]
2. By cohabitation with the mother.[96]

Guardianship rights arise by operation of law where an unmarried legal parent has cohabited with the child's mother for a period of 12 months, including cohabitation of *at least* three months after the birth of the child.[97] Section 6F of the GIA allows such parents to apply to court for a declaration that they have guardianship rights on this basis, but they do not need to do so because the rights arise by operation of law.

Tobin has criticised this provision because it does not give second parents who are in a committed relationship guardianship rights from birth.[98] The imposed three-month delay could be significant if parents are in disagreement about medical decisions following the birth of their child.[99] Moreover, parents who are in a committed relationship but not actually cohabiting at the same address will fall outside this provision.[100] CSO figures show that between 2016 and 2020, fewer than 27% of children born to unmarried parents had parents living at the same address.[101]

---

93 Guardianship of Infants Act 1964, s 6A.

94 ibid, s 6B.

95 Guardianship of Infants Act 1964, ss 2(3) and 6B(1)(b).

96 ibid, s 2(4A) or s 6B(2)(b).

97 ibid.

98 Brian Tobin, 'The (D)evolving Nature of Guardianship Rights for Unmarried Fathers under Irish Law?' (2020) 30 Child and Family Law Quarterly 285.

99 Geoffrey Shannon, *Children and Family Relationships Law in Ireland* (Clarus Press 2016) 204.

100 ibid, 192.

101 See CSO, Vital Statistics Yearly Summary 2016 (Table 5) available at https://www.cso.ie/en/releasesandpublications/ep/p-vsys/vitalstatisticsyearlysummary2016/; CSO, Vital Statistics Yearly Summary 2017 (Table 5), available at https://www.cso.ie/en/releasesandpublications/ep/p-vsys/vitalstatisticsyearlysummary2017/; CSO, Vital Statistics Yearly Summary 2018 (Table 5), available at https://www.cso.ie/en/releasesandpublications/ep/p-vsys/vitalstatisticsyearlysummary2018/; CSO, Vital Statistics Yearly Summary 2019 (Table 5), available at https://www.cso.ie/en/releasesandpublications/ep/p-vsys/vitalstatisticsyearlysummary2019/; CSO, Vital Statistics Yearly Summary 2020 (Table 5), available at https://www.cso.ie/en/releasesandpublications/ep/p-vsys/vitalstatisticsyearlysummary2020/ [last accessed 29 November 2021]. Indeed, in most regions from 2016-2020 less than 25% of children born to unmarried parents were born to unmarried parents living at the same address,

3. By making a joint statutory declaration with the mother.[102]

Guardianship rights can be conferred on a second parent by a declaration made by both parents in accordance with the Guardianship of Children (Statutory Declaration) Regulations 2020.[103] This straightforward and inexpensive procedure[104] requires the child's mother to consent to making a statutory declaration appointing the legal father or second female parent as a guardian. Parents jointly fill out a form and have their signatures witnessed by a person authorised by law.[105] Changes made by the Children and Family Relationships Act 2015[106] now allow Registrars registering a child's birth to witness a statutory declaration conferring guardianship rights. However, there is no *statutory duty* on the Registrar to either provide information about the statutory declaration or the statutory declaration form itself to parents when they are registering the birth of a child. Many parents are still unaware of this mechanism for conferring guardianship or why it might be useful.[107]

No central registry for statutory declarations exists. Parents must keep their own copies. In *ER O'B (a minor) v Minister for Justice, Equality and Law Reform.*[108] a father challenged the absence of a public register on guardianship as a failure by the State to protect the rights of children and parents. The court held that while a public register would be a desirable social reform, its absence was not a breach of constitutional or convention rights.

4. By successful application for a court order[109]

---

except in the South East region (25.3% in 2016; 25.7% in 2017; 26.5% in 2018 and 26.1% in 2019) and the Midlands region (25.1% in 2018 and 25.8% in 2019), where the relevant figures were just slightly over 25%.

102 Guardianship of Infants Act 1964, s 2(4) or s 6B(4).

103 See SI 210/2020.

104 Rules of the Superior Courts (fees payable to commissioners for oaths), 2003, SI 616/2003 limits the fee chargeable for witnessing a statutory declaration to €10 per signature witnessed.

105 Statutory Declaration Act 1938, s 1 and Civil Registration Act 2004, s 27A.

106 s 97 of the Children and Family Relationships Act 2015, inserting s 27A into the Civil Registration Act 2004, was commenced on 6 October 2019 by s 1(7) of the Children and Family Relationships Act 2015, as amended by s 12 of the Civil Registration Act 2019.

107 In 2015, the then Minister for Justice, Frances Fitzgerald, highlighted in the Oireachtas that 'the existing mechanism of making a statutory declaration is a simple and inexpensive one but there is insufficient awareness of its existence and many parents simply do not use it', Select Committee on Justice, Defence and Equality, 5 March 2015, available at: https://www.oireachtas.ie/en/debates/debate/select_committee_on_justice_defence_and_equality/2015-03-05/2/?highlight%5B0%5D=children&highlight%5B1%5D=family&highlight%5B2%5D=relationships&highlight%5B3%5D=bill&highlight%5B4%5D=2015&highlight%5B5%5D=commit [last accessed 25 March 2022].

108 [2009] IEHC 423.

109 Guardianship of Infants Act 1964, s 6A.

Section 6A of the Guardianship of Infants Act 1964 enables a father or second female parent to apply to the court to be appointed a guardian of their child. When deciding whether or not to make a guardianship order, the court must consider the best interests of the child as the paramount consideration.[110] The court must consider the checklist of factors outlined in s 31 including the views of the child that are ascertainable.

Historically, the courts considered the strength of a father's relationship with the mother to be important in determining whether guardianship rights should be granted.[111] The current legal test for guardianship places the emphasis squarely on the best interests of the child and not the deservedness of parents. The vast majority of unmarried fathers are successful in their guardianship applications.[112]

Key case– *JMcD v PL*[113]

(**Warning:** Although this is the leading case on guardianship, it was decided before the introduction of the best interests principle and the s 31 checklist of factors into Guardianship of Infants Act 1964. The approach of the court is child-centred, but the court centres the child's welfare as the first and paramount consideration rather than using the new best interests test. The case also pre-dates the introduction of civil partnership, marriage equality and statutory regulation of DAHR.)

This case involved a dispute amongst the parents of a 3-year-old boy about their appropriate parental roles. The boy was born through assisted reproduction which took place outside a clinical setting and his parents entered into a co-parenting agreement. It was agreed that the child's mother and her long term female partner would act as the child's primary parents. The father agreed to donate his sperm and be involved in the child's life as a 'favourite uncle' but not to influence the child's upbringing.[114] Following the birth of the boy, the father wanted greater involvement in the child's life and applied for guardianship and access.

---

110 ibid, s 3.

111 *JK v VW* [1990] 2 IR 437, 446.

112 See discussion Law Reform Commission, *Consultation paper: Legal Aspects of Family Relationships* (LRC CP 55-2009) [3.07]. In 2015, 76% of applications by fathers for guardianship were granted (1808 out of 2,367). Court Service Annual Report 2015, 44. These statistics are no longer included in the Courts Service Annual Reports.

113 *JMcD v PL* [2010] 2 IR 99.

114 ibid, 211.

Both the High Court and Supreme Court denied the father's application for guardianship on the basis that it would not promote the child's welfare.[115] In the High Court, Hedigan J ordered a s 47 report which advised against guardianship or access because of the disruption that the father's interference would cause to the child's life.[116] Hedigan J ruled that there should be no guardianship or access for the father. The child lived in a loving, secure family and the presence of the father was likely to cause conflict and disruption.[117]

The Supreme Court held that the High Court had not given enough weight to the benefit to a child of having a relationship with his father.[118] Moreover, the court held that the father's relationship with the child's mother should not determine the outcome of the case.[119] This commentary is significant as it shows that the courts are now considering the direct benefits of an applicant parent's relationship with the child rather than considering the nature of the relationship between the parents as the important signifier of commitment to the child.

The Supreme Court ruled that access was appropriate in these circumstances[120] and left it open for a fresh application to be made on the issue of guardianship if the circumstances changed.[121] It is possible that the Supreme Court judges felt that if the access arrangements put in place resulted in the child establishing a strong attachment to its father over time, then a guardianship application might one day succeed. However, on return to the High Court to decide on the details of access, Hedigan J made the access arrangements conditional on the father's undertaking not to seek a parental role in the little boy's life.[122]

3.4 Critical thinking point: Should all parents have equal rights of guardianship?

The rules of automatic guardianship discriminate on the basis of gender and marital status. While mothers always have automatic guardianship rights from birth, fathers do not unless they are married to the child's mother. The second legal parent in a DAHR arrangement is in the same position as a father.

---

115 ibid, 239, 276, 284.
116 ibid, 224.
117 ibid, 239.
118 ibid, 276, 284.
119 ibid, 276, 320.
120 ibid, 276-277.
121 ibid, 276.
122 *JMcD v PL* [2010] IEHC 120.

Multiple incremental reforms to the law since 1987[123] have made a father's position in relation to guardianship rights better, but not the same as that of a mother.[124] The strength of the father's relationship with the child's mother still influences his prospects of becoming a guardian. Marriage or cohabitation will result in guardianship by operation of law, whereas a statutory declaration can be made with the mother's agreement.

This differential treatment of fathers, although much criticised[125] has been upheld as compatible with the ECHR. In *B v UK*[126] the ECtHR upheld English law which did not automatically grant guardianship rights to all fathers as ECHR compliant. The court held that the relationship between an unmarried father and his child can vary from 'ignorance and indifference' to a close stable relationship.[127] This was considered an objective and justifiable reason for the difference between married and unmarried fathers and so there was no violation of art 14 in conjunction with art 8 of the ECHR as long as procedures exist by which a father could obtain parental rights. In *Sporer v Austria,*[128] the court warned that very weighty reasons are required to justify a difference in treatment of fathers based on marital status.[129] But again the court upheld provisions of Austrian law which gave automatic custody rights to mothers and not to fathers where unmarried parents lived apart. This was again justified because of the different life situations into which children whose parents are not married are born.[130]

Policy arguments for automatic guardianship rights include the argument that it would encourage more fathers to take a meaningful role in their children's lives[131] and give committed fathers who are already in such roles, the formal legal authority to make decisions for their children.[132] It would also recognise the *prima facie* benefit to the child of having a relationship with both parents. However, automatic guardianship could

[123] Status of Children Act 1987, s 12; Children Act 1997, s 4; Children and Family Relationships Act 2015, s 97.

[124] Brian Tobin, 'The (d)evolving nature of guardianship rights for unmarried fathers under Irish law?' (2020) 32 Child and Family Law Quarterly 291-294.

[125] See Brian Tobin, 'Guardianship and Unmarried fathers in Ireland: One Step Forward, Two Steps Back?' (2020) 23(4) Irish Journal of Family Law 87; Jennifer White, 'Unmarried Fathers – The Need for Legislative Change in Ireland' (2015) 18(3) Irish Journal of Family Law 70.

[126] [2000] 1 FLR 1 [44].

[127] See also *Mc Michael v UK* (1995) 20 EHRR 205.

[128] [2011] 1 FLR 2134.

[129] ibid [75].

[130] ibid [85].

[131] Jennifer White, 'Unmarried Fathers – The Need for Legislative Change in Ireland' (2015) 18(3) *Iri*sh Journal of Family Law 70.

[132] Anne Egan, 'Are Fathers Discriminated against in Irish Family Law? An Empirical Study' (2011) 14(2) Irish Journal of Family Law 38, 47.

also increase the ability of non-resident parents to interfere in the lives of their ex-partners and children, potentially requiring court intervention.

Automatic legal guardianship from birth following a 10 month period of cohabitation with the child's mother was proposed as part of the reforms made by the Child and Family Relationships Act.[133] However, concerns were expressed that giving fathers automatic guardianship rights from birth on the basis of cohabitation rather than marriage would render the legislation unconstitutional by downgrading marriage as a preferential status.[134] It seems highly unlikely that giving unmarried fathers guardianship rights equivalent to married fathers upon the birth of their child would discourage people from marrying. Moreover, Tobin argues that the recognition of children's rights under Article 42A should have required the State to promote a child-centred approach to guardianship rights and allow fathers to acquire guardianship rights quickly and easily regardless of marital status.[135]

All parents could simply be given automatic guardianship rights from their child's birth by operation of law[136] as is the law in Australia.[137]

Another option for reform is to allow guardianship to arise by registration of the father's name on the child's birth certificate, where the mother consents to registration. This is the law in England and Wales,[138] Scotland and Northern Ireland where a substantial majority of unmarried fathers acquire parental responsibility through registration.[139] Guardianship through birth registration attaches a new legal meaning to birth certificates which then become a source of parental rights as well as proof of parental status.

3.5 Guardianship for persons who are not legal parents

A person who is not recognised as the legal parent of a child can apply

---

133 See Head 31 (1) and (3) and Head 37 (1) and (2) of the General Scheme of the Children and Family Relationships Bill 2014, available at: https://www.justice.ie/en/JELR/General%20Scheme%20of%20a%20Children%20and%20Family%20Relationships%20Bill.pdf/Files/General%20Scheme%20of%20a%20Children%20and%20Family%20Relationships%20Bill.pdf [last accessed 7 February 2022].

134 Dáil Deb, 12 March 2015.

135 Brian Tobin, 'The (d)evolving nature of guardianship rights for unmarried fathers under Irish law?' (2020) 32 Child and Family Law Quarterly 300, 301.

136 Law Reform Commission, Consultation Paper, Legal Aspects of Family Relationships (LRC CP 55-2009) 64-65; Law Reform Commission, *Report on Illegitimacy* (LRC 4-1982), 85.

137 Family Law Reform Act 1995, s 61C.

138 Adoption and Children Act 2002, s 111.

139 ibid. Parental Responsibility is the equivalent of guardianship in England and Wales.

to the court to be appointed as an *additional guardian* under s 6C of the 1964 Act. This is open to two different categories of non-parent:

- **Step-parents** (i.e. people who are married to the parent of the child or have cohabited with them for over three years) who have shared responsibility for the child's day to day care for more than two years.
- **Adults who have acted in the place of parents for a continuous period of more than 12 months**. People in this category have provided the child's day-to-day care for over 12 months in a situation where the child has no parent or guardian willing or able to care for them. This category includes informal kinship carers such as grandparents but foster parents of children who are in state care must wait five years before applying for guardianship.[140]

These mechanisms are an important change to the law and allow recognition of more diverse family forms in Ireland.[141] Guardianship rights bring stability and formality to a situation where a kinship carer is looking after a child or where a partner is involved in making decisions about the care of a child. These mechanisms can also be used as a 'work around' for intending parents of surrogate-born children who do not qualify for legal parentage under Irish law. These intending parents will have to wait for two years after the child is born before the person who is not recognised as a legal parent can apply for guardianship in order to satisfy the statutory requirements of being involved in or responsible for the child's care.

In order to make a guardianship order under s 6C, the court must have the consent of each existing guardian, but the court can dispense with the need for the consent of an existing guardian 'if it is satisfied that the consent is unreasonably withheld and that it is in the best interests of the child' to make the order.

In deciding whether or not to make an order under s 6C, the s 3 best interests principle and the s 31 checklist apply. In addition, s 6C expressly requires the court to ensure that the child has the opportunity to make his or her views known to the extent possible given his or her age and understanding. The court must also have regard to the overall number of people who have guardianship rights for the child and the degree to which they are involved in the child's upbringing.[142]

---

140 Child Care Act 1991, s 43A.

141 Clare Murray, 'Recognising the Modern Family: Extending Legislative Guardianship Rights in Ireland' (2012) 15 Irish Journal of Family Law 39.

142 Guardianship of Infants Act 1964, s 6C(8)(b).

Where an additional guardian is appointed by the court, the rights of pre-existing guardians are not affected unless the court otherwise orders.[143] Where one or both of the parents of the child are still living, the guardianship rights of the new additional guardian are limited to rights and responsibility outlined in s 6C(11)[144] and can be further limited by the court.[145] This means that an additional guardian may enjoy a more limited form of guardianship than parent guardians.

3.6 Temporary and testamentary guardianship

'Qualifying guardians' have the right to nominate an additional temporary guardian to act in their place and make decisions for the child if they become incapable due to serious illness or injury.[146] A qualifying guardian includes a parent guardian with custody of a child or a non-parent guardian with custody of a child to the exclusion of any living parent of the child. Temporary guardianship allows guardians with day-to-day care of the child to make contingency plans in the event that they become incapable of providing care. For example, a grandmother with guardianship rights who is caring for her grandchildren may nominate a family member to take over if she becomes ill and enters palliative care.

The nomination by the qualifying guardian must be in writing and may specify limits on the rights and responsibilities of guardianship that the temporary guardian may exercise.[147] It is then up to the nominated person to apply to the court for an order granting them guardianship rights if they consider that the qualifying guardian who has nominated them has become incapable of exercising the rights and responsibilities of guardianship.[148] Where such an application is made, all the child's existing legal parents and guardians must be informed, as well as Tusla.[149]

When deciding whether or not to make an order for guardianship, the court must consider the s 3 best interests principle and the s 31 checklist. Section 6E(5) additionally requires the court to be satisfied that the qualifying guardian is incapable of exercising the rights and responsibilities of guardianship, that the nominated person is fit and proper to exercise the rights and responsibilities of temporary guardianship and that it is in the best interest of the child for that particular person to become their temporary guardian.

---

[143] ibid, s 6C(5).
[144] Outlined above.
[145] Guardianship of Infants Act 1964, s 6C(9).
[146] ibid, s 6E.
[147] ibid, s 6E(2).
[148] ibid, s 6E(3).
[149] ibid, s 6E(4).

Once appointed, a temporary guardian takes custody of the child and acts jointly with any other guardian including the qualifying guardian.[150] The rights and responsibilities of the temporary guardian may be limited by court order.[151] If the qualifying guardian becomes capable of exercising the rights and responsibilities of guardianship again, the temporary guardian is required to apply to court to have the order of guardianship revoked.[152]

Some guardians also have the power to appoint a person by deed or in their will to act in their place as guardian in the event of their death. This option is open to all parent guardians and to a guardian who is not a parent of the child but who has custody of the child to the exclusion of any living parent.[153] On the death of the appointing guardian, there is no need to apply for a court order, the testamentary guardian is automatically empowered to act jointly with any surviving guardian of the child.[154] However, if a surviving guardian objects to the appointment of the testamentary guardian, or if the testamentary guardian considers the surviving guardian unfit to have custody of the child, an application may be made to the court. The court then has a range of options available to it: it may make an order revoking the appointment of the testamentary guardian; it may order the testamentary and surviving guardian(s) to act jointly; or it may make an order that the testamentary guardian act as the child's guardian to the exclusion, as far as the court considers proper, of the surviving guardian.[155] Where the court makes an order for the testamentary guardian to act to the exclusion of other guardians, it may also make orders in respect of custody, access or maintenance.[156]

When making any decision relating to the guardianship of a child, the court must consider the best interest of the child as the paramount concern and consider the factors outlined in the s 31 checklist including the views of the child that are ascertainable.

3.7 Disputes between guardians

It is very common for a child to have two or more guardians. All parent guardians have equal decision-making status unless conditions have been placed on their decision-making powers by court order. In *CO'S v Doyle*[157] the Supreme Court held that a father who had acquired guardianship by

---

150 ibid, s 6E(8) .
151 ibid, s 6E(7).
152 ibid, s 6E(9).
153 ibid. See s 7(2) of the Guardianship of Infants Act 1964, as substituted by s 50 of the Children and Family Relationships Act 2015.
154 Guardianship of Infants Act 1964, s 7.
155 ibid, s 7(5).
156 ibid, s 7(6).
157 [2013] IESC 60 [33].

court order was not subordinate in status to the child's mother when it came to decision-making.

In the case of non-parent guardians, their powers are limited to the rights and responsibilities outlined in s 6C(11) and may be further limited by court order. Temporary and testamentary guardians may also have limited guardianship rights.

Guardians may act individually to make decisions for children and do not generally have to confer or agree. However, there are situations where the consent of more than one guardian is required by statute, for example, s 14(1) of the Passport Act 2008 requires the permission of two guardians before a passport can be issued for a child.[158] For health care decisions, the HSE usually accept the consent of one parent to medical treatment.[159] However, where there is a dispute between guardians about healthcare choices for their child, the HSE will try to reach consensus and where this is not possible may make an application to court to allow treatment.

Where guardians disagree on a particular decision about a child, they can apply to court under s 11(1) to resolve the dispute. In making its decision, the court must apply the s 3 best interests principle and the s 31 checklist.

Example case – *BB v AA* [2013] IEHC 394

The parents, who were separated, could not agree on which of two secondary schools their twelve year old son should attend. Hogan J centred the welfare of the child and considered all relevant circumstances, including the boy's wishes to attend school B. Hogan J found that the child should attend school B which was fee paying but was best suited to the child's abilities and needs.

Court orders can restrict guardians from being involved in specified future decisions about their child. For example, in *MG v FR*[160] where the parents were separated, the mother refused permission to enrol her daughter in an Irish speaking pre-school. The father wanted the child to attend the Irish speaking pre-school so that she would become eligible for a place in an excellent Irish speaking primary school. The court held that attending the pre-school would be in the child's best interests and made an order dispensing with need for the mother's consent to taking up a place in the Irish speaking primary school when it became available.

158 Consent of a guardian can be dispensed by court order and in other exceptional circumstances; Passport Act 2008, s 14.

159 HSE, *National Consent Policy* (2022), 51 available at https://www.hse.ie/eng/about/who/national-office-human-rights-equality-policy/consent/hse-national-consent-policy.pdf [last accessed 2 August 2023].

160 [2015] IEHC 857.

3.8 Removal of guardianship status

An extreme solution to resolve entrenched disputes between guardians is the removal of guardianship status. A guardian, or proposed guardian, may apply to the court seeking the removal of another guardian.

Mothers and second parents who are married to the child's mother have automatic guardianship rights by operation of law and cannot be removed as the guardian of a child by court order.[161] Specific exercises of their guardianship rights may be restricted by court order, but their guardianship rights will endure until their child turns 18, unless an adoption order is made.

Where a guardian has acquired guardianship rights by court order, statutory declaration, cohabitation, will or deed, or by operation of law in another country, their guardianship rights can be removed by an order of the court.[162] Such a guardian can only be removed where there is another guardian, it is necessary and desirable, it is in the best interest of the child to do so and, the guardian to be removed consents, is unwilling or unable to exercise the powers of guardianship or has failed in their duties.[163]

A private law application by a guardian for the removal of guardianship status from another person is not an appropriate solution for child protection issues which are dealt with by public law remedies.

4. Custody and Access

Disputes about parenting often involve issues of custody and access. Custody is seen as an adult right to exercise physical day-to-day care and control over a child who lives with them.[164] In contrast, access is viewed as a right of the child[165] that allows them to maintain contact with their parents, siblings and other persons involved in their care and upbringing.[166]

Married parents,[167] mothers[168] and other guardians[169] have rights of custody over their children as against non-guardians unless a custody order is in place. For example, if a child was living with extended family,

---

161 Guardianship of Infants Act 1964, s 8(6).
162 ibid, s 8(4) and 8(6).
163 ibid, s 8(7).
164 *RC v IS* [2003] 4 IR 431, 439.
165 Article 9(3) UNCRC; *MM v GM* [2015] IECA 29.
166 *MD v GD* [1992] FLJ 34; [1992] WJSC-HC 3403; [1992] 7 JIC 3002.
167 *In Re J* [1966] IR 295; *G v An Bord Uchtála* [1980] IR 32, 85 (Henchy J).
168 *State (Nicolaou) v An Bord Úchtálá* [1966] IR 567, 644.
169 Guardianship of Infants Act 1964, s 10(2).

his parents or guardians could seek to enforce their rights of custody by having the child returned to their care.[170]

Where there is a dispute about where a child should live the court may be called upon to decide. In deciding disputes about custody and access, the court must regard the best interests of the child as the paramount consideration.[171] The statutory checklist of factors under s 31(2) must also be considered in determining what outcome is in the best interest of any individual children who are the subject of a dispute.

Most custody and access arrangements do not go to court but are arranged privately by parents.[172]

4.1 Who can apply to court for orders relating to custody and access?

Legal guardians can apply to court for an order regarding custody or access.[173] Parents without guardianship rights can also apply for custody and access to their children.[174] A wide category of people who are not legal parents or guardians can also apply to court for custody. This greater flexibility in the law makes it easier for kinship carers and social parents who are not recognised as legal parents to formalise a caring situation, giving them more certainty and stability.

Section 11E of the Guardianship of Infants Act 1964 allows three categories of non-parent to apply for custody:

- **Relatives,** defined as grandparents, brothers, sisters, uncles or aunts.
- **Step-parents,** (i.e. people who are married to the parent of the child or have cohabited for over three years) who have shared responsibility for the child's day-to-day care for more than two years.
- **Adults who have acted in the place of parents for a continuous period of more than 12 months**. People in this category have provided the child's day-to-day care for over

---

170 ibid, s 14.

171 ibid, s 3.

172 Simone McCaughren, Stephanie Holt, Aisling Parkes and Soma Gregory, *Research Report on guidance of contact time for infants and young children in separated families* (December 2022), 83 available at http://www.tara.tcd.ie/bitstream/handle/2262/101861/FINAL%20OneFamily%20TCD%20UCC%20Report%2012Dec22v2.pdf?sequence=1&isAllowed=y [last accessed 2 August 2023]; One Family, *Ireland's first National Shared Parenting Survey: Results and Recommendations* (2017), 5 available at https://onefamily.ie/wp-content/uploads/2017/01/One-Family_Shared-Parenting_Results-and-Recommendations_FINAL-REPORT_Online.pdf [last accessed 2 August 2023].

173 Guardianship of Infants Act 1964 s 11(2).

174 ibid, s 11(4).

12 months in a situation where the child has no parent or guardian willing or able to care for them.

The court must have the consent of all the child's guardians before making an order granting custody to a non-parent[175] unless it is satisfied that it is in the best interests of the child to dispense with a guardian's consent.[176]

An order for access is required where people with custody rights over the child refuse to facilitate the child spending time with a particular person. Section 11B of the Guardianship of Infants Act 1964 allows an even broader category of people to apply to court for leave to apply for access, including any person with whom the child resides or has formerly resided, and adoptive relatives. However, the legislation prompts the court to consider why the access is being opposed. The court must consider all the circumstances including, the applicant's connection with the child, the risk that the application might disrupt the child's life to the extent that the child would suffer harm, the wishes of the child's guardians and the need for an access order when deciding whether or not to allow these applicants to proceed with their application.

4.2 Ascertaining best interests in custody and access disputes

Section 31(1) requires the court to look at *all relevant circumstances* when determining what is in the best interests of the child. The statutory checklist of factors outlined in s 31(2) draws the courts attention to particular issues which demonstrate the importance of maintaining relationships and parental co-operation.

Key legislation – Guardianship of Infants Act 1964, s 31

(1) In determining for the purposes of this Act what is in the best interests of a child, the court shall have regard to all of the factors or circumstances that it regards as relevant to the child concerned and his or her family.

(2) The factors and circumstances referred to in subsection (1) include:

(a) the benefit to the child of having a meaningful relationship with each of his or her parents and with the other relatives and persons who are involved in the child's upbringing and, except where such contact is not in the child's best interests, of having sufficient contact with them to maintain such relationships;

(b) the views of the child concerned that are ascertainable (whether in accordance with section 32 or otherwise);

[175] ibid, s 11E(3).
[176] ibid, s 11E(4).

(c) the physical, psychological and emotional needs of the child concerned, taking into consideration the child's age and stage of development and the likely effect on him or her of any change of circumstances;
(d) the history of the child's upbringing and care, including the nature of the relationship between the child and each of his or her parents and the other relatives and persons referred to in paragraph (a), and the desirability of preserving and strengthening such relationships;
(e) the child's religious, spiritual, cultural and linguistic upbringing and needs;
(f) the child's social, intellectual and educational upbringing and needs;
(g) the child's age and any special characteristics;
(h) any harm which the child has suffered or is at risk of suffering, including harm as a result of household violence, and the protection of the child's safety and psychological well-being;
(i) where applicable, proposals made for the child's custody, care, development and upbringing and for access to and contact with the child, having regard to the desirability of the parents or guardians of the child agreeing to such proposals and co-operating with each other in relation to them;
(j) the willingness and ability of each of the child's parents to facilitate and encourage a close and continuing relationship between the child and the other parent, and to maintain and foster relationships between the child and his or her relatives;
(k) the capacity of each person in respect of whom an application is made under this Act—
  (i) to care for and meet the needs of the child,
  (ii) to communicate and co-operate on issues relating to the child, and
  (iii) to exercise the relevant powers, responsibilities and entitlements to which the application relates.

The statutory checklist emphasises the value to the child of having a meaningful relationship with both parents and continuing relationships with relatives and other people involved in their upbringing. In *HO'R v MR*[177] Abbott J held that the court is required to consider how best to optimise the child's existing relationships in the particular circumstances. The court is asked to consider the willingness and ability of parents to facilitate and encourage such relationships. Where one parent is unwilling to do this, there is a risk that their custody and access will be curtailed by

[177] [2016] IEHC 781 [7]-[8].

the court.[178] Co-operation between the parents is also of key importance to the court in determining a good outcome.

The court should identify the different types of needs of an individual child with regard to their age and any special characteristics[179] and the history of the child's upbringing and care. The court must consider the capacity of the applicant adult to care for the child, communicate and co-operate with other people and to exercise their responsibilities. The court is prompted to consider the effect on the child of changes in circumstances and alerted to the risk of harm from household violence and the need to protect the child's safety and psychological wellbeing.

The statutory checklist also requires the court to consider the ascertainable views of the child. This obligation is considered in further detail below.

Example case

In *Z v Z*[180] the High Court stressed the need to consider and apply the s 31 checklist in custody and access cases. Here, the court refused a father's application for custody and access where his 11-year-old son lived in another country and there had been no contact between father and son for over five years. The court found that there was no evidence that the father had the capacity to care for his son and meet his needs. The boy was well settled and did not want to see his father.

The court acknowledged that facilitating a meaningful relationship between a child and his father is generally desirable, but this must take second place to ensuring the best interests of the individual child.[181] In this case, where there had been a finding that the father had perpetrated physical and sexual abuse on the child, the court feared that contact with the father would be unnecessarily disruptive and would not protect the child's safety and psychological well-being.

4.3 Joint custody and typical custody arrangements

Section 11 of the Guardianship of Infants Act 1964 allows the court to make an order for joint custody for both parents. Research suggests that this is the most common court ordered custody arrangement following divorce or judicial separation in the Circuit Court.[182] Sole custody orders

---

[178] ibid [17]-[18]

[179] Guardianship of Infants Act 1964, s 31(2)(c), (e) and (f).

[180] [2021] IEHC 20 [79]-[97]

[181] ibid [86]–[88].

[182] Evelyn Mahon and Elena Moore, *Post-separation parenting: A study of separation and divorce agreements made in the Family Law Courts of Ireland and their implications*

are generally used where one of the parents is unfit to care for the children, is no longer involved or where there is a record of serious violence.[183] Joint custody does not necessarily mean that the child spends equal amounts of time with each adult carer. Instead, joint custody grants both parents equivalent legal status in relation to day-to-day rights and responsibilities.

Joint custody is awarded in cases where the court feels that the parents have the capacity to agree specific arrangements in relation to the daily care of their children. For example, in *S v D*[184] an order for joint custody was made where the father had not yet finalised his living arrangements allowing the parents flexibility in making day to day arrangements once the living situation became clear.

Joint custody is also appropriate to clarify rights in cross-border cases. For example, in *AN v KN,*[185] an order for joint custody was made on the basis that the children's habitual residence and home was in Ireland with their mother, but it was envisaged that they would travel frequently to Australia to spend time with their father.

Joint custody may also be used in high conflict cases in the hope that such equality of status will encourage parents to resolve any acrimony between them.[186]

Court orders for parenting arrangements where the children spend equal amounts of time with both parents are made[187] but it is more typical for children to spend more time with their mothers.[188] Ann Egan and Carol Coulter both suggest that this is due to practical concerns,[189] in part because women are more likely to work part-time and have time to care for the children.

---

for parent-child contact and family lives (Office of the Minister for Children and Youth Affairs 2011) 60–64.

183 Carol Coulter, *Family Law in Practice: A Study of Cases in the Circuit Court* (Clarus Press 2009) 63-68; Evelyn Mahon and Elena Moore, *Post-separation parenting: A study of separation and divorce agreements made in the Family Law Courts of Ireland and their implications for parent-child contact and family lives* (Office of the Minister for Children and Youth Affairs 2011) 61–62.

184 [2022] IEHC 594.

185 [2022] IEHC 528.

186 *DFO'S v CA* [1999] IEHC 147.

187 See *McA (D) v McA (K)* [2002] 12 JIC 1705.

188 Evelyn Mahon and Elena Moore, *Post-separation parenting: A study of separation and divorce agreements made in the Family Law Courts of Ireland and their implications for parent-child contact and family lives.* (Office of the Minister for Children and Youth Affairs 2011) 62; Carol Coulter, *Family Law in Practice: A Study of Cases in the Circuit Court* (Clarus Press 2009) 103.

189 Anne Egan, 'Are Fathers Discriminated against in Irish Family Law? An Empirical Study' (2011) 14(2) Irish Journal of Family Law 38, 47.

Section 11E allows the court to make an order for joint custody between a parent and a non-parent and to specify where and with whom the child should live and for what periods of time.

4.4 Court-ordered access arrangements

The best interests checklist promotes the value of children having ongoing relationships with both parents and relationships with other family members.[190] In *MM v GM*,[191] Hogan J held that children have a right to the care and company of each parent, where contact is judged objectively to be in their best interests. The courts are generally favourable to access applications.[192]

Access orders will often specify the type, quality and timing of access that is to take place between the child and their parent or family members. The courts must consider the best interests of the child as the paramount consideration when deciding access applications. Children are entitled to the care, company and support of both parents where possible in order to have a meaningful relationship with both of them. This usually means that children should have appropriate overnight access to a parent they don't normally live with. In *MM v GM*,[193] Hogan J suggests that overnight access with both parents should generally be considered as the child's entitlement, preserving the 'normal, carefree element of family life'.[194] Research by Sinéad Conneely et al suggests that overnight access was granted by the court in about 40% of cases observed.[195] Research by Simone McCaughren et al, who looked at both privately arranged access and court ordered access arrangements for children under six suggests that overnight access is the most common type of access arrangement, reported by 69% of participating parents.[196]

Depending on the circumstances, access might take the form of overnight stays at a parents' house, face to face activities, holidays with a parent who lives abroad or it may be more restricted. Courts may order supervised access where there is concern about the wellbeing of a child. Ireland

---

[190] Including grandparents see Anne Egan and Richard MacNamara, 'Grandparents and the Law in Ireland' (2010) 13 Irish Journal of Family Law 27.

[191] [2015] IECA 29 [13].

[192] Sinéad Conneely, Róisín O'Shea and Shane Dempsey, 'Custody and Access in the District Court' (2021) 24 Irish Journal of Family Law 84.

[193] [2015] IECA 29.

[194] ibid [14].

[195] Sinéad Conneely, Róisín O'Shea and Shane Dempsey, 'Custody and Access in the District Court' (2021) 24 Irish Journal of Family Law 84.

[196] Simone McCaughren, Stephanie Holt, Aisling Parkes and Soma Gregory, *Research Report on guidance of contact time for infants and young children in separated families* (One Family December 2022), 83 available at http://www.tara.tcd.ie/bitstream/handle/2262/101861/FINAL%20OneFamily%20TCD%20UCC%20Report%2012Dec22v2.pdf?sequence=1&isAllowed=y [last accessed 2 August 2023].

has no public system of supervised access services[197] which means that supervision must be provided by a neutral family member or by private professional services. The lack of support for parents in managing difficult access arrangement is a big safety concern for judges.[198] In very difficult situations, indirect contact such phone or video calls may be considered most appropriate in the best interests of the child. Irish courts are very reluctant to order no access, even in hostile circumstances.[199]

The courts may attempt to increase contact in a series of stages. For example, in the high conflict case of *McN v McN*[200] the court outlined a structure for weekly video calls between a father and each of his three children for a period of three months. The court hoped to progress contact if this system worked satisfactorily but emphasised that any further access would have to be risk assessed and supervised until the court was fully satisfied that there was proper and useful engagement for the children.

4.4.1 Variation and enforcement of custody and access orders

Custody and access orders are never final and can be varied or discharged by the court where this is in the best interests of the child.[201] A change in circumstances or new information can justify the variation or discharge of such orders allowing arrangements to change with the child's evolving needs.

A parent or guardian of a child who has been granted a court order for custody or access to a child may apply to the court for an enforcement order where custody or access is unreasonably denied by another parent or guardian.[202] The option of applying to the court for an enforcement order under s 18A is not available to relatives or other persons who are not guardians, even though such people are entitled to apply for custody and access and such rights might be frustrated by a parent or guardian of the child.

---

197 Barnardos and One Family ran pilot services for supervised access centres between 2011–2013 but these services are now closed, see https://onefamily.ie/how-we-support-families/child-contact-centres/https://onefamily.ie/how-we-support-families/child-contact-centres/ [last accessed 2 August 2023]; Simone McCaughren, Stephanie Holt, Aisling Parkes and Soma Gregory, *Research Report on guidance of contact time for infants and young children in separated families* (One Family December 2022) 71-73 available at http://www.tara.tcd.ie/bitstream/handle/2262/101861/FINAL%20OneFamily%20TCD%20UCC%20Report%2012Dec22v2.pdf?sequence=1&isAllowed=y [last accessed 2 August 2023] .

198 ibid 110–111.

199 Evelyn Mahon and Elena Moore, *Post-separation parenting: A study of separation and divorce agreements made in the Family Law Courts of Ireland and their implications for parent-child contact and family lives* (Office of the Minister for Children and Youth Affairs 2011) 66–70.

200 [2021] IEHC 556.

201 Guardianship of Infants Act 1964, s 12.

202 ibid, s 18A.

The court may make an enforcement order where it is satisfied that custody or access has been unreasonably denied and the order is in the best interests of the child.[203] Such an order may grant the applicant additional access to the child to make up for the time that has been missed[204] but only if the child, to the extent possible given his or her age and understanding, has had the opportunity to make his or her views known to the court and these views are taken into account.[205] An enforcement order may require the parent who has been denied access or custody to be reimbursed for any expenses incurred trying to exercise their rights of custody and access. The enforcement order may also provide that the parents or guardians attend a parenting programme or family counselling and/or that they receive information on the possibility of availing of mediation as a means of resolving their parenting disputes.[206]

Custody and access orders can also be enforced by way of contempt of court proceedings. The court will take into account the best interests of the child and may be reluctant to imprison a parent, even for repeated breach of orders.

Example case – Contempt of court proceedings

In *PM v EM*,[207] a father with custody of his daughter repeatedly disrupted court-ordered access with the child's mother. The mother brought attachment and committal proceedings. The court found that the father had deliberately used the Covid-19 public health crisis to frustrate access and disrupt the relationship between his daughter and her mother. However, the court held that committing the father to prison would not be in the best interests of the child and would serve to drive a wedge between mother and daughter. Instead, the court gave the following warning to the father:

> 'The father has acted throughout in a determined, premeditated and intelligent way. It is a real concern that he has largely succeeded to date in having his way despite the Court Orders made. If he continues to behave in defiance of Court Orders then he may well find himself falling into that category of rare cases where the sanction of incarceration is the last option available to the court to show to him and others that Court Orders are made to be obeyed'.[208]

[203] ibid, s 18A(3).
[204] ibid, s 18A(4)(a).
[205] ibid, s 18A(5).
[206] ibid, s 18A(4).
[207] [2020] IEHC 700.
[208] ibid [81].

5. The views of the child in private law disputes

Article 42A.4.2° requires provision to be made by law to ensure that in respect of any child who is capable of forming his or her own views, the view of the child shall be ascertained and given due weight having regard to the age and maturity of the child.

Conor O'Mahony[209] outlines three parts to the court's constitutional duty:

1. The court must establish whether the child is capable of forming relevant views.
2. If so, the court must ascertain what the child's views are
3. The court must then decide how much weight to give the child's views depending on the age and maturity of the child.

Judges have had discretion to take children's wishes into account since 1997[210] and the child's procedural right to be heard and have their wishes taken into account is established in Irish case law.[211] However, research suggests that children's voices are rarely heard by the courts in private law disputes.[212] Section 31 of the Guardianship of Infants Act 1964 now obliges the court to take into account the child's views 'that are ascertainable'.[213] Section 32 of the Guardianship of Infants Act 1964 allows the court to appoint an expert to determine and convey the child's views but does not require the court to do so. As O'Mahony points out, this wording is too weak to ensure that the court's constitutional obligations are fulfilled. The appointment of an expert is at the court's discretion and there is no guidance as to how to ascertain the child's views in cases where a report is not ordered.[214]

Examples of judicial best practice in hearing children's views in private law cases can be found in child abduction cases, where art 11(2) of Brussels II *bis*[215] places a stronger mandatory positive obligation on the

---

[209] Conor O'Mahony, *Annual Report of the Special Rapporteur on Child Protection 2020*, 91 available at https://www.gov.ie/pdf/?file=https://assets.gov.ie/108822/caa4c294-0d99-4d35-8560-c7555588e1ac.pdf#page=null [last accessed 2 August 2023].

[210] Guardianship of Infants Act 1964, s 25 as amended by the Children Act 1997, s 11.

[211] *FN v CO* [2004] 4 IR 311, 322.

[212] Elaine O'Callaghan, 'Realising the Child's Right to be Heard in Private Child Contact Disputes: Progress in Practice?' (2010) 13 Irish Journal of Family Law 94-101.

[213] Guardianship of Infants Act 1964, s 31(2)(b).

[214] Opening Statement of Dr Conor O'Mahony, Senior Lecturer, School of Law, University College Cork Oireachtas Committee on Justice and Equality, 20 February 2019, 2-4 available at https://data.oireachtas.ie/ie/oireachtas/committee/dail/32/joint_committee_on_justice_and_equality/submissions/2019/2019-02-20_opening-statement-dr-conor-o-mahony-senior-lecturer-in-constitutional-and-child-law-school-of-law-university-college-cork_en.pdf [last accessed 2 August 2023].

[215] Council Regulation (EC) No 2201/2003 of 27 November 2003 concerning jurisdiction and the recognition and enforcement of judgments in matrimonial matters and the

court to provide a child with an opportunity to be heard, unless this appears inappropriate. These types of cross-border cases are examined in Chapter 12.

The Guardianship of Infants Act 1964 does not give the court any guidance on how to establish whether or not a child is capable of forming their own views. This seems to be a matter for the individual judge in each case. In *N v N*[216] Finlay Geoghegan J held that normal six-year-olds are capable of forming their own views about many matters of direct relevance in their ordinary everyday life. Whereas, in *RP v SD*[217] the court held that a child who was not yet five would not be capable of forming relevant views on the facts of the case. Research by McCaughren et al, suggests that children under six are not generally heard in private law disputes.[218]

In practice, there are limited mechanism for children's views to be heard in private law cases. There is no statutory provision for the appointment of a guardian *ad litem,* as is the case in public law cases.[219] The court may, at its discretion, appoint an expert to determine and convey the child's views.[220] Judges are not bound to accept the recommendations of such reports but must give adequate and sustainable reasons for rejecting them as evidence.[221] In preparing a report for the court the expert may interview the children and observe the family.[222] However, the cost of an expert report must be met by the parents. The UNCRC has recommended that additional state resourcing is required to guarantee that the views of the child are taken into account.[223] McCaughren et al have also expressed concern about inconsistent use of reports and the use of unregulated private practitioners as experts.[224]

---

matters of parental responsibility, repealing Regulation (EC) No 1347/2000. This obligation is now found in art 21 of Brussels II ter Council Regulation (EU) 2019/1111 of 25 June 2019 on jurisdiction, the recognition and enforcement of decisions in matrimonial matters and the matters of parental responsibility, and on international child abduction (recast) OJ L 178, 2.7.2019, 1–115.

216 [2008] IEHC 28 [32].

217 [2012] IEHC 188 [40].

218 Simone McCaughren, Stephanie Holt, Aisling Parkes and Soma Gregory, *Research Report on guidance of contact time for infants and young children in separated families* One Family December 2022), 112–116 available at http://www.tara.tcd.ie/bitstream/handle/2262/101861/FINAL%20OneFamily%20TCD%20UCC%20Report%2012Dec22v2.pdf?sequence=1&isAllowed=y [last accessed 2 August 2023].

219 Children Act 1997, s 11 does provide for this but has not commenced. It only provides for GALS to be appointed in special circumstances.

220 Guardianship of Infants Act 1964, s 13; Guardianship of Infants Act 1964 (Child's Views Expert) Regulations 2018; Family Law Act 1995, s 47.

221 *DK v PIK* [2022] IECA 246 [124].

222 eg *DK v PIK* [2022] IECA 246.

223 Committee on the Rights of the Child , Concluding Observations on the Combined Third and Fourth Periodic Reports of Ireland – CRC/C/IRL/CO/3-4 2016, [32]–[33]

224 Simone McCaughren, Stephanie Holt, Aisling Parkes and Soma Gregory, *Research Report on guidance of contact time for infants and young children in separated*

Finally, a judge may decide to talk directly to children. Such informal discussions can raise evidential problems. For example, in *AS (orse DB v RB)*[225] the trial judge saw two children in his chambers without the parents or their legal representatives present. The Supreme Court was clear that the only evidence that a trial judge can rely on in family law proceedings is evidence given on oath or in the presence of both parties, therefore any information obtained from the children was not admissible in making a decision. In *O'D v O'D*[226]Abbott J set out some guidelines to assist judges when speaking to children including the need to agree the terms of reference of the meeting with the parents in dispute and to make a proper record of the meeting with the children.[227] These principles were endorsed by the Court of Appeal in *DK v PIK*[228] who confirmed that what is said to a judge by a child in a meeting conducted in the absence of the parties to the dispute or their representatives cannot properly be relied upon as evidence.[229]

6. Child maintenance

Child maintenance refers to financial support paid to cover the everyday costs of bringing up a child. It is usually paid by a non-resident parent to the resident parent (i.e. the parent with whom the child lives), following parental separation. The primary legal responsibility to financially provide for children lies with their parents but the State has a secondary role in ensuring that children's needs are meet.

Article 27 of the UNCRC recognises the right of every child to a standard of living 'adequate for the child's physical, mental, spiritual, moral and social development'. The primary responsibility to secure this right lies with parents under the UNCRC. However, States Parties are under an obligation to assist parents in financially providing for their children and must also provide social assistance programmes to feed, house and clothe children where necessary. Article 27(4) specifically requires the State to take all appropriate measures to recover maintenance for the child from their parents.

In *Attorney General v Dowse*, the High Court confirmed that Article 42.1 places a constitutional obligation on parents to financially provide for

families (One Family December 2022), 15–20 available at http://www.tara.tcd.ie/bitstream/handle/2262/101861/FINAL%20OneFamily%20TCD%20UCC%20Report%2012Dec22v2.pdf?sequence=1&isAllowed=y [last accessed 2 August 2023].

225 [2002] 2 IR 428.

226 [2013] 3 IR 189.

227 ibid [261]–[327].

228 [2022] IECA 246 [133].

229 ibid [143].

their children.[230] However, child maintenance is generally treated by the law as a private obligation between two adults rather than a child's right that must be protected by the State. Many parents will come to private agreements about child maintenance, sometimes through mediation or other forms of collaborative law but these agreements are not enforceable unless made into an order of court.[231] No state support is provided to help parents with calculation or collection of maintenance payments. The onus is on parents who cannot agree to bring their own individual court proceedings. Legal enforcement mechanisms to collect child maintenance are particularly problematic and received international criticism from the Committee on the Elimination of Discrimination Against Women in 2017.[232] In 2022, the *Report of the Child Maintenance Review Group* concluded that the child maintenance system is 'fundamentally unsatisfactory' and in need of 'urgent and radical reform'.[233]

The legislation relating to child maintenance law in Ireland is complicated. Different statutes apply depending on the context in which child maintenance is considered by the court. Child maintenance can be considered during divorce or judicial separation proceedings[234] as part of the court's obligation to ensure that provision has been made for dependents of a marriage.[235] Child maintenance can also be considered as a standalone issue under the Guardianship of Infants Act 1964 or the Family Law (Maintenance of Spouses and Children) Act 1976. These two mechanisms can be used for all children, regardless of whether or not their parents are married to each other. Section 42 of the Family Law Act 1995 now gives the court jurisdiction to make a lump sum payment either 'instead of' or 'in addition to' periodical payments orders made under the 1964 Act or the 1976 Act.

This section will focus on the large numbers of child maintenance applications made under the Family Law (Maintenance of Spouses and Children) Act 1976 (5,451 applications in 2021).[236] Such applications are nearly exclusively heard in the District Court but can also be brought in

---

[230] [2006] IEHC 64 [74].

[231] See Chapter 5.

[232] Committee on the Elimination of Discrimination against Women, *Concluding observations on the combined sixth and 7th periodic reports of Ireland,* 57 available at https://digitallibrary.un.org/record/863874?ln=en' [last accessed 2 August 2023].

[233] Report of the Child Maintenance Review Group (November 2022) available at https://www.gov.ie/en/publication/f01cd-report-of-the-child-maintenance-review-group/ [12.1.9] [last accessed 2 August 2023].

[234] Under the Judicial Separation and Family Law Reform Act 1989 or the Family Law (Divorce) Act 1996.

[235] See Chapter 4.

[236] Court Service, Annual Report 2021, 64. These figures include applications for spousal maintenance as well as child maintenance.

the Circuit Court.[237] There is very little formal reporting of such cases. The District Court is limited to a maximum financial award of €150 per week per child[238] or a lump sum of €15,000.[239] In contrast, no financial limits apply in the Circuit Court or High Court where child maintenance is more commonly considered as part of judicial separation, divorce cases and cohabitation cases.

The Family Law (Maintenance of Spouses and Children) Act 1976 was initially designed exclusively for married families. It has now been extended to include all parents and children, but different sections of the Act apply depending on whether or not the adults liable to pay child maintenance are married to each other.

6.1 Who is liable to pay child maintenance?

The Family Law (Maintenance of Spouses and Children) Act 1976 ('the 1976 Act') imposes a broad liability on adults for child maintenance which extends beyond their legal or biological children and includes unrelated children where the adults have voluntarily taken on the obligation of financial support. Spouses are liable under the 1976 Act for 'dependent children of the family'[240] which includes children born to the couple, children adopted by the couple and children to whom both spouses are acting in the place of parents. It also includes the child of just one spouse, a child adopted by just one spouse and a child to whom just one spouse is acting in the place of parents as long as the other spouse, being aware that he or she is not the parent of the child, has treated that child as a member of the family.[241]

The liability of parents who are not married to each other is slightly narrower. They are liable for their legal or biological children[242] but they are only liable to pay child maintenance to support the children of their cohabiting partner[243] if they have been legally appointed as the child's guardian.[244]

Child maintenance is owed to 'dependent children'. This includes all children under the age of 18 and children under the age of 23 where they are in full-time education or seeking maintenance to support full-time education. The obligation to pay child maintenance endures indefinitely

---

237 Family Law (Maintenance of Spouses and Children) Act 1976, s 23.
238 ibid, s 23(2).
239 Family Law Act 1995, s 42.
240 Family Law (Maintenance of Spouses and Children) Act 1976, s 5.
241 ibid, s 3.
242 ibid, s 5A.
243 ibid, s 5B.
244 Under s 6C of the Guardianship of Infants Act 1964, see above.

where a child is suffering from a mental or physical disability to such extent that it is not reasonably possible for them to fully financial maintain themselves in adulthood. Where the liability to pay child maintenance depends on guardianship, any maintenance order made ceases once the child turns 18[245] when guardianship lapses, regardless of the needs of the child.

6.2 Who can apply for a child maintenance order under the 1976 Act?

Applications for child maintenance order are generally brought by the resident parent (who is usually the mother) against the non-resident parent.[246] The 1976 Act also allows applications for child maintenance to be brought by third parties where the parents have failed to provide such maintenance as is proper in the circumstances.[247] This third party might include a relative, social worker or the child themselves. Applications by older children seeking financial support for higher education are not uncommon. Where the parents are married to each other, the court can only make a child maintenance order on the application of a third party where one of the spouses is dead or the spouses are living separately and apart.[248]

An application to have an existing maintenance order discharged or varied can be made to the court if there is a change in circumstances or new information.[249]

6.3 How is the level of child maintenance determined by the court?

In order to make an award of child maintenance, the court must be satisfied that the liable adult has failed to provide such maintenance **'as is proper in the circumstances'**.[250] In determining the appropriate payment level the court has total discretion but must have regard to all the circumstances of the case, including the relevant statutory checklist of factors. Different checklists apply depending on the marital status of the child's parents : section 5(4) where the child's parents are married to each other, section 5A(3) where the parents are not married to each other and sections 5B(3) and 5C(3) where the court is considering the liability of cohabiting partner who is the guardian of the child. The court is not required to consider the best interest of the child or the child's views.

In all situations, the court must consider the income, earning capacity

---

[245] Family Law (Maintenance of Spouses and Children) Act 1976, s 6(3A).
[246] ibid, ss 5 and 5A.
[247] ibid, ss 5(1)(b) and 5A(2).
[248] ibid, s 5(1)(b).
[249] ibid, s 6.
[250] ibid, ss 5, 5A and 5B.

and other financial resources of both adults and any dependent children, the financial responsibilities of each adult to spouses or cohabitants and the needs of any other dependent children. The court is expressly instructed to disregard any state benefit or allowance granted in respect of dependent children to either parent in its determination. In cases involving parents who are married to each other, the court may also consider the conduct of each spouse.[251]

There is very little judicial guidance on how a court should exercise its discretion in determining an appropriate level of child maintenance. In *RH v NH,*[252] Finlay CJ set out five practical considerations for courts to consider when determining maintenance for a wife and children following parental separation including; the inevitability that all parties would suffer a drop in their standard of living, the need for the court to identify the minimum reasonable requirements of the wife and children, the earning capacity of the wife, the true take home pay of the husband and the reasonable living expenses of the husband.

In *Attorney General v Dowse,*[253] the court used powers under s 7(1B) of the Adoption Act 1991[254] to order wealthy adoptive parents who had abandoned their adoptive child to pay child maintenance. In these highly unusual circumstances, McMenamin J considered the standard of living of both parents to be relevant and made maintenance orders to give the child parity with the standard of living of their other children.[255]

The Child Maintenance Review Group suggest that the average weekly amount of child maintenance received is €58 per week per child[256] which is consistent with research by Conneely on the average payments ordered by the District Court.[257] In 2011, Mahon and Moore found that average child maintenance payments ordered by the Circuit Court in divorce and judicial separation cases were slightly higher at approximately €60-€100 per week per child.[258] These Circuit Court awards were made in a context where the housing needs of the child and the financial maintenance of the primary care giver may have been secured by other financial orders.

---

251 ibid, s 5(4)(c).

252 [1986] ILRM 352, 354–355.

253 [2006] IEHC 64.

254 This power is now found in Adoption Act 2010, s 92(3).

255 *Attorney General v Dowse* [2006] IEHC 64 [86]-[87].

256 *Report of the Child Maintenance Review Group* (November 2022) [8.2.4.12].

257 Sinead Conneely, Róisín O'Shea and Shane Dempsey, 'Child Maintenance and the District Court' (2021) 24 Irish Journal of Family Law 31–36.

258 Evelyn Mahon and Elena Moore, *Post-separation parenting: A study of separation and divorce agreements made in the Family Law Courts of Ireland and their implications for parent-child contact and family lives* (Office of the Minister for Children and Youth Affairs 2011).

6.4 How are child maintenance orders enforced?

Effective enforcement of child maintenance orders is highly challenging for resident parents and can involve multiple trips to court. Where child maintenance is not paid, the resident parent can apply again to court for an attachment of earnings order which requires child maintenance payments to be deducted at source from the other parent's salary, pension or state benefits.[259] The effectiveness of an attachment of earning order is limited. Where the paying parent changes employers, the order ceases to have effect and the resident parent must return to court with information about the new employer for a new order. Attachment of earnings orders have no application at all where the non-resident parent is self employed. In Sinead Conneely's study, attachment of earnings orders were made in only 6.2% of cases. The authors suggest that attachment of earnings orders were not requested in their sample because of their futility where the payer was unemployed or had frequent changes of employment.[260]

The resident parent can apply for an enforcement order if the maintenance is not paid following the attachment of earnings order[261] but this requires them to make yet another application, return to court and secure a new court date.[262]

An alternative option for enforcement of maintenance orders is to take proceedings for contempt of court. The court can order imprisonment for non-payment of child maintenance but this is rare.[263]

6.5 Proposals for reform

There have been multiple calls for the establishment of an administrative body[264] to calculate and collect child maintenance payments as is the case in many other countries including Northern Ireland. The Child Maintenance Review Group were divided in their recommendations on this issue. Four out of seven Group members were in favour of the establishment of a properly funded State Child Maintenance Agency to

---

259 Family Law (Maintenance of Spouses and Children) Act 1976, s 10.

260 Sinead Conneely, Róisín O'Shea and Shane Dempsey, 'Child Maintenance and the District Court' (2021) 24 Irish Journal of Family Law 31–36, 33.

261 Family Law (Maintenance of Spouses and Children) Act 1976, s 20.

262 Women's Aid, Submission to the Child Maintenance Review Group (March 2021), 5 available at https://www.nwci.ie/learn/publication/nwc_submission_to_the_child_maintenance_review_group [last accessed 2 August 2023].

263 Conor O'Mahony, *Annual Report of the Special Rapporteur on Child Protection* (June 2021), 209.

264 Report of the Child Maintenance Review Group (November 2022), 86–93 available at https://www.gov.ie/en/publication/f01cd-report-of-the-child-maintenance-review-group/ [last accessed 2 August 2023].

deal with standalone maintenance cases.[265] The remaining three Group members favoured extensive reform of the existing court-based system including additional resourcing.

7. SUMMARY

Parentage rules by manner of conception

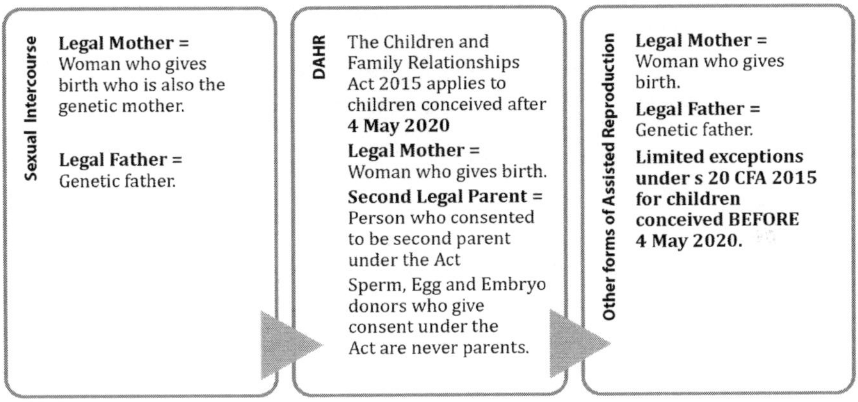

Surrogacy

- Surrogacy is, as yet, unregulated in Ireland.
- Legislative proposals must balance the competing interests of intended parents, children and surrogates and be international human rights compliant.
- Current legislative proposals lean towards a post-birth legal order model with a pre-birth authorisation stage.

Guardianship

- Automatic guardianship rights attach to mothers, married fathers and married second parents following DAHR.
- Fathers and second parents who are not married to the mother must acquire guardianship through cohabitation, by agreement or through a court order.
- Non-parents can also acquire guardianship by court order under s 6C in certain circumstances.
- In deciding whether or not to make an order for guardianship the

[265] ibid [12.6].

court must consider the best interests of the child, the best interests checklist and the child's ascertainable views.

- Where guardians disagree and bring an issue to the court to resolve, the court will make the decision in the best interests of the child. (ss 3 and 31 apply and the child's views should be taken into account where ascertainable).

Custody and access

- Parental disputes about guardianship, custody and access are mainly decided in the District or Circuit Court.
- The Court must determine the dispute according to the best interests principle in s 3 and consider the statutory 'checklist' in s 31.
- The court must also ascertain and consider the wishes of a child who is capable of forming relevant views.

Maintenance

- Child maintenance is treated as a private legal obligation between adults in Irish law.
- Under the Family Law Act 1976, adults are liable to pay child maintenance for their legal and biological children and to unrelated children where they have already taken on the obligation of financial support.
- The court has a great deal of discretion in deciding how much child maintenance is proper in the circumstances but must refer to a statutory checklist of factors. The best interests principle does not apply.
- Child maintenance orders can be enforced through attachment of earnings orders, enforcement orders or contempt of court but the Child Maintenance Review Group 2022 suggests that current mechanisms are inadequate.
- There are calls to introduce an administrative body to calculate and collect child maintenance payments.

8. Further Reading

8.1 Legal parentage

Lydia Bracken, *LGBTI+ Parent Families in Ireland: Legal Recognition of Parent-Child Relationships,* University of Limerick, 2021, 28, available at https://www.ul.ie/research/lgbti-parent-families-ireland-legal-recognition-parent-child-relationships [last accessed 8 March 2022].

Conor O' Mahony, *A Review of Children's Rights and Best Interests in the Context of Donor-Assisted Human Reproduction and Surrogacy in Irish Law* (Department of Children, Equality, Disability, Integration and Youth 2021).

Maebh Harding, 'LGBT+ Family Rights in Ireland: Stretching Traditional Conceptions of Parenthood' in June Carbone and Robin Fretwell (ed) *International Survey of Family Law* (Intersentia 2022) 206-229.

Brian Tobin, 'Assisted Reproductive Techniques and Irish Law: No Child Left Behind?' (2020) 64 The Irish Jurist 138.

8.2 Surrogacy

Joint Committee on International Surrogacy, *Final Report of the Joint Committee on International Surrogacy* (Joint Committee on International Surrogacy 2022).

Conor O'Mahony, *A Review of Children's Rights and Best Interests in the Context of Donor-Assisted Human Reproduction and Surrogacy in Irish Law* (2020) available at https://www.gov.ie/en/publication/3e601-a-review-of-childrens-rights-and-best-interests-in-the-context-of-donorassisted-human-reproa-review-of-childrens-rights-and-best-interests-in-the-context-of-donor-assisted-human-reproduction-and-surrogacy-in-irish-law-duction-and-surrogacy-in-irish-law/ [last accessed 2 August 2023].

Bronagh O'Hanlon, Katie Winder and Chloe O'Reilly, 'A Snapshot of Surrogacy in Ireland with a Comparative Look at international Practices' (2020) 4 Irish Judicial Studies Journal 25 available at https://ijsj.ie/assets/uploads/documents/pdfs/2020-Edition-02/2.%20O'Hanlon%20Winder%20O'Reilly.pdf [last accessed 2 August 2023].

Lydia Bracken, 'The Position of the Surrogate in the Health (Assisted Human Reproduction) Bill' (2022) Irish Journal of Family Law 45.

Brian Tobin, *The Legal Recognition of Same-Sex Relationships: Emerging Families in Ireland and Beyond* (Hart 2023) ch 4.

8.3 Guardianship

Brian Tobin, 'Guardianship and Unmarried fathers in Ireland: One Step Forward, Two Steps Back?' (2020) 23 (4) Irish Journal of Family Law 87.

Clare Murray, 'Recognising the Modern Family: Extending Legislative Guardianship Rights in Ireland' (2012) 15 Irish Journal of Family Law 39.

8.4 Views of the child

Simone McCaughren, Stephanie Holt, Aisling Parkes and Soma Gregory, *Research Report on guidance of contact time for infants and young children in separated families* (One Family December 2022).

Aoife Daly, 'The Judicial interview in Cases of Children's Best Interests-Lessons for Ireland' (2017) Irish Journal of Family Law 66.

8.5 Custody and access

Sinéad Conneely, Róisín O'Shea and Shane Dempsey, 'Custody and Access in the District Court' (2021) 24 Irish Journal of Family Law 84.

Stephanie Holt, 'A Case of Laying Down the Law: Post-Separation Child Contact and Domestic Abuse' (2011) Irish Journal of Family Law 87.

Evelyn Mahon and Elena Moore, *Post-separation parenting: A study of separation and divorce agreements made in the Family Law Courts of Ireland and their implications for parent-child contact and family lives.* (Office of the Minister for Children and Youth Affairs 2011) 66.

8.6 Maintenance

Kathryn O'Sullivan, 'Child Maintenance Reform in Ireland: Lessons from Abroad' (2022) 34 Child and Family Law Quarterly 41.

Sinead Conneely, Róisín O'Shea and Shane Dempsey, 'Child Maintenance and the District Court' (2021) 24 Irish Journal of Family Law 31.

Report of the Child Maintenance Review Group (November 2022) available at *https://www.gov.ie/en/publication/f01cd-report-of-the-child-maintenance-review-group/* [last accessed 2 August 2023].

Chapter 10

Public Child Law

Maebh Harding

With thanks to Aisling Parkes and Joseph Mooney for comments on the draft.

LEARNING OBJECTIVES

By the end of this chapter, students will be equipped to:

- Outline the different orders and mechanisms available under the Child Care Act 1991 to intervene into family life to protect children.
- Evaluate the extent and appropriateness of state intervention into family life to protect children.
- Analyse the need for children's rights to be prioritised in public child law proceedings.
- Contextualise Ireland's modern law of child protection within an historical legacy of institutionalisation.

CRITICAL THINKING POINTS

- What do we really know about everyday care proceedings?
- Is the voice of the child adequately heard within care proceedings?

1. Introduction

Public child law raises difficult questions about the roles of the state and parents in protecting and safeguarding children and their rights. Tensions arise between the need to ensure that children are protected from harm and the need to prevent the State from interfering unjustifiably in the family unit. Children have rights to live in a family and parents have prima facie rights to care for, and make decisions about, their children's upbringing. Constitutional protection afforded to the family unit under Article 41 has historically led to a reluctance on the part of the State to interfere in the privacy of the family. The law works on the assumption that, generally speaking, the best place for children is in the family because most families provide a loving environment. But where a particular family environment is negatively impacting the child's welfare and development, the State has legal obligations to protect that child's individual rights and, in appropriate cases, to intervene to promote the child's welfare and development. The law must strike an appropriate balance between the ideal position that children are best off with parents with the reality that some parents cannot provide appropriate care for their children.

In international law there is also policy of deference to the family unit. For example, art 18 (1) of the United Nations Convention on the Rights of the Child (UNCRC) acknowledges the **primary role of parents**:

> States Parties shall use their best efforts to ensure recognition of the principle that both parents have common responsibilities for the upbringing and development of the child. Parents or, as the case may be, legal guardians, have the primary responsibility for the upbringing and development of the child. The best interests of the child will be their basic concern.

However, art 19 acknowledges that children **are not** always protected within their families. States Parties must work with families to safeguard children and provide supports. State intervention is a necessary last resort:

> States Parties shall take all appropriate legislative, administrative, social and educational measures to protect the child from all forms of physical or mental violence, injury or abuse, neglect or negligent treatment, maltreatment or exploitation, including sexual abuse, while in the care of parent(s), legal guardian(s) or any other person who has the care of the child.
>
> Such protective measures should, as appropriate, include effective procedures for the establishment of social programmes to provide necessary support for the child and for those who have the care of the child, as well as for other forms of prevention and for identification, reporting, referral, investigation, and follow-up of instances of child maltreatment and, as appropriate, for judicial involvement.

The European Convention on Human Rights (ECHR) safeguards the right to family life in art 8 but also protects children from abuse through the prohibition on torture in art 3. The State must balance these rights by implementing policies that protect children but also respect the autonomy of the family. In extreme situations, the risk of harm to children outweighs the need to respect the privacy of the family unit and the best solution for children is to be removed from family care. Deciding the appropriate point for state intervention raises difficult questions.

Tragedies result both from excessive state intervention into family life and from failure to intervene.

For example, in *K & T v Finland,*[1] a newborn baby was removed from his mother who suffered from schizophrenia and was having a mental health crisis. The European Court of Human Rights (ECtHR) found that the Finnish authority's failure to make efforts to reunite mother and child when her health improved was a violation of art 8. Whereas in *Z v UK*[2] the failure of British child protection services to protect four children who had suffered appalling abuse from their parents was found to be in violation of art 3.

Article 42A of the Irish Constitution recognises and affirms the natural and imprescriptible rights of all children and requires the State, as far as practicable, to protect and vindicate those rights in its law. As examined in Chapter 8, Article 42A.2 permits state intervention in families where parents have failed in their duties towards their children to such extent that the children's safety or welfare is likely to be prejudicially affected. The substantive legal requirement of parental failure is known as the legal *threshold* for state intervention. It prevents over-interference by the state into the family. Where state intervention is permitted it must always be proportionate, that is, the intervention should be the minimum required to protect children's rights.

The Child Care Act 1991 places a duty on the Child and Family Agency (Tusla) to promote the welfare of children who are not receiving adequate care and protection. This duty is fulfilled by providing support to children and families, but also, where necessary, by making formal supervision arrangements or by taking children into the care of the state. This can happen with the agreement of the parents (**voluntary care**) or without such agreement (**involuntary care**). A high evidential benchmark must be met before a child can be taken into involuntary care, this is discussed in detail below.

Where a child is removed from their family and placed in state care, the State must continue to protect them and ensure their safety and wellbeing. Tusla acts in the place of the child's parents in these situations. In 2021, 962 children were admitted to state care, 77% were admitted due to neglect or safety concerns, whereas 23% entered care because of abuse.[3] By the end of 2021, there were 5,863 children in state care in Ireland. Before the implementation of modern legislation, most children in the care of the State were placed in large institutions where they were

---

1 [2000] ECHR 174.

2 [2002] 34 EHRR 97.

3 Tusla, *Review of Adequacy Report 2021* (2022) available at https://www.tusla.ie/publications/review-of-adequacy-reports/ 58–60, [last accessed 3 August 2023].

often exploited and abused. Today 90% children in state care are placed with foster carers and there are legal safeguards for their protection.[4]

2. Ireland's legacy of institutionalisation as child protection

Modern child protection legislation has evolved as a reaction to a legacy of institutionalisation. The Children Act 1908 ('the 1908 Act')[5] extended the state's ability to remove children from their parents and place them into institutional care, eroding parental rights of custody. This was also the first legislative attempt to protect children from cruelty, creating the first criminal offences for child abuse. The 1908 Act was the basis of child protection law for most of the 20th century.[6] Until the 1970s, state support for children in need was focused on institutionalisation and little direct financial or welfare support was provided to allow these children to stay with their families.

The 1908 Act provided the regulatory basis for Reformatory Schools intended to provide an alternative for children who would otherwise be sent to adult prisons.[7] The Industrial Schools Act 1868 set up state endorsed residential schools in which children received industrial training. For girls, this involved sewing and laundry and for the boys, preparation for manual trades was the priority. Most children who were sent to industrial schools entered because they were destitute or in poor social circumstances and remained until they were 16 years of age. Industrial schools and Reformatory schools were run by religious orders on behalf of the State, but the Department of Education had clear legal responsibility under the 1908 Act for children committed to Industrial and Reformatory Schools.[8]

Children could be placed in Industrial Schools voluntarily by parents or guardians, but they could also be sent there by different organs of the State without parental permission.[9] Between 1936 and 1970, at least

---

4 ibid 64.

5 An Act to consolidate and amend the Law relating to the Protection of Children and Young Persons, Reformatory and Industrial Schools, and Juvenile Offenders, and otherwise to amend the Law with respect to Children and Young Persons. Children Act 1908 Edw. VII 8 c.67.

6 As amended by the Children Act 1929 and the Children Act 1941.

7 The Reformatory Schools (Ireland) Act 1858.

8 Rules and Regulations for Certified Industrial Schools in Saorstát Éireann 1933.

9 Children could be committed to Industrial schools under a detention order made by a court under s 58 of the Children Act 1908. The court could also commit children to industrial schools for non-attendance at school where their parents had made all reasonable efforts to send the child to school, s 17(4) of the School Attendance Act 1926. The Health Act 1953, s 55 allowed the Health Authorities to place orphans and abandoned children in Industrial schools without any court order.

42,000 children were admitted to Industrial Schools.[10] The Ryan Report[11] found that the conditions in industrial schools amounted to neglect as children were often given inadequate education and exploitative industrial training. Many children also suffered serious physical, emotional, and sexual abuse in institutional state care.

Following the Report of the Committee of Enquiry into Reformatory and Industrial Schools' Systems ('the Kennedy Report')[12] in 1970, there was clear consensus that Ireland's dated child protection framework was unfit for purpose and that a co-ordinated approach to child protection was required. The committee called for the abolition of the institutional system of residential care and highlighted the need for Ireland to have an up-to-date comprehensive Children Act.

The Child Care Act 1991 is now the primary statute regulating the placing of children into state care.

3. Constitutional protection of the marital family and the need for Article 42A

The Irish Constitution defers to the marital family. Article 41 protects the marital family from attack and Article 42.5, as originally drafted, placed a strong emphasis on parental rights of autonomy with very little recognition of the individual rights of children. From the 1970s onwards, the courts began to give more weight to parental autonomy, deferring to the rights of marital families in child protection situations. In 1985, the Supreme Court in *Re JH*[13] declared a constitutional presumption that the welfare of a child is to be found in their constitutional family unless there are *compelling reasons* why this cannot be achieved. This deference to the marital family unit over children's individual rights, resulted in state intervention being limited to very extreme circumstances, leaving children at risk of abuse and neglect within the marital family.[14]

The Thirty-first Amendment to the Irish Constitution is an express

---

10 *The Report of the Commission to Inquire into Child Abuse* (2009) (The Ryan Report) Vol 1, Chapter 3 available at http://childabusecommission.ie/?page_id=241 [last accessed 3 August 2023]. See correction by Eoin O'Sullivan to initially reported figures available at https://childabusecommission.ie/?p=1763 [last accessed 3 August 2023].

11 *The Report of the Commission to Inquire into Child Abuse* (2009) (The Ryan Report) available at http://childabusecommission.ie/?page_id=241 [last accessed 3 August 2023].

12 *Reformatory and Industrial Schools System Report* (1970) available at https://www.lenus.ie/handle/10147/77793 [last accessed 3 August 2023].

13 [1985] IR 375.

14 *Northern Area Health Board v HW and DW* [2001] 3 IR 622; *N v HSE and others* [2006] 4 IR 374; Máiréad Enright 'Interrogating the Natural Order: Hierarchies of Rights in Irish Child Law' (2008) 11 Irish Journal of Family Law 3; see Chapter 11.

acknowledgment of children's rights and the wording is influenced by Ireland's international children's rights obligations.[15] Article 42A.2 ensures a consistent approach to state intervention for all children and focusses on the effect of parental failure on children. State intervention must be made with due regard for the rights of the child.

Article 42A.4 additionally requires that provision shall be made *by law* for the best interests of the child to be the paramount consideration in public child law proceedings and for the views of the child to be heard and given due weight. These safeguards required changes to the Child Care Act 1991, some of which are not yet in force.

Key Constitutional provision – Article 42A

1 The State recognises and affirms the natural and imprescriptible rights of all children and shall, as far as practicable, by its laws protect and vindicate those rights.

2 1° In exceptional cases, where the parents, *regardless of their marital status,* fail in their duty towards their children *to such extent that the safety or welfare of any of their children is likely to be prejudicially affected,* the State as guardian of the common good shall, *by proportionate means* as provided by law, endeavour to supply the place of the parents, but always with due regard for the natural and imprescriptible rights of the child [emphasis added].

....

4 1° Provision shall be made by law that in the resolution of all proceedings—

- i brought by the State, as guardian of the common good, for the purpose of preventing the safety and welfare of any child from being prejudicially affected, or
- ii concerning the adoption, guardianship or custody of, or access to, any child,

the best interests of the child shall be the paramount consideration.

2° Provision shall be made by law for securing, as far as practicable, that in all proceedings referred to in subsection 1° of this section in respect of any child who is capable of forming his or her own views, **the views of the child shall be ascertained and given due weight** having regard to the age and maturity of the child.

Article 42A must be interpreted alongside Article 41's protection for the marital family. As discussed in Chapter 8, there is still debate about the

15 Thirty-first Amendment of the Constitution (Children) Act 2012, signed into law on 28 April 2015.

effect of the children's rights referendum on the courts' determination of the appropriate constitutional threshold for state intervention. However, it is now clear that the judiciary must take a child-focussed approach to state intervention and the constitutional threshold test.

Key case

In *Re JJ*[16] a young boy, John, suffered devastating brain injuries in an accident. The hospital wanted to end life-sustaining treatment, but the child's parents objected. The hospital applied to court for state authority to override the parents' decisions about John's medical treatment.

The Supreme Court held that there was an exceptional case for state intervention into parental decision-making within the meaning of Article 42A.2.1° and authorised the end-of-life treatment proposed by the hospital. This case established that the touchstone for state intervention is the *harmful effect* of parental failure on the safety or welfare of a child.[17] This parental failure must amount to more than just a finding that a child might be better off if parents made a different decision for their child.[18] The court emphasised that it is usually to the child's benefit to be part of their family unit and that a significant and high threshold remains before the State can override parental decision-making.[19]

4. The Child Care Act 1991 – overview

The Child Care Act 1991 ('the 1991 Act') pre-dates Ireland's ratification of the UNCRC, the Children's Rights referendum and Article 42A but must be interpreted in light of the new guiding constitutional principles for state intervention into family life to protect children. Some important changes have recently been made to the 1991 Act by the Child Care (Amendment) Act 2022. A government review of the 1991 Act is ongoing[20] and the General Scheme of the Child Care (Amendment) Bill 2023 has now been published.

Under the Child Care Act 1991, the Department of Health is the main provider of child protection services, a role which is now fulfilled by the

16 [2021] IESC 1; Conor O'Mahony, 'The Same but Different? Article 42A and the Threshold for State Intervention in Family Life: In Re JJ' (2022) 4 Irish Supreme Court Review 141.

17 *Re JJ* [2021] IESC 1 [135].

18 ibid [143].

19 ibid [133].

20 Department of Children, Equality , Disability, Integration and Youth, *Review of the Child Care Act 1991* available at https://www.gov.ie/en/publication/97d109-review-of-the-child-care-act-1991/#:~:text=The%201991%20Act%20is%20a,the%20Child%20and%20Family%20Agency [last accessed 3 August 2023].

Child and Family Agency, which is known as Tusla. Co-operation and engagement with families is the first priority of the 1991 Act. Timely family support aims to prevent children entering the state care system.

The 1991 Act outlines the duties of the State towards children for the first time and these legal obligations fall on Tusla. Section 3 creates a general **duty to promote children's welfare.** Section 16 creates a specific **duty to intervene** to protect children. The role of Tusla is a proactive one, the agency must apply for care or supervision orders where children are at risk of harm and require care or protection that they are unlikely to receive without state intervention. Tusla must provide appropriate evidence to the court as to the risk of harm to the child before intervention can be legally permitted. The level of evidence required is slightly different depending on what type of court order is required and this is explored below.

The 1991 Act creates two legal pathways into state care:

1. **Voluntary Care**: where children are in state care in accordance with ongoing parental permission and there is no need for a court order.
2. **Involuntary Care:** Tusla must provide suitable evidence to the court that a risk of harm to the children exists, and it is in the children's best interests to enter state care. A court order allowing state intervention is made.

In 2021, 54% of admissions to care were voluntary whereas 46% followed a court order.[21] 4,626 children were in care under an order of the court at the end of 2021 whereas 1,237 children were in care under a voluntary arrangement.[22]

4.1 Guiding principles for decision-making under the 1991 Act

Part of the ongoing Government Review of the 1991 Act is focussed on drafting more explicit and coherent guiding principles for making decisions about children.

Section 24 of the 1991 Act, recently amended by the Child Care (Amendment) Act 2022, sets out guiding principles for the *court* when making decisions about children. The court must regard the best interests of the child as the paramount consideration.[23] The court is referred to a list

---

[21] Tusla, *Review of Adequacy Report 2021* (2022) available at https://www.tusla.ie/publications/review-of-adequacy-reports/ 58 [last accessed 3 August 2023].
[22] ibid, 70.
[23] s 24(1).

of factors that it must consider in determining what is in the best interests of the child. This list is not exhaustive, and the court may consider other relevant circumstances:

Section 24 – Best interests 'checklist'

The court shall have regard to all of the factors or circumstances that it considers relevant to the child including—

(a) the child's age, maturity and any special characteristics of the child,
(b) the benefit to the child of having a meaningful relationship with his or her parents and with any other relatives and persons who are involved in the child's upbringing,
(c) the views of the child where he or she is capable of forming, and has chosen to express, such views,
(d) the physical, psychological and emotional needs of the child,
(e) the social, intellectual and educational needs of the child,
(f) the religious, spiritual, cultural and linguistic upbringing and needs of the child, and
(g) any harm which the child has suffered or is at risk of suffering, including harm as a result of household violence, and the protection of the child's safety and psychological well-being.

This checklist requires the court to take into account the views of the child where they have been expressed. Section 5 of the Child Care Amendment Act 2022 inserts new s 24A into the Child Care Act 1991 which will place a stronger obligation on the court to consider the ascertainable views of a child, but this has not yet commenced. Section 24A will require the court to determine the best means by which the child's views may be expressed to the court and give due weight to such views, having regard to the age and maturity of the child. This obligation will apply unless the child is not capable of forming views.

The General Scheme of the Child Care (Amendment) Bill 2023 proposes a list of guiding principles which will apply to decisions made by Tusla. These new principles, if implemented, will centre the best interests of the child and the voice of the child in all decision-making processes under the Act giving effect to the requirements of Article 42A. In the meantime, s 3 still gives primacy to parental rights, requiring Tusla to have regard to the rights and duties of parents before regarding the *welfare* of the child as the first and paramount consideration.[24] This approach reflects constitutional case law predating Article 42A. Section 3 also requires Tusla to give due consideration the wishes of the child as far as is practicable, having regard to his age and understanding.

[24] ss 3 and 24.

Key legislation – Navigating the Child Care Act 1991

1. **Governing principles for Tusla:** Tusla's legal duties towards children are set out in ss 3, 4 and 16.

   Section 3 requires Tusla, when making decisions, to have regard to
   - the rights and duties of parents
   - the welfare of the child as the paramount concern
   - the wishes of child
   - best interests of the child to be brought up in their own family.

   Section 3 also sets out Tusla's general duty to **promote the welfare** of children who are not receiving adequate care and protection.

   Section 4 sets out Tusla's obligations to provide Voluntary Care.

   Section 16 sets out Tusla's obligations to apply for a court order to take a child into state care.

2. Parts III-IVA outline the legal requirements for the different legal mechanisms for placing children in **involuntary state care.**
   - Garda Powers – s 12
   - Emergency Care Orders – s 12
   - Interim Care Orders – s 17
   - Care Orders – s 18
   - Supervision Orders – s 19
   - Special Care Orders – s 23F

   There are specific evidential requirements for each order which must be satisfied before the court can authorise state intervention.

3. **Governing principles for the court are found in s 24:**
   - s 24 courts must consider the best interests of the child as the paramount concern.
   - s 24A (when enacted) will require the court to facilitate the expression of the child's views and give those views due weight, having regard to the age and maturity of the child.

4.2 The broader legal framework for child protection

The Child Care Act 1991, as amended, is the key statute in public child law proceedings, but it is part of a broader child protection framework. As examined above, all national legislation must be interpreted in light of constitutional obligations and international children's rights obligations under the ECHR and UNCRC.

The Children Act 2001 primarily governs how children are treated by the criminal justice system but also provides for the establishment of special care facilities for children who require secure accommodation for their own protection. Provisions for making Special Care Orders were inserted into the Child Care Act 1991 and this type of order is discussed in more detail below. Section 246 of the Children Act 2001 criminalises some forms of child abuse.

The Children First Act 2015 requires the Minister to publish guidelines in respect of the protection and welfare of children[25] which are now found in the *Children First, National Guidance for the Protection and Welfare of Children* (2017).[26] *Children First Guidance* covers the recognition of child abuse and neglect, how to make reports to Tusla and outlines best practice for organisations working with children on how to keep children safe while using their services. *Children First Guidance* describes the four main types of abuse (neglect, emotional abuse, physical abuse and sexual abuse) and sets out the steps which should be taken to ensure that the child or young person is protected from harm.

The Children First Act 2015 places statutory obligations on specific groups of professionals[27] to report child abuse and neglect. The introduction of mandatory reporting obligations under this legislation was highly controversial. While it represents a clear commitment by the State to take child abuse seriously, mandatory reporting also generates huge numbers of reports to Tusla. 73,069 referrals were made in total in 2021 (about 200 per day) and 73% of these were mandated reports.[28] The most common source of referrals is An Garda Síochána[29] who made 37% of all referrals in 2021 followed by social workers, teachers and parents. In 2021, 52% of referrals related to child welfare concerns while 35% were made for child protection reasons such as abuse or neglect.[30]

Reports made to Tusla are reviewed by a duty social worker within 24 hours. They may proceed to a preliminary enquiry to see if social work intervention is required. In 2021, 50% of all referrals were closed following

---

25 Children First Act 2015, s 6.

26 https://www.tusla.ie/uploads/content/Children_First_National_Guidance_2017.pdf (last accessed 3 August 2023) and online safety addendum available at https://www.tusla.ie/uploads/content/Final_2019_Addendum_CF_Guidance.pdf [last accessed 3 August 2023].

27 Children First Act 2015, s 14. Including: professionals working with children in the education, health, justice, youth and childcare sectors, registered foster carers and members of the clergy or pastoral care workers of a church or other religious community. Adult counsellors and people working in adult psychiatry.

28 Tusla, *Review of Adequacy Report 2021* (2022), 21-22 available at https://www.tusla.ie/publications/review-of-adequacy-reports/ [last accessed 3 August 2023].

29 This arises where someone reports to An Garda Síochana who report to Tusla.

30 Tusla, *Review of Adequacy Report 2021* (2022), 27 available at https://www.tusla.ie/publications/review-of-adequacy-reports/ [last accessed 3 August 2023].

screening and 8,780 referrals progressed to a preliminary inquiry.[31] A small number will proceed to initial assessment where Tusla gathers evidence to see if there is a risk of harm to the child. In 2021, only 184 referrals resulted in the child's admission to state care in the same calendar year (including voluntary care).[32] An even smaller number will result in an application to court for a care order. Ireland has a relatively low rate of referrals to state care compared to Northern Ireland, Scotland and England.[33] It has been suggested by Gerard Brophy, Chief Social Worker at Tusla, that this is partly because of poor resourcing. Ireland has only 1.4 social workers per thousand people in the Irish population which is well below the relative numbers in Northern Ireland or England and Wales.[34] In 2016, in its concluding observations, the UNCRC expressed concern that Tusla had not been provided with sufficient power or resources.[35]

Care orders are made at District Court level except for Special Care Orders which are made in the High Court. Carol Coulter's research[36] suggests that there is significant regional variation in how cases are listed and managed. Her work also suggests there is no precision in the District Court about the level of evidence required by Tusla to grant a care order[37] and that not all District Judges consider constitutional law or ECHR rights. Changes proposed by the Family Court Bill 2022 will hopefully improve things for children and parents by providing specialist and appropriate venues for care proceedings.[38]

4.3 Critical thinking point: What do we really know about everyday care proceedings?

Although public child law is an important and significant area of law,

---

31 Tusla, *Review of Adequacy Report 2021* (2022), 33–34 available at https://www.tusla.ie/publications/review-of-adequacy-reports/ [last accessed 3 August 2023].

32 (Note that this is out of a total of 962 admissions to care in 2021) Tusla, *Review of Adequacy Report 2021* (2022), 35 available at https://www.tusla.ie/publications/review-of-adequacy-reports/ [last accessed 3 August 2023].

33 Eamon Furey and John Canavan, *A Review on the availability and comparability of statistics on child protection and welfare, including children in care, collated by Tusla*: Child and Family Agency with statistics published in other jurisdictions (March 2019) available at https://www.tusla.ie/uploads/content/COMPWELFINALREPORTMARCH29_-_Final.pdf [last accessed 3 August 2023].

34 *Irish Examiner*, 'Tusla's Chief Social Worker says Ireland needs to recruit more', (October 2022) available at https://www.irishexaminer.com/news/arid-40727370.html [last accessed 3 August 2023].

35 CRC/C/IRL/CO/3-4 (2016), 8.

36 Carol Coulter, *District Court Child Care Proceedings: A National Overview* (2019).

37 Child Care Law Reporting Project Submission to Department of Children and Youth Affairs on Review of Child Care Act 1991 (2018) available at https://assets.gov.ie/73953/a6bec28b0574424bab86affec465942c.pdf [last accessed 3 August 2023].

38 Maria Corbett, 'Child Care is Crying Out for a Specialist, Separate and Unified Family Court' (2022) 25 Irish Journal of Family Law 3.

until recently, not much has been know about how it functions.[39] Tusla publishes annual statistics[40] in relation to child protection services, family support services and children entering and leaving state care, but poor reporting of public child law cases makes it very difficult to understand how the system of care orders actually works.

Care proceedings are heard by the District Court, meaning there are few written judgments. The *in camera* rule requires cases to be held in private and there are restrictions on reporting.[41] This can make it difficult to access court reports of child care proceedings. In recent years, a limited number of District Court rulings are available on courts.ie[42] and some cases have been reported by the Child Care Reporting Project.[43] Care proceeding issues also feature in the annual Special Rapporteur on Child Protection reports.[44] These are important sources for the study of public child law and allow new insights into this area of law.

Research from the Child Care Proceedings Group at University College Cork[45] and from the Child Care Law Reporting Project has highlighted significant concerns about how consistently public child law operates in practice[46] and the need for specialist family courts and specialist training for judges.[47]

There is much that we still don't know about child protection proceedings. For example, there is evidence to suggest that ethnic minority children[48]

---

39 Conor O'Mahony, Caroline Shore, Kenneth Burns and Aisling Parkes, 'Child Care Proceedings in the District Court: What Do We Really Know?' (2012) 15 Irish Journal of Family Law 49–55.

40 https://www.tusla.ie/publications/review-of-adequacy-reports/ [last accessed 3 August 2023].

41 Child Care Act 1991, ss 29(1) and 31.

42 https://www.courts.ie/judgments.

43 https://www.childlawproject.ie/publications/.

44 Available at: https://www.gov.ie/en/collection/51fc67-special-rapporteur-on-child-protection-reports/ [last accessed 3 August 2023].

45 Available here: https://www.ucc.ie/en/appsoc/resconf/res/childcareproceedingsinthedistrictcourt2012-2019/ [last accessed 3 August 2023].

46 Carol Coulter, *District Court Child Care Proceedings: A National Overview* (March 2019) available at https://www.childlawproject.ie/wp-content/uploads/2019/03/CCLRP-regional-report-2019_FINAL.pdf [last accessed 3 August 2023].

47 Conor O'Mahony, Caroline Shore, Kenneth Burns and Aisling Parkes, 'Child Care Proceedings in Non-Specialist Courts: Lessons from Ireland' (2016) 30 International Journal of Law Policy and the Family 131.

48 Maria Corbett and Carol Coulter, *Ripe for Reform: An Analytical Review of Three Years of Court Reporting on Child Care Proceedings* (October 2021) [2.7] available at https://www.childlawproject.ie/wp-content/uploads/2021/11/CCLRP-Ripe-for-Reform-Report-October-2021.pdf [last accessed 3 August 2023]; Carol Coulter, *Final Report Child Care Law Reporting Project* (November 2015), 12–13 available at https://www.childlawproject.ie/wp-content/uploads/2015/11/CCLRP-Full-final-report_FINAL2.pdf [last accessed 3 August 2023].

such as Mincéirí, Roma and children of African descent[49] are significantly over-represented within care proceedings. Yet not much is known about why this is the case and official statistics on ethnicity of children in state care is not available.

There are also discrepancies between official sources of information. For example, Tusla's data suggest that 442 children entered care following care orders in 2021[50] but the court statistics for the same year[51] record that 871 care orders, 1369 interim care order and 325 emergency care orders were made in the same year. This inconsistency may be due to differences in time frames of data collection but makes it difficult to get a clear picture of what is going on in care proceedings.

5. The role of Tusla

Tusla has primary responsibility for child protection and welfare services in Ireland.[52] As part of its role, Tusla works with families to support children. Section 3(3) of the 1991 Act requires Tusla to provide general child care and family support services, including services like family resource centres which are open to all families. Tusla also has a role in monitoring situations where children are cared for by friends[53] by private agreement with the child's parents but no such obligation arises where children are cared for by relatives.[54]

As outlined in the introduction, the 1991 Act places three different legal duties on Tusla to take action in relation to vulnerable children. These are examined in turn:

5.1 Section 3 – Duty to promote welfare

Section 3(1) of the 1991 Act places a duty on Tusla to **promote the welfare** of children who are not receiving adequate care and protection.

49 AkiDwA, *It takes a village to raise a child: Children of African Descent in Irish State Care* (September 2022), 9 available at https://akidwa.ie/wp-content/uploads/2022/09/It-Takes-a-Village-to-Raise-a-Child-Children-of-African-Descent-in-Irish-State-Care-11.pdf [last accessed 3 August 2023].

50 Tusla, *Review of Adequacy Report 2021* (2022), 58; available at https://www.tusla.ie/publications/review-of-adequacy-reports/ [last accessed 3 August 2023].

51 Courts Service, *Annual Report 2021*, 69 (2022) available at https://www.courts.ie/acc/alfresco/24bce47c-3cc6-4e86-b647-04cdc64c2445/Courts_Service_Annual_Report_2021.pdf/pdf#view=fitH [last accessed 3 August 2023].

52 Child and Family Agency Act 2013.

53 Child Care Act 1991, s 230. Excludes care where the parent or guardian is on holidays, as long as it is not longer than 42 days.

54 Kenneth Burns, Conor O'Mahony and Rebekah Brennan, '"Private Family Arrangements" for Children in Ireland: The Informal Grey Space In-Between State Care and the Family Home' (2021) 51 The British Journal of Social Work 1203.

The courts have been clear that Tusla has a proactive duty to protect against future risks to a general class of children[55] and that this duty is very broad.[56] Tusla must take steps to identify children who are not receiving adequate care and protection and co-ordinate information relating to them.

Tusla's *Meitheal* model brings together different services to provide support to children and families with additional needs who may be having problems at school or struggling with behaviour or mental health. This voluntary early intervention programme allows Tusla to support children and promote family wellbeing. 2,373 Meitheal processes were requested in 2021 either directly by the family themselves or by referral.[57]

Tusla has a great deal of discretion in how it fulfils its s 3 statutory duties but is subject to legal challenge where it fails to fulfil its statutory functions, negligently fulfils its statutory functions, or fails to protect the rights of children or adults. Section 3 of the Child Care Act 1991 imposes obligations on Tusla to investigate child abuse complaints and mitigate risks to the child. However, there is currently no statutory framework for conducting such investigation. In *MQ v Gleeson*,[58] the court found that while investigating allegations of child abuse fell within the remit of Tusla's s 3 duties, a robust process for investigating and reporting allegations of abuse was needed to comply with broader principles of constitutional justice and fair procedures.

Following *MQ v Gleeson*, there have been many judicial review challenges to Tusla's investigative processes for child abuse complaints.[59] An Expert Assurance Group in 2019[60] concluded that s 3 is an inadequate statutory basis for Tusla's investigative powers, a view shared by former Special Rapporteur Conor O'Mahony.[61] In 2022, Tusla introduced a new Child Abuse Substantiation Procedure (CASP).[62] The General Scheme of the

---

55 *MQ v Gleeson* [1998] 4 IR 85.

56 *CFA v AA* [2018] IEHC 112 where it was accepted that disclosing the HIV status of a child to a third party could potentially fall within Tusla's s 3 powers.

57 Tusla, *Review of Adequacy Report 2021* (2022), 111 available at https://www.tusla.ie/publications/review-of-adequacy-reports/ [last accessed 3 August 2023].

58 [1998] 4 IR 85.

59 eg *EE v Child and Family Agency* [2018] IECA 159 and *WM v CFA* [2017] IEHC 587.

60 *Final Report of the Expert Assurance Group established to oversee and advise on the implementation of the recommendations of the Health Information and Quality Authority's "Report of the investigation into the management of allegations of child sexual abuse against adults of concern by the Child and Family Agency (Tusla) upon the direction of the Minister for Children and Youth Affairs"* (September 2019) available at https://assets.gov.ie/48194/18906f6d5e294c12a8ba9f62b729181b.pdf [last accessed 3 August 2023].

61 Available at https://www.tusla.ie/CASP/ [last accessed 3 August 2023].

62 https://www.tusla.ie/uploads/content/Child_Abuse_Substantiation_Procedure_(CASP).pdf [last accessed 3 August 2023].

Child Care (Amendment) Bill 2023 proposes placing CASP on a statutory footing.

5.2 Section 4 – Voluntary care

Section 4 allows Tusla to take a child into state care without the need for a court order as long as they have permission from their parents, guardians and/or those *in loco parentis.*[63] The majority of children enter state care through voluntary arrangements.[64] Tusla must have regard to the wishes of parents while providing this care[65] and where the parents want to end the arrangement, the child must be returned to the care of their parents or a court order must be made.[66] Section 4(4) allows children to be taken into voluntary care without explicit consent where the child is lost, or the parent is missing. In such cases, Tusla must try to reunite the child with his parents where this appears to be in his best interest.

> Section 4 gives Tusla a great deal of discretion as to when it needs to take a child into voluntary care. 'Where it appears to Tusla that a child requires care or protection that he is unlikely to receive unless he is taken into its care, it shall be the duty of Tusla to take him into its care under this section'.[67]

This contrasts with grounds for compulsory care orders or emergency care orders where the evidential criteria are narrowly defined. Section 8 outlines situations where children are in need of 'care and protection' including children whose parents are dead or missing, children whose parents have deserted or abandoned them, children who are homeless, children who are at risk of being neglected or ill-treated, and children whose parents are unable to care for them due to ill-health or for any other reason. Tusla must conduct a thorough and conscientious assessment of the child in order to ascertain what action should be taken and should explore less interventionalist avenues first. Tusla is also obliged to hold regular childcare reviews.[68]

Voluntary care under s 4 is usually an approved foster care arrangement. Fostering involves a change in legal **custody.** Parents sign a 'reception into

---

63 *O'H v HSE* [2007] IEHC 175 – a father who did not have custody of the child but had guardianship rights must be consulted.

64 Tusla, *Review of Adequacy Report 2021* (2022), 58 available at https://www.tusla.ie/publications/review-of-adequacy-reports/ [last accessed 3 August 2023].

65 s 4(3).

66 s 4(2).

67 s 4(1).

68 arts 17 and 18 of relevant regulations. Child Care (Placement of Children in Foster Care) Regulations 1995. Child Care (Placement of Children in Residential Care) Regulations 1995. Child Care (Placement of Children with Relatives) Regulations 1995.

care' form. The child lives with the foster parents who have day to day decision making powers. There is no automatic transfer of **guardianship** to foster parents, but foster parents can apply for legal guardianship after five years.[69]

As Corbett[70] outlines, voluntary care is quick, flexible and inexpensive when compared to care proceedings. It has significant advantages for short-term respite and situations where parents have a positive relationship with Tusla. However, there are disadvantages to the use of voluntary care. There are no duration limits on voluntary care and although the review process for all state care placements should be the same, it is reported that children in voluntary care are not prioritised by overloaded Tusla workers.[71] This means that such children may drift in placements that do not suit them.[72] A voluntary placement may lack stability and safety for children if parents revoke consent suddenly. Where there isn't enough time to get an emergency care order the child might be sent home to an unsafe environment. There is also an inherent power imbalance when a social worker confronts a parent with a suspicion of neglect or abuse and parents have reported soft coercion from Tusla in the use of voluntary care.[73] There are sometimes concerns over a parent's capacity to agree to voluntary care where there are mental health issues, or cognitive impairment.[74]

Research by Rebekah Brenna, Conor O'Mahony and Kenneth Burns[75] recommends a complete overhaul of s 4, suggesting a maximum duration for voluntary care placements, a formal review before the expiry of a placement, and regular reviews and participation of children in reviews. Conor O'Mahony also called for the cancellation of voluntary care agreement to be subject to a 72-hour notice period.[76] The proposed General Scheme of the Child Care (Amendment) Bill 2023 places a requirement on Tusla to review voluntary care placements after 6 months

---

69 s 43A of the Child Care Act 1991.

70 Maria Corbett, 'Children in Voluntary Care: An Essential Provision but one in need of reform' (2018) 21 Irish Journal of Family Law 9.

71 Rebekah Brennan, Conor O'Mahony and Kenneth Burns, 'The Rights of the Child in Voluntary Care in Ireland: A call for reform in law, policy and practice' (2021) 125 Child and Youth Services Review 1.

72 See for example *Child and Family Agency v MC* [2015] IEDC 10.

73 Conor O'Mahony, Rebekah Brennan and Kenneth Burns, 'Informed consent and parental rights in voluntary care agreements' (2020) 32 Child and Family Law Quarterly 373–396.

74 See *M v F* [2012] IEDC 14.

75 Rebekah Brennan, Conor O'Mahony and Kenneth Burns, 'The Rights of the Child in Voluntary Care in Ireland: A call for reform in law, policy and practice' (2021) 125 Child and Youth Services Review 1.

76 Conor O'Mahony, *Annual Report of the Special Rapporteur on Child Protection* (June 2020), 87.

and allows Tusla to keep a child in voluntary care for three working days after consent has been withdrawn.

5.3 Care proceedings and evidential requirements

Section 16 places a legal duty on Tusla to apply for a court order to take a child into care where such action is necessary for the child to receive the care and protection that they require.

Section 16 of the Child Care Act 1991

Where it appears to Tusla that a child requires care or protection which he is unlikely to receive unless a court makes a care order or supervision order in respect of him, it shall be the duty of Tusla to make application for a care order or a supervision order.

Tusla have discretion to decide what kind of care order is most appropriate in the circumstances. However, in order for the court to grant an order, the statutory evidential test for that particular order must be satisfied, that is Tusla must provide appropriate evidence of risk of harm to justify proportionate state interference with parental care. Because each of the different types of care orders represents a different type of intervention, each order has different evidential requirements which must be met to justify that level of state intervention. For example, Tusla will respond to emergency situations by applying for an emergency care order. In such situations, a full assessment is not possible, but an emergency care order will be granted if it is clear that the child is at immediate and serious risk. A more comprehensive assessment will be required to satisfy a court that long term care order under s 18 is appropriate. Tusla will often apply for an interim care order while long term care planning for a child is underway.

Evidential difficulties arise in practice. Social workers and courts weigh the evidence but in assessing risk to a child and dealing with future possibilities they must engage in the impossible task of predicting a child's future. Good social work practice and communication between professionals working with child are essential.

The next section of the chapter goes through the different types of care orders and other legal mechanisms available, outlining the appropriate legal test and analysing their typical use.

6. Emergency protection

The 1991 Act provides three different mechanisms which may be appropriate to protect children in **emergency situations**; Garda Powers (where no court order is necessary), the Emergency Care Order and the Interim Care Order.

6.1 Section 12 – Garda powers

Section 12 grants a Garda the power to enter any building or vehicle without warrant to remove a child to safety where there are **reasonable grounds** for believing that:

There is an **immediate and serious risk to the health or welfare of the child**

AND

It would not be sufficient to wait for an emergency care order to be made.

This power allows Gardaí to remove children from dangerous situations where it is not suitable to wait for Tusla to apply for an emergency care order. Children must be placed in the care of Tusla as soon as possible.[77] Tusla must within three days either return the child to its home or make an application to keep the child in state care.[78]

There is no judicial consideration of Garda powers because no court order is required to remove the children. The power is exercisable on the judgment of a Garda alone after evaluating the evidence reasonably available to him or her at that time. Following a 2014 investigation by the Ombudsman for Children into the use of Garda power to remove children from the Roma Community who did not physically resemble their parents,[79] the Gardaí and Tusla have updated their joint working protocol to improve interagency co-operation and give effect to the *Children First Guidance*.[80] Children removed by Gardaí are usually placed in emergency foster care prior to a court hearing for an emergency care order. Tusla's

---

[77] s 12(3).

[78] s 12(4).

[79] Emily Logan, *Garda Síochána Act 2005 (Section 42) (Special Inquiries relating to Garda Síochána) Order 2013* July 2013) available at https://www.iasw.ie/download/205/d44782c2-d5b4-4aa7-afb1-50df7337780a.PDF [last accessed 3 August 2023]. A report of one of the emergency care order applications can also be found on the Child Care Reporting Project website available at https://www.childlawproject.ie/publications/emergency-care-order-for-roma-child-withdrawn-after-dna-test/ [last accessed 3 August 2023].

[80] Joint Working Protrocol for An Garda Síochána/Tusla–Child and Family Agency Liaison available at https://www.tusla.ie/uploads/content/CF_Joint_Protocol.pdf [last accessed 3 August 2023].

Emergency Out of Hours Service, established in 2015, provides an out of hours social work service for the Gardaí.

There have been two research projects into the use of these Garda powers. In 2017, Geoffrey Shannon interviewed Gardaí who had exercised s 12 powers, as well as analysing PULSE data.[81] He found that Gardaí felt they had inadequate training in child protection or on cultural diversity. Gardaí also highlighted inadequacies in the out of hours service which meant that children had to wait in unsuitable surroundings such as Garda stations.

In 2020, Carmel Devaney et al from NUI Galway published an analysis of 452 uses of Garda powers involving 382 children.[82] They interviewed 28 Tusla child protection workers. The report found that the local relationship between the Gardaí and Tusla was very important and emphasised the importance of joint training on the use of s 12. They found that the Gardaí contacted Tusla prior to invoking s 12 powers in the vast majority of cases. Section 12 powers were most often used in relation to children where there were issues around parental mental health and parental substance misuse. For young people, aged between 13 and 17 years of age, s 12 powers were also used because of teenage behavioural issues. The report raised concerns that emergency foster care is often unsuitable for children with behavioural issues and that there is a very limited supply of emergency beds in residential units.

6.2 Section 13 – emergency care orders

An emergency care order does not have to be preceded by Garda intervention, but Tusla must apply for an emergency care order if they do not want to return children, removed by Gardaí, to their families. In most applications looked at in Devaney's study, an emergency order or interim care order was granted but some applications for Emergency Care Orders (ECOs) after Garda intervention ended in no order.[83] A total of 325 applications for ECOs were made in the District Court in 2021.[84]

---

[81] Geoffrey Shannon, *Audit of the Exercise by An Garda Síochána of the provisions of section 12 of the Child Care Act 1991* (2017) available at https://www.lenus.ie/handle/10147/621405 [last accessed 3 August 2023].

[82] Carmel Devaney, Rosemary Crosse, Leonor Rodriguezand Charlotte Silke, *A study of Tusla – Child and Family Agency's actions and decision-making process following An Garda Síochána's application of Section 12 of the Child Care Act 1991* (UNESCO Child and Family Research Centre, National University of Ireland Galway 2020) available at https://www.gov.ie/en/publication/687d3-publication-of-a-study-of-tusla-child-and-family-agencys-actions-and-decision-making-process-following-an-garda-siochanas-application-of-section-12-of-the-child-care-act-1991/ [last accessed 3 August 2023].

[83] ibid.

[84] Courts Service, *Annual Report 2021*, 69.

The evidential requirements for emergency care orders are lower than that for care orders. This reflects the urgency of the order and is balanced by the short duration of the emergency order. A District Court judge can make an emergency care order where there is ***reasonable cause*** to believe that:

There is an **immediate and serious risk to the health or welfare of a child**

OR

There is likely to be such a risk if a child is not removed.[85]

However, Tusla must establish both the **immediacy of risk** and the **serious nature of that risk** as well as demonstrating that the proposed intervention is proportionate. The court must also consider the child's best interests as the paramount concern.[86]

Cases reported by the Child Care Law Reporting Project show that emergency care order cases typically feature maternal mental health issues or addiction issues.[87] They are used to prevent a child with non-accidental injuries being removed from hospital.[88] Another typical use is where mothers agree pre-birth to put a child in voluntary care and then change their minds. Emergency Care Orders are most often refused where the evidential requirement that the risk is immediate is not satisfied.[89]

Emergency care orders are a draconian intervention and have been referred to by the courts as a 'nuclear option'.[90] Applications can be made *ex parte,* ie without notice to the parents. Emergency care orders can be made other than in a public sitting of District Court such as in a District Judge's private house.[91] However, emergency care orders are very short,

---

85 s 13(1).

86 s 24.

87 https://www.childlawproject.ie/publications/emergency-care-order-following-mothers-mental-health-relapse/ [last accessed 3 August 2023];https://www.childlawproject.ie/publications/emergency-care-order-where-mother-detained-under-mental-health-act/ [last accessed 3 August 2023]; https://www.childlawproject.ie/publications/emergency-care-orders-for-two-children-due-to-mothers-addiction-and-homelessness/ [last accessed 3 August 2023].

88 https://www.childlawproject.ie/publications/emergency-care-order-for-baby-with-non-accidental-injury/ [last accessed 3 August 2023].

89 See https://www.childlawproject.ie/publications/emergency-care-order-refused-for-child-at-moderate-risk-of-suicide/ (last accessed 3 August 2023); and_https://www.childlawproject.ie/publications/emergency-care-order-refused-for-african-child/ [last accessed 3 August 2023].

90 *SOTA v CFA* [2018] IEHC 714 [71].

91 s 13(4)(d).

lasting a maximum of eight days[92] or for shorter periods which will be specified by the District Court in the order.[93] If further time is required, Tusla must apply for an interim care order which has higher evidential requirements. Emergency care orders are so short that they are nearly invariably followed by an application for an Interim Care Order.

Moreover, parental rights are protected during an emergency care order. Generally speaking, Tusla must inform parents of the whereabouts of their children[94] and there is a presumption of contact.[95] The court may make directions under the emergency care order not to inform the parents of the child's location[96] but this is not done lightly.[97]

Example case

The High Court reviewed the proportionality of an emergency care order in *SOTA v CFA*.[98] Here an *ex parte* emergency care order for two days was granted in respect of a newborn baby. The infant was removed by Gardaí from hospital, placed in emergency foster care and an interim care order was subsequently granted. There was a history of physical injury and neglect to the parents' other nine children who were the subject of care orders. The mother had mental health issues and claimed that demons, spirits, and angels were coming for her and her baby. The case for the State was that the mother posed an immediate and serious risk to her baby who she might harm under a delusional belief. There was also a risk that the parents would abscond from the hospital and take the baby to an unknown location. Oral evidence was presented to the court by a midwife as to the mother's mental state and by a social worker as to the family's history.

The court held that *ex parte* emergency care orders should only be used after all other less intrusive alternatives had been considered and eliminated for good reason. In this case, there had been no consideration of keeping the baby at the hospital as a temporary measure. The emergency care order was held not to be constitutionally proportionate nor compliant with obligations under the ECHR.

---

92 The General Scheme of the Child Care (Amendment) Bill 2023 proposes extending the maximum duration of Emergency Care Orders to 15 days.

93 s 13(2).

94 s 14.

95 *State (D and D) v Groarke* [1990] 1 IR 305.

96 s 13(7)(a).

97 *State (D and D) v Groarke* [1990] 1 IR 305, 319.

98 [2018] IEHC 714.

6.3 Section 17 – interim care orders

Interim care orders are typically made in three different situations: where an emergency care order is about to lapse and Tusla does not think it appropriate to return the child; to prevent a child being removed from voluntary care; or, to remove a child from parental care where the risk is not so immediate as to warrant an emergency care order. Such orders are sought where Tusla is anticipating that a full care order will be sought but does not yet have enough evidence to make a full care order application.

Interim care orders last for a maximum of 29 days but can be extended with parental consent or by court order. 747 applications for interim care orders were made to the District Court in 2021 alongside 5,704 applications for extensions of interim care orders.

Under s 17, a District Judge must be *satisfied* that three evidential components have been proved on the balance of probabilities:

A care order application has been made or is about to be made.

AND

There is **reasonable cause** to believe the child is being assaulted, ill-treated, neglected or sexually abused.

OR

The child's health, development or welfare is being avoidably impaired or neglected OR **is likely to be** avoidably impaired or neglected.

AND

The child requires care or protection which is unlikely to be received without a court order.

The court must also consider the best interests of the child as paramount and the constitutional proportionality of the order.

Parents must usually be given two days' notice of an interim care application[99] but they can exceptionally be made with abridged notice or ex *parte*.[100]

---

[99] District Court (Child Care) Rules 2015, SI 143/2015.

[100] s 17(3).

Example case

In *Child and Family Agency v ES & AJ,*[101] Judge Horgan considered the evidential threshold for an interim care order. The Child and Family Agency (CFA) sought an interim care order for two children aged six and four. It was claimed that the mother could not meet the emotional needs of the children and was hostile and aggressive to the CFA. The mother had paranoid schizophrenia coupled with alcohol abuse and had verbal and physical altercations with her partner. The CFA's case hinged on the emotional impact of the mother's mental health condition on her children.

The children were subject to a child protection plan and there was a scaffolding of support services including the Public Health Nurse, Community Mental Health Services, Family Support Workers and Social Work Department oversight. In addition, a family member resided with the mother and another family member visited daily.

Applying the s 17 threshold test, Judge Horgan found no evidence of assault, neglect or sexual abuse. There was no evidence that the children's health development or welfare were currently being avoidably impaired but there was reasonable cause to believe the children's health, development and welfare would be avoidably impaired in the future through unintentional exposure to conflict. However, Judge Horgan was not satisfied that the interim care order would provide the children with the care and protection they needed. The evidence was that the children were thriving, and the risk of future harm was not greater than the harm the children would suffer through abrupt separation from their mother. The Child and Family Agency had failed to demonstrate the third component of the threshold test, i.e. that an interim care order would improve the children's situation.

Once an interim care order has been made, the child is placed in the care of Tusla[102] but reflecting the temporary nature of the order, day to day decision-making rights regarding the child are not transferred to Tusla but remain with the parents. Interim care orders typically last for 29 days unless parental permission is given for a longer order. Where an application is made for extension by court order, Tusla does not have to make the case again, but must provide evidence that the circumstances giving rise to the original interim care order continue.[103]

The proposed General Scheme of the Child Care (Amendment) Bill 2023

[101] [2015] IEDC 5.
[102] s 17(2).
[103] *KA v HSE* [2012] 1 IR 794.

allows interim care orders to be granted where Tusla is in the process of considering whether it is appropriate to apply for a care order. It also extends the maximum term of an interim care order to 12 months.

7. Longer term state intervention

Where longer term state intervention is required, Tusla must apply for a full care order under section 18 or a supervision order under s 19. 523 applications for care orders were made to the District Court in 2021 alongside 267 applications for supervision orders.[104]

7.1 Section 18 – care orders

The evidential requirements for a full care order are higher than for an emergency protection or interim order. The court must be satisfied that:[105]

The child has been or is being assaulted, ill-treated, neglected or sexually abused.

OR

The child's health, development or welfare has been or is being avoidably impaired or neglected,

OR

The child's health, development or welfare **is likely to be** avoidably impaired or neglected,

AND

The child requires care or protection which he is unlikely to receive unless the court makes an order under this section.

In addition, the court must consider the child's best interests as paramount,[106] and consider whether the proposed action is proportionate.

The burden of proof lies on Tusla who must prove their case on the balance of probabilities (ie more likely than not). In order to satisfy the evidential requirements for a care order, evidence of specific types of abuse must be proven or Tusla must make the more general case that the child's welfare or development has been, is being or is likely to be

[104] Courts Service, *Annual Report 2021*, 69.
[105] s 18(1).
[106] s 24.

avoidably impaired and neglected. There is no need to prove malevolence or ill intent by the parents but the threat to the health or development of the children must be avoidable. Article 42A requires parental failure before state intervention into the family is constitutionally permitted and this is relevant to how the evidential requirements are understood. The types of abuse outlined in s 18 reflect the categories of harm in the Children First Act 2015 and in the *Children First Guidance* 2017. The General Scheme of the Child Care (Amendment) Bill 2023 proposes an additional ground for a care order where the court is satisfied that the child is likely to be assaulted, ill-treated, neglected or sexually abused.

Making the case that a child **is likely to be** avoidably impaired or neglected can be quite nuanced, as Tusla must base its case on evidence that is proved to the court on the balance of probabilities. This means that they must rely on past behaviour or evidence of the current situation to show that there is future risk that the child's health, development or welfare will be avoidably impaired or neglected. For example, evidence that a parent has harmed other children in the past and currently refuses to comply with safeguarding measures may be enough to prove that the child's health welfare or development is at risk, depending on the circumstances. There is no Irish case law on this point but the most recent guidance from the UK Supreme Court suggests that such evidence must show that there is '[a] real possibility that the child would suffer harm in the future'.[107]

Irish judicial commentary on the evidential requirements for making a care order is rare. In *Child and Family Agency v LH,*[108] Judge Horgan set out the roles of Tusla and the court in care proceedings and the need to consider the constitutional rights of parents and children. The onus is on Tusla to establish that a particular care order is necessary to protect the safety and welfare of a child and the standard of proof is the balance of probabilities. The court must only make care orders that are proportionate in the particular circumstances. The court must not to intervene in family life unless it is truly necessary and then to the least possible extent necessary to protect the child.[109]

A care order commits a child into the care of Tusla and can last until the child turns 18 years of age[110] although the court should consider whether a shorter order is more proportionate.[111] A care order gives Tusla decision making powers and responsibilities over the child, and these are spelled out within the Act. Section 18(3) gives Tusla control over the child as if it

---

[107] *Re B (Care Proceedings: Appeal)* [2013] UKSC 33.
[108] [2017] IEDC 17.
[109] ibid [15].
[110] s 18(2).
[111] *CFA v CH & SC* [2017] IEDC 4.

were his parent but also requires Tusla to do what is reasonable for the purposes of safeguarding or promoting the child's health, development or welfare in the circumstances of the case. In particular, Tusla is empowered to 1) decide the type of care to be provided to the child, 2) give consent to any necessary medical or psychiatric examination, treatment or assessment and 3) give consent to the issue of a passport for the child to enable him to travel abroad for limited periods.

7.2 Section 19 – supervision orders

Supervision orders are different to care orders in that the child is not taken away from his home but is instead visited regularly by Tusla. Support and advice can also be provided to the child's parents or carers.[112] A court can make a supervision order instead of a care order under s 18(5) where the evidential requirements for a care order have been met but the court is satisfied that a care order is not necessary and a supervision order is desirable instead.[113]

Where Tusla directly apply for a supervision order under s 19 the court must be satisfied *that there are reasonable grounds for believing:*

The child has been or is being assaulted, ill-treated, neglected or sexually abused.

OR

The child's health, development or welfare has been or is being avoidably impaired or neglected.

OR

The child's health, development or welfare **is likely to be** avoidably impaired or neglected.

AND

It is desirable that the child be visited periodically by or on behalf of Tusla.

7.3 Part IVA – special care orders

Special care orders are used where the problem is not parental care but the behaviour of children themselves. Many of these children will have health problems, mental health disorders and/or substance abuse

---

112 s 19(2).
113 s 18(5).

issues.[114] Their behaviour means that they cannot stay at home or be placed in foster care because of the risk they pose to themselves or others.

Special care orders constitute a deprivation of liberty for the child. There was no power of detention in the Child Care Act 1991 as enacted. Instead, children in need of secure therapeutic care were placed in St Patrick's Institution using the inherent jurisdiction of the High Court. In *DG v Eastern Health Board*[115] the Supreme Court upheld an order detaining a teenage boy in St Patrick's as lawful and necessary to protect his constitutional rights but emphasised that such orders should only be used for short periods. However, in 2002, The European Court of Human Rights found that the detention of DG in St Patrick's breached his right to liberty and security under art 5 of the ECHR.[116] The court held that if the State chooses a system of educational supervision it is obliged to put in place appropriate institutional facilities which meet the security and educational demands of that system. St Patrick's did not have appropriate educational facilities and was eventually closed in 2017.

The Child Care (Amendment) Act 2011 amended the 1991 Act to provide for children in need of special care or protection and was commenced in 2018. Section 23B places a duty on Tusla to provide and maintain special care units. Where Tusla is satisfied that a child over the age of 11 requires special care it may apply for a special care order.[117] In making this determination, Tusla must **be satisfied that:**

1) There is reasonable cause to believe that the behaviour of the child poses a real and substantial risk of harm to his or her life, health, safety, development or welfare.

AND

2) That having regard to that behaviour and risk of harm that state care or mental health treatment will not adequately address the child's risk of harm and care requirements.

AND

3) That a special care order from the High Court is required.

Special Care Orders can only be made by the High Court and are heard by the 'Minors in Special Care List' on a weekly basis. Section 23H requires the High Court to **be satisfied that:**

---

[114] Clare Barry, *Children in Special Care in Ireland: The Role of the Court in the Protection and Vindication of their Rights* (PhD thesis) (August 2021), 118.
[115] [1997] IESC 7.
[116] *DG v Ireland* (Application No 39474/98).
[117] Child Care Act 1991, s 23F.

The child has attained the age of 11 years.

AND

The behaviour of the child poses a real and substantial risk of harm to his or her life, safety, development or welfare.

AND

Mental health services and care orders would not adequately address the risk of harm.

AND

The child requires special care to adequately address that behaviour and risk of harm and those care requirements cannot be provided unless a **special care order** is made.

Special Care orders last three months[118] but can be extended to six months[119]and are reviewed every 4 weeks.[120] They place the child into the care of Tusla and direct Tusla to detain the child in a special care unit and provide special care.[121]

Example case

In *Child and Family Agency v ML (otherwise G)*[122] the court considered a special care order made in relation to a 17-year-old, G, who had assaulted a social worker in a car. The child had been born into a house of extreme violence and had been taken into care at the age of 10.

It was argued that G's behaviour could not be the basis of a special care order because it concerned risk to the social worker and not to G herself. The court held that this behaviour did give rise to a real and substantial risk of harm to the development, welfare, safety and health of G because in order to live a meaningful life she needed a degree of socialisation. The special care order was upheld as necessary, proportionate and validly made.

It is not clear from court statistics how many special care orders are made every year. In Clare Barry's observational study of 31 special care order cases[123] all applications for special care were granted by the High Court

118 ibid, s 23H(2).
119 ibid, s 23J.
120 ibid, s 23I.
121 ibid, s 23H(2).
122 [2019] IECA 109.
123 i.e cases under the 1991 Act statutory framework.

and Barry suggests that special care is a resource driven service.[124] There are only three secure care units in Ireland with a maximum of 26 beds in total which are not always available.[125] At the end of 2021 there were 16 children in special care.[126] Children are regularly sent abroad to the UK for secure care. Colfer and Coulter's research[127] suggests that special care orders remain vulnerable to challenge under the ECHR because appropriate educational facilities are not always available. They caution that transitioning from special care is also problematic for children as there are no appropriate onward placements.

8. Critical Thinking Point: Is the Voice of the Child Adequately Heard within Care Proceedings?

Care proceedings are legally structured as being about the removal of parental rights. The child is the subject matter of the dispute and not an active participant or a party to the case. Today, Article 42A.4 of the Constitution requires that provision is made by law for securing the views of a child, who is capable of forming views, in care proceedings and that due weight is given to those views so that children can have an input into a decision that will have a very serious impact on their lives. As discussed above, the Child Care Amendment Act 2022 will insert a new s 24A into the Child Care Act 1991 to require the court to determine the means by which the child should express their views in the proceedings and to give due weight to such views.[128] As O'Mahony suggests, these changes to the 1991 Act will require the court to take a three-step approach: 1) establish whether the child is capable of forming relevant views, 2) decide how those views should be expressed to the court and 3) rule on how much weight those views should be given in the particular circumstances taking into account the age and maturity of the child.

Existing research suggests that children are routinely excluded from the decision-making process in care proceedings in Ireland.[129] Social work

---

[124] Clare Barry, *Children in Special Care in Ireland: The Role of the Court in the Protection and Vindication of their Rights* (PhD thesis) (August 2021), 121.

[125] https://www.gov.ie/en/policy-information/118b86-special-care-units/.

[126] Tusla, *Review of Adequacy Report 2021* (2022), 79; available at https://www.tusla.ie/publications/review-of-adequacy-reports/ [last accessed 3 August 2023].

[127] Lisa Colfer and Carol Coulter, *High Court oversight of children's complex needs* (July 2020) available at https://www.childlawproject.ie/latest-volume/high-court-oversight-of-childrens-complex-care-needs [last accessed 3 August 2023].

[128] Child Care Amendment Act 2022, s 5 which has not yet been commenced.

[129] Elaine O'Callaghan, Conor O'Mahony and Kenneth Burns, '"There is nothing as effective as hearing the lived experience of the child"; Practitioners' Views on Children's Participation in Child Care Cases in Ireland' (2019) 22 Irish Journal of Family Law 2; Aisling Parkes, Caroline Shore, Conor O'Mahony and Kenneth Burns, 'The right of the child to be heard? Professional experiences of child care proceedings in the Irish District Court' (2015) 27 Child and Family Law Quarterly 423.

practitioners encourage children to submit their views directly to the judge as best practice.[130] However, many barristers and solicitors surveyed in 2017 felt that it was not part of their role to meet with the child in care proceedings as they represented the parents or the guardian *ad litem*.[131] All professions cited inadequate training and the lack of a child friendly environment as barriers to the greater involvement of children in decisions about care proceedings.

Children don't generally give evidence directly in care proceedings, instead their views are conveyed to the court in less direct ways. The most common way in which children's views are conveyed in care proceedings is through the appointment of a guardian *ad litem* (GAL).[132] A child can be made a party to a case where necessary in the interests of justice, and legal representation may be appointed[133] however the 1991 Act does not currently allow children to be represented in proceedings AND have a GAL.[134] This may explain why research by Corbett and Coulter[135] and Parkes et al[136] suggests that making children a party to child care proceedings is very rare. Children may be permitted to speak to a judge in chambers or write to them directly. The practice of arranging direct conversations between children and judges varies from court to court.[137]

Section 26 of the Child Care Act 1991 allows for the appointment of a GAL in care proceedings where a) the child is **not a party to the proceedings** and b) the court is satisfied that it is necessary **in the best interests of the child** and **in the interests of justice** to have a guardian appointed.

---

130 Danielle Kennan, Bernadine Brady and Cormac Forkan, 'Space, Voice, Audience and Influence: The Lundy Model of Participation (2007) in Child Welfare Practice' (2019) 31 Social Work in Action 205.

131 Elaine O'Callaghan, Conor O'Mahony and Kenneth Burns, '"There is nothing as effective as hearing the lived experience of the child": Practitioners' Views on Children's Participation in Child Care Cases in Ireland' (2019) 22 Irish Journal of Family Law 2

132 Child Care Act 1991, s 26.

133 ibid, s 25.

134 ibid, s 26(4). See discussion Conor O'Mahony, *Annual Report of the Special Rapporteur on Child Protection* (June 2020), 88-116.

135 Maria Corbett and Carol Coulter, *Child Care Proceedings: A Thematic Review of Irish and International Practice* (2009), 99, available at https://www.gov.ie/pdf/?file=https://assets.gov.ie/27780/a770243297774574af9171c5226fdf74.pdf#page=1 [last accessed 3 August 2023].

136 Aisling Parkes, Caroline Shore, Conor O'Mahony and Kenneth Burns, 'The right of the child to be heard? Professional experiences of child care proceedings in the Irish District Court' (2015) 27 Child and Family Law Quarterly 423.

137 Maria Corbett and Carol Coulter, *Child Care Proceedings: A Thematic Review of Irish and International Practice* (2009), 100.

Pending legislation – The Child Care (Amendment) Act 2022

The Child Care (Amendment) Act 2022 will insert a new Pt VA into the Child Care Act 1991 to regulate GALs.[138]

The Act creates a presumption in favour of the appointment of a GAL in proceedings in the District Court and makes the appointment of a GAL mandatory in the High Court.[139]

The twin role of the GAL is outlined in the **proposed** s 35E:

35E. (1) The functions of a guardian *ad litem* appointed for a child shall be—

(a) in so far as practicable and where the child is capable of forming his or her own views, to ascertain the views of the child in relation to any matter to which the proceedings relate, and

(b) to make recommendations to the court regarding what is in the best interests of the child— (i) where the child has expressed views referred to in paragraph (a), after having considered those views, or (ii) where the child is not capable of forming or expressing his or her views or is unwilling to express his or her views.

Although the court may call the GAL as a witness,[140] the GAL is not a party to the proceedings.[141] It will be possible for the child to have a GAL and be party to proceedings[142] if the court deems it appropriate.

The Act gives the Minister the powers to make regulations on the qualifications and experience that are required to act as a GAL[143] and provides for the establishment of a national GAL service to provide a high-quality standardised service for children.

While legislative reform to regulate guardians *ad litem* has now taken place in the form of the Child Care (Amendment) Act 2022, until it is commenced, there is still no regulation of GALs.[144] The 1991 Act does not set out any criteria for the court to take into account in appointing a GAL,

138 Child Care (Amendment) Act 2022, s 7 which has not yet been commenced.

139 New s 35B of Child Care Act 1991 as proposed by s 7 Child Care (Amendment) Act 2022.

140 New s 35E(8) of Child Care Act 1991 as proposed by s 7 Child Care (Amendment) Act 2022.

141 New s 35E(10) of Child Care Act 1991 as proposed by s 7 Child Care (Amendment) Act 2022.

142 New s 35H of Child Care Act 1991 as proposed by s 7 Child Care (Amendment) Act 2022.

143 New s 35L of Child Care Act 1991 as proposed by s 7 Child Care (Amendment) Act 2022.

144 Nicola Carr, 'Guiding the GALs: A Case of Hesitant Policy-making in the Republic of Ireland' (2009) 12 Irish Journal of Family Law 60; Ann McWillams and Claire Hamilton,

no qualifications are required to act as a GAL, and the exact status and role of the GAL in care proceedings is unclear.[145] The High Court has recognised that the GAL has two distinct functions, which may conflict; acting as an advocate for the child and providing an independent assessment of what is the child's best interests.[146]

It is hoped that the legislative changes made to the GAL role will, when commenced, ensure that children's views are routinely heard in care proceedings and given meaningful weight.

9. After the care order

This section considers what happens to children after a care order is made and how the wellbeing of children in state care is monitored and reviewed.

Section 36(1) of the Child Care Act 1991 outlines the different options available to Tusla in providing alternative care for a child.

Section 36(1) of the Child Care Act 1991
Where a child is in the care of Tusla, the Agency shall provide such care for him, subject to its control and supervision, in such of the following ways as it considers to be in his best interests— (a) by placing him with a foster parent, or (b) by placing him in residential care (whether in a children's residential centre registered under *Part VIII*, in a residential home maintained by the Agency or in a school or other suitable place of residence), or (c) in the case of a child who may be eligible for adoption under the Adoption Acts, 1952 to 1988, by placing him with a suitable person with a view to his adoption, or (d) by making such other suitable arrangements (which may include placing the child with a relative) as the Agency thinks proper.

Tusla's latest statistics[147] show that out of 5,863 children in care at the end of 2021, 90% were in foster care (including 1,502 children who were in relative foster care), 7.7% were in a residential placement with

'There isn't anything like a Gal: The Guardian ad Litem Service in Ireland' (2010) 10 Irish Journal of Applied Social Studies 31.

145 Although there is some discussion in *AO'D v Judge Constantine O'Leary* [2016] IEHC 555.

146 *Health Services Executive v DK* [2007] IEHC 488.

147 Tusla, *Review of Adequacy Report 2021* (2022), 68 available at https://www.tusla.ie/publications/review-of-adequacy-reports/ [last accessed 3 August 2023].

tiny numbers of children in special care placements, detention schools, disability units or other rehabilitation centres.

9.1 Care plans

Tusla is obliged to prepare a plan for the care and upbringing of children. This care plan must be prepared before placing a child in residential care or with foster parents. Care plans should outline: the care arrangements for the child; the aims and objectives of the placement; the support to be provided by the HSE and Tusla to the child and parents (where appropriate); arrangements for contact with parents and siblings; and arrangements to review the plan.

Care plans are examined by the court in s 18 care proceedings and must be reviewed by Tusla at regular intervals.[148] Tusla has a Child and Youth Participation Strategy which commits to involving children and young people in decision making.[149] Children have the right to attend their child in care reviews with their social worker and should be given a 'child in care' review form before the meetings and be permitted to see their care plan. They may also bring an advocate from an organisation like Empowering People In Care (EPIC) to the review or another adult.

Research by Olivia McEvoy and Martine Smith in 2011[150] suggests that children were not routinely involved in their care reviews and did not feel that their voices were heard. Work by Caroline O Meara found that only 71 out of 324 in-care reviews were attended by children in 2017 indicating that this is an area where culture change is required.[151]

The **Health Information and Quality Authority (HIQA)** inspects children's social care services to determine whether they are meeting national standards.[152] In a recent report on foster care services,[153] HIQA found that only one out of 17 service areas was fully compliant in having a

---

148 Child Care (Placement of Children in Foster Care) Regulations 1995, ss 11 and 18; Child Care (Placement of Children with Relatives) Regulations 1995, ss 11 and 18; Child Care (Placement of Children in Residential Care) Regulations 1995, s 23.

149 https://www.tusla.ie/services/family-community-support/prevention-partnership-and-family-support-programme/participation/child-and-youth-participation-strategy/ [last accessed 3 August 2023].

150 Olivia McEvoy and Martine Smith, *Listen to our Voices! Hearing Children and Young People in the Care of the State* (Department of Children and Youth Affairs 2011) Executive Summary– available at https://www.lenus.ie/bitstream/handle/10147/139489/LTOVreport.pdf?sequence=3 [last accessed 3 August 2023].

151 https://www.irishexaminer.com/news/arid-30989784.html [last accessed 3 August 2023].

152 Health Act 2007.

153 HIQA, *Overview report on statutory foster care services 2019-2020* (2021) available at https://www.hiqa.ie/reports-and-publications/key-reports-investigations/overview-report-statutory-foster-care-services [last accessed 3 August 2023].

written plan for each child in foster care and having the child and her family participate in preparing the care plan. The report found that not all children were given feedback on the decisions made in their reviews, nor were changes to their care plan always discussed with them. It also highlighted the lack of appropriate, child-friendly accommodation for hosting meetings. HIQA also issued questionnaires to all children in care over the age of six years and visited children in their foster care households. Most children said they had a care plan and had been spoken to about it by their social worker. However, children had mixed views about their care plan and care plan reviews.

9.2 Section 47 court powers of review

While care orders give Tusla decision making powers for the child, s 47 gives the courts some powers to monitor a child in care. Under s 47, the District Court may give directions and make such order on **any question affecting the welfare of the child** as it thinks proper where a child is in the care of Tusla. Such directions and orders relate to the child's upbringing, health, development or care and are sometimes used by the District Court to support the terms of a care order. Section 47 directions and orders can be made by the court at its own motion or on application by another person. The court has no jurisdiction to make section 47 directions once the child has turned 18 years of age.

The extent of the court's supervisory power under s 47 has been subject to litigation. In *Eastern Health Board v McDonnell*[154] the High Court considered District Court orders directing the Eastern Health Board to prepare full care plans (i.e., something they should have been doing anyway). McCracken J held that Article 40 of the Constitution required the court to preserve the personal rights of the citizen. This meant that s 47 gave overall control of children in care to the District Court. McCracken J was clear that this did not mean that the District Court should interfere in day-to-day decisions relating to care, but rather that the court could intervene where matters of concern are brought to the attention of the court. The directions that there should be no change of foster parents or social workers without leave of the District Court were upheld.

---

[154] [1999] 1 IR 174.

Example case

CFA v MM[155] provides a good example of the court adding nuance to a care order with directions *on its own motion*. This case concerned Baby T who was an infant under 12 months old. The mother was homeless and had heroin addiction issues. She had refused to be admitted to a drug treatment facility during pregnancy. The child was removed post birth and the mother was reluctant to have any contact with the child. The mother had consented to foster care until the child was 18 years old because she could not see herself being in a position to resume care. The court made a care order on the basis that Baby's T health development and welfare was likely to be avoidably impaired or neglected into the future. The court also found that a care order up to 18 years of age was proportionate to ensure continuity of care and avoid the possible effect on the child of disruption.

However, the court felt that if the mother's circumstances changed, reunification could be in the best interests of the child. It made a direction for the mother to be provided with 'all supports necessary' to assist her to participate meaningfully with access visits. The court also directed that the case was to be re-entered before the court if the child's foster placement broke down or if the Child and Family Agency sought to change the child's foster care placement.

Key case

VQ v Horgan & Anor[156] explored the limits of the District Court's supervisory jurisdiction. In this case, foster carers applied to get dental treatment for a 14-year-old boy who was being bullied about his teeth. No public funding was available for the dental treatment. The foster parents sought funding from Tusla but were told to take it out of their fostering allowance. They applied to the District Court for a s 47 direction, but this was refused. The District Court held that it was the function of the executive to decide how funding was spent. On appeal, the High Court upheld the decision. It confirmed that the District Court has an overall supervisory and directory jurisdiction in regard to the exercise by Tusla of its powers. The District Court can make all decisions relating to the care and welfare of the child subject only to the proviso that the court ought not to interfere unless matters arise which require consideration of the welfare and interests of the child. The question for the District Court is whether the treatment was merely desirable, or necessary in the best interests of the child.

155 [2018] IEDC 2.
156 [2016] IEHC 631.

9.3 External scrutiny of care

The Ombudsman for Children (OCO) has jurisdiction to investigate complaints about how children are treated by public services including Tusla and investigates about 1,500 complaints per year.[157] It can make findings of fact and make recommendations. Recently, in a *Report on Jack's Case*[158] it investigated a complaint about residential care placements. Jack was an 8-year-old boy who was profoundly disabled and required full time care. He had spent three years in hospital after being fit for discharge because no appropriate placement was available. The OCO found that failure of the HSE and Tusla to work together to meet Jack's needs had had a negative impact on Jack's life. The investigation highlighted systemic failures by the HSE to provide adequate support and services to many children like Jack, with disabilities, who were living in inappropriate settings. The OCO made recommendations to both Tusla and the HSE and called for a national review.

10. After care and outcomes

Section 45 of the Child Care Act 1991 requires Tusla to prepare an aftercare plan for an *eligible* child or adult, where Tusla forms a view that there is a need for assistance. To be eligible for aftercare support a person needs to have spent minimum periods in state care.[159] Even where a need for assistance has been identified, aftercare can be limited on the basis of a lack of resources.[160] Some judges direct an aftercare review before the child turns 18 but this very *ad hoc.* 3,059 children and young adults were in receipt of aftercare services at the end of 2021, 82% had an aftercare plan.[161]

International research suggests that children leaving the care of the State have lower levels of educational attainment and higher levels of unemployment and social disadvantage than the general population, but little is known about the educational experience and outcomes of children in care in Ireland. Exploratory research by Marieke Darmody *et al*[162]

---

157 Ombudsman for Children Act 2002, ss 8 and 9.

158 The full report is available at https://www.oco.ie/library/ombudsman-for-children-launches-report-on-jacks-case/ [last accessed 3 August 2023].

159 Outlined in s 45 of the Child Care Act 1991 and Tusla, National Aftercare Policy for Alternative Care (2017) available at https://www.tusla.ie/services/alternative-care/after-care/national-aftercare-policy-for-alternative-care/ [last accessed 3 August 2023].

160 *LH v Child and Family Agency* [2014] IEDC 08.

161 Tusla, *Review of Adequacy Report 2021* (2022), 95 available at https://www.tusla.ie/publications/review-of-adequacy-reports [last accessed 3 August 2023].

162 ESRI, *Education of Children in Care in Ireland: An Exploratory Study by the Economic and Social Research Institute* (2013) available at https://www.esri.ie/system/files/publications/BKMNEXT235.pdf [last accessed 3 August 2023].

found that stable care placements provided a supportive environment and could encourage children to do well at school whereas multiple care placements could be disruptive of schooling. However, it was not possible for the authors to generate a clear profile of attendance, participation and attainment rates in education among children in care or to compare them with the general population of children. There is ongoing pressure for a large-scale **longitudinal study** of children in care as proposed in 2009 following the Ryan Report.[163] Carmel Devaney *et al*[164] did a small study of 27 participants in 2017. They found that children's experiences of care were very different and that some children did have good experiences. They also highlighted that the common social narrative that care is a universally bad experience is stigmatising for children in care and care leavers.

11. Summary

- Tusla has a duty to promote the welfare of children who are not receiving adequate care and protection. This is fulfilled by providing support to parents and families and by taking children into state care where appropriate.
- Children can be placed into state care with the agreement of their parents (voluntary care) or without parental agreement if such measures are approved by court order (involuntary care).
- State intervention into family life must be legitimate and proportionate. Article 42A.2 permits state intervention into families only where parents have failed in their duties to such extent that the children's safety or welfare is likely to be prejudicially affected. The various care orders under the Child Care Act 1991 require strict evidential requirements to be satisfied before state intervention without parental permission can be authorised.
- Before making any type of care order, the court must consider the child's best interests as the paramount concern.
- Article 42A.4 requires that provision is made by law for securing the views of children within public law proceedings. A new s 24A of the Child Care Act 1991 (when commenced) will require the court to

---

163 Carmel Devaney and Cliona Rooney, *The Feasibility of Conducting a Longitudinal Study on Children in Care or Children Leaving Care within the Irish Context* (2018), available at https://www.tusla.ie/uploads/content/Feasibility_Study_on_Longitudinal_Study.pdf [last accessed 3 August 2023].

164 Carmel Devaney, Lisa Moran, Caroline McGregor, *Outcomes for Permanence and Stability for Children in Care in Ireland* (2017) available at https://www.tusla.ie/uploads/content/Outcomes_for_permanence_and_stability_in_children_in_long_term_care_Practice_Guide_2017_Digital.pdf [last accessed 3 August 2023].

determine the means by which a child should express their views and give due weight to such views.

- Guardians *ad Litem* are commonly used to convey the wishes and interests of the child to the court in public child law proceedings. A new Pt VA of the Child Care Act 1991 will (when commenced) provide more robust regulation of this role and improve the supports for hearing children's views within public law proceedings.
- Children in long term care in Ireland are usually placed in foster care.

12. Further reading

Ursula Kilkelly, 'Learning Lessons from the Past: Legal Issues Arising from Ireland's Child Abuse Reports' (2012) 12 Irish Journal of Applied Social Sciences 8.

Conor O'Mahony, 'The Same but Different? Article 42A and the Threshold for State Intervention in Family Life: In Re JJ' (2022) 4 Irish Supreme Court Review 141.

Conor O'Mahony, Aisling Parkes, Kenneth Burns, Caroline Shore, 'Child Care Proceedings in Non-Specialist Courts: Lessons from Ireland' (2016) 30 International Journal of Law, Policy and the Family 131.

The Care Experience Podcast explores the experiences of people who grew up in care. This important perspective is missing from most academic writing, available at https://thecareexperience.libsyn.com/ [last accessed 3 August 2023].

12.1 Voluntary care

Rebekah Brennan, Conor O'Mahony and Kenneth Burns, 'The rights of the child in voluntary care in Ireland: a call for reform in law, policy and practice',(2021) Children and Youth Services Review 1–38.

Kenneth Burns, Conor O'Mahony and Rebekah Brennan, 'Private Family Arrangements' for Children in Ireland: The Informal Grey Space In-Between State Care and the Family Home' (2021) 51 The British Journal of Social Work 1203.

Conor O'Mahony, Rebekah Brennan and Kenneth Burns, 'Informed consent and parental rights in voluntary care agreements' (2020) 32 Child and Family Law Quarterly 373.

12.2 Emergency care

Children in immediate danger: emergency removals in Finnish and Irish child protection' Lamponen, Tuuli; Pösö, Tarja; Burns, Kenneth 'Children in immediate danger: emergency removals in Finnish and Irish child protection' (2019) 24 Child and Family Social Work 486.

12.3 Voice of the child

Aoife Daly, *Children, Autonomy and the Courts beyond the Right to Be Heard* (Brill Nijhoff 2018)

Elaine O'Callaghan, Conor O'Mahony and Kenneth Burns, '"There is nothing as effective as hearing the lived experience of the child" : Practitioners' Views on Children's Participation in Child Care Cases in Ireland' (2019) 22 Irish Journal of Family Law 2.

Aisling Parkes, Caroline Shore, Conor O'Mahony and Kenneth Burns, 'The right of the child to be heard? Professional experiences of child care proceedings in the Irish District Court' (2015) 27 Child and Family Law Quarterly 423.

Olivia McEvoy & Martine Smith *Listen to our Voices! Hearing Children and Young People in the Care of the State* (Department of Children and Youth Affairs 2011) Executive Summary available at https://www.lenus.ie/bitstream/handle/10147/139489/LTOVreport.pdf?sequence=3 [last accessed 3 August 2023].

Chapter 11

Adoption

Fiona Broughton Coveney and Deirdre McGowan

LEARNING OUTCOMES

On completion of this chapter, students will be equipped to:

- Contextualise the purpose and effect of the Birth Information and Tracing Act 2022.
- Identify the key rights protections applicable to adoption.
- Outline the statutory framework governing adoption.

CRITICAL THINKING POINTS

- Does Irish law strike an appropriate balance between the privacy rights of parents and an adopted person's identity rights?
- Should open adoption be supported by legislation?

1. Introduction

An adoption order made by the court permanently changes who a child's parents are in law. It removes all legal connections between a child and one or more of their parents and transfers those connections to one or more adoptive parents. This is an impactful process that can have serious consequences for the child's understanding of who they are and how they fit into a broader familial and cultural network. Although Ireland now has a modern rights informed framework of laws governing adoption, this was not always the case. Indeed, the most recent legislative change relating to adoption was the result of campaigning by those affected by historic, secret and, often, illegal adoption practices.

The **Adoption Act 2010** ('the 2010 Act') takes a child-centred, rights-informed approach to adoption, facilitating adoption with and without the consent of parents. It also governs the adoption of children from other countries (inter-country adoption), giving effect to the Hague Convention on Intercountry Adoption.[1] In practical terms, children may

[1] Hague Convention on Protection of Children and Co-operation in Respect of Intercountry Adoption.

be adopted following placement in long-term foster care or adopted by a step-parent. Although very common in the past, new-born babies are rarely placed for adoption now. There were 101 domestic adoption orders made in 2021, of which 65 were step-parent adoptions and 24 related to children in long term foster care. There were just 16 intercountry adoption orders made in 2021.[2]

Permanently transferring parental rights and responsibilities from birth parents to adoptive parents engages a range of rights under the United Nations Convention on the Rights of the Child (UNCRC) and the European Convention on Human Rights (ECHR). There are also specific provisions in the UNCRC relating to the process of adoption. In addition, Article 42A of the Constitution requires the State to implement a legislative framework for adoption with the best interests of the child as the paramount consideration in the resolution of adoption proceedings.

Until very recently, Irish adoption law did not give adopted people a right to access information about the circumstances of their birth. Although recent practices around adoption mean that adopted persons often know this information, this was not always the case. The breach of identity and other rights occasioned to people affected by historic adoption practices has led to the enactment of the **Birth Information and Tracing Act 2022.** This legislation gives adopted persons a statutory right to birth information, and thus acknowledges that adoption is a process for the benefit of children and not a service to birth or adoptive families.

2. Rights Framework Applicable to Adoption

The UNCRC is the cornerstone for many recent constitutional and legislative changes that have taken place in Ireland relating to adoption and other children's rights issues. Several articles of the UNCRC express rights of the child that are significant in the adoption process. The best interests principle in art 3 of the UNCRC, the right of the child to be heard in art 12, and other guiding principles of the UNCRC described in detail in Chapter 8 apply to adoption. Other relevant UNCRC provisions include the right of the child to know and be cared for by his or her parents,[3] the right of the child to his or her identity, including the right to family relations without unlawful interference[4] and the right of the child not to be separated from his or her parents against their will with

---

[2] Statistics from Adoption Authority of Ireland, available at https://www.aai.gov.ie/images/2022/Domestic_Adoption_Statistics_2017_2021.pdf; https://www.aai.gov.ie/images/2022/Intercountry_statistics_2021.pdf [last accessed 10 March 2023].

[3] art 7.

[4] art 8.

certain lawful exceptions.[5] The UNCRC also provides for the right of the child who is separated from their parents to maintain personal relations and direct contact with their parents in certain situations.[6] Article 20 relates to children 'temporarily or permanently deprived of his or her family environment' and provides that States Parties should ensure care for such a child, including adoption.[7] Article 21 specifically provides for States Parties' duties in relation to adoption, stating that, in the context of adoption, 'the best interests of the child shall be the paramount consideration'. Other provisions in art 21 concern the authorisation of adoptions by competent bodies and informed consent;[8] the recognition of inter-country adoption as a means to care for a child;[9] safeguards and standards[10] and the promotion of bi-lateral and multi-lateral arrangements and agreements relating to adoption between countries.[11]

Article 42A of the Constitution, discussed in detail in Chapter 8, has both general and specific applicability to adoption. Its enactment in 2015 required significant amendments to the 2010 Act. Article 42A.2.2° requires provision to be made by law for the adoption of *any* child where the parents have failed in their duty to the child and where the best interests of the child require. This represents an important child centred change in the law as discussed in Chapter 8. Further, Article 42A.3 requires provision to be made by law for the voluntary placement for adoption and adoption of *any* child. Previously, different rules applied to different categories of children, and it was very difficult for the children of married parents to be adopted.

The ECHR, ratified by Ireland in 1953, protects a child's right to identity as part of their right to a family and private life. In *Odiévre v France* the European Court of Human Rights (ECtHR) described the right to identity as including the right to know one's parentage.[12] As noted above, the UNCRC makes more specific reference to identity rights providing that children have the right, from birth, to a name and the right to acquire a nationality as well as the right to know and be cared for by their parents as far as possible. Further, art 8 of the UNCRC requires States Parties to respect a child's right to preserve their identity including their name, nationality and family relations as recognised by law and without unlawful interference.

---

5 art 9(1).
6 art 9(3).
7 art 20(3).
8 art 21(a).
9 art 21(b).
10 art 21(c)–(d).
11 art 21(e).
12 App No 42326/98 (ECHR, 13 February 2003.)

Although a right to identity is not specifically mentioned in the Irish Constitution, it has been recognised as a personal right under Article 40.3.1°. In the context of adoption, the Supreme Court held in *I'OT v B* that the child's right to identity must be weighed against the parents' right to privacy.[13] Irish legislation has, until recently, placed greater weight on parental privacy by not giving adopted persons a right to access to information about the circumstances of their birth and early life. The Birth Information and Tracing Act 2022, discussed in detail below, effects a significant change in direction in providing a statutory right to birth information for adopted persons.

3. Identity rights and historical practices

Until recently, the constitutional privacy rights of parents took precedence in Irish law and practice meaning that adopted persons had no right to obtain their birth records. Identifying information would only be disclosed to them with the permission of their birth parents. This preferencing of privacy rights was a legacy of how adoption was understood historically, not as serving the best interests of children, but as a solution to the 'problem' of children born to unmarried parents. Pregnancy outside marriage was considered shameful and this shame attached to pregnant women and their children, resulting in significant negative repercussions for both.[14] From the foundation of the State until 1987, children born to unmarried parents carried the legal status of illegitimate.[15] This affected inheritance and other legal rights,[16] but also impacted upon the day to day lives of children and mothers. Unmarried pregnant women and girls were hidden from society, went abroad, or were incarcerated in one of a network of Mother and Baby Homes and other institutions. It was almost impossible for an unmarried woman to raise a child alone[17] and most women left these homes without their children who were, often without parental consent, incarcerated in industrial schools, boarded out in foster homes, or handed over to Irish and overseas married couples to raise as their own. Finding new parents for a child was seen as a way to protect them from the stigma of illegitimacy, but no vetting of prospective adopters was undertaken, and the entire process was shrouded in secrecy.[18]

---

13 [1998] 2 IR 321.

14 Clara Fischer, 'Gender, nation, and the politics of shame: Magdalen Laundries and the institutionalisation of feminine transgression in modern Ireland', (2016) 41(4) *Signs* 821.

15 The Status of Children Act 1987 abolished the status.

16 Maria Luddy, 'Unmarried Mothers in Ireland, 1880-1973' (2011) 20(1) *Women's History Review* 109, 110. In relation to succession, see *OB v S* [1984] IR 316.

17 No financial support was provided by the State to unmarried mothers and their children until a social welfare allowance was introduced in 1973.

18 Simone Mc Caughren and Fred Powell, 'The Fate of the "Illegitimate" Child: An Analysis

A scandal involving the adoption of an Irish child by an American film star pushed the government of the time to implement adoption legislation in 1953.[19] Prior to the passage of the Adoption Act 1952, Ireland had no legislation governing adoption. Although it was possible to record an adoption by deed, many children were transferred to new families by registering the new parents as birth parents. This practice was a criminal breach of the Birth and Deaths Registration Act 1874 but continued until well into the 1970s despite the passage of the Adoption Act 1952. An independent review commissioned by the Minister for Children in 2019, estimated that up to 20,000 children were the subject of illegal adoption practices between 1946 and 1996.[20] As well as being illegal, the falsification of birth records meant that many people did not know that the people who raised them were not their birth parents and where they did know, had no way to obtain information about their genetic and social identity.

Despite significant improvement in the legal framework governing adoption with the enactment of the Adoption Act 1952 and subsequent reforming legislation, adopted children still had no right to access information about the circumstances of their birth. The National Adoption Contact Preference Register was established on a non-statutory basis in 2005. This allowed people affected by adoption to make known their preferences regarding contact with family members. It operated by matching people based on their expressed willingness to provide or not provide information or to connect with family members. It therefore presupposed that adopted persons had some information about the circumstances of their birth and relied on the good will or consent of others in providing information. The basic information recorded on birth certificates has always been available because these are public records generally available on payment of a small fee. A legally adopted person who requests a copy of their birth certificate after the age of 18 will be advised that additional information is available and can then obtain their original birth certificate. For those adopted illegally, the position was much more complicated.

In 2021, the Special Rapporteur on Child Protection, Conor O'Mahony, made proposals for a state response to illegal birth registrations, including recommendations in relation to access to birth information.[21] Some of these recommendations have been incorporated into the Birth

---

of Irish Social Policy, 1750-1952' in Niamh Howlin and Kevin Costello, *Law and the Family in Ireland 1800-1950* (Palgrave 2017).

19 ibid, 208.

20 Conor O'Mahony, *Proposals for a State Response to Illegal Birth Registrations in Ireland*, Department of Children, Equality, Disability, Integration and Youth (2021).

21 https://www.gov.ie/en/publication/6ff84-proposals-for-a-state-response-to-illegal-birth-registrations-in-ireland/ [last accessed 1 March 2023].

Information and Tracing Act 2022 ('the 2022 Act')[22] which provides a new statutory framework for accessing birth information including for the first time a statutory right to access birth information.

3.1 Critical thinking point: Does Irish law strike an appropriate balance between the privacy rights of parents and an adopted person's identity rights?

The 2022 Act provides a statutory right of access to birth certificates,[23] birth, early life and care information,[24] and medical information[25] for 'relevant persons' who were adopted, boarded out, the subject of an illegal birth registration or resident in one of the institutions listed in the schedule to the Act. However, where a parent has registered a desire not to be contacted, the adopted person requesting information via the statutory scheme must attend an information session with a representative of the Adoption Authority or Tusla where they will be told of their parent's wishes and that the expression of such wishes represents the exercise of their right to privacy.[26]

Organisations representing adopted persons argue that the requirement to attend an information session represents a disproportionate interference with information and identity rights and that it is discriminatory in treating some adopted people differently to the general public, particularly in relation to access to birth certificates which are freely available from the Civil Registrar's office on payment of a small fee. Some adopted people have sufficient information to identify their original birth registration from the public birth register but those without such information must use the statutory system and thus could be required to attend the sessions. Further, the Clann project argues that the definition of 'relevant person' in the 2022 Act excludes a large number of persons impacted by illegal practices including those resident in institutions not listed in the schedule to the Act, many people adopted abroad, and some whose births were illegally registered.[27]

The legislation does, however, recognise that illegal adoptions took place and makes provision to ensure that the illegality does not adversely affect an adopted person's legal status. It provides that illegally adopted people, despite the absence of a legal transfer of parentage, may identify as the

---

22 Commenced between July and October 2022.
23 2022 Act, ss 6–8.
24 ibid, ss 9–12.
25 ibid, ss 15–16.
26 ibid, s 17.
27 Claire McGettrick, Maeve O'Rourke, Loughlin O'Nolan, *Clann Project: Birth Information and Tracing Bill 2022, Briefing Note and Amendments 28 February 2022* available at http://clannproject.org/ [last accessed 17 March 2023].

children of their adoptive parents. It confirms their right to be identified as a member of their social family[28] and confirms that they have succession rights in relation to both their adoptive and original families.[29] Provision is also made for the amendment of the Register of Births where information becomes available indicating that an incorrect entry has been made. Any amendments made will be recorded in a separate register searchable by the person affected, a small number of specified relatives and any other person whom the Civil Registrar in their discretion determines.[30] These provisions represent a practical solution to the significant legal issues that can arise from the practice of illegal birth registration.

The 2022 Act also establishes a tracing service for people wishing to make contact or share or seek information,[31] an updated Contact Preference Register[32] and measures to address issues for any person whose birth was subject to an illegal registration.[33] Support, including counselling is available free of charge under the Act for any person affected.[34] The Act also provides for the safeguarding of all relevant records.[35] The Contact Preference Register allows relevant persons to make contact,[36] accept contact,[37] request privacy,[38] seek information[39] or share information.[40] The Adoption Authority of Ireland facilitates the Register and all preferences held by the Adoption Authority, under the old National Adoption Contact Preference Register, transferred to the new Contact Preference Register and remain valid.

This legislation represents a significant improvement in the position of some people subject to historical adoption practices and prioritises a child's right to identity over a parent's right to privacy. There has been some criticism on the grounds that families placing children for adoption

28 2022 Act, s 59
29 ibid, Pt 8, ss 52-57.
30 Civil Registration Act 2004, s 30F as amended by Birth Information and Tracing Act 2022, s 57.
31 Birth Information and Tracing Act 2022, Pt 5.
32 2022 Act, Pt 6.
33 2022 Act, s 59. The Act amends the Succession Act 1965 (Pt 8 of 2022 Act) and the Civil Registration Act 2004 (Pt 9 of 2022 Act) to address issues that arise for persons affected by illegal birth registrations. The aim is to vindicate the rights of those persons to an accurate birth registration. The relevant person is entitled to live under whichever identity they choose (their accurate birth identity or the identity they have lived all of their lives) and to have their social parents recognised in law under a register. Part 8 addressed any inheritance issues arising for affected persons.
34 2022 Act, ss 63 and 69.
35 ibid, Pt 7.
36 ibid, s 38(11)(a).
37 ibid, s 38(11)(b).
38 ibid, s 38(11)(c) and (e).
39 ibid, s 38(11)(d).
40 ibid, s 38(11)(e).

in the past were assured privacy. However, as groups representing adopted people point out, providing birth information is not the same as instigating or encouraging contact between adopted people and their families of origin.

4. Modern adoption legislation

The Adoption Act 1952 was the first Irish legislation governing adoption and it remained in place, with amendments, until 2010. The 1952 Act established An Bord Uchtála, which had oversight of the adoption process and was empowered to make adoption orders. The adoption process and regulatory framework was significantly reformed with the enactment of the 2010 Act, commenced on 1 November 2010. This legislation aimed to improve standards in domestic and intercountry adoption. It repealed the Adoption Act 1952 and reformed related legislation.[41] The 2010 Act established the **Adoption Authority of Ireland** (the Adoption Authority), which is now empowered to make adoption orders.[42] It also facilitates compliance with the terms of the Hague Convention on the Protection of Children and Co-operation in respect of Inter-country Adoption, 1993 (the Hague Convention)[43] which Ireland ratified on the same day that the 2010 Act became law.[44] The Convention, coupled with the 2010 Act, facilitates inter-country adoptions between Ireland and other signatory countries or countries with which Ireland has Convention compliant bilateral agreements.[45] Following the enactment of the Children's Rights Amendment, some amendments were made to the Act in 2017 to ensure compliance with the new constitutional provisions.[46]

Reflecting international rights and constitutional obligations, s 19(1) of the 2010 Act provides that in adoption matters, applications and proceedings, the Adoption Authority and the court will regard the **best interests of the child** as the paramount consideration. Further, s 19(3) provides that a child capable of forming views has the right for his or her views to be ascertained and for those views be given due weight having regard to the age and maturity of the child.

---

41 For example, the Adoptive Leave Act 1995; Child Care Act 1991; Civil Registration Act 2004; Freedom of Information Act 1997; Guardianship of Infants Act 1964; Married Women's Status Act 1957; Ombudsman for Children Act 2002; Parental Leave Act 1998; Status of Children Act 1987; Succession Act 1965.

42 The Child and Family Agency (Tusla) is the competent body for the assessment of adoptions.

43 The Hague Convention came into force on 1 May 1995 and became part of Irish law under the 2010 Act.

44 The 2010 Act, s 9 states that '[T]he Hague Convention has the force of law in the State'.

45 ibid, Pt 9.

46 Adoption (Amendment) Act 2017.

4.1 Adoption orders

Section 58 of the 2010 Act, sets out the effect of an **adoption order**. When an adoption order is made by the Adoption Authority, guardians and 'relevant non-guardians' lose all parental rights and duties in relation to the child. These rights and duties transfer to the adopting parents.

Key legislation – s 58 of the Adoption Act 2010

58.— Subject to Section 58A, upon an adoption order being made, or the recognition under this Act of an intercountry adoption effected outside the State—

(a) the child concerned shall be considered, with regard to the rights and duties of parents and children in relation to each other, as the child of the adopters, and

(b) with respect to the child –

(i) the mother or guardian of the child, and

(ii) every relevant non-guardian of the child,

shall, subject to section 57, lose all parental rights and be freed from all parental duties in respect of the child.

However, where an adopter is a step-parent intending to have joint parental responsibilities with a parent, an adoption order has a slightly different effect as set out in s 58A. This section was introduced in 2017 to remedy the previous situation whereby for a child to become the child of a step-parent, the parent and step parent needed to adopt jointly, erasing and then re-granting parental rights and responsibilities to the parent. Now, a step-parent can adopt a child without affecting the parental rights and responsibilities of the other parent.

Key legislation – s 58A of the Adoption Act 2010 (Step-parent adoption)

(1) Section 58 shall not apply where the adopter of a child is a step parent of the child and, in that case, upon an adoption order being made—

(a) the child concerned shall be considered, with regard to the rights and duties of parents and children in relation to each other, as the child of—
   (i) the adopter and the adopter's spouse,
   (ii) the adopter and the adopter's civil partner, or
   (iii) the adopter and the adopter's co-habitant,
   and
(b) with respect to the child—
   (i) the mother or guardian, unless such mother or guardian is a person referred to in subparagraph (i), (ii) or (iii) of paragraph (a), and
   (ii) every relevant non-guardian of the child,

shall, subject to section 57, lose all parental rights and shall be freed from all parental duties in respect of that child.

(2) Nothing in this section shall operate to affect the legal parent-child relationship of a person, being a mother or guardian secondly referred to in paragraph (b) (i), with regard to his or her child, who is the subject of the adoption order referred to in subsection (1).]

4.2 Types of domestic adoption

Children are most commonly adopted by a step-parent or by their long term foster parents. Where children are being adopted by foster parents, this will often happen just before a child turns 18. A step-parent for the purpose of the Act is a spouse, civil partner or cohabitant of a parent of the child.[47] The stereotypical situation of a young unmarried woman placing an infant for adoption at birth is now very unusual. Even where an infant is placed for adoption at birth, this will often be the result of an intervention by Tusla prior to the child's birth (see Chapter 10).

The 2010 Act (as amended) implements the constitutional statement that provision shall be made by law for a child to be placed for adoption in two main situations:

1. Where parents have voluntarily placed the child for adoption.
2. Where the parents have failed for a specified period of time

[47] 2010 Act, s 37.

in their duty toward the child and where the best interests of the child so require.

Most adoptions will fall under the **'voluntary placement'** category in the sense that the relevant parent or guardian agrees to the child being placed for adoption. Occasionally, a parent will change their mind after an initial voluntary placement and withdraw their consent. The adoptive parents can choose to accept this and withdraw from the process, or to apply to the court to have the consent of the parents dispensed with. Despite the need for an application to the court, this remains a 'voluntary placement' adoption for the purposes of the legislation. In **failure of duty** cases, the child is placed for adoption by the State following an intervention by Tusla (see Chapter 10). Such involuntary adoptions always require an order of the court to affirm that the parents have failed in their duty to the child and that the adoption is in the child's best interests. The specific process for each type of adoption is detailed later in this chapter.

4.2.1 Children who may be adopted

Section 23 of the 2010 Act sets out the categories of children who may be adopted. Only children under 18 years of age on the date of the adoption order and resident in the State may be adopted.[48] Where the proposed adopter is a step-parent of the child, the child must have lived with their parent and the step-parent or been in the care of the step-parent for a continuous period of two years at the date of application,[49] although the Adoption Authority may, having regard to the circumstances of the case, accept a shorter period.[50] For involuntary adoptions, the child must have lived with the prospective adopters for a minimum period of 18 months.[51]

4.2.2 Persons who may adopt

Prospective adopters must fulfil the **eligibility and suitability** criteria set out in the 2010 Act. In order to be eligible, the applicants must be a married couple living together,[52] civil partners living together,[53] a cohabiting couple who have lived together for at least 3 years,[54] a parent,[55]

---

48 ibid, s 23(1)(a).
49 ibid, s 23(1)(b).
50 ibid, s 23(2).
51 ibid, s 54(2A)(e).
52 ibid, s 33(1)(a)(i).
53 ibid, s 33(1)(a)(ia).
54 ibid, s 33(1)(a)(ib) and S3(1).
55 ibid, s 33(1)(a)(ii). A parent for the purpose of the Act includes a mother or father of the child or a woman (other than the mother) who is the parent of a donor conceived child within the meaning of s 5 of the Children and Family Relationship Act 2015.

step-parent[56] or relative of the child.[57] Other persons may adopt if they can satisfy the Adoption Authority that the adoption is desirable and in the best interests of the child.[58] Where an applicant is married, in a civil partnership or cohabiting, the consent of their spouse, civil partner or cohabitant will normally be required for the adoption if they are not also adopting the child.[59] Proposed adopters must, in most cases, be over 21 years of age[60] and habitually resident in the State.[61]

In addition to meeting eligibility requirements, prospective adopters must be suitable persons 'to have parental rights and duties in respect of a child'.[62] Section 34(a) refers to a number of factors of relevance to a determination of suitability including good moral character, good health and of an age that they can expect to fulfil their duties to the child throughout childhood. They must demonstrate a capacity to promote and support the child's development and wellbeing, safeguard their welfare, provide necessary health, social, educational, and other interventions for the child and value the child's needs in relation to their identity, ethnic, religious and cultural background. In addition, they must have adequate financial means to support the child and have been provided with adequate information, advice and counselling concerning adoption.[63] In practical terms, prospective adopters apply to Tusla for a suitability assessment. Tusla make a report which is forwarded to the Adoption Authority for the purpose of making a suitability declaration.[64] This declaration remains valid for two years but can be extended for an additional one year.[65] The Adoption Authority can include a statement in the declaration in relation to the age or state of health of a child that the Authority deems the applicant suitable to parent.[66]

4.3 Voluntary adoption

The voluntary adoption process is based on the concept of **consent**, with the default position being that the mother/guardians of the child give informed consent to both the placement of the child for adoption and the final adoption order. Other relevant non-guardians, including a non-guardian father, will be consulted in relation to the adoption, but

56 As defined by s 37, see above.
57 A relative of a child is a grandparent, brother, sister, uncle or aunt of the child and includes the spouse of any such persons: s 3(1).
58 2010 Act, s 31(1)(b).
59 ibid, s 33(3).
60 ibid, s 33(4), with some limited exceptions.
61 ibid, s 33(5).
62 ibid, s 34(a).
63 ibid, s 34(b) and (c).
64 ibid, s 39(1).
65 ibid, s 41(1).
66 ibid, s 40(3)

their consent is not required. The court has power to dispense with the consent of the mother/guardian where the mother/guardian withdraws consent after initial placement, and it is in the best interests of the child to dispense with consent.[67]

4.3.1 Placement for voluntary adoption

Adoptions are managed by an accredited body which can be an adoption agency registered with the Adoption Authority or Tusla.[68] The first stage of the process is known as **placement for adoption**. This is where the mother/guardian of the child gives consent to the commencement of an adoption process. The child may already be living with the prospective adopter(s) as a step-child or foster child at this stage, but before the formal adoption process can be begin the mother/guardian of the child must give informed consent to placement. The adoption agency must provide the mother/guardian with specific information in writing, including that a placement for adoption is the beginning of the adoption process and the effect of a placement for adoption on the rights of guardians. They must also ensure that the mother/guardian understands this information and that they sign a document confirming their understanding. The agency is also required to provide information, advice and counselling to the mother/guardian.[69] It is the responsibility of the adoption agency to ensure that a child directly placed with them by a mother/guardian is appropriately cared for before being placed with prospective adopters. Any child placed for adoption must be at least six weeks old.[70]

Next, the adoption agency must take such steps as are practicable to consult with any relevant non-guardian.[71] A relevant non-guardian is a father of the child who has not been appointed guardian, a person appointed as temporary guardian by the court, a person appointed guardian by the court without the right to object to an adoption, or a parent of a child born through DAHR who is not a guardian of the child.[72] Consultation includes the provision of information regarding the legal implications of, and procedure for, adoption.[73] If the relevant non-guardian indicates that they have no objection, the placement will proceed.[74] Where an objection is made however, the adoption agency will defer the placement until the non-guardian has had an opportunity

---

67 ibid, s 31(2).
68 ibid, s 11.
69 ibid, s 14(a) to (c).
70 ibid, s 13(a).
71 ibid, s 17(2)
72 ibid, s 3.
73 ibid, s 17(2).
74 ibid, s 17(3)(a).

to apply to the court for appointment as guardian.[75] If the application is successful, then they can, as guardian, object and the placement will not proceed. Where the Adoption Authority believes that it is inappropriate to consult with the relevant non-guardian it can, with the approval of the High Court, authorise the placement without consultation.[76] In circumstances where a relevant non-guardian cannot be contacted despite reasonable efforts, the Authority can authorise the placement.[77] Where the mother of the child will not disclose the identity of the father, the adoption agency must counsel her regarding the implications of such non-disclosure, including the possibility of delays, the potential for the father to object at a later stage and that the lack of medical, genetic and social background information may adversely impact the health development and welfare of the child.[78] Where the mother does not know the identity of the father, she can provide a declaration to that effect. When the identity of the father is not known or not disclosed, the High Court on application by the Adoption Authority, can dispense with the consultation requirement.[79]

These provisions regarding consultation with non-guardians were a response to a finding by the ECtHR in *Keegan v Ireland* that Irish law breached the ECHR by, at that time, allowing a child to be adopted without their father's knowledge.[80] In this case, the father of a child placed for adoption by the mother applied for guardianship in an attempt to block the adoption of his child. His application for guardianship was refused and the adoption proceeded.[81] The Supreme Court decided that the welfare of the child was best served by remaining with the prospective adopters. The 2010 Act, in addition to providing for consultation, enables a father to notify the Adoption Authority if he is concerned that his child may be placed for adoption without his knowledge. The Adoption Authority will then notify him if the child is placed for adoption.[82]

The initial consent to placement does not operate as a consent to adoption. An adoption order will not be made until a final consent by the child's mother/guardian is provided or such consent is dispensed with by the High Court.[83] This final consent must be given in writing after the child has reached the age of 6 weeks and within three months of the

---

75 ibid, s 17(3)(b).
76 ibid, s 18(4).
77 ibid, s 18(2).
78 ibid, s 18(5).
79 ibid, ss 18(6), 18(7).
80 App no 16969/90 (ECtHR, 26 May 1994)
81 *JK v VW* [1990] 2 IR 437.
82 2010 Act, s 16.
83 ibid, s 26(1) provides for the setting aside of consent to adoption in a number of circumstances.

application for an adoption order.[84] Consent can be withdrawn at any time before the adoption order is made.[85] When giving final consent, the mother/guardian must be advised that they can withdraw it, that they are entitled to be heard at the adoption hearing and that the High Court can authorise the authority to dispense with their consent if it is subsequently withdrawn.[86]

Section 26(4) of the 2010 Act allows the mother/guardian to withdraw consent at any time before the making of the adoption order. However, because the Adoption Authority is an administrative body rather than a judicial one, it cannot resolve disputes between adoptive parents and the mother/guardians. Therefore, if consent is withdrawn and the adoptive parents wish to proceed with the adoption, an application will be made to the High Court under s 31 to dispense with the mother/guardian's consent.[87] In considering an application, the best interests of the child must be the paramount consideration and the court must have regard to a number of factors including:

> (i) the relationship between the applicants and the child [...];
> (ii) the relationship between the child and his or her mother or guardian [...] and the efforts made by any of those persons to develop or maintain a relationship with the child;
> (iii) the proposed arrangements of the applicants and the mother or guardian or other person whose consent [...] is necessary [...] for the future care of the child;
> (iv) the rights, whether under the Constitution or otherwise, of the persons concerned (including the natural and imprescriptible rights of the child);
> (v) any other matter which the court considers relevant [...].[88]

In addition to these considerations, the High Court is required to have regard to the child's views having regard to the age and maturity of the child[89] and to ensure that 'the best interests of the child shall be the paramount consideration' in their decision.[90]

---

84 ibid, s 28(1).
85 ibid, s 26(4).
86 ibid, s 27(1)
87 See case-law such as *G v An Bord Uchtála* [1980] IR 3; *EF & FF v An Bord Uchtála and SD* [1980] IR 32; *McF v G & G & Sacred Heart Adoption Society* [1983] ILRM 228 and *N & N v G & G HSE* [2006] IEHC 278 (Baby Ann case).
88 2010 Act, s 31(4)(a).
89 ibid, s 31(4)(b).
90 ibid, s 31(4)(b) as amended by Adoption (Amendment) Act 2017, s 14C.

Key case – *N & N v HSE, G & G, and An Bord Uchtála* [2006] IESC 60

The main case dealing with the withdrawal of consent is *N v HSE*[91] (the 'baby Ann' case), which was decided before Article 42A was inserted into the Constitution and the 2010 Act updated to reflect its provisions.[92] In this case, a child had been placed for adoption immediately after her birth and the mother had signed the final consent to adoption less than a year later. The mother then withdrew her consent and requested the return of the child. The mother had married the child's father in the interim and they successfully argued that as a marital family, the child's welfare was best served by being returned to their custody. Article 42A and the provisions of s 31 now require the child's best interests to be the paramount consideration in dispensing with consent. Although this change of emphasis may not have changed the outcome in this specific case, the nature of the arguments and reasoning would be significantly different in focusing on the best interests of the child rather than the marital status of the parents.

4.4 Involuntary adoption

Involuntary adoptions generally arise where a child is in the care of the State and an application is made for an adoption order in respect of the child. This most commonly arises where foster carers wish to adopt a child in their care. If the prospective adopters meet the eligibility and suitability requirements set out in the 2010 Act the Adoption Authority will consult with Tusla, the child, the mother of the child, the father of the child, other guardians, relatives and persons caring for the child.[93] Once the Authority is satisfied that an adoption is appropriate, the prospective adopter may request Tusla to make an application to the High Court to dispense with the consent of the parents.[94] Tusla may proceed with the application only if it is satisfied that every reasonable effort has been made to support the parents and it believes it is 'proper to do so'.[95] On application by Tusla, the High Court may dispense with the consent of the parents where the court is satisfied that:[96]

(a) the parents have for a period of at least 3 years failed in their duty to the child to such an extent that the safety and welfare of the child is likely to be prejudicially affected, and
(b) there is no reasonable prospect that the parents will be able

---

91 *N & N v HSE, G & G, and An Bord Uchtála* [2006] IESC 60.
92 By the Adoption (Amendment) Act 2017.
93 Adoption Act 2010, s 53(1)(a).
94 2010 Act, s 54(1)
95 2010 Act, s 54(1)(a) and (b).
96 2010 Act, s 54(2A).

to care for the child in a manner that will not prejudicially affect his or her safety or welfare, and

(c) the failure constitutes an abandonment on the part of the parents of all parental rights, whether under the Constitution or otherwise with respect to the child, and

(d) by reason of the failure, the State, as guardian of the common good, should supply the place of the parents, and

(e) the child is living with the proposed adoptive parents at the time of the application and for not less than 18 months prior to the application, and

(f) the adoption of the child by the adoptive parents is a proportionate means by which to supply the place of the parents.[97]

The court in considering the application must have regard to the constitutional rights of all parties as well as the views of the child, in so far as practicable having regard to the age and maturity of the child. It must also, in the resolution of any dispute, consider the best interests of the child as the paramount consideration. The recent Supreme Court decision in *Child and Family Agency & Ors v Adoption Authority of Ireland*[98] indicates the difficulty inherent in meeting the threshold test set out in s 54(2A) and explains why many adoptions from long term foster care occur very close to the child's eighteenth birthday.[99]

Key case – *Child and Family Agency and B v Adoption Authority of Ireland and C and Z* [2023] IESC 12

In this case, Ms B had been placed in voluntary foster care shortly after her birth. She suffered foetal alcohol syndrome and as a result had developmental delays. She was cared for by a foster carer, Ms A, for her entire childhood and when Ms B was 17 years old, Ms A applied to adopt her. The Adoption Authority made a declaration pursuant to s 40 of the 2010 Act that Ms A was both eligible and suitable to act as an adoptive parent, but her birth parents, Ms C and Mr Z, refused to consent to the adoption. The Child and Family Agency then applied to the High Court for an order under s 54(2) of the Adoption Act 2010 to dispense with the parents' consent.

Ms C and Mr Z had been married to each other at the time of Ms B's birth and Ms C was the victim of significant domestic abuse and had developed an alcohol addiction. Ms B was taken into care as were two

97 2010 Act, s 54(2A) as amended by the Adoption (Amendment) Act 2017, s 24.

98 [2023] IESC 12.

99 See also *Child and Family Agency & Ors v Adoption Authority of Ireland* [2022] IEHC 269.

other, older children, of the marriage. The older children were returned to Ms C after she had undergone treatment for her addiction and other issues. There was some contact between Ms B and her mother, but there was no contact with the father.

In the High Court, Barrett J refused the application to dispense with Ms Cs consent because he was not satisfied that the statutory proofs required by s 54(2A) of the 2010 Act were satisfied. He held that because Ms C had demonstrated general parenting competencies in relation to her other children, that it would be an over-reach by the State to supply her place and an adoption would be disproportionate. He also held that adoption would not in the best interests of the child given that she was just 10 weeks away from turning 18 and would gain no significant benefits from an adoption.

The majority of the Court of Appeal reversed this decision, and the Supreme Court affirmed the reversal. In the Supreme Court, Hogan J went through each of the factors in s 54(2A) in turn. In relation to (a) he noted that Ms C had never exercised any decision-making role in relation to Ms B and that this amounted to a failure of duty meeting the relevant threshold. As there was no reasonable prospect that Ms C would ever be in a position to care for Ms B in a way that would not prejudicially affect her welfare, factor (b) was also met. Ms C had agreed to the continuing care of Ms B by her foster carer and had left all critical decisions to her. This constituted an abandonment of parental rights as required by (c). In relation to the necessity of state intervention, Hogan J referred to Ms C's difficulties at the time the child was placed into voluntary care noting that 'this is a clear case of where the State had to supply the place of the parents'[100] as required by (d). Ms B was in the care of the proposed adopters as required by (e). Regarding (f), Hogan J referred to adoption as an institution intended to meet human needs for family stability, security and love in situations where the birth parents have not been able to provide an appropriate environment.

Hogan J pointed out that the requirements in (b) and (c) are difficult to establish in early childhood when 'ideally ... adoption orders should preferably be made in order to advance the best interests of the child in question.'[101] He suggested that the legislative framework did not adequately reflect the changes brought about by Article 42A, 'one of the objectives of which was to facilitate the adoption of children in foster care.'[102]

---

[100] ibid [71].
[101] ibid [77].
[102] ibid [78].

4.5 The adoption order and hearing

An Adoption Order is the formal order transferring parental rights to the adoptive parents and extinguishing those of the birth parents. It is granted following a hearing before the Adoption Authority. The purpose of the hearing is to ensure that all relevant statutory requirements have been met. The child and adoptive parents attend, and the adopters give sworn evidence as to identity and eligibility. Where an application to the Court is necessary to dispense with consent in either a voluntary or involuntary adoption, the Adoption Authority will process the adoption application to the point where it is in a position to make an Adoption Order should the High Court authorise it.

After the Adoption Order is made, an adoption certificate is issued by the Registrar General's Office. This adoption certificate has the same legal status as a birth certificate. An entry is made in the Adopted Children's Register, which contains all the details relevant to the adoption including the child's name; PPS number; date of birth; adopter's details and the date of the adoption order.[103]

5. Open adoption

Despite significant evidence of the harm caused to adopted people by the secretive and often illegal adoption practices of the past, Irish legislation still provides for the possibility of birth information being withheld from a child until they can make an application under the Birth Information and Tracing Act 2022. In addition, the adoption system remains 'closed', meaning there is no legal framework to facilitate formal contact between a child, birth parents and adoptive parents after the adoption order is made. Where contact occurs informally, any agreements made between birth and adoptive parents are unregulated and unenforceable. Although many adoptions now occur in situations where child may have had contact with their birth parents and extended family prior to the order, an adoptive family can cease contact after the order, potentially ending important familial connections in a way that may not be in the best interests of the child.[104] The ECtHR case of *Bogonosovy v Russia* illustrates the potential impact of fully closed adoption practices.[105] In this case, a grandfather who had cared for a child for 5 years after her mother died was denied any contact with the child after she was adopted. The Court held that in failing to assess the familial ties between the grandfather and child when she began living with her adoptive family, the national Court had breached his right to respect for his family life under Article 8. This

103 2010 Act, s 84 and Sch 3 amended by the Adoption (Amendment) Act 2017, s 41.
104 Parents can, of course, do likewise.
105 App No 38201/16(ECHR 9 September 2019).

case focused on the grandfather, as he had made the application, but the child had also been denied the opportunity to continue a relationship with her birth family because of the closed nature of the adoption.[106]

5.1 Critical thinking point: Should open adoption be supported by legislation?

An open approach to adoption, where appropriate, is considered to be a more child centred way to manage the process. 'Open adoption' is an umbrella term denoting a continuum of forms of contact and communication between birth families and adoptive families. This can range from the exchange of information or items such as letters and photographs (semi-open adoption) to post adoption contact between members of birth and adoptive families of a child under 18.[107] Section 42 of the Adoption (Amendment) Act 2017 required the Minister for Children and Youth Affairs to initiate a 'review and consultation in respect of the potential introduction of open or semi-open adoption'. The results of this review were published in November 2019.[108] The review noted that although there is no formal post-adoption contact support service, Tusla does support contact arrangements. Challenges encountered by children and adults are addressed as they arise, and support and intervention are provided to both birth and adoptive families.[109] Tusla aims to ensure that post-adoption contact is in the best interests of the child and that the child's views are considered as appropriate.[110] The report noted the lack of a formal approach could breach children's rights under the UNCRC and their right to identity under the UNCHR and fail to promote their best interests as required by Article 42A of the Constitution.[111]

The aim of the review was to consider how a more open form of adoption might work in the Irish context. It examined the Irish legal and policy context, forms of open or semi-open adoption in other jurisdictions and evidence on impacts and outcomes. The main recommendation of the review was that that legislation be enacted to support voluntary forms of post-adoption contact. This would facilitate contact where all parties agree and where it is determined to be in the best interests of the child, essentially a formalisation of existing practices. The legislation would be

---

[106] In Ireland, s 11B of the Guardianship of Infants Act 1964 would facilitate an application for leave to seek access by the grandfather in this situation.

[107] Department of Children and Youth Affairs, 'Review and Consultation in respect of the Potential Introduction of Open or Semi-Open Adoption in Ireland', Report produced in accordance with s 42 of the Adoption (Amendment) Act 2017 (November 2019), 9.

[108] ibid.

[109] ibid, 29.

[110] ibid, 50.

[111] ibid, 51

supported by a set of guidelines to govern the process of establishing whether contact is in the best interests of the child and how contact should plans operate.[112] As a consent-based proposal, this legislation would make existing practices rights compliant, but no further action has been taken by government to implement the recommendations in the report. There is provision in the Guardianship of Infants Act 1964 to allow relatives and people with whom a child has formerly resided to apply to the court for leave to make an application for access to the child. This provision offers an avenue for post-adoption contact in some situations. In considering an application the court will consider the applicants connection with the child, the risk of disruption to the child's life, the wishes of the child's guardians, the views of the child and whether making the order is necessary.[113]

As noted in the review, open adoption practices will only be useful in promoting a child's best interests if all parties agree. Secrecy was a significant motivation for many adoptions in the past and some birth parents may wish to exercise their right to privacy by refusing to participate in any form of contact. The Birth Information and Tracing Act 2022 recognises the right to privacy of birth parents in allowing them to register a preference for no contact, but birth information will nonetheless be made available to the child on request once they reach the age of 16. The balancing of rights is therefore in favour of the provision of information to promote the identity rights of the child whilst protecting the privacy rights of parents by not facilitating contact between child and birth parents post adoption.

6. Intercountry adoption

Intercountry adoption occurs where a resident of Ireland adopts a child who is habitually resident in another country.[114] Intercountry adoption was initially placed on a statutory footing in 1991 but is now governed by the 2010 Act, which implemented the State's obligations under the Hague Convention on Intercountry Adoption. Under the 2010 Act, Irish residents can only adopt from countries that have also ratified the Hague Convention or from non-Hague countries with which Ireland has a bi-lateral agreement so long as the agreement has 'regard for the principles of the Hague Convention'.[115]

The Hague Convention establishes safeguards and promotes co-operation amongst states to protect children and families in the context of cross-

[112] ibid, 3–4.
[113] Guardianship of Infants Act 1964, s 11B. See Chapter 9 for more on access orders.
[114] See Chapter 12 for a discussion of the meaning of 'habitually resident' in this context.
[115] 2010 Act, s 73.

border adoption. It puts the best interests of the child to the fore of decision-making and thus gives practical effect to art 21 of the UNCRC (on adoption) as well as art 3 (best interests) and art 12 (right to be heard) in the context of adoption.

Article 2 of the Hague Convention explains the remit of the Convention as follows:

Key treaty provision – Article 2, Hague Convention on Intercountry Adoption

(1) The Convention shall apply where a child habitually resident in one Contracting State ('the State of origin') has been, is being, or is to be moved to another Contracting State ('the receiving State') either after his or her adoption in the State of origin by spouses or a person habitually resident in the receiving State, or for the purposes of such an adoption in the receiving State or in the State of origin.

The Central Authorities of the two relevant states work in tandem to complete the adoption process in accordance with the Convention.[116] The Adoption Authority is the Central Authority for Ireland. There are specific procedures that must be followed in intercountry adoption. First, prospective adopters must apply for, and obtain a declaration of eligibility and suitability and decide from which country they wish to adopt.[117] They then work with the appropriate accredited agency in their chosen country to identify a suitable child.[118] The Adoption Authority sends an art 15 report to the Central Authority in the country of origin of the child[119] which includes an assessment report on the prospective adopter(s).[120] If the Central Authority is satisfied with the art 15 report, it matches the prospective adopter(s) with a child and sends an art 16 child study report to the Adoption Authority to be considered. This report includes information regarding the child's eligibility, birth circumstances, needs, birth parent counselling, birth parent decisions, the matching process, and the relevant art 15 report on the prospective adopter(s).[121] The Adoption Authority considers the child study report and if satisfied sends an art 17 child placement agreement notice to the Central Authority

116 Hague Convention, arts 17–22.

117 In compliance with art 14 of the Hague Convention.

118 See the Adoption Authority of Ireland website for Country Information on the name of the appropriate agencies in relevant countries.

119 Under art 22 of the Hague Convention 1993 the functions outlined in ss 15, 16 and 17 may be delegated to an approved accredited body.

120 In compliance with art 5 of the Hague Convention.

121 Hague Convention, art 4.

of the country of origin. This allows the child to be placed with the prospective adopter(s).

The legislation of the country of origin will dictate the procedure for the granting of the adoption order. When the order is granted, the Central Authority in the country of origin issues an art 23 certificate. This confirms that an adoption has taken place in accordance with the Hague Convention. The adoption must be registered on the Register of Intercountry Adoptions in Ireland no later than three months after the child enters Ireland following his or her adoption.[122]

7. Summary

- Historic and illegal adoption practices created a legacy of secrecy and shame around adoption and have made it difficult for adopted people to access information about their identity. The Birth Information and Tracing Act 2022 attempts to deal with some of the issues around access to information created by historical practices.
- Adoption engages a number of provisions of the UNCRC including the best interests principle in art 3, the right of the child to be heard in art 12, the right to know and be cared by for his or her parents (art 7), a right to their identity and family relations (art 8), to not be separated from their parents against their will save in certain lawful situations and to maintain personal relations and direct contact with their parents (art 9). Article 21 specifically relates to adoption. Article 42A of the Irish Constitution specifically references adoption and identity rights are protected by Article 40.3.1°. The ECHR right to private and family life (art 8) protects a child's right to identity in the adoption process.
- The Adoption Act 2010 is the principal legislation governing adoption. It establishes the Adoption Authority of Ireland and provides for voluntary and involuntary forms of adoption. The process of adoption facilitated by the Adoption Act 2010 is based on principles of consent, constitutional and human rights, and compliance with the Hague Convention on Intercountry Adoption.

8. Further reading

8.1 Historical adoption practices

Maria Luddy, 'Unmarried Mothers in Ireland, 1880-1973' (2011) 20(1) *Women's History Review* 109.

---

[122] 2010 Act, s 90.

Mairead Enright and Aoife O'Donoghue (eds) *Mother and Baby Homes Commission of Investigation Report: Draft Alternative Executive Summary* (2021) available at https://www.tudublin.ie/media/website/news/2021/main-news/Draft-September-24.pdf [last accessed 3 August 2023].

Simone Mc Caughren and Fred Powell, 'The Fate of the "Illegitimate" Child: An Analysis of Irish Social Policy, 1750-1952' in Niamh Howlin and Kevin Costello, *Law and the Family in Ireland 1800-1950* (Palgrave 2017).

8.2 Modern adoption

Valentina Immacolata Cagliani, 'A New Society Needs a new Concept of Adoption: Open Adoption' (2020) 23(1) *Irish Journal of Family Law* 21.

Department of Children and Youth Affairs, 'Review and Consultation in respect of the Potential Introduction of Open or Semi-Open Adoption in Ireland', Report produced in accordance with s 42 of the Adoption (Amendment) Act 2017 (November 2019).

Simone McCaughren and Caroline McGregor, 'Reimagining adoption in Ireland: a viable option for children in care?' (2018) 24 (3) *Child Care in Practice* 229.

Valerie O'Brien and Angela Palmer, 'Adoption and the Irish Care System: Context and Drivers for Change?' (2015) 18(3) *Irish Journal of Family Law* 52.

Aisling Parkes and Simone McCaughern, 'Viewing Adoption through a Child's Rights Lens: Looking to the Future of Adoption Law and Practice in Ireland' (2013) 17(4) *Irish Journal of Family Law* 99.

Chapter 12

Irish Family Law in a Cross-Border Context

Máire Ní Shúilleabháin

LEARNING OBJECTIVES

By the end of this chapter, students will be equipped to:

- Appreciate the legal complexities that arise where family relationships and family disputes occur in a cross-border context.
- Apply Irish, EU and international rules of private international law to cross-border family situations.
- Use the language and methodology of private international law in a family law setting.
- Distinguish between the concepts of domicile and habitual residence.

CRITICAL THINKING POINTS

- How should Irish law on recognition of foreign divorces be reformed?
- Does the 1980 Hague Child Abduction Convention, as applied by the Irish courts, provide appropriate support for the best interests of the child?

1. Introduction

This chapter explores the legal complexities which arise where there is an international dimension to a family law dispute.[1] Where children have lived in another country before moving to Ireland, or where a couple have married or divorced abroad, rules of **private international law** come into play. There are three categories of private international law to be considered:

1. *rules on jurisdiction* determine where a family law dispute should be litigated i.e. in an Irish court or in a foreign court.
2. *rules on choice-of-law* determine if an Irish court should apply

[1] Inter-country adoption is discussed in Chapter 11.

foreign family law instead of Irish family law in a cross-border situation,

3. *rules on judgment recognition* determine when Irish courts should recognise judgments handed down by foreign courts in a family law case.

Private international law enables Irish judges and authorities to respond appropriately to international dimensions in a family situation. This has become more important as Ireland becomes an increasingly diverse society. Preliminary results for the 2022 census estimate that net inward migration to Ireland between 2016 and 2022 was 190,333.[2] This figure includes Irish citizens returning to Ireland after a period of living abroad and non-citizen families moving to Ireland for the first time. In the 2016 census, it was recorded that 810,406 Irish residents were born outside of Ireland (17.3% of the population), an increase by 43,636 on the 2011 figure.[3] These statistics reflect global trends: it was estimated in 2019, that there were almost four times as many people living outside of their country of birth across the world than in 1960.[4]

Private international law rules applied in Ireland come from a variety of sources. Some are traditional common law rules from Irish and English case law, some are part of Irish legislation, some come from EU law and others come from conventions adopted by the Hague Conference on Private International Law and given the force of law in Ireland. The application of these measures is influenced by the European Convention on Human Rights (ECHR) as interpreted by the European Court of Human Rights (ECtHR) and by other human rights instruments.

2. Cross-Border Marriage and Civil Partnership

Most countries have developed choice-of-law rules that apply to the formation of marriage. These rules are relevant where an Irish couple has married abroad or where a couple with strong connections to another legal system marries in Ireland. These rules are usually designed with certain objectives in mind. The first is to ensure consistent recognition of marriages across national borders and avoid **limping marriages.** A limping marriage is valid and recognised in one connected country but

[2] Central Statistics Office, *Census of Population 2022 – Preliminary Results* (2022) available at https://www.cso.ie/en/releasesandpublications/ep/p-cpr/censusofpopulation2022-preliminaryresults/ [last accessed 30 November 2022].

[3] Central Statistics Office, *Census 2016 Summary Results – Part 1* (2017) 46 available at https://www.cso.ie/en/media/csoie/newsevents/documents/census2016summaryresultspart1/Census2016SummaryPart1.pdf [last accessed 30 November 2022].

[4] Joseph Chamie, 'International Migration amid a World in Crisis' (2020) 8 Journal on Migration and Human Security 230, 232.

is not recognised in another country, a situation that is considered highly undesirable. However, state authorities also want to safeguard their own domestic policies on marriage, and this may require non-recognition of certain marriages.[5]

In Irish private international law, the formalities of marriage or **formal validity** are governed by the law of the place of celebration,[6] while the impediments to marriage or **essential validity** are governed by the law of each party's **domicile** at the time of marriage.[7] The impediment test is known as the **dual domicile** test because it asks whether each spouse had the capacity to marry the other under the law of their own domicile. The concept of domicile is discussed further below.

As has been seen in Chapter 2, formalities of marriage relate to the mechanics of how marriage is constituted: whether the intending spouses must give notice of their intention to marry, whether the ceremony must take place in a particular kind of building and in the presence of a designated solemniser, whether witnesses and registration and the presence of the spouses are required. Different countries have different views on how marriage should be formalised, ranging from countries like Ireland with strict rules on notice and the mode of celebration to those which take a much more flexible and lenient approach. In some countries marriage may be lawfully celebrated by a private exchange of vows, or by way of a ceremony which is not attended by either spouse.[8]

Irish law requires the parties to a marriage be aged 18 years, to have the capacity to consent, not to be closely related. Other countries will have different views of these matters: perhaps permitting marriage at a younger age,[9] or marriage between close relatives.[10] Under a foreign marriage law, a parent's consent to marriage may suffice in circumstances where an adult child is incapable of giving consent.[11] The marriage of a same sex couple, permissible under Irish law, is prohibited in many overseas legal orders.[12]

---

5 Dagmar Coester-Waltjen, 'Marriage' in Jürgen Basedow and others (eds), *Encyclopaedia of Private International Law* (Edward Elgar 2017) 1227.

6 *Hamza v Minister for Justice, Equality and Law Reform* [2013] IESC 9 [54].

7 *Hamza v Minister for Justice, Equality and Law Reform* [2010] IEHC 427 [28]; *M v F* [2011] IEHC 415 [27].

8 Prakash Shah, 'Inconvenient Marriages, or What Happens When Ethnic Minorities Marry Transjurisdictionally' (2010) 6 *Utrecht Law Review* 17, 24 *et seq*; *McCabe v McCabe* [1994] 1 FLR 410.

9 See United Nations Statistics Division, Minimum Age for Marriage available at https://data.un.org/documentdata.aspx?id=336 [last accessed 3 December 2022].

10 See *Cheni (Orse Rodriguez) v Cheni* [1965] P 85 where the marriage in Egypt of a woman and her uncle, valid under Egyptian law, was recognised in England.

11 *City of Westminster v IC* [2008] EWCA Civ 198, [2009] Fam 11 [35].

12 See ILGA Europe, *Rainbow Europe Map and Index 2022* (2022) available at https://

Questions of legal recognition of foreign marriage may arise in any context where a party to an alleged marriage claims to be entitled to be a spouse for the purposes of Irish law. This may be in the context of family reunification where the spouse has a right of entry under s 18 of the Refugee Act 1996,[13] or for the purpose of enjoying spousal property[14] or taxation rights[15] under Irish law.

There are three stages to consider in determining whether a foreign marriage may be recognised in Ireland. First, it must be sufficiently similar in its fundamentals to Irish marriage to be classified as marriage for the purposes of Irish private international law rules. Secondly, the marriage must be formally valid under the law of the country where it was celebrated. Thirdly, under the dual domicile test, each of the spouses must have complied with their own domiciliary law on impediments to marriage.

Some relationships described as marriage in other countries may be considered fundamentally different to the conception of marriage envisaged by Irish law. For example, Iranian law allows for temporary marriage.[16] A man is permitted to marry multiple wives in Lebanon and many other countries.[17] Before an Irish court will consider the formal and essential validity of a foreign marriage under the choice-of-law rules described above, the Irish court must be satisfied that it can be classified as marriage for the purposes of Irish private international law. Temporary marriage is unlikely to qualify because of the Irish emphasis of a *permanent* commitment.[18] A polygamous marriage is disqualified from classification as marriage in Ireland because monogamy and gender-equality are core values of marriage[19] The Irish Supreme Court has ruled

---

www.ilga-europe.org/report/rainbow-europe-2022/ [last accessed 8 December 2022], for a list of the European countries allowing/not allowing same sex marriage under their domestic laws.

13 See e.g. *Hamza v Minister for Justice, Equality and Law Reform* [2010] IEHC 427 [2]–[4].

14 *Conlan v Mohamed* [1987] ILRM 172 (HC); [1989] ILRM 523 (SC).

15 *Zappone and Gilligan v The Revenue Commissioners* [2006] IEHC 404, [2008] 2 IR 417.

16 Prakash Shah, 'Inconvenient Marriages, or What Happens When Ethnic Minorities Marry Transjurisdictionally' (2010) 6 *Utrecht Law Review* 17, 30.

17 *HAH v SAA* [2017] IESC 40, [2017] 1 IR 372 [6] (O'Malley J); *Hamza v Minister for Justice, Equality and Law Reform* [2010] IEHC 427 [43] (Sudan); *IH (Afghanistan) v Minister for Justice and Equality* [2020] IECA 241 (Pakistan) [2].

18 Máire Ní Shúilleabháin, 'Overseas Marriage and Divorce in Islamic Form: A Critical Perspective on the Development of Irish Private International Law' in K O'Sullivan (ed), *Minority Religions under Irish Law: Islam in National and International Context* (Brill 2019) 138-139.

19 *HAH v SAA* [2017] IESC 40 [113]-[114]. The Supreme Court (O'Malley J at [104]–[111]) confirmed that the husband's marriage to his *first* wife was entitled to recognition in Ireland.

out any legal recognition for second and subsequent wives even if a polygamous marriage is valid under the foreign legal order.[20]

The choice-of-law rules for formal and essential validity will now be discussed in more detail.

2.1 Formal validity of marriage

The formal validity of a marriage is determined by reference to the law of the place of celebration. This approach is justified on the basis that it avoids limping marriages because most other countries adopt the same approach. It also corresponds with the reasonable expectations of the parties.[21] A person, marrying in a particular country, would expect to do so in accordance with local laws.

Applying the law of the place of celebration means that Irish courts and authorities will recognise many foreign marriages celebrated in forms which are substantially different to those required in Irish domestic law. In *Hamza v Minister for Justice, Equality and Law Reform* it was confirmed that a marriage celebrated abroad in a proxy form, with one spouse, or possibly even both spouses, absent, could be recognised in Ireland.[22] It was accepted that while the fact of consent is a question of essential validity, the method of giving consent is a matter of form.[23] Irish law could accept the proxy form used here because it was a valid method of marrying in the place of celebration, Sudan.[24] The Irish High Court has also extended recognition to a marriage celebrated in a traditional customary form in Zimbabwe.[25] Zimbabwean law accepted Shona customary rites involving notification of the village headman, use of a go-between to procure familial agreement, payment of bride-price and attendance of other villagers. This meant that the validity of the customary marriage could be recognised in Ireland.[26]

The place of celebration rule may also result in the *invalidation* of marriages celebrated in relatively familiar forms. For example, in the 1950s, thirty-three Irish Catholic couples married in religious ceremonies in Lourdes, France.[27] French law required a civil ceremony, and so these

---

20 *HAH v SAA* [2017] IESC 40.

21 Jonathan Hill and Máire Ní Shúilleabhain, *Clarkson & Hill's Conflict of Laws* (5th edn, Oxford University Press 2016) 360.

22 *Hamza v Minister for Justice, Equality and Law Reform* [2010] IEHC 427 [17], [23], [26]; *Hamza v Minister for Justice, Equality and Law Reform* [2013] IESC 9 [53].

23 *Hamza v Minister for Justice, Equality and Law Reform* [2010] IEHC 427 [26].

24 It is possible that proxy marriages may be denied recognition in certain circumstances: see *RC (Afghanistan) v Minister for Justice and Equality* [2019] IEHC 65 [13], [29].

25 *M v F* [2011] IEHC 415.

26 *M v F* [2011] IEHC 415 [8], [18]–[20].

27 William Binchy, *Irish Conflict of Laws* (Butterworth 1988) 223.

couples were not validly married according to French law. Consequently, under the place of celebration rule, they could not be considered validly married as a matter of Irish law – until the Oireachtas intervened and legislated for the retrospective validation of these marriages celebrated in Lourdes.[28]

Where there is breakdown in civil administration in the country of celebration, for example, in circumstances of war, the authorised methods for celebrating marriage may be unavailable. When it is impossible to marry in accordance with domestic formalities in an overseas country, a private exchange of marital vows may be recognised at common law.[29] Couples who marry in accordance with legal formalities prescribed by the place of celebration may rely on a common law presumption of validity of a marriage if a collapse in civil administration makes it impossible to get a marriage certificate or other direct proof of compliance.[30]

2.2 Domicile and essential validity of marriage

The essential validity of a marriage is determined by reference to the **dual domicile test:** there must be no impediment to marriage under the domiciliary law of either spouse.

Broadly speaking, domicile corresponds to the idea of a permanent home.[31] A person is assumed to be domiciled in the country where their father was domiciled at the time of their birth.[32] This is known as their domicile of origin. Where a person moves to a particular country and forms a settled purpose of residing indefinitely in that country, they become domiciled there.[33] Where a person moves from one country to another and has no settled long-term plan as to where they will live, their domicile of origin revives. Domicile tends to link a person with a country and a legal system to which they have an abiding attachment.

The dual domicile test can be justified on the basis that a person should comply with the impediments to marriage under the law with which they have a long-standing personal and cultural connection. The test also has an anti-evasion rationale: if an Irish-domiciled couple attempts to side-

---

28 Marriage Act 1972, s 2.

29 *Hassan v Min for Justice* [2013] IESC 8 [38]-[48] (Fennelly J).

30 *Hassan v Min for Justice* [2013] IESC 8 [31], [48]–[52] (Fennelly J).

31 *In re Sillar, Hurley v Wimbush* [1956] IR 344, 350 (HC) cited in *PK v TK* [2002] IESC 15 (Fennelly J).

32 Where a child is born to parents not married to each other, the traditional view is that the child's domicile is determined by reference to the mother's domicile at the time of the child's birth. See Lauren Clayton Helm, 'Out with the Old and In with the New: Bringing the Law of Domicile into the Twenty-First Century' (2020) 7 Journal of International and Comparative Law 199.

33 *DT v FL* [2004] 1 ILRM 509, 519 (SC).

step the Irish prohibition on marriage between a man and his stepmother by marrying in a country where there is no equivalent impediment, they will find that the marriage contracted abroad will not be recognised in Ireland.[34]

The precise scope of the dual domicile test is somewhat uncertain, and it has been qualified by statute. Section 31 of the Family Law Act 1995 sets a minimum age of 18 for marriages celebrated in Ireland, but also for marriages celebrated abroad if either party is ordinarily resident in Ireland. Thus, the overseas marriage of two 17 year olds will *not* be recognised under Irish law if either was ordinarily resident in Ireland at the time of the marriage ceremony. The same marriage would be recognised if neither resided in Ireland at that time, and 17 was considered a sufficient age for marriage under the domiciliary law of each spouse.

The dual domicile test can lead to the non-recognition of same sex marriages contracted abroad. Section 12(1) of the Marriage Act 2015 provides that '[a] marriage under the law of a place other than the State shall not be precluded from being recognised as a marriage by reason of the sex of the parties to the marriage'. The Dáil Debates suggest that the legislative intention was to create an exception to the dual domicile rule to allow for recognition of foreign same sex marriages even if one of the spouses was domiciled in a country prohibiting this kind of marriage.[35] However, s 12 can also be interpreted as simply allowing the recognition of foreign same sex marriage as marriage something which was previously prohibited[36] without offering any exemption from the usual requirement of full compliance with the domiciliary laws on capacity to marry.[37]

The doctrine of public policy also impacts on the application of the dual domicile test. Foreign law may be inapplicable if it is significantly at variance with Irish fundamental values.[38] Irish courts emphasise the need for pluralism and tolerance of difference in the treatment of foreign marriages,[39] but marriage impediments are closely intertwined with values enjoying protection under the Constitution[40] and the ECHR.[41]

---

34 The foundational case of *Brook v Brook* (1861) 9 HL Cas 193 concerned an English-domiciled couple who sought to escape English affinity restrictions by marrying in Denmark.

35 Dáil Deb 23 September 2015, vol 890 (per Minister Frances Fitzgerald).

36 Under s 5 of the Civil Partnership and Certain Rights and Obligations of Cohabitants Act 2010, foreign same sex marriages were classified as civil partnerships.

37 See Maebh Harding, 'Marriage Equality: a Seismic Shift for Family Law in Ireland?' in Bill Atkin (ed), *The International Survey of Family Law* (Family Law 2016), 273.

38 *HAH v SAA* [2017] IESC 40 [2.8] Clarke J.

39 See *Aslam v Minister for Justice* [2011] IEHC 512 [22] citing O'Donnell J in *Nottinghamshire County Council v KB* [2011] IESC 48.

40 See Articles 40.1 and 41 discussed in *HAH v SAA* [2017] IESC 40.

41 See art 8 (right to respect for private and family life), art 12 (right to marry) and art

The public policy doctrine can require Irish *recognition* of a marriage which is invalid under the dual domicile test eg, where the domiciliary law prohibits inter-religious marriage. Public policy can also require the *non-recognition* of a foreign marriage which satisfies the domiciliary law e.g. the marriage of a young teenager[42] or of an adult lacking capacity to consent.[43]

EU free movement doctrine and ECHR obligations may significantly shape the future development of the common law rules relating to the essential validity of foreign marriages in Ireland. In *Coman* the Court of Justice of the EU (CJEU) determined that spousal rights of entry and residence under EU law extended equally to same sex spouses, and there were some suggestions of a wider obligation of marriage recognition under art 21 of the Treaty on the Functioning of the European Union (TFEU) (on free movement of persons).[44] In *Orlandi v Italy* the ECtHR found that Italy had violated art 8 ECHR in refusing to recognise or protect the marital status of same sex couples who had married outside of Italy.[45] A number of further complaints to the ECtHR relating to non-recognition of foreign marriages are pending.[46]

2.3 Civil partnership

Civil partnership was introduced into Irish law by the Civil Partnership and Certain Rights and Obligations of Cohabitants Act 2010 ('the 2010 Act') but, with the introduction of marriage equality and the Marriage Act 2015 ('the 2015 Act'), was discontinued for new entrants.[47] Section 5 of the 2010 Act allowed for recognition of overseas registered partnerships as civil partnerships in Ireland by ministerial order. However, following the adoption of the 2015 Act, no such recognition is given to partnerships registered outside of Ireland after 16 May 2016.[48] This means that many overseas registered partnerships are at risk of limping if the partners move to Ireland which may be a violation of the ECHR.[49] The Irish courts

---

14 (non-discrimination in the enjoyment of ECHR rights).

42 *HAH v SAA* [2017] IESC 40 [2.11] Clarke J (but subject to the possibility of subsequent affirmation as an adult). See also *ZH and RH v Switzerland* App no 60119/12 (ECtHR, 8 December 2015).

43 *City of Westminster* [2008] EWCA Civ 198 [32], [59]. See also s 38 of the Domestic Violence Act 2018 which creates offences relating to conduct bringing about forced marriages abroad.

44 Case C-673/16, *Coman v Inspectoratul General pentru Imigrări*, ECLI:EU:C:2018:385.

45 *Orlandi v Italy* App nos 26431/12, 26742/12, 44057/12 and 60088/12 (ECtHR, 14 December 2017).

46 See e.g. *Coman v Romania* App no 2663/21 (communicated 9 February 2021); *AB and KV v Romania* App no 17816/21 (communicated 19 October 2021).

47 Marriage Act 2015, s 8.

48 Marriage Act 2015, s 13, inserting a new s 5A into the 2010 Act.

49 See Máire Ní Shúilleabháin, 'Private International Law Implications of "Equal Civil

might recognise these overseas registered partnerships as marriage for the purposes of Irish law – but this approach might not be considered a satisfactory solution for couples who consciously chose registered partnership in preference to marriage in the country of origin, and sits uncomfortably alongside the legislative policy of non-recognition expressed in the 2015 Act.

3. Cross-border divorce and financial obligations

Where a couple has divorced abroad or where a spouse with strong connections to an overseas legal order applies for divorce in Ireland, domestic and EU legislative rules on international divorce jurisdiction and divorce recognition become relevant.

3.1 Cross-border divorce under Brussels II*ter*

Council Regulation (EU) 2019/1111,[50] known as the Brussels II*ter* Regulation,[51] determines jurisdiction to grant divorce in EU Member States excluding Denmark. Article 3 sets out the circumstances in which the national courts of EU Member States are competent to hear actions for divorce, annulment or judicial separation.

Divorce jurisdiction is based on habitual residence and nationality grounds, but art 2(3) of the regulation provides that the concept of domicile[52] replaces the concept of nationality for Ireland. Thus, under art 3 Brussels II*ter*, an Irish court may only pronounce divorce where both spouses are domiciled in Ireland (art 3(b)), or one spouse is habitually resident in Ireland and any additional requirements of art 3(a) are satisfied.[53] Because of the substitution of domicile for nationality under art 2(3) Brussels II*ter*, Irish nationality is irrelevant in determining divorce jurisdiction in Ireland.

Partnerships"' (2019) 68 International and Comparative Law Quarterly 161, 167 *et seq*.

50 Council Regulation (EU) 2019/1111 of 25 June 2019 on jurisdiction, the recognition and enforcement of decisions in matrimonial matters and the matters of parental responsibility, and on international child abduction [2019] OJ L178/1.

51 A similar legislative scheme was previously laid down under the 'Brussels II' Regulation 1347/2000 [2000] OJ L160/19 and, its successor, the Brussels II*bis* Regulation 2201/2003 [2003] OJ L338/1. Brussels II*ter* came into force (replacing Brussels II*bis*) on 1 August 2022 (art 105 Brussels II*ter*).

52 'Domicile' in the context of art 3 Brussels II*ter* means common law domicile discussed above.

53 The Irish courts may also, on occasion, have residual jurisdiction based on the domicile of one party only: see art 6 Brussels II*ter* and s 39 of the Family Law (Divorce) Act 1996.

Key legislation – Art 3 Council Regulation (EU) 2019/1111 of 25 June 2019 on jurisdiction, the recognition and enforcement of decisions in matrimonial matters and the matters of parental responsibility and on international child abduction (recast)

In matters relating to divorce, legal separation or marriage annulment, jurisdiction shall lie with the courts of the Member State:

(a) in whose territory:
  (i) the spouses are habitually resident
  (ii) the spouses were last habitually resident, insofar as one of them still resides there
  (iii) the respondent is habitually resident
  (iv) in the event of a joint application, either of the spouses is habitually resident
  (v) the applicant is habitually resident if he or she resided there for at least a year immediately before the application was made, or
  (vi) the applicant is habitually resident if he or she resided there for at least six months immediately before the application was made and is a national of the Member State in question; or

(b) of the nationality of both spouses.

Habitual residence is a much more straightforward concept than domicile, focussing on the 'here and now' of a person's life. While the CJEU has described the concept as 'essentially a question of fact',[54] judicial interpretation may be required in difficult cases.[55] Habitual residence refers to where a person is currently living, where they have their centre of interests[56] and everyday life[57] based on a presence which is sufficiently stable[58] and with a degree of integration into a social and cultural environment.[59] In *IB v FA* the CJEU determined that a person may only have one single habitual residence[60] and so it may be difficult to determine the habitual residence of a person who splits their time evenly between two countries. In an era of high mobility, 'habitual residence' is thought to be a fair and appropriate connecting factor for divorce, allowing migrant communities the same access to their local divorce courts as longer-standing residents.[61]

---

54 Case C-289/20 *IB v FA* ECLI:EU:C:2021:955 [52].

55 Máire Ní Shúilleabháin, *Cross-Border Divorce Law: Brussels II bis* (Oxford 2010), 41 ff.

56 Case C-289/20 *IB v FA* ECLI:EU:C:2021:955 [42].

57 Case C-501/20 *MPA v LCDNMT* ECLI:EU:C:2022:619 [57].

58 Case C-289/20 *IB v FA* ECLI:EU:C:2021:955 [57].

59 ibid, [60].

60 ibid, referring to identical provisions in Brussels II *bis*.

61 Máire Ní Shúilleabháin, 'Article 3' in Ulrich Magnus and Peter Mankowski (eds), *Brussels IIter Regulation* (Otto Schmidt, Cologne 2023) 110.

Article 3 Brussels II*ter* allows the Irish courts to hear a divorce action where both spouses are habitually resident in Ireland, or both were, and one still is.[62] The Irish courts are also competent to grant a divorce if only the respondent is habitually resident in Ireland because, in that case, the other spouse has initiated and is consenting to proceedings in Ireland.[63] Where only the applicant is habitually resident in Ireland, and the respondent never resided here, there is a concern that divorce litigation in Ireland may be unfair to the respondent – and that is why art 3 requires additional fortifying connections to establish jurisdiction in Ireland. In these circumstances the applicant must show, in addition to habitual residence at the time of commencement of proceedings, either residence for the previous year,[64] or residence for the previous six months and domicile in Ireland.[65] The CJEU has recently suggested that residence is a much looser requirement than habitual residence.[66]

These additional requirements give the respondent some protection against **forum shopping**; a strategic choice of Ireland as the divorce venue on the basis that it serves the applicant's interests. Where the Irish court has jurisdiction to pronounce divorce, it also acquires jurisdiction to award maintenance[67] and other financial relief,[68] and so an applicant may favour an Irish divorce court over a foreign divorce court if they think they will get a more favourable financial solution from the Irish courts.[69]

Article 3 Brussels II*ter* does not make any provision to allow the spouses to agree a divorce jurisdiction, for example, by way of a choice-of-court clause in a pre-nuptial agreement. There is strong support for the facilitation of jurisdiction agreements of this kind because they provide predictability for mobile couples, and protect against forum shopping.[70]

---

62 Brussels II*ter*, art 3(a)(i) and (ii).

63 ibid, art 3(a)(iii).

64 ibid, art 3(a)(v).

65 ibid, art 3(a)(vi).

66 Case C-289/20 *IB v FA* ECLI:EU:C:2021:955 [59]-[61].

67 art 3(c) of the Maintenance Regulation (Council Regulation (EC) No 4/2009 of 18 December 2008 on jurisdiction, applicable law, recognition and enforcement of decisions and cooperation in matters relating to maintenance obligation) [2009] OJ L7/1.

68 As a matter of domestic law Ireland is not participating in the Matrimonial Property Regulation (Council Regulation (EU) 2016/1103 of 24 June 2016 implementing enhanced cooperation in the area of jurisdiction, applicable law and the recognition and enforcement of decisions in matters of matrimonial property regimes [2016] OJ L183/1).

69 An applicant may also forum shop in pursuit of more lenient divorce laws (see eg *Rapisarda v Colladon* [2014] EWFC 35) but this is unlikely in the Irish context where the requirement of two years' separation is relatively more onerous than most foreign divorce laws.

70 Máire Ní Shúilleabháin, 'Article 3' in Ulrich Magnus and Peter Mankowski (eds), *Brussels IIter Regulation* (Otto Schmidt, Cologne 2023) 103, 114-115.

The EU Commission was in favour of this kind of party autonomy, but, in the end, because of political disagreement on the recognition of same sex marriage within the EU, it was decided not to reform the divorce jurisdiction rules under Brussels II*ter*.[71] It remains unclear as to whether same sex spouses may avail of divorce jurisdiction under art 3 Brussels II*ter*.[72]

If one of the art 3 bases is satisfied, the Irish courts will have jurisdiction to grant a divorce even if a couple have much stronger connections to another EU Member State, or to a non-EU country. However, where another EU Member State also has jurisdiction under art 3 Brussels II*ter*, and proceedings commenced earlier in that other Member State, Ireland is strictly obliged to yield to the other Member State.[73]

Where an Irish court has divorce jurisdiction under art 3 Brussels II*ter*, it will apply Irish divorce law[74] even if, for example, both spouses are French and the respondent spouse lives in France. In other EU Member States, courts may apply foreign divorce laws including Irish divorce law in international cases. The choice-of-law rules for divorce have been harmonised through the Rome III Regulation[75] in 17 EU Member States but Ireland did not participate in this regulation due to concerns about the constitutional implications of applying foreign divorce law.

While Irish judges will always apply the domestic Irish rules of divorce, they may apply foreign maintenance laws in determining financial relief. This is because Ireland is party to the 2007 Hague Maintenance Protocol which allows for the application of the maintenance laws of the habitual residence of the maintenance creditor, even if that is a foreign law.[76] The 2007 Hague Maintenance Protocol allows a couple to agree in advance

---

71 See COM (2006) 399 final, COM (2014) 225 final and SWD (2016) 207 final.

72 While Case C-673/16, *Coman v Inspectoratul General pentru Imigrări*, ECLI:EU:C:2018:385 favours a gender-neutral interpretation of 'spouses', the principle of 'continuity of interpretation' suggests that 'spouses' in Art 3 Brussels II*ter* has the same meaning as it had in art 2 Brussels II back in 2000 when no country in the world allowed same sex couples to marry. If same sex spouses are not covered by art 3 Brussels II*ter*, then divorce jurisdiction depends on one spouse showing ordinary residence in Ireland for one year, or domicile in Ireland (s 39 of the Family Law (Divorce) Act 1996).

73 art 20 Brussels II*ter*. In the same vein, other EU Member States with jurisdiction under art 3 Brussels II*ter* must decline to hear a case where the same divorce action was previously commenced in Ireland.

74 Máire Ní Shúilleabháin, 'Marriage, Divorce and Stagnation in the Irish Conflict of Laws' (2014) 52 *Irish Jurist* 68,73.

75 Council Regulation (EU) No 1259/2010 of 20 December 2010 implementing enhanced cooperation in the area of the law applicable to divorce and legal separation [2010] OJ L343/10.

76 Protocol of 23 November 2007 on the Law Applicable to Maintenance Obligations, art 3(1).

on the applicable maintenance law[77] and the EU Maintenance Regulation 4/2009 gives effect to spousal agreements on maintenance jurisdiction.[78] Thus, in maintenance matters, but not in divorce itself, party autonomy is accommodated.

The Brussels II*ter* Regulation also provides for mutual recognition of divorces between EU Member States. People divorced in other Member States will have their new marital status recognised in Ireland, and divorces granted in Irish courts enjoy automatic recognition throughout the EU. This includes both court-pronounced divorces,[79] and private divorces by agreement and registration.[80] Under Brussels II*ter*, recognition may be refused in exceptional circumstances such as where the Member State divorce offends Irish public policy or where it was obtained without notice to a spouse who objects to recognition[81] but these exceptions are likely to apply only in the rarest of cases.

The Maintenance Regulation facilitates the enforcement of Irish maintenance orders across the EU.[82] Maintenance orders made in other EU Member States enjoy automatic recognition in Ireland and may be enforced here against the assets or income of the debtor spouse.

3.2 Recognition of divorces obtained outside the EU

A divorce from a non-EU[83] country is only recognised in Ireland if either spouse was domiciled in the country where the divorce was granted.[84] If same sex spouses are excluded from Brussels II*ter,* as discussed above, then s 5 of the Domicile and Recognition of Foreign Divorces Act 1986 provides the *sole* basis for recognition of their foreign divorces whether obtained in the EU or elsewhere.

Irish law was traditionally very restrictive in its recognition of foreign divorces due to the constitutional ban on divorce in Ireland.[85] In the 1970s, the Supreme Court accepted that recognition of foreign divorces based on

---

77 art 8 (for adult maintenance).

78 Maintenance Regulation, art 4 (for adult maintenance).

79 art 30. This obligation extends to divorces pronounced in EU Member States since 1 March 2001: see further art 100(2) Brussels II*ter*.

80 Case C-646/20, *Senatsverwaltung für Inneres und Sport, Standesamtaufsicht v TB* ECLI:EU:C:2022:879; arts 64-68 Brussels II*ter*.

81 Brussels II*ter*, arts 38 and 68. See also *Chaudhry v An tÁrd-Chláraitheoir* [2015] IEHC 522.

82 art 17 of the Maintenance Regulation.

83 Although the UK has withdrawn from the EU, UK divorces still enjoy automatic recognition or something close to automatic recognition under s 126 of the Withdrawal of the United Kingdom from the European Union (Consequential Provisions) Act 2020.

84 s 5(1) of the Domicile and Recognition of Foreign Divorces Act 1986.

85 *Mayo Perrott v Mayo Perrott* [1958] IR 336.

domicile was constitutionally permissible.[86] In *H v H* the Supreme Court rejected the idea that judicial interpretation of common law rules could allow the recognition of foreign divorce based on residence, domicile was the only permitted basis.[87]

The Thirty-eighth Amendment of the Constitution (Dissolution of Marriage) Act 2019 has now amended the Constitution allowing provision to be made by law for the recognition of foreign divorces. This removes any constitutional obstacle to legislation allowing foreign divorces to be recognized more easily in Ireland, but no legislation has been enacted save that following Brexit legislation was passed to allow British divorces to be recognized on almost the same terms as under EU legislation.[88] The Law Reform Commission is undertaking a more general examination of the law on recognition of foreign divorces and will issue recommendations for reform.[89]

3.3 Critical thinking point: How should Irish law on recognition of foreign divorces be reformed?

The Central Statistics Office reported a strong inward flow of 30,200 Irish nationals returning to live in Ireland in the year to 2021.[90] Inevitably some of those Irish nationals will have divorced whilst living in a non-EU country, but some will be unable to establish that they were domiciled in the country where they were living, and the divorce will not be recognised unless their (ex-)spouse was domiciled in that country.

In 2007 the Ombudsman reported on a number of complaints from individuals affected by Ireland's restrictive divorce-recognition policy, highlighting delays and expense for those wishing to remarry, and concerns that an ex-spouse might have inheritance rights.[91] The inherent ambiguity of domicile often resulted in inconsistent determinations from state authorities.[92] In one case described by the Ombudsman, the

---

86 *Gaffney v Gaffney* [1975] IR 133.

87 *H v H* [2015] IESC 7; [2015] 1 ILRM 453.

88 The Withdrawal of the United Kingdom from the European Union (Consequential Provisions) Act 2020, Pt 19.

89 Law Reform Commission, *Report: Fifth Programme of Law Reform* (LRC 120-2019) 16.

90 Central Statistics Office, *Population and Migration Estimates, April 2021* available at https://www.cso.ie/en/releasesandpublications/ep/p-pme/populationandmigrationestimatesapril2021/mainresults/ [last accessed 28 January 2023].

91 Ombudsman, *Complaints Against the General Register Office: Investigation Report* (Oct 2007) available at https://www.ombudsman.ie/publications/reports/complaints-against-the-gr/ [last accessed 21 December 2022].

92 ibid.

complainant spent seven years seeking to establish the validity of her second marriage following a foreign divorce.[93]

Recognition of foreign divorce based on either spouse's habitual residence will ameliorate most of the practical problems described above. Where a person was living in the foreign country where they divorced, there should be no difficulty in establishing habitual residence.

Ireland has experienced substantial inward migration from countries with religious and customary divorce systems[94] such as Pakistan,[95] India[96] or Ghana.[97] In such countries divorce may be obtained with minimal formality, and without any court involvement. In *MY v AA*[98] it was suggested *obiter* that certain informal Islamic *talaq* divorces may be incapable of recognition under the Domicile and Recognition of Foreign Divorces Act 1986.

Irish law must find a way of ensuring recognition of religious and customary divorces where spouses have divorced in accordance with their local norms and organised their lives around their new marital status. The situation is complicated where the informal or religious divorce method does not align with ECHR expectations on gender-equality and due process. For example, in *Pellegrini v Italy*[99] the ECtHR ruled that the Italian authorities ought to have reviewed Vatican annulment proceedings for their compliance with Article 6 ECHR (fair trial rights) prior to recognising an annulment in Italy.

In England and Wales the Family Law Act 1986 sets down separate, more restrictive criteria for recognition of overseas divorces obtained 'otherwise than by means of proceedings'. This legislation was drafted with the aim of protecting immigrant women, but has resulted in much case law about the meaning of proceedings and a realisation that the presence of proceedings does not necessarily safeguard the interests of women.[100] In Germany and Spain, human rights concerns only result in non-recognition if the disadvantaged party is demanding non-

---

93 ibid. For a recent example of the administrative difficulties (and practical disadvantages) experienced by those who have divorced overseas, see *McGovern v Chief Appeals Officer* [2021] IEHC 202.

94 Central Statistics Office, *Census of Population 2016 – Profile 7 Migration and Diversity* available at https://www.cso.ie/en/releasesandpublications/ep/p-cp7md/p7md/p7anii/ [last accessed 21 December 2022].

95 *Quazi v Quazi* [1980] AC 744.

96 *NP v KRP (Recognition of Foreign Divorces)* [2013] EWHC 694 (Fam).

97 See *Botwe v Brifa* [2021] EWHC 2307 (Fam).

98 *MY v AA* [2017] IEHC 227 [93].

99 (2001) 35 EHRR 44.

100 See Máire Ní Shúilleabháin, '"A Peculiarly Pointless Line of Division": Recognition of Proceedings and Non-Proceedings Divorces under the Family Law Act 1986' in Andrew

recognition[101] and perhaps this might be the solution recommended by the Law Reform Commission.

Part III of the Family Law Act 1995 already allows ex-spouses, whose marriages have been dissolved abroad, to apply for financial provision, so ensuring proper provision for former spouses should not be a concern.

4. Cross-border parentage and surrogacy

As noted in Chapter 9, Irish couples are travelling abroad to use surrogacy services in other countries. The intended parents may be named as the child's parents on the birth certificate issued in the country of the child's birth. However, Irish authorities generally treat international surrogacy arrangements in the same way as domestic surrogacy arrangements,[102] allowing the genetic father to apply for a declaration of parentage,[103] and the other intended parent (if any) to apply for guardianship after caring for the child for two years.[104]

The Supreme Court has recently confirmed that the parentage of an intended parent may be recognised in Ireland where there has been a foreign adoption order.[105] The ECtHR has been very active in condemning the non-recognition of a child's relationship with their genetic father taking the view that the child's right to private life under art 8 ECHR demands such recognition[106] but the ECtHR has been much more guarded in developing obligations of recognition in all other circumstances.[107] There has been much less support under the ECHR for the recognition of the parentage of an intended mother – whether her own ovum was

Dickinson and Edwin Peel (eds), *A Conflict of Laws Companion: Essays in Honour of Adrian Briggs* (Oxford 2021).

101 See Cristina González Beilfuss, 'Islamic Family Law in the European Union' in Johan Meeusen and others (eds), *International Family Law for the European Union* (Intersentia 2007) 433.

102 See the Guidance Document provided by the Department of Foreign Affairs on 'Citizenship, Parentage, Guardianship and Travel Document Issues in Relation to Children Born as a Result of Surrogacy Arrangements Entered into Outside the State' available at https://www.dfa.ie/media/dfa/alldfawebsitemedia/childrens-issues-surrogacy-guidance-document.pdf [last accessed 14 February 2023]. On international surrogacy and nationality, see *A, B and C v Minister for Foreign Affairs and Trade* [2023] IESC 10.

103 ss 35 and 38 of the Status of Children Act 1987, as amended.

104 s 6C Guardianship of Infants Act 1964, as amended.

105 *In Re A (a minor) and B (a minor)* [2023] IESC 6.

106 *Mennesson v France* App no 65192/11 (ECtHR, 26 June 2014).

107 See *Paradiso v Italy* App No 25358/12 (ECtHR, 24 January 2017); *D v France* App No 11288/18 (ECtHR, 16 July 2020); *Valdís Fjölnisdóttir v Iceland* App No 71552/17 (ECtHR, 18 May 2021); *AM v Norway* App No 30254/18 (ECtHR, 24 March 2022).

used in conceiving the child or not[108] – and for the recognition of a second intended parent more generally.[109]

It seems likely that there will be significant change in the handling of international surrogacy over the coming years. The CJEU has indicated that the right of free movement (under art 21 TFEU) requires cross-border recognition of the child's same sex parents.[110] Meanwhile, the EU Commission has issued a proposal for a Regulation on recognition of parenthood,[111] and at the Hague Conference, the Experts' Group on the Parentage/Surrogacy Project has issued its Final Report on 'The Feasibility of One or More Private International Law Instruments on Legal Parentage'.[112] At domestic level, the Joint Oireachtas Committee on International Surrogacy issued its Final Report in July 2022, recommending that intended parents should be able to apply for a parental order to secure recognition of a parent-child relationship in Ireland.[113] Such order would be conditional on the surrogate's post-birth consent and on the child having a genetic relationship with at least one of the intended parents.[114] The Government has committed to implementing the Committee's recommendations by way of amendments to the Health (Assisted Human Reproduction) Bill 2022.[115]

5. Cross-border parental responsibility

Where a child or their family has strong connections to another country, a question may arise as to whether legal proceedings in relation to the child should be determined in Ireland or elsewhere, what law should be

[108] Although the obligation to facilitate recognition is somewhat stronger where the intended mother's ovum is used: see Grand Chamber Advisory Opinion, Request No P16-2018-001 (ECtHR, 10 April 2019) [47].

[109] But see also *DB v Switzerland* Apps No 58252/15 and 58817/15 (ECtHR, 22 November 2022)

[110] Case C-490/20 *VMA v Stolichna obshtina, rayon 'Pancharevo'* ECLI:EU:C:2021:1008.

[111] Proposal for a Council Regulation on jurisdiction, applicable law, recognition of decisions and acceptance of authentic instruments in matters of parenthood and on the creation of a European Certificate of Parenthood COM (2022) 695 final.

[112] Parentage/Surrogacy Experts' Group, *Final Report: The Feasibility of One or More Private International Law Instruments on Legal Parentage* (Prel Doc No 1 of November 2022) available at https://assets.hcch.net/docs/6d8eeb81-ef67-4b21-be42-f7261d0cfa52.pdf [last accessed 14 February 2023].

[113] Houses of the Oireachtas, *Final Report of the Joint Committee on International Surrogacy* (July 2022).

[114] ibid.

[115] See the Government Press Release, 'Government approves policy proposals on international surrogacy and recognition of past surrogacy arrangements' (13 December 2022) available at https://www.gov.ie/en/press-release/b5e0d-government-approves-policy-proposals-on-international-surrogacy-and-recognition-of-past-surrogacy-arrangements/ [last accessed 14 February 2023].

applied and whether an arrangement put in place in another country should be recognised and enforced under Irish law.

The Brussels II*ter* Regulation[116] lays down rules of jurisdiction and recognition and enforcement for guardianship, custody, access and public care matters which are all categorised as **parental responsibility** matters within the regulation.[117] The jurisdictional rules relating to parental responsibility are ordered into a strict hierarchy within Brussels II*ter*.[118]

The general jurisdiction rule, laid down in art 7(1), grants parental responsibility jurisdiction to the courts of the Member State where the child is habitually resident. This focus on habitual residence is intended to ensure that the court or authority is closely connected to the circumstances of the child when making decisions.[119] The decision-maker(s) should have ease of access to those caring for the child, to the child's school environment, to any social workers who have been engaging with the child – and to the child themselves. The delays entailed in taking evidence across borders are avoided, and the burden of international travel is removed.[120]

In determining the child's habitual residence, the focus is on the day-to-day life of the child,[121] and the core ingredients are stable presence[122] with a degree of social integration.[123] This is similar to the assessment of an adult's habitual residence. However, where children are concerned, there is a greater focus on the family environment, and parental intention is an important[124] factor. The assessment of the child's habitual residence will also vary with age: for a new-born infant the residence and intentions of the primary care-giver will be highly significant. For an older child, connections to school[125] and the child's own state of mind are more important.[126] Where a child is habitually resident in Ireland, the Irish courts will have jurisdiction to determine matters of parental responsibility under the general rule.

---

[116] Council Regulation (EU) 2019/1111.

[117] See the definition in art 1(2).

[118] arts 7-15 Brussels II*ter*.

[119] Recital 20 Brussels II*ter*.

[120] Thomas Garber, 'Article 7' in Ulrich Magnus and Peter Mankowski (eds), *Brussels IIter Regulation* (Otto Schmidt, Cologne 2023) 127–128.'

[121] Case C-512/17 *HR v KO* ECLI:EU:C:2018:513 [42], [45].

[122] Presence is a *sine qua non* of habitual residence: a child cannot be habitually resident in a country where they have never been: Case C-499/15 *W v X* ECLI:EU:C:2017:118 [61].

[123] See *Mercredi v Chaffe* ECLI:EU:C:2010:829 [47]-[49].

[124] *Mercredi* [50]–[53].

[125] *Mercredi* [53]–[55].

[126] *Re LC (Children)* [2014] UKSC 1 [37].

Brussels II*ter* specifies a number of exceptions to this general jurisdiction rule recognising that art 7(1) might not *always* provide the ideal forum and that the particular circumstances of an individual child may occasionally require proceedings to be dealt with elsewhere.

The courts of the country of habitual residence must defer to the courts of another Member State with jurisdiction under art 10 Brussels II*ter*. Article 10 jurisdiction arises where:

1) the child has a substantial connection to the relevant Member State,
2) there is party agreement on this forum, AND
3) this exercise of jurisdiction outside of the Member State of habitual residence is in the best interests of the child.

The child is considered to have a substantial connection to another Member State if the child is a national of that state, or was previously habitually resident there, or if at least one of the holders of parental responsibility is habitually resident there.[127] Article 10 therefore allows for a degree of party autonomy and allows parental responsibility proceedings to be joined with other related family proceedings taking place abroad[128] but only where this is in the best interests of the child.

Under art 12 Brussels II*ter*, an Irish court with art 7(1) general jurisdiction may exceptionally transfer proceedings to another Member State with which the child has a particular connection, if the second court accepts jurisdiction and is better placed to assess the best interests of the child. Article 12 allows for a degree of flexibility in circumstances where the child has moved away from Ireland *since* the commencement of proceedings in Ireland;[129] or where a child residing in Ireland has much stronger connections with another Member State.[130] Thus, the Irish courts might transfer parental responsibility proceedings to the French courts if a French child has moved back to France after proceedings commenced in Ireland. Such a transfer might also be considered by the Irish courts, if a French child, still living in Ireland, has only recently become habitually resident in Ireland, and where, for example, the child lived for many years in France, only speaks French, and had previously been supported by French social workers.[131]

---

[127] art 10(1)(a) Brussels II*ter* (a non-exhaustive list).

[128] Recital 23 Brussels II*ter*.

[129] art 12(4)(a) Brussels II*ter*.

[130] See the (exhaustive) list of 'particular' connections laid down in art 12(4) Brussels II*ter* (also recital 26).

[131] Pursuant to art 13 Brussels II*ter* other courts may themselves request a transfer from the courts of habitual residence.

Articles 11 and 15 are intended to ensure that there is never any gap in protection and that the child is never prejudiced by the absence of jurisdiction. Article 11 caters for the possibility that a child might not have any habitual residence at a particular moment in time, for example, where a child is born unexpectedly and prematurely to a Swedish-resident woman while she is in Ireland on business.[132] Where the habitual residence of the child cannot be established, the courts for the place where the child is present shall have jurisdiction.[133]

Under art 15, a child's presence in Ireland allows the Irish courts to adopt temporary emergency measures to protect a child – even if the child is clearly habitually resident in another Member State – but only until the courts of the habitual residence take over. This power, might be important where, for example, a German-resident family, on holidays in Ireland, were involved in a car accident and the parents, but not the children, were seriously injured.[134]

There is another important international instrument dealing with parental responsibility. This is the **1996 Hague Convention on Protection of Children**[135] given force of law in Ireland by the Protection of Children (Hague Convention) Act 2000. The 1996 Hague Convention applies in 54 Contracting States, including the 27 EU Member States. It allocates parental responsibility jurisdiction on terms which mostly echo those laid down in Brussels II*ter*. The courts of the child's habitual residence will ordinarily have jurisdiction under art 5.

Beyond the rules of jurisdiction laid down in Brussels II*ter* and in the 1996 Hague Convention, the Irish courts may exceptionally issue parental responsibility orders with respect to Irish citizen children who are residing in a non-EU country which is not party to the 1996 Hague Convention.[136]

Brussels II*ter* and the 1996 Hague Convention provide for the mutual recognition and enforcement of parental responsibility orders as between participating states.[137]

---

[132] This example draws on European Commission, *Practice Guide for the Application of the Brussels IIB Regulation* (Luxembourg 2022) 81 available at https://e-justice.europa.eu/287/EN/ejn_s_publications [last accessed 21 February 2023].

[133] art 11 Brussels II*ter* is also subject to the condition that jurisdiction cannot be determined on the basis of art 10.

[134] This example is adapted from European Commission, *Practice Guide for the Application of the Brussels IIB Regulation* (Luxembourg 2022) 53–54.

[135] Hague Convention on Jurisdiction, Applicable Law, Recognition, Enforcement and Co-operation in Respect of Parental Responsibility and Measures for the Protection of Children 1996.

[136] Pursuant to art 14 Brussels II*ter*; *O'M v S* [2020] IEHC 541.

[137] See art 39 Brussels II*ter* and art 23 of the 1996 Hague Convention.

Brussels II*ter* makes no provision for choice-of-law – and so the 1996 Hague Convention is the sole reference point on such matters.[138] Under Chapter III of the 1996 Hague Convention, the applicable law is normally the law of the forum and the application of foreign law is unusual.

Cross-border child maintenance matters are regulated by the EU Maintenance Regulation,[139] the 2007 Hague Maintenance Protocol and by the 2007 Hague Child Support Convention.[140] Article 3(d) of the Maintenance Regulation confers maintenance jurisdiction on the court that is hearing a parental responsibility matter ensuring, in most cases, that the courts of the child's habitual residence can deal with parental responsibility and maintenance together. Where a child maintenance action is brought as a standalone proceeding, both the courts of the applicant's and the respondent's habitual residence have jurisdiction.[141] Within the EU, the Maintenance Regulation provides for recognition and enforcement of child maintenance orders and for administrative cooperation.[142] At global level, the 2007 Hague Convention supports the cross-border enforcement of child maintenance between 45 Contracting States.

6. International Child Abduction

Each year children are taken to Ireland and from Ireland by a parent without the permission of the child's second parent or guardian.[143] Where a child is taken from the country where they are habitually resident,[144] a parent, guardian or state authority with parental responsibility may apply for the return of the child.[145] A rapid return process known as **summary return** is facilitated by the 1980 Convention on Civil Aspects of International Child Abduction (the 1980 Hague Convention) in force in 103 countries globally. In Ireland the 1980 Hague Convention is given the force of law by the Child Abduction and Enforcement of Custody Orders Act

---

138 See Recital 92 Brussels II*ter*.

139 Regulation 4/2009.

140 Convention of 23 November 2007 on the International Recovery of Child Support and Other Forms of Family Maintenance.

141 art 3(a) and 3(b) of the Maintenance Regulation.

142 See arts 17 and 51 of the Maintenance Regulation.

143 See Courts Service, *The Courts Service Annual Report for 2021* (July 2022) 67 reporting the number of incoming applications for 1980 Hague Convention return orders between 2016 and 2021 (32 in 2021, 21 in 2020, 34 in 2019, 37 in 2018, 36 in 2017, and 47 in 2016) available at https://www.courts.ie/news/courts-service-annual-report-2021 [last accessed 24 February 2023].

144 On the child's 'habitual residence' in the context of the 1980 Hague Convention, see *KW v PW* [2016] IECA 364.

145 The applicant must have a right of custody, a mere right of 'access' will not suffice (see arts 3 and 5 of the 1980 Hague Convention) – but the identification of 'custody' rights is not always straightforward: see eg *J Le L v AT* [2021] IEHC 219.

1991. This Convention applies when the child is taken unlawfully which is known as **wrongful removal**. The Convention also applies where a child is taken abroad lawfully e.g. for a short holiday and is not returned. This is known as **wrongful retention.**[146]

Within the EU, the operation of the 1980 Hague Convention is supplemented by a number of additional requirements laid down in the Brussels II*ter* Regulation.[147] These supplementary rules apply where both the **requested State** that has been asked to return the child and the **requesting State** where the child was habitually resident prior to the abduction are EU Member States.[148]

Under art 12 of the 1980 Hague Convention, the requested State is obliged to order return of the child where less than a year has elapsed between the abduction and the commencement of the return proceedings. Where more than a year has elapsed, then the requested State must order the return of the child, unless it is demonstrated that the child is now settled in its new environment.[149] Further exceptions to return may be invoked by the abducting parent under art 13.

Key legislation – Art 13 1980 Hague Convention on the Civil Aspects of International Child Abduction

Notwithstanding the provisions of the preceding Article, the judicial or administrative authority of the requested State is not bound to order the return of the child if the person, institution, or other body which opposes its return establishes that –

(a) the person, institution or other body having the care of the person of the child **was not actually exercising the custody rights** at the time of the removal or retention, or had **consented** to or subsequently **acquiesced** in the removal or retention; or

(b) there is a **grave risk** that his or her return would expose the child to physical or psychological harm or otherwise place the child in an intolerable situation.

The judicial or administrative authority may also refuse to order the return of the child if it finds that **the child objects** to being returned and has attained an age and degree of maturity at which it is appropriate to take account of its views. ... [emphasis added]

---

146 art 3 of the 1980 Hague Convention.

147 See arts 22-29 Brussels II*ter*.

148 art 22 Brussels II*ter*.

149 On the 'settlement' defence under Art 12 1980 Hague Convention, see *P v B (No 2)* [1999] 4 IR 185 (SC).

The Hague Good Practice Guide[150] envisages that these art 13 exceptions will be interpreted restrictively. The Irish courts have generally been slow to accept arguments based on art 13 and have emphasised their discretion to return the child even if one of these exceptions is made out.[151] All of these exceptions are very strictly construed.

A finding that the left-behind parent was not actually exercising their custody rights will be extremely rare. Even if the left-behind parent was imprisoned at the time of the abduction, they will usually be considered to have been exercising their custody rights if they had limited interaction with the child.[152] Only where there is a prolonged period with no attempt to contact the child will the non-exercise of custody rights exception be established.[153]

The difference between consent and acquiescence is one of timing: consent precedes the abduction, acquiescence postdates it. The Irish courts have emphasised the need for evidence of an actual subjective intent to acquiesce or else a communication which clearly and unequivocally led the other parent to believe that the left-behind parent was not going to assert their right to return.[154]

Non-return based on grave risk is rare. Where the abducting parent invokes this exception, and provides credible evidence of instances of physical violence by the left-behind parent, the Irish courts will generally seek to secure undertakings from that left-behind parent to allow for a safe return: for example, an undertaking to vacate the family home to allow the abducting parent and children to reside there separately pending a custody hearing in the requesting State, and, if necessary, an undertaking to provide financial support.[155] Where the abductor makes allegations that the left-behind parent sexually abused the child, the requested Irish court will usually return the child to the requesting State if the allegations have already been assessed and rejected by the authorities in the requesting State.[156] The prospect of the child's separation from the abducting parent will not normally satisfy the grave risk exception, even if the abducting parent has been the child's primary carer since birth.[157]

---

150 HCCH, *1980 Child Abduction Convention: Guide to Good Practice: Part VI: Article 13(1) (b)* (2020) 24 available at https://assets.hcch.net/docs/225b44d3-5c6b-4a14-8f5b-57cb370c497f.pdf [last accessed 24 February 2023].

151 *CMW v SJF* [2019] IECA 227 [65].

152 *DM v VK* [2022] IEHC 252 [5.9]; *MSH v LH* [2000] 3 IR 390 (SC).

153 *MJT v CC* [2014] IEHC 196.

154 *R v R* [2015] IECA 265 [23] citing *Re H (Abduction: Acquiescence)* [1998] AC 72.

155 *R v R* [2015] IEHC 573.

156 *CDG v JB* [2018] IECA 323; *PL v EC* [2009] 1 IR 1 (SC). On allegations of sexual abuse and the use of undertakings to safeguard the child, see also *AS v PS* [1998] 2 IR 244 (SC).

157 *R v R* [2015] IECA 265 [57]; *CMW v SJF* [2019] IECA 227 [52], [61]–[62]. But see also

Separation might occur where that parent is reluctant to return to the requesting State, or because of immigration restrictions in the requesting State,[158] or because of a risk of prosecution for the abduction,[159] or for financial reasons,[160] or because the abducting parent has formed a new relationship in the requested State.[161]

The child's disruption and upset and anxiety in being returned and removed from a now-familiar environment in the requested state[162] is not enough to satisfy the grave risk exception. The Irish court may delay the enforcement of the return order so as to minimise the negative impact on the child e.g. waiting until the end of the school term.[163] In an extreme case, where there has been very extensive delay in the return proceedings, and where the child has put down very deep roots in the requested state, the delayed return may of itself pose a grave risk.[164]

The child's own objection may justify non-return but the courts will be careful to assess the 'intensity of feeling', and to distinguish a true objection to return from a more ambiguous expression of reluctance or a mere preference for living with one parent.[165] The courts are also conscious of the possibility of the child having been influenced by the abducting parent.[166] A child's objection with a 'cogent and rational' basis will be more persuasive.[167] There is no fixed minimum age for hearing children in child abduction proceedings. The child must have the capacity to form a view and the more mature the child, the more weight their view will carry.[168] The clear objection of a seven year old child may suffice to refuse return.[169] Where an older child objects to return, the court may also refuse to return a younger sibling, to avoid the separation of siblings In these circumstances, the refusal to return the younger child is based on the grave risk exception.[170]

MS v AR [2018] IECA 181 [32], [87] where it was clear that the abducting mother would not return and where the Court of Appeal declined to return the child; and *ML v JC* [2013] IEHC 641 where there was evidence that return would have a serious detrimental effect on the abducting mother's psychiatric health.

158 *VR v CO'N* [2018] IECA 220.

159 *R v R* [2015] IECA 265) [57]; *CDG v JB* [2018] IECA 323 [41]–[44], [53], [81]-[82]; *CMW v SJF* [2019] IECA 227 [64].

160 *CMW v SJF* [2019] IECA 227 [70].

161 *C v G* [2020] IECA 233 [144]–[145].

162 *R v R* [2015] IECA 265 [60]–[61].

163 *R v R* [2015] IECA 265 [67]–[68].

164 *DM v VK* [2022] IECA 207 [112].

165 *J v QI* [2020] IECA 302 [49], [69], [101]–[102]; *MS v AR* [2018] IECA 181 [84].

166 *MS v AR* [2018] IECA 181 [67], [71].

167 *J v QI* [2020] IECA 302 [49].

168 *MS v AR* [2018] IECA 181 [28]–[31]; *MS v AR* [2019] IESC 10 [64].

169 *MS v AR* [2018] IECA 181 [31], [77].

170 *MS v AR* [2018] IECA 181 [94], [89].

Article 20 the 1980 Hague Convention also allows for a refusal of return if return 'would not be permitted by the fundamental principles of the requested State relating to the protection of human rights and fundamental freedoms'. The Irish Supreme Court has set a very high threshold[171] for this exception. It will only apply in very exceptional circumstances where what is proposed 'departs so markedly from the essential scheme and order envisaged by the Constitution and is such a direct consequence of the Court's order that return is not *permitted* by the Constitution'.[172]

6.1 Critical thinking point: Does the 1980 Hague Child Abduction Convention, as applied by the Irish courts, provide appropriate support for the best interests of the child?

The 1980 Hague Convention is designed to the deter acts of abduction, protecting children from the trauma of being removed from their familiar environment. The summary return procedure promotes a speedy restoration of the status quo minimising the disruption to the child's life and encouraging an orderly resolution of parental responsibility.[173] However, summary return may also be deeply harmful to the child, for example, where the abduction was a response to domestic violence which then continues following the return of the child – or where the primary carer abductor does not return with the child for fear of imprisonment for the act of abduction.[174] The Irish courts' reluctance to refuse return based on allegations of domestic violence or the risk of separation is understandable: the requesting court is often in a much better position to determine the veracity of allegations of abuse, and the risk of separation argument could be raised by every abductor. The requested court is not permitted to undertake a full best interests analysis, this is done by the requesting State authorities following the return of the child. The summary return process is designed to get the child back to the court best placed to make a best interests decision. Nonetheless, return orders are sometimes made and enforced in circumstances which do not serve the best interests of the individual child at hand.

The ECtHR responded to some of these concerns in the *Neulinger* decision of 2010. In this case the Grand Chamber ruled that the enforcement of a

---

171 *CMW v SJF* [2019] IECA 227 [40].

172 *Nottinghamshire County Council v KB* [2011] IESC 48,[54] (O'Donnell J). See also *VR v CO'N* [2018] IECA 220; *CDG v JB* [2018] IECA 323; *CT v PS* [2021] IECA 132.

173 On relocation applications before the Irish courts, see *SK v AL* [2019] IECA 177; *K v K* [2022] IECA 246.

174 See Marilyn Freeman and Nicola Taylor, 'Domestic Violence and Child Participation: Contemporary Challenges for the 1980 Hague Child Abduction Convention' (2020) 42 Journal of Social Welfare and Family Law 154; Rhona Schuz, *The Hague Child Abduction Convention: A Critical Analysis* (Hart 2013) 66–67, 280–284.

return order – on the particular facts of the case – would violate the art 8 ECHR rights of the abducting mother and child, and the ECtHR indicated that requested courts should conduct an 'in-depth examination of the entire family situation'.[175] This suggestion was widely criticised because it had the potential to derail the effectiveness of summary return and to undermine the primary jurisdiction of the requesting court in determining the custody dispute.[176] In a subsequent case, *X v Latvia*, the Grand Chamber by a majority of nine to eight held that the Latvian authorities had violated art 8 ECHR in failing to adequately assess grave risk and in ordering the return of the child.[177] However, in *X v Latvia* the ECtHR accepted that there is no need for the requested court to conduct an in depth examination of the entire family situation but still insisted that art 8 ECHR requires an effective examination of any exceptions invoked, and a reasoned judgment on the issue of return.[178] In subsequent cases differing views have been expressed as to how the risk of separation from the primary carer ought to be handled with some suggestions that art 8 ECHR requires a proper examination of any barriers to the abductor's return with the child.[179]

The EU's interventions into the area of international child abduction have also been controversial. The supplementary rules laid down in Brussels II*ter* are widely welcomed as streamlining the return process,[180] ensuring cooperation in facilitating a safe return[181] and for requiring the child's views to be heard.[182] However, Brussels II*ter* allows the requesting court to issue a mandatory return order which overrides a non-return order made under art 13 of the 1980 Hague Convention.[183] This EU override mechanism has attracted criticism.[184] Some requested states have refused to enforce the overriding mandatory return orders as required by EU law.[185] When Brussels II*bis* was being revised, many commentators recommended the abolition of this override mechanism, and the reversion to the traditional approach under the 1980 Hague Convention,

---

175 *Neulinger and Shuruk v Switzerland* (2012) 54 EHRR 31 [139].

176 See eg *In the Matter of S (A Child)* [2012] UKSC 10 [38].

177 *X v Latvia* (2014) 59 EHRR 3.

178 X v Latvia (2014) 59 EHRR 3. [105]–[107].

179 See *GN v Poland* App no 2171/14 (ECtHR, 19 July 2016); *Royer v Hungary* App No 9114/16 (ECtHR, 6 March 2018); *Satanovska and Rogers v Ukraine* App no 12354/19 (ECtHR, 28 Jan 2021); *Thompson v Russia* App no 36048/17 (ECtHR, 30 March 2021).

180 arts 23, 24 and 28 Brussels II*ter*.

181 art 27(3)–(5) Brussels II*ter*.

182 art 26 Brussels II*ter*.

183 art 11(8) Brussels II*bis*; art 29 Brussels II*ter* (the procedure is now confined to situations where the non-return order is based on grave risk or the child's objection).

184 See Thalia Kruger et al, 'Current-Day International Child Abduction: Does Brussels IIb Live Up to the Challenges?' (2022) 18 Journal of Private International Law 159.

185 Paul Beaumont, Lara Walker and Jayne Holliday, 'Conflicts of EU Courts on Child Abduction: the Reality of Article 11(6)-(8) Brussels IIa Proceedings Across the EU' (2016) 12 Journal of Private International Law 211.

whereby the issuance of the non-return order is final.[186] However, this did not happen. Brussels II*ter* has introduced new provisions whereby the requested State may exceptionally refuse to enforce the mandatory return order issued in the requesting State.[187] Brussels II*ter* thus allows for multiple rounds of litigation in both connected states, a situation which may increase parental conflict and generate a prolonged period of instability for the child.[188]

7. Summary

- Where family relationships or disputes arise in a cross-border context, three key legal questions may arise:
  - Does the Irish court have jurisdiction to hear the dispute?
  - Should the court apply Irish law or foreign law?
  - How should existing foreign judgments be recognised and enforced in Ireland?
- Domicile and habitual residence are important connecting factors. A person is usually domiciled in a country where they are living with the intention of remaining permanently or indefinitely. Habitual residence is focussed on the here and now of a person's life, where they currently have their main residence and day-to-day life.
- A foreign marriage will usually be recognised in Ireland if it was celebrated in compliance with the formalities laid down in the country of celebration, and there were no impediments to marriage under the laws of the countries where the spouses were domiciled at the time of the marriage. Recognition of foreign civil partnerships is much more limited and uncertain.
- A foreign divorce from an EU Member State is normally recognised in Ireland without any difficulty, but divorces from non-EU countries are only recognised if there is a connection of domicile to the country where the divorce was obtained. There is a lot of uncertainty as to the rules governing divorce jurisdiction and recognition for same sex spouses.
- Irish law is uncertain in its treatment of certain kinds of parentage established abroad, particularly parentage of children born abroad through surrogacy. The ECtHR and CJEU are developing obligations of cross-border recognition of parentage – based on the right to

---

[186] ibid 258.

[187] arts 50, 56–57 Brussels II*ter*.

[188] Paul Beaumont, Lara Walker and Jayne Holliday, 'Conflicts of EU Courts on Child Abduction: the Reality of Article 11(6)-(8) Brussels IIa Proceedings Across the EU' (2016) 12 Journal of Private International Law 211, 258.

respect for private and family life (art 8 ECHR) and the doctrine of free movement of persons (art 21 TFEU).

- The courts of the country where a child is habitually resident will hear any dispute concerning custody, access, guardianship, or public care. Exceptionally, another country which has a strong connection to the child may be empowered to exercise jurisdiction.
- Under the 1980 Hague Child Abduction Convention, a child who is habitually resident in one Contracting State and has been abducted to another Contracting State, must be returned to the first Contracting State. The return of the child may be refused if it would entail a grave risk for the child or if the child objects.

8. Further reading

8.1. Irish academic sources

Lydia Bracken, 'Recognition of LGBTQI+ Parent Families Across European Borders' (2022) 29(3) Maastricht Journal of European and Comparative Law 399.

Patricia Brazil, 'Recent Developments Concerning Transfer of Child Care Proceedings under Brussels II Revised' (2014) 51 Irish Jurist 181.

Maebh Harding, 'Ireland' in Katarina Trimmings and Paul Beaumont (eds), *International Surrogacy Arrangements: Legal Regulation at the International Level* (Hart 2013).

Houses of the Oireachtas, *Final Report of the Joint Committee on International Surrogacy* (July 2022).

Eimear Long, 'The Hague Convention on the Protection of Children – What's New?' (2008) 11(4) Irish Journal of Family Law 92.

Richard McNamara and Frank Martin, 'Brussels Calling: The Unstoppable Europeanisation of Irish Family Law' (2006) 9(3) Irish Journal of Family Law 8.

Máire Ní Shúilleabháin, 'Marriage, Divorce and Stagnation in the Irish Conflict of Laws' (2014) 52 Irish Jurist 68.

Máire Ní Shúilleabháin, 'Foreign Divorce Recognition and Residence: A Critical Analysis of H v H' (2017) 57 Irish Jurist 162.

Jane Reddin, 'An Unhappy Marriage: The EU and the Divorce Jurisdiction

System under Brussels II Bis' (2020) 20 University College Dublin Law Review 39.

8.2 International books and articles which discuss the handling of cross-border family matters in other legal orders, and under EU/international instruments applicable in Ireland and elsewhere

Paul Beaumont, Lara Walker and Jayne Holliday, 'Conflicts of EU Courts on Child Abduction: the Reality of Article 11(6)-(8) Brussels IIa Proceedings Across the EU' (2016) 12 Journal of Private International Law 211.

James Fawcett, Máire Ní Shúilleabháin and Sangeeta Shah, *Human Rights and Private International Law* (Oxford University Press 2016).

Jonathan Hill and Máire Ní Shúilleabhain, *Clarkson & Hill's Conflict of Laws* (5th edn, Oxford University Press 2016).

Thalia Kruger et al, 'Current-Day International Child Abduction: Does Brussels IIb Live Up to the Challenges?' (2022) *18* Journal of Private International Law 159.

Ulrich Magnus and Peter Mankowski (eds), *Brussels IIter Regulation* (Otto Schmidt 2023).

Jörg Pirrung, 'Improvements to International Child Protection as a Result of the 1996 Hague Child Protection Convention' (2012) International Family Law (March) 70.

Rhona Schuz, *The Hague Child Abduction Convention: A Critical Analysis* (Hart 2013).

Prakash Shah, 'Inconvenient Marriages, or What Happens When Ethnic Minorities Marry Transjurisdictionally' (2010) 6 Utrecht Law Review 17.

Index